A NORMAL LIFE

The struggles and escapes of a wanted man

by Vassilis Palaiokostas,
with introduction by Polykarpos Georgiadis

English translation by The Colleagues'
Publications (ΟΙ ΕΚΔΟΣΕΙΣ ΤΩΝ
ΣΥΝΑΔΕΛΦΩΝ) and Freedom Press, 2021

Edited by Rowan Tallis Milligan,
Alex Roberts and Rob Ray

Design by Rob Ray

© All rights reserved by the author

Printed 2021

ISBN 978-1-904491-40-8
All rights reserved

Published by
Freedom Press
84b Whitechapel High St,
London
E1 7QX
freedompress.org.uk

CONTENTS

ABOUT THIS BOOK

The idea of the social bandit has somewhat fallen out of popular useage in Britain in modern times, often being relegated to cinematic outings of Merry Men amid a sea of often simplistic cops 'n' robbers and gangland turf warring.

Not so in Greece, where Vassilis Palaiokostas and his brother Nikos, the mountain-born sons of a goat herding family who became the nation's most successful illegalists and prison escape artists, are household names. Vassilis in particular, thanks to his famous double helicopter escape from the supposedly high-security Korydallos Prison and habit of handing wads of cash robbed from the rich to the poor, is popularly known as The Uncatchable, or The Greek Robin Hood. His exploits filled newspapers and TV discussion shows for two solid decades, turning him into a folk hero for a broad swathe of the public and especially for Greece's large and very active anarchist movement, which dubbed him St Basil — the Greek Santa.

These names, and the sentiments behind them, draw on a particular phenomenon of Greek culture, rooted in a history of rebellion against occupying powers, that has bled through into a popular anti-authoritarian streak which drives both a constant struggle against State domination and deep distrust of capitalist bosses. In his foreword, written from prison, Polykarpos Giordadis examines this social history and the place of his friend Vassilis within it.

The core of this book, and what drew Freedom Press to publish it in English for the first time, is simple. Palaiokostas tells a hell of a life story. He writes about outrageous events like others would about going down the shops, and does so from the perspective of one who prizes freedom from the restrictions of the State above all else. His shopping list includes the biggest bank heist in Greek history, the first boss ransom, a tour of the Greek prison system and its character, and no less than three spectacular escapes, the last of which made headlines around the world. He has never killed anyone (though this was perhaps sometimes more by luck than design), and his targets are the rich, rather than the poor. He fought the law rather than bow before it and, just for once, the law lost.

But while the story is simple, the author himself, his place in Greek history and his attitudes, are not. In many ways a straightforwardly macho presence, his immense braggadocio is levened by a form of romantic libertarian leftism, a wry sense of humour and an absolutely damning tale to tell about the cruelty and corruption of Greece's justice system.

Freedom Press is, as a rule, more used to carrying political histories and philosophical ideas than telling the blockbuster tale of a wanted man, however Vassilis' urge to reject and confound the rules set by our lords and masters is ultimately the urge to be free. His story, and incidentally that of illegalism in Greece, the rebels and politicals who would rather die on their feet than live on their knees, is worth telling in more detail.

TIMELINE

Childhood
1960: Nikos Palaioikostas born
1966, May 17: Vassilis born in Moschofyto village, the fourth of five children
1979: Family moves to Trikala, the region's largest town

80s
1982: Nikos' first arrest, for property damage
1986: Vassilis gets his cards marked by police after theft arrest
1986-87: Military conscription for six-and-a-half months in armoured division
1987: Nikos arrested and jailed
1988 (winter): Nikos escapes after Vassilis throws rope over wall of old Trikala jail
1989: Nikos re-arrested

90s
1990, early: Vassilis meets Kostas 'The Artist' Samaras
　　　April: They try to free Nikos from Larissa prison by ramming a stolen truck into the prison walls, but are both arrested and later jailed
　　　December: Nikos escapes under cover of a major riot
1991, January: Kostas escapes
　　　August: Vassilis transferred to Chalkida Prison after his escape plan is ratted out, and subsequently escapes with a bedsheet rope and coat hanger grapple
1991-95: Vassilis and Nikos spending much of their time in Europe
1991-99: Police accuse the pair of a number of armed robberies
1992, June: Kalabaka bank robbery. It's the biggest heist in Greek history and humiliates local cops. Becomes one of the country's most wanted men
1995, December 15: Kidnap and ransom of Alexander Haitoglou
1999, May 8: Escapes from police trap at Trikala gate
　　　December 20: Involved in car crash, recognised and arrested

00s
2000: Convicted of kidnap and three bank robberies and sentenced to 25 years
2002: Helps organise a hunger strike over prison conditions
2003: Transferred to Korydallos Prison after discovery of escape plan
2006: June 4: First helicopter escape from Korydallos
　　　Autumn: Nikos caught by a road block, eventually sentenced to 16 years
2008, June 9: Kidnap and ransom of industrialist George Mylonas
　　　August 2: Vassilis recaptured after cops track him back to ransom safehouse
2009: January: Huge supportive crowds turn out for Vassilis' pre-trial hearing
　　　February 22: Escapes from Korydallos Prison for second time by helicopter.
　　　March: Unusual robbery in Trikala takes 250,000 euros, Vassilis blamed

10s-20s
2010: Robberies of National Bank in February and October are blamed on Vassilis
　　　June: Seemingly in an effort to tarnish his reputation, authorities say they found his fingerprint on a letterbomb which killed a postal worker. Critics point out that not only is there no prior history of him being remotely interested in such tactics (in fact he prides himself on being non-lethal), there is no way a fatally large explosion would have left prints. Nevertheless, a €1 million bounty is placed on his head.
2011, February: Last alleged sighting of Palaiokostas in Greece
2019: Autobiography comes out in Greece, is instant bestseller
2021: Still free and on the run, 18 years still pending on his original convictions

FOREWORD

by Polykarpos Georgiadis
writing from Larissa Prison, 2021

I often ponder and laugh at the characterisations given to some of us by the judicial authority. It calls us callous delinquents and dangerous criminals, with the same ease it characterises the free sharks and hyenas of capital as law abiding citizens! They call me a robber, while I believe I carried out an act of humanitarian significance within a society of inequality.
~ Theodoros Tsouvalakis, 1978*

Who is Vassilis Palaiokostas, really? The State has put a huge bounty on him amidst the bankruptcy of its capitalist economy, the inflation of State debt and a tough policy of austerity for the social majority. The Hellenic Police have created a special persecution team that deals exclusively with the campaign to arrest him, after his second helicopter escape in 2009. He is even a target of the "anti" terrorist force. The mass media have crafted a legend around him, with journalistic clichés coming one after another: "The Phantom", "The Uncatchable", "The Robin Hood of the Poor".

Despite their ruthless hunt, Vassilis Palaiokostas has won the all-around liking and acceptance of society, but also the respect of his persecutors, who he has ridiculed quite a few times. There are several instances where cops and prison guards have expressed their wish that Vassilis Palaiokostas stay free, without hiding the fact they like him. Once, a cop in the holding cells said to me: "You should know that we do not want to come up against Vassilis. We do not want to arrest him. He has never bothered a citizen, he does not deserve prison".

So, who is this strange robber? In order to answer that, we have to take a small dive into the past ...

II

In the 1950s historian Eric Hobsbawm introduced the concept of "social banditry" in order to define a specific manifestation of delinquency. The social bandit participates in life as a regular member of the community, representing a figure of revenge and individual uprising, however they are not a revolutionary. They do not have a program for changing social relations. They do not clash with institutions, but with the bagmen of those institutions. The idealised figure of the social bandit is that of a wronged and persecuted farmer forced to become an outlaw, transforming before the eyes of the dominated "into a hero, protector, avenger, fighter for justice, maybe even a liberator, and definitely a

---

*   Tsouvalakis, along with his brother Nikos, was one of the first bank robbers in modern Greek history.

person who deserves admiration, help and support". The main characteristics of a social bandit are:

Direct bonds with local populations who live in their field of action. After all, the State for many years viciously attacked "bandit supporters", using the logic of "strike the periphery in order to pressure the centre".

They express, through their person, society's wider resentment towards the cruelty of authority, the rich, the loan-sharks and the judicial authorities. They act as an avatar for the defence of pre-capitalist agricultural and pastoral communities against the onslaught of the capitalist way of production and the centralised State.

They have a powerful localistic feeling, unstable attitudes towards authority (alternating between hostility and cooperation) and claim to alleviate its outrageous inequalities and injustices, but not the system of inequality and injustice. That is beyond their horizon. A part of the loot is used to redistribute power and resources from top to bottom: the bandit helps the agricultural community by building churches or mosques (since they share the same moral values and religious beliefs), they pay for poor girls' marriages, they give money to families and fund public works.

In Greece the period of "banditocracy" begins after the gaining of national independence, as an inheritance of the guerrilla struggle against the Ottoman Empire*. The old "thieves" (the veterans of the revolution) were repressed by king Otto, resulting in an uprising in 1834. As Nikos Belogiannis (a famed communist executed by the Greek State in 1952) notes: "Thousands took to the mountains and banditry took the character of unorganised popular resistance against the Prelates".** This phenomenon of banditry was so extensive that, according to prominent sociologist Stathis Damianakos, "when studying this phenomenon one gets the sense that the Greek people in their entirety become outlaws". Despite a brutal campaign of repression the Greek State did not succeed in erasing that phenomenon for decades. Dictator Theodoros Pangalos*** eventually managed a powerful blow to the "banditocracy" of the countryside however, causing the self-extermination of bandits, via a "smart" legal framework offering amnesty to those bandits who delivered the heads of their fellow travellers to the authorities.

At the same time, the development of capitalist production, the industrialisation of Greece's economy, the modernisation of its road network and the gradual

---

*   Greece was part of the Roman and Byzantine empires from 27 BC through to the 14th century, when it was progressively ceded to first the Serbs and then the Ottomans, which dominated the region until a successful war for independence in 1821-32. A succession of monarchs, Hellenic Republics and a Nazi occupation followed, through to the modern period. In 1967 a military dictatorship, known as the Junta, took power in a coup, which lasted until 1974 when it collapsed in the wake of the Athens Polytechnic Uprising. It was replaced by the Third Hellenic Republic, which was for many years a two-party system swapping between social-democratric party PASOK and conservative New Democracy. PASOK was largely replaced by Syriza in 2015, and as of 2021 the country is again run by New Democracy

**   Provincial governors of Greek Christian communities, either directly appointed by Ottoman authorities or elected by village chiefs.

***   Pangalos declared himself president in a 1925 coup and was deposed in 1926.

transition to a different form of social organisation removed the fertile ground on which social banditry could grow. From the 1930s the phenomenon declined and integrated into forms of popular resistance or political enlistment (sometimes in favour of the State). The stance of the bandit gangs during the Nazi occupation is characteristic. Many robbers (like the legendary Karolivanos) joined the movement of resistance and the popular army of ELAS* that was created by the Communist Party, while other bandits were integrated in nationalistic anti-communist groups that cooperated with occupation forces. This completely different form of enlistment also reflects the often self-conflicting phenomenon of social banditry, balanced between conservatism and resistance.

The question that arises is: is Vassilis Palaiokostas a "social bandit"? The answer is no. Palaiokostas has clear references to the phenomenon of social banditry, something that is also evident in his book. Social banditry, however, encompasses a completely different era to ours, expressing the "romantic" resistance of agricultural-pastoral communities against a constantly changing world. Vassilis Palaiokostas is the distant echo of that resistance, but his field of action is completely different. Our era is completely different. Illegality, in an era when capitalist production has colonised every corner of social life, is completely different.

III

Between 1860 and 1862 Karl Marx wrote a small text regarding the economic function of crime. After his death, it was included in his Theories of Surplus Value (*Das Kapital*, chapter four). For Marx, crime was one more productive sector that multiplies national wealth. It produces new professional sectors, gives a push to new inventions and creates motives for the development of productive forces:

> The effects of the criminal on the development of productive power can be shown in detail. Would locks ever have reached their present degree of excellence had there been no thieves? Would the making of bank-notes have reached its present perfection had there been no forgers? Would the microscope have found its way into the sphere of ordinary commerce but for trading frauds? Doesn't practical chemistry owe just as much to adulteration of commodities and the efforts to show it up as to the honest zeal for production?
>
> Crime, through its constantly new methods of attack on property, constantly calls into being new methods of defence, and so is as productive as strikes for the invention of machines. And if one leaves the sphere of private crime: would the world-market ever have come into being but for national crime? Indeed, would even the nations have arisen? And hasn't the Tree of Sin been at the same time the Tree of Knowledge ever since the time of Adam?

---

* The Greek People's Liberation Army, which fought against the fascists in World War II.

During that era Marx would have been impressed by the development and modernisation of crime, and its transformation into a structured and organised form of "illegal capital". A huge percentage of global GDP comes from criminal activities, with "black" and "white" accumulation of capital being intertwined. The figure of bandit-avenger has given over its place, then, to the figure of a tough illegal capitalist, while the idyllic atmosphere of the countryside as a field of action is replaced by the noisy big cities. The anti-authoritarian nature of "social banditry" (partly true, partly an idealised myth) is today displaced by a tough hierarchy that governs so-called "organised crime". This transition from forms of popular delinquency, like "social banditry", to a "useful and controlled criminality", is described by Michel Foucault in *Discipline and Punishment*.

Contrary to "social banditry", which under its particular conditions acquires clear anti-plutocratic characteristics, modernised criminality, "structured on a penal system with prison as its centre, represents a diversion of lawlessness, suitable for the circuits of profit and the authority of ruling class". Criminality, as defined by the State covering the petty crime of the poor, is thus transformed into one more tool for social discipline, aimed at creating submissive individuals who are economically useful and politically obedient. The purpose of the "justice system" is not to fight crime, but to include delinquent activity in a general strategy of subordination. In this way authority avoids popular delinquency feeding into social struggles and integrates occasional offenders into a controlled environment of designated roles.

Police repression, judicial authority, imprisonment and criminality are four interacting poles. Through a self-reinforcing spiral the police deliver the offender to the judges, who decide to store them in jails, where they are integrated into the hierarchy of illegal capital and delivered back to society as stigmatised and branded criminals. Within this complex, authority and crime are two opposite poles of the same battery, which supplies power to a complicated process of social discipline. Through this process criminality becomes a tool to deflect and control popular delinquency, which is transformed into a privileged tool of authority.

Thus emerges an "outlaw" authoritarian function, that not only sets working class and popular delinquency within boundaries that are harmless to authority, but also generates a force of illegal police, a reserve army of impoverished lumpens. From this source authority can enlist snitches, collaborators, thugs and professional scabs/strike breakers. Its greatest accomplishment however is an artful channelling of delinquency among the lower classes onto paths that are harmless to authority: the thousands of proletarians and poor who fill these correctional slaughterhouses become pawns of illegal capital on one side, while on the other they direct difficult behaviour against their class brothers and sisters rather than the rich, the State and the apparatus of their own oppression.

Therefore, the question arises: is Vassilis Palaiokostas a criminal? The answer is again, no.

Vassilis belongs to a generation of outlaws that tends to be buried underneath the spectacle of professionalised crime. This generation, having connections with radical political manifestations and drawing inspiration from the tradition of social banditry, had, and has, an infallible principle that obstructs its integration to the capitalism of crime (which is an inseparable part of the crime of capitalism) — their violence is never channelled downwards, towards the poor and powerless. It is always channelled upwards, towards plutocrats, banks, the powerful, the persecution apparatus.

Inevitably, a third question arises. Is Vassilis Palaiokostas a revolutionary?

The answer is no, once more. The delinquent actions of Vassilis might be distinguished by an intense class instinct, being a natural ally of revolutionary action, however it cannot in any way be said that he is part of a comprehensive and coherent revolutionary strategy, nor that he aims at social subversion and the transformation of social relations. The action of Vassilis is an anomaly, it cannot be poured into a political mould. However, his inclinations cannot be hidden. In his cell Vassilis had flags with Che Guevara and Aris Velouchiotis,* and has always expressed how much likes the anarchists — though he has never himself claimed to be a Communist or anarchist.

Who is, then, Vassilis Palaiokostas?

We do not have to answer this question. We will find the answer in his voluminous autobiographical book, which describes just one part of his life. There is still a great deal of his past that is waiting for the right time to come to the surface, and plenty of future yet to be lived. The only thing for sure is that no matter how many persecutory battalions the authorities unleash, how many times they put a bounty on him, how many times they shoot at him, they can never arrest his dignity.

IV

I met Vassilis for the first time in Korydallos Prison in 2004. Three things made an impression on me: his particular, and razor sharp, humour, his ambitions for the reclaiming of his freedom, and the small library he had in his cell, full of books by Nietzsche, Dostoyevski and historical studies about social banditry.

The penultimate time was on August 20th, 2008. We had drunk a bit of tsipouro,** philosophising and contemplating and were getting ready to watch Monty Python and the Holy Grail. A few days earlier we had seen Life of Brian and Vassilis (consciously an atheist) had been excited by the particular humour of Python. The police special forces, however, had a different opinion, since they are not known for their sense of humour.

The last time I saw him was in the holding cells of the Thessaloniki General Police Directorate, a few days after our arrest. Despite the various police and media scenarios, I have not seen Vassilis since then. So, this small foreword is also an opportunity to send one more signal of solidarity: good luck comrade, and may you always be free!

---

*   Velouchiotis (1905-45), a (later expelled) Communist activist and journalist, was a leader of the Greek People's Liberation Army and National Liberation Front. He was killed by rightist paramilitaries during the 1944-45 Greek Civil War.
**   A strong spirit made from wine press residue, or a type of moonshine.

We had taken on this foreword together with anarchist comrade Giannis Dimitrakis. However, Giannis has a "disadvantage": he never bowed his head to any authority, legitimate or illegitimate. The result of this "disadvantage" was his objective inability (for reasons I cannot describe here) to participate in writing this text. For all the reasons of the world, therefore, I dedicate this foreword to my beloved friend and comrade Giannis Dimitrakis.

And in memory of Spyros Dravilas, of course ...

Polykarpos was arrested in 2008 and imprisoned for his part in protecting Vassilis while on the run, also attracting charges over the kidnapping of industrialist Yorgos Mylonas. He is a well-known figure in Greek anti-fascist and anti-imperialist struggle.

Giannis Dimitrakis is one of the most famous anarchist bank robbers in Greece having, among many other exploits, been arrested and convicted for a 2006 heist at the Athens National Bank. During his most recent stint in prison he has been a notable organising force, including a hunger strike in solidarity with 17 November prisoner Dimitris Koufontinas in early 2021. He is currently in recovery after suffering a near-fatal attack in Domokos Prison.

Spyros Dravilas was a close comrade of Vassilis, and involved in his first escape from Korydallos Prison. His life and death are described more fully by Vassilis in the chapter 'Return to Korydallos and the first helicopter escape'. Appositely, an anarchist action marked the aftermath of his passing by burning police vehicles.

PROLOGUE

She's furious! I can't restrain her. A ruthless predator, just like a peregrine falcon, she glides and attacks. She dives into the darkness of sleeping memories, grabs and tears apart her prey, placing it piece by piece in front of me, still alive, with a single command: you must turn all this into human words.

How can I accept, and how can I bear the weight of such a responsibility, being unlettered? Still, do I have a choice in the face of such a command? I'll try my best, whether I like it or not ...

I suddenly find myself the host of a feast, my cellar filled with the purest worldly goods, but knowing neither how to cook nor serve them to my guests. So I'll serve them as my winged one brings them to me. Raw. Still dripping blood. Some may find this meal heavy for their delicate stomachs. They shouldn't worry. It's because it doesn't include chemical additives and it hasn't undergone any mutations or third-party interference. Be it as it may — let them trust me.

These chosen segments of my life and struggle carry the marks of solid, hard truth. With those marks as a guide, I will try to guide you, reader, to this truth. Don't stumble and don't waste time in the wrongs of my writing. Follow its pulse. The living, rhythmic pulse of a soul that through twenty years of being wanted and seven-and-a-half years of confinement, which found itself in the middle of an incessant, brutal pursuit by brazen authorities that have no heart, no pulse, and no flow.

By rights, this book belongs to me, so allow me to dedicate it to all those who, through my hardships, became my valued friends. They are the people who opened their homes, arms, and hearts to me. They give me a reason to still believe and have hope in humanity. I owe them all thanks because, aside from everything else, they remain committed to the values and beliefs that give meaning to the human condition.

They're still swimming against the current.

To you, B.N.CA.

A NORMAL LIFE

The struggles and escapes of a wanted man

Greece is broken up into thirteen Regional Units. Shown here are both the regions and most of the major towns and cities which act as local capitals, which are frequently referenced by Vassilis as he describes his various journeys. Not shown, but noteworthy, is the Pindus mountain range which runs from the Albanian border down to Patras. Some additional locations mentioned in the book are marked and noted below:

1. Diavata	(jail)	5. Livadeia	(arrest, car chase)
2. Kalabaka	(robbery)	6. Malandrino	(jail)
3. Katerini	(car chase)	7. Moschofyto	(birthplace)
4. Korydallos	(jail)	8. Parga	(car chase)

NIKOS' ESCAPE
FROM OLD TRIKALA PRISON

It was 1988, and I had dedicated the whole year to Nikos' release from prison. I had become his shadow. I'd been sneaking inside the toilets of courthouses leaving fretsaw blades and burglary tools, which he never managed to get his hands on. On one occasion I went to the vacant lot of the Lamia police department and left a defensive grenade for him there, stuck between a barred toilet window and a thin iron net. He didn't manage to get that either. I descended twice into the large tunnels beneath the old Trikala prison, trying to locate a smaller, temporary brick tunnel that was there (according to Nikos, who had seen it from the inside). Yet, no matter how hard I searched, I couldn't locate it.

It was summer, and I was planning to leave another grenade inside a toilet flush at the Trikala Courthouse. Nikos was transferred to the examining magistrate's office on the second floor and asked to use the bathroom, but was not given permission.

The window behind the examining magistrate's desk was open, however, and overlooked the courthouse's entrance.

He decided to take the risk. Walking behind the examining magistrate, he jumped out of the window. He was unlucky. As he fell, he landed on a small step, straining his foot. He didn't manage to get far and was promptly arrested. Because of this little snag, his escape would have to be postponed for six months, until he had healed.

By the time winter came he had fully recovered — in fact, he had begun exercising hard to be in better shape. I visited him every other day because we had already begun crafting a new escape plan. Although the prison was old, built within the city limits and not heavily guarded, no prisoner had managed to break out from it before. Because of its age it had neither an interior nor an outer dead zone. Its sole security measure was a tall stone wall and the guards patrolling its top, placed quite near one another.

Our plan was simple and bold. I would throw a knotted rope over a specific spot on the wall, which Nikos would then use to climb over and meet me down the road, where I would be waiting for him with a car. That simple.

Not yet having any experience in stealing cars, or driving them for that matter, I asked an acquaintance for help. He volunteered to lend us his, changing the licence plates. We set the escape for a winter Sunday, near four in the afternoon. A few days earlier I bought a pretty thick rope, made knots on it, each placed two feet apart from the other, tied a weight on one end and began practicing, throwing it over a wall of about the same height. After quite a few tries, I became sure that, at least as far as this part of the plan was concerned, there would be no problem. Yet a problem did arise, and it involved the guy who had agreed to help us. He was the first of many I would meet through my years in action who made promises before weighing up their decision, and when they eventually changed their mind, thought that a simple "I've reconsidered" would suffice. It was Friday, only two days before the escape, when he told me he had indeed changed his mind. I was paralysed. I visited Nikos, and we decided not to postpone the attempt, despite the sudden obstacles that were looming up. It started snowing heavily on Saturday morning and by nightfall at least six inches of snow accumulated in the city of Trikala. That was good and bad at the same time. In a city, snow may prove to be an obstacle for the fugitive, but so does for his pursuers.

It was five to four on Sunday morning when I arrived across the spot of the prison wall where the escape was to take place, holding a supermarket bag. There was a kiosk there. For a while, I stood there, waiting for the time to come. The snow on the road was now almost twelve inches tall, and the city had been paralysed. Only the main roads remained open, and those were difficult to drive on. Few cars were to be seen and even fewer people. I was wearing a beanie, covering my forehead and my ears, and a scarf to cover the rest of my face. The guard was inside his post, listening to a sports commentary on a loud portable radio. He seemed to care for nothing else.

At four sharp I crossed the road swiftly and reached the prison wall. I got the rope out of the bag, slipped the noose around a streetlamp, retreated back to the middle of the road and threw the weight over the wall, mere inches away from the guard post. The rope followed the course of the weight, crossing to the other side of the wall. I grabbed the now empty bag, shooting one last look at the guard who hadn't noticed anything, and broke into a run, towards the city's snowy streets. Tracks created by the townspeople helped me get away quickly.

After a few minutes, I reached an abandoned house, where I had left a change of clothes. I put them on, threw the ones I had been wearing in a dumpster a little further down the road and, now neat as could be, headed towards the city centre to meet my friends. I had been walking along the snow-covered sidewalk on the city's main road for a while already when I noticed an unmarked cop car tailing me. In it were three plainclothes. They had their windows rolled down, and they were staring at me. I halted. They did too.

"Can I help you, boys?"

"Get inside. The chief wants to see you".

"Today?"

"Why not today?"

"Because it's snowing, that's why".

"Come. Get inside!"

I got in the back of the car.

"Where are you coming from?"

"Home".

"On foot?"

"How else in this weather?"

"And where are you off to? In this weather".

"My friends are waiting for me".

"Where?"

I gave them the name of the coffee shop.

While they were bombarding me with their seemingly innocent questions, the car took a right turn, heading towards the prison.

"I think the police station is in the opposite direction", I said to them rather casually.

"We'll make a stop at the prison to have a few words with Nikos. You'll have the chance to see him too. How does that sound?"

"Are you playing me?"

"No, you've been playing us since the moment you entered this car. Don't you know that Nikos broke out?"

"When?"

"Fifteen to twenty minutes ago! Don't worry, though, we've located him. Soon he'll be back behind bars!"

That was good news. Nikos had managed to climb over the wall and twenty minutes were more than enough for him to disappear. It was Sunday afternoon, the station was understaffed, and most of the city's roads were closed; they'd have a hard time locating him. It would be a piece of cake for Nikos. Saying they had found him ... they were just bluffing.

The unmarked cop car stopped near the kiosk, across the spot where the breakout had taken place only a few minutes earlier.

"Come, let us show you where he escaped from, in case you don't already know!" they said to me as they got out of the car.

I followed them, knowing that at that very same moment they were showing me to the kiosk's occupant (the only eyewitness), hoping he'd identify me. Its window would have allowed him to watch Nikos' escape from start to finish. Yet he couldn't possibly identify me. I was a different person. You never know, though, when it comes to eyewitnesses. They sometimes take their role a bit too seriously. Their momentary illusion could become a judge's alibi, translated into a lengthy prison sentence.

The rope was still intact. Still there. Exactly as I had thrown it, only a bit more stretched. From the plainclothes' incessant blabbing, I learned that Nikos wasn't alone when he escaped. A Serbian inmate had seized the opportunity and followed him.

We re-entered the unmarked car and this time we did drive to the police station. We got to the security department. The chief and the deputy director were waiting for us in the former's office. Although I had no prior criminal record, I knew them both. Because of Nikos' struggle we had met quite a few times. They urged me to take a seat. I saw a defensive grenade, strategically placed on the desk so that I'd notice — I recognised it at once. It was the same grenade I had left inside the toilet flush at the examining magistrate's office last summer. They thought they could have me down cold. Me!

The chief was furious with the escape; he lost his temper. He verbally assaulted me, throwing relentless accusations: "You helped him escape ... you're the moral instigator of his crimes. You're his fence. I'll gather all necessary evidence and lock you up ... I'll get a hundred men if I have to and hunt Nikos across Greece until I catch him ... blah blah blah".

When his rant was finally over, I said: "You'll first have to prove your accusations before throwing them at me. For the time being, I don't see any evidence whatsoever. What you do with Nikos is your own business; I don't need to know. So if we're done here, my friends are waiting for me. They'll be worried".

"Leave. But you won't get away with it ... I'll be watching you!"

He kept his word. He had it out for me. About two years later, unable to make good on his threat with evidence, he resorted to underhand methods to achieve his goal.

In the meantime, Nikos and his former cellmate — now companion — were living their own adventure. They walked for hours, heading north, following the railroad. Around midnight they reached the outskirts of Kalabaka.

Michael lived in a nearby village and knew the surrounding area well enough. Having been informed about the planned breakout, he had made all the necessary preparations. He located an abandoned hermitage in a rocky area around Meteora and equipped it with food, water, bed sheets, firewood, even binoculars. The hermitage was actually a cave dug high above the ground in a massive rock, at the north side of Meteora. There were narrow steps sculpted on the sides of the enormous rock, beginning at its roots and climbing to its top, leading to a small, habitable chamber. It had a single large window, — one side of which was fixed on the natural stone wall of a fireplace, which afforded a panoramic view of most of the villages in the Kalabaka flatland as well as the surrounding mountains. It was to this shelter that Michael led the two fugitives that cold night.

They spent a whole week there, gazing at the endlessly white winter landscape, next to the lit fireplace, while the snowfall continued. At nightfall, they would hear signal whistling and shortly after, on a rudimentary path carved into the thick snow blanket, three figures would appear, climbing up the mountain with apparent difficulty. It was Michael and his two dogs. He was bringing them their daily supplies. He never forgot to bring them some tsipouro along with traditional local nibbles, to accompany their long conversations by the fireplace.

What more, what greater prize could the two fugitives expect from life and freedom, for their courage to do the obvious as human beings?

ATTACK PLAN FOR LARISSA PRISON, AND MY ARREST

Meeting Kostas*

It was early in the spring of 1990, and we were devising a new plan to break Nikos out of prison. This time it was Larissa.** Nikos had been a prisoner there for more than a year, having been arrested just outside the city of Ioannina*** as a fugitive from Trikala.

At the time, I was a law-abiding citizen and, being a relative of his, visited him often to discuss the details of the endeavour. Larissa prison wasn't as simple a case as the one in Trikala. At the time it was considered state-of-the-art in terms of security and escape prevention; the best facility the State system had to offer. It was located next to a school complex, far from any residential area, in the heart of the Thessalian Plain, surrounded by barren hills. A single country road ran along its front side, connecting Larissa with the town of Palamas in Karditsa and the surrounding villages.

The prison was built of cement and steel, surrounded by a heavily guarded tall wall. It had an interior dead zone surveilled by security cameras and another one, just outside the wall, the fencing of which was built of metal posts and steel nets, on top of which were strung many lines of concertina razor wire.

All the prison complex's security measures, along with its barren surroundings, discouraged any bold thoughts of escape, whether expressed by inmates or by others who might wish to orchestrate an armed attack, to free one or more people. It wasn't a coincidence that nobody had broken out of this prison in the past, which was why any attempt to free Nikos had to be thoroughly examined, methodically organised, and executed perfectly.

Planning to attack a prison is rather easy; organising and carrying through the plan, on the other hand, depends on a lot of factors. First, you have to find the right people to take part in the operation. The said people ought not to be lacking in skill and bravery. I had a partner that had neither skill nor was known for his courage. Yet, to his credit, he wanted in on the job, to do whatever he could do. Nikos had a partner as well. He suggested that we meet and discuss the whole situation. I travelled to Athens and met with him. He was interested, and wanted to be part of Nikos' breakout.

Kostas was himself a fugitive, a wanted man. Experienced in lawlessness, he could prove helpful. He was very resourceful, able to find solutions to all kinds

---

*   Kostas Samaras, also known as The Artist, was well-known at the time for a line in intricately-planned and spectacular heists. He is broadly credited in the Greek press as a mentor to the young Vassilis.
**   Situated between Thessaloniki and Athens, Larissa is Thessaly's largest city and Greece's fifth-largest with a population of 140,000.
***   Ioannina is the capital of Epirus region in north-western Greece, near the border with Albania.

of frustrating problems. A skilful car thief, aside from everything else, he knew all the escape routes in Thessaly region, which could prove very useful to all of us in the future. I asked him whether we could find one or two more people to participate in the attempt.

"Don't bother", he said. "If it's a paid job, everyone's jumping at the opportunity. When it comes to breaking out an inmate, no one's interested. Don't put your hopes in others. What we do, we do it on our own". It was a fact I'd have to face many times in the future.

It was early April when we met again, at a prearranged meeting in Larissa. This time I brought Thanasis with me so that they could meet in person. We decided that for the planning stage of our attempt to break Nikos out, we'd need lodgings nearby. Without further delay, we rented a two-bedroom penthouse at the heart of the city, which would serve as our headquarters.

Plan and preparations

Nikos spent his yard time at the north-west of the prison complex. The last guard shift change was at eight in the evening, just a few minutes before the yard closed. After days of surveillance, he realised that when their shift ended the guards descended from their posts through an interior dead zone, a few minutes before the new guards arrived — which left the corner guard post unwatched for a little while.

Over the next few days we walked the surrounding hills to get a better look at the area. We discovered some dirt tracks — which were not in perfect condition since they were used only by agricultural machines and ran relatively close to the prison compound. One of them sloped down the hill and, passing close to the north-west corner guard post, continued along its exterior dead zone, leading to the main road that ran in front of the prison.

It was the kind of access we needed, and we had finally found it. After this welcome development we devised a detailed attack plan. Taking advantage of the momentary absence of the guard, Kostas, posing as a truck driver, would knock down the outer fencing. Moving backwards, he would park the truck at the wall, right underneath the corner guard post. Heavily armed and hidden in the back, I would climb up into the guard post using a collapsible steel ladder and take it over. I would have a rolled-up, custom-made rope ladder with me. After securing the guard post, I would let the ladder unravel to the floor of the interior dead zone. Nikos, in turn, would have to find his way to the interior iron-barred wall and climb up the rope ladder to the guard post. If he was lucky and the guard left the door open, it shouldn't be that hard. Then he'd have to quickly climb down to the back of the truck using the steel ladder, where guns would be waiting for him as well.

In the meantime, I'd have to keep the two closest guards occupied and make sure no others approached. I had a flair for such stuff; it was right up my alley. I wouldn't have a problem. When Nikos had armed himself, I'd drop back into the truck, and we would drive uphill, where a four-door Opel would be waiting for us on the other side. Then, via the dirt road, which was in relatively good shape, we would head to Terpsithea, where another car would be waiting for us, and we could vanish into thin air.

My partner, Thanasis, would take on an easier yet equally important job. While the attack was taking place he'd be stationed at a vantage point on top of the hill facing the entrance of the prison, with a view of the whole complex and its surrounding dirt roads. From there, he could give us live updates on the guards' and police's reactions and movement, using a radio transmitter. He was also in charge of finding his way to and away from the vantage point. When the party was over, he'd return to headquarters.

I visited Nikos to inform him of the proposed plan. Nikos agreed to it all but he didn't hide his worries about the logistics. His concern stemmed from the fact that only two people would attack the exterior guardhouse. Deep down he too believed that two skilled people are better than a thousand good-for-nothings. I was young, a total spitfire. I wanted this attack really badly, to take over the guard post and break Nikos free. Of course, I had an added incentive — Nikos is my brother, he had fallen into the hands of the authorities and was asking for my help. I had a moral obligation to free him, and that's why I had taken on the most challenging part of the plan. I bid him farewell, promising that in a week I'd be back to tell him whether everything was ready.

The following week we worked feverishly. We drove Kostas' Opel Ascona outside Thessaly and stole a 4x4 van, perfect for the dirt roads of the Thessalian Plain. We drove and left it in one of Larissa's suburbs. The second vehicle we needed was the large truck we'd use to breach the prison walls. This ought to have doubled back wheels as the concertina razor wire would naturally cause some damage when we demolished the wall. Kostas was tasked with stealing and driving the truck, yet he had never stolen or driven such a truck before.

Seek, and you shall find …

We had to find a quiet spot for the theft, the warm-up, and the initial driving tests until he got the hang of it. Only an unguarded quarry would cut it. After checking several we finally chose one on top of the mountain, just outside the town of Anchialos in Volos.

One of the following nights, the Opel's headlights illuminated the quarry's locked boom barrier. It was past midnight and four watchdogs welcomed us, barking. We put down our windows and began throwing grilled chicken at them. After a little while even the wariest among them would protect us from unwelcome visitors. I got out and cut the barrier's padlock using a large bolt cutter, then Kostas drove through and parked his Opel in the far distance.

Inside the quarry were a couple of large trucks with metal trailers, perfect for our job. What made an impression on us were the two massive loading machines, with their huge tires wrapped with thick chains, each of which must have weighed more than fifty tonnes. If only we knew how to drive them! We could have demolished the whole prison! Still, we didn't. After looking at the steel beasts for a while longer, we broke a small padlock and entered a little house that was there. Searching the place using our flashlights, we discovered two large vaults filled with gunpowder rolled and ready to be used, a handful of detonators, safety fuses and detonating fuses. Those would certainly come in handy! We carried them outside and carefully placed them in the Opel's trunk.

It was time for us to focus on what we really wanted: the truck. We picked the newest one as its tires were in better condition, and Kostas soon started it up. After a few back-and-forths, we began. Kostas was leading the way, and I was following close behind, so I had the chance to see first-hand how boldness beats experience. Balancing between life and death, he got the truck to a vacant lot in the western part of the city of Larissa and parked it there.

The following day, we bought a collapsible steel ladder and placed it in the back. Using steel pipes and climbing rope, we built a seven yard long rope ladder. We also made a handful of special nails, which could come in handy in a potential car chase to slash the cop cars' tires.

Over the next few days, having finished this preparatory stage of the operation, we focused on our available firepower. The explosives we'd found in the quarry were an unexpected gift, as long as we found out how we could use them in the best possible way. We tested them, timing the safety fuses, and cut ten pieces of equal size, with a burn time of about seven to ten seconds. We placed them in ten detonators, which in turn we put in ten packs of gunpowder. Then, we bought a steel pipe, the inside diameter of which was equal to that of the gunpowder pack, and we cut that into ten pieces, to the length of the gunpowder packs. After carving them circularly using a grinding disk, creating small rectangular openings on their surface, we placed the gunpowder packs inside. So we had ten little bombs ready to be used, which would give us a huge advantage.

As far as weapons were concerned, we had a 9mm submachine gun, several pump-action shotguns, and some rifles. Back then, guns were not easy to come by (especially in the countryside). The only person who had a handgun was Kostas. We obtained many cartridges of various types and drove to a secluded part of Elassona to test them. The test was to be done on a thick folding sheet iron, which we intended to place on the Opel's back seat, as a protective measure from enemy fire.

The machine gun was in perfect condition. It never once jammed throughout the test. It certainly was one of the guns I'd take with me during the takeover of the guard post. The rifles were brand new, having been recently obtained from the gun shop. They worked perfectly well. Shotguns, when you saw off one-third of the barrel and add a pistol grip, are handy, and also scary, guns to use. Especially when one knows how to properly use them. I decided that if I were to take a back-up gun with me, it would be a pump-action shotgun with eight cartridges.

The sheet iron survived even the single-shots, then it was time for us to test our newly-obtained "super-gun".

Lighting up the fuse and throwing the bomb down the ravine brought to mind my first contact with explosives. I was about eight to ten years old when they began building a forest road to connect the remote residential areas of Pindus to the rest of the world. A world-changing event for us young lads. Sitting on the neighbouring hilltops, we watched enthusiastically as the steel creations of man mercilessly attacked Pindus' resisting rock. When the drills stopped, we already knew what was to follow. We always heard a loud voice, resounding again and again: "Big blast!" At once we saw the culprits, having done their dirty work, run like rats into hiding. We waited for a while and then, out of nowhere, colourful boulders of stone exploded from the bowels of the earth, surrounded by thick patches of dust. Boosh! The deafening sound crawled violently inside our ears, shaking us to our cores. We immediately turned our eyes to the sky to watch the shattered stones fall all around.

Our mischief, apart from messing up with the road construction machines, included stealing explosives so that we could use them when fishing. Using baking paper we would make funnels, placing a stone, some dynamite with a detonator, and a lit fuse inside them. We would throw them inside the large gorges, where we wouldn't normally be able to fish, and run to cover. A little while later thousands of gallons of water would rain down on us, soaking us to the bone. There was no antiterrorist act back then! Fortunately, reason still prevailed. If there's a sentence I would accept without complaint, it would be for this crime of mine against nature, even if I committed it when I was ten.

The near-attack and getting arrested

We returned to headquarters, finally ready for the great attempt. I visited Nikos once again, to tell him about the final details. The die had been cast; the breakout would take place two days from now, at eight sharp. We had two days to double check everything and see whether we needed to make any adjustments to our plan. In the end, we thought it wise for the second getaway car waiting for us behind the hill to be the Opel. For this reason, the night before the attempt, we drove the 4x4 to Terpsithea. We parked it on the village's main road, making sure it didn't obstruct those living nearby.

The next day, at a quarter to eight, we were ready for action. Hidden behind the hill, the truck's engine running, with me in the back of the truck and Kostas in the driver seat, we waited, tuned in to a set radio transmitter frequency, for Thanasis to give us the go-ahead. At five to eight we heard his voice, telling us that the guard had left his post.

Kostas had another big surprise for me. Instead of starting the car, he called me from the window to give me another short-range transmitter, keeping another for himself, so that we too could communicate. I couldn't figure out why he did that. In the future, having to cooperate with him again, I'd realise that though he was good at making plans, he wasn't as good when it came to putting them to action.

"It's ok, Kostas! If I need something, I'll shout through the window".

He insisted, and not wanting to clash with him at this time, I took the transmitter. The absurdity went on.

"Do you copy?"

"Yes, do you?"

And so on and so forth.

The transmitters were not set up, and we were trying to tune them when we ought to be on our way to take over the guard post. Still unmoved, we heard Thanasis' voice informing us that the new guard had entered the guard post. I could barely control my anger. What had just happened was inconceivable. I just couldn't wrap my head around it. Yet I had to restrain myself so as not to spoil our partnership. We'd just have to postpone the operation for a different day. Misfortunes never come singly, however, and this day had a lot of troubles still in store for me.

We left the truck at an opening half a mile away for the night and drove the Opel to pick up Thanasis. We found him at the root of the dirt road. The van that had been parked at Terpsithea since the previous night had to be moved, since the villagers knew one another's cars and it would raise suspicions if it stayed there any longer. Terspithea was a small village. We reached the first houses using the rural route and made a stop for Kostas and Thanasis to get out. The van was parked on the first parallel road. I couldn't see the van from that spot, yet the village was tranquil. A traditional coffee-shop about a hundred yards ahead seemed closed. So there was nothing to be worried about. The guys, taking a shortcut through a trail of sorts, went to pick up the 4x4, taking the submachine gun with them. Picking up the van, they would come back, and we would all drive to Larissa.

Ten yards away from where I had parked, down a slope, was a construction site; the perfect place to take a leak. I got out of the car and headed there. Having finished, I walked back, slouched. Raising my gaze, I found myself in a completely different environment. I realised I was surrounded by approximately ten men. I was dumbstruck. I was caught off guard! I had no gun on me. The rifle was inside the car, next to the gearshift. Things were taking a turn for the worse. One of them tried to ask me something, I tried to answer, and they attacked me. I didn't stand a chance; they were too many. So, out of nowhere, I found myself handcuffed. Moral of the story: when taking a leak, make sure to watch your back.

They took me to the seemingly closed coffee-shop and turned on the lights. As I came to realise, listening to them, they had located the stolen van, slashed one of its rear tires and hid inside the café, waiting to arrest whoever came to get it. When I went to take a leak, they ran towards my car in total silence and waited for me. Out of the ten, only three of them were actually policemen; the rest were plain villagers acting the part. I don't know why they didn't attempt to arrest the two other guys, but from conversations I overheard through their transmitters, I discovered that the guys had driven the 4x4 away, with the police searching for them in the surrounding area.

At last some good news! In my pocket, they found my wallet, with my ID card inside. It was a mistake having it with me.

"Headquarters ... this guy has an ID", one of them said in a thick country accent.

"Give us his information, officer".

"Palaiokostas Vassilios, of Leonidas and ..."

"That's enough, officer. To all units, we are searching for said fugitives. They have a 4x4 Nissan. Notify headquarters as soon as you locate them. They are extremely dangerous. They are heavily armed. All officers should follow self-protection measures ... blah blah blah".

In the meantime ...

"Is this your identity?"

"I think so, yes!"

"No, he's one of the others ... how did they call him from headquarters?"

"You should ask him if you catch him".

"Being a smartass, hey? You'll fess up everything when we get to the station".

The village was swarming with cop cars. They forced me inside one of them, and formed a big convoy around us, then we were off to the Larissa police department. All the cars' emergency lights and their sirens were turned on. The calmness and clarity of mind with which I was facing this tough situation scared me. I hadn't expected to react this way. It was my first arrest, and my offences were severe. They fell under anti-terrorist laws only recently voted through by the government of Konstantinos Mitsotakis,* a Peer of Greece and a profound democrat, whose descendants would also identify their political action with anti-terrorist laws. It's contract work really. Even if there are no terrorists, some must be invented to justify repressive legislation. For the majority of the country's politicians, the ideal regime is repressive, vindictive, and totalitarian. With this in mind, they pass their laws. This is the tragic consequence of politics being regarded as a private initiative within a family business, with all the said family's members considered as having been born able political leaders! Because, apart from being of "royal descent", they all act entitled as well, of course. The whole world revolves around them, and the sun rises to shine over their feats.**

Detainment, an immoral offer and imprisonment

They threw me in a holding cell, nobody came to see me for many hours until at last, a guy came over. They unlocked the door, and he entered.

"I'm a lawyer", he said. "Kostas sent me to tell you he called the police himself and told them where to find the 4x4 and that you had nothing to do with any of this. He asked me to tell you that he is now safe and that you should put the blame on him".

---

*   Konstantinos' son Kyriakos became Prime Minister under the New Democracy government of 2019.

**   Author's Note: nepotism is so deeply rooted in Greece's political system that it has become widely accepted as a normal condition. The Greek people keep electing the offspring of known political families. These families' have control of all the State's mechanisms, actively abolishing the very same notion of democracy. They exercise their authority to serve their personal interests, maintaining and expanding a corrupted, crony system at the very core of Greek society.

"The blame for what? Are we accused of something?"

"Look, Vassilis, things aren't good. They found the truck, the ladders, the explosives etc. You'll be held in custody based on the antiterrorist law. We have to come up with a story, to …"

"We don't have to do anything. I don't want to lie to anyone. Can you call the chief? I want to talk to him".

"Don't you want to tell me as well? If I'm to legally consult you, I need to know".

"Do as I ask. I know what I'm doing. It's my call", I stopped him. In conscious illegality, other things come before legal ploys. I didn't know him, and I just couldn't trust him.

He left disappointed. My distrust for lawyers went back to the beginning of Nikos' struggle when we assigned his defence to a promising young lawyer from Trikala. I had already started suspecting him from one of our first unsupervised visits at the prison (visits he arranged, taking advantage of his reputation). It was me, him, and Nikos, alone in one of the prison's chambers. He didn't allow us to talk in private, on the pretext that since he was the one arranging these meetings, they ought to be strictly focused on Nikos' line of defence. He even urged us to speak in code in front of him. When we tried it, his eyes would fly wide open, and he'd be all ears.

By an odd coincidence, during one of my visits to his office, the landline rang. He seemed uncomfortable in my presence while talking on the phone. He was secretive, speaking in code. He concluded, saying:

"I believe we'll soon have sound developments. At your service … it was my pleasure, chief". He had blurted out that last one by accident. I was really young and completely impulsive back then. Even now, as I'm writing about this incident, I can't figure out how I controlled myself so as not to step on his head like the snake he was. Instead, I calmly asked that he give me Nikos' judicial documents, announcing his dismissal.

The time I spent alone in that holding cell was enough for me to piece together a story which sounded logical, albeit not wholly believable. Kostas was a sentenced man and also a fugitive. To him, this case was of no legal interest. Thanasis and I had no prior criminal records. I had no delusions concerning my fate; my pre-trial detention was certain. Thanasis, however, had to be protected no matter the cost, because he had nothing to do with the orchestration of the plan. The story I had come up with didn't hurt Kostas while it muddied the waters concerning Thanasis. However, I had yet to make a decision. At the mere idea that my partners would think that I wavered or that I acted selfishly, was inclining towards not testifying or answering any of the cops' questions.

What the lawyer had said to me, had, in a sense, untied my hands, from a moral perspective. He had confirmed I was on the right track. Many hours had gone by since the lawyer left when the chief of police appeared outside my cell, followed by a handful of guards.

"Your lawyer told me you wish to speak to me", he said as if I'd spoiled his morning.

"I don't want to talk to you in particular. I just want to testify and clear everything up concerning this case".

"The police will decide when you will testify, not you! Don't be hasty".

"If you're not in a rush, then I'm not either. But I might change my mind later on".

He nodded at the guard to unlock the cell.

"Come on then", he ordered me.

With a legion of cops surrounding me, we climbed several floors until we reached a spacious room, with an oblong table in its middle. They made me sit at the narrow side of the table. Two cops sat across from me wearing plain clothes, pens and papers in their hands. The chief sat to my right and across him sat some butt-face I hadn't seen before. A consultant. The other cops remained standing around us, keeping their distance from the table. What struck me were the four or five people standing together in the corner, staring at me. They were probably civilians, called by the police to identify me. I didn't like that. I concluded that the cops were equally ready for my testimony.

My story was short and plain. Kostas phoned me and asked to see me as a friend of Nikos. We had an appointment at the Larissa bus stop, since I would be getting there by bus. Never in my life had I seen him before. He offered to drive me to prison, giving me some money for Nikos (I had indeed visited Nikos the same day, giving him money). When visiting hours were over, he picked me up to drive me back to Trikala (since it was on his way). We'd only make a quick stop to drop his friend, Thanasis (whom I had also never seen before) at Terpsithea, where he lived.

When I finished my story, I was bombarded with questions and threats. I made it clear that I wouldn't answer any questions.

"This is the one and only truth. If you doubt it, dispute it with evidence. The story will remain the same even if you hang me upside down and skin me alive!" I announced.

"No, we don't do such things ..."

At the time, the Larissa Police Department was notorious for assaulting detainees. To be fair, they treated me rather well. Of course, it was also a publicity matter. They paid attention to such stuff. This doesn't mean they are nice to everybody. This goes for the whole Hellenic Police.

The district attorney indicted me and ordered that I'd be transferred to the examining magistrate. There, a complete novice, I'd learn the way law and legal culture allow their officers to make immoral offers to defendants. When the questioning ritual was over, the examining magistrate began his sermon: "You're a young man, and you don't deserve to go to prison. Based on the charges against you, your future looks really bleak when, being the young man you are, you could create, fall in love and have a family ... a prison sentence is irreversible, you won't get a second chance, you can't turn the clock back" etc.

Then he began speaking using archaic language. Was it legal jargon? I'm not sure; I didn't understand a thing. I think he did it on purpose because right afterwards, he turned to my lawyer and nodded as if saying: "Translate to your little rook".

After a thoughtful silence, my lawyer said:

"Vassilis, can we talk in private for a moment?"

We walked to the corner of the office, and he translated the government official.

"What the examining magistrate is saying is that if you provide evidence for Kostas' arrest, he'll let you go home, immediately".

"What an interesting offer! Are you sure this is what he said?"

"What the hell! I'm a lawyer, I know legal terminology".

"Legal terms ... these are the terms of the devil! Tell that prick, in his language, to go fuck himself.

My pre-trial detention was a one-way street.

BREAKING OUT OF CHALCIS PRISON

A man in uniform

When they arrested me in Larissa they confiscated a small identification tag I wore on my hand, which was a gift from a loved one. The police urged a vengeful goldsmith from Pyrgos, Elis, to identify the gift as having been stolen from his shop, which Nikos had previously robbed. Without requesting any documents that the tag had indeed been taken from the goldsmith, the cops registered it as stolen goods and handed it back to him. Without my knowledge, a file was created against me, portraying me as an accomplice in the robbery. The district attorney of Patra issued five subpoenas over six months and sent them to the Trikala police department to forward to me, so that I could appear and refute the charges. They never notified me, despite knowing where to find me.

After five subpoenas, the district attorney had to issue an arrest warrant against me. Only then did the conniving pricks locate me — and then they were quick about it. The arrest warrant coincided with one of the times I reported to the police station concerning the Larissa incident (which I did every first and fifteenth of the month), where they handcuffed me. They replied to my protests by saying that my mother had received the subpoenas. What a dirty, cheap lie! Yes, my mother was so illiterate that she couldn't even sign her own name (something they knew well enough), but she was also very smart and clued-up. So it couldn't possibly be true. And if it was, she would have told me, since I had been living with her the whole time. Even more so, I reported to the police station twice a month. They could have given me at least one if not all of them.

Nikos meanwhile was once again a fugitive, having managed to break out of Korydallos Prison along with eighty others, after a riot the previous Christmas. By coincidence, in between his escape and my malicious arrest, two incidents had taken place in the city of Trikala, in which we had no involvement. A burglary at a central jewellery shop, for which the police suspected (and they told me so) Nikos, and the burning of the deputy chief's car (he was really nice after all), for which their suspicions fell on me.

Since they couldn't manage to build a case against us and they couldn't even locate Nikos, they found an easy and dirty solution to lock me up. This vile set-up would lead me, a day before Easter, to the Prisoner Transfer Division in Patra.

The building's sole, huge hall was completely empty. As it was Easter Holliday, all inmates had been transferred to the prisons that would permanently house them. As I would later find out, the district attorney and examining magistrate had already decided on my pre-trial imprisonment. This was not proper legal procedure, according to which the defendant has to be made aware of the charges before any decision is made, and given a chance to to refute them. They detained me without doing this so they could go on vacation with their families, where they'd surely have a great time. Your pain, my happiness.

They intended to send me to Patra Prison, but it was too late. Because of the holiday, the prison had stopped receiving inmates. I'd have to spend the three-day holiday alone at the Transfer Division hall. On Easter Day, a forty-year-old lieutenant (I think) was on duty, vehemently cursing his luck for having to work such a day because of me. When, however, I explained to him how his colleagues from Trikala, along with the civil servants at Patra had set me up, he forgot his own problems at once. Curiously enough, he believed I was ready to take my own life, and he wouldn't let me out of his sight. He made sure I had everything I needed and always found nice (at least according to him) subjects for us to talk about. He just couldn't put himself in my shoes, he couldn't understand my reasoning. He mistook it for a self-destructive tendency.

At four, someone else arrived to take over from him, but before he left, he walked to the cell's gate to encourage me:

"Don't worry, Vassilis. Everything in this life ends at some point, this will too!"

"Even life itself", I retorted on purpose.

For a moment, he stared at me, trying to decipher what I was thinking.

"Don't do anything stupid. You're a young man!" he said with the stern look of a patron, and he left. Or so I thought.

Not an hour had gone by when I saw him enter the office, holding two bags. He said something to the officer on duty, and then they both walked over to my cell.

"Vassilis! I brought you some roasted lamb from home. And some Easter bread", he said before whispering, in a conspiratory manner: "I've brought you a few beers as well. Don't say a word."

Before I could thank him, he fumbled inside his pockets and brought out two red Easter eggs. He slipped his hand inside the bars and gave me one of them.

"Come on, let's crack them! Happy Easter!" he exclaimed.

***

More than two months later, I found myself back at the Prisoner Transfer Division in Patra. It took the opium-addicted legal system that long to get going. Its depositaries had finally decided to learn why I was in prison. To ask me for a change.

I did not intend to leave their questions unanswered. Knowing they would summon me to make a plea at some point, I had been preparing an escape. This would be my resounding response to their reasonable, albeit belated, queries. When you're dealing with subhumans who misuse their authority in such a dirty way, escaping is the only option. I had a handcuff key with me, and I was fit as ever. I had been told by some other prisoners that the courthouse was near, around two to three hundred yards from the Prisoner Transfer Division building. Most times, they escorted the prisoners summoned there by the examining magistrate or the district attorney on foot. I couldn't let such an opportunity go to waste.

The hall of the Transfer Division was extremely overcrowded, to the point I missed those three days of solitude. At some point, I heard the barker's steel voice.

"Palaiokostas ... which one are you?"

"That's me!"

"Come outside. The examining magistrate is waiting for you".

He unlocked the door, and I exited. The salaried servant of good handcuffed me (hands to the front) and escorted me outside the offices, where a familiar face appeared. It was the lieutenant that had kept me company on Easter day. The one who had brought me roasted lamb. He didn't recognise me. Working there, he saw hundreds of people come and go every day. And I now had a two-month-old beard. I didn't remind him either. He would be one of the two officers to escort me to the courthouse, and I didn't like that at all.

"Ready, partner?"

"Let's go …"

We climbed down the stairs and stood at the entrance of the building. The lieutenant looked at his colleague:

"I've got it. You don't have to come".

"Are you sure? Don't let him escape".

"And go where? He seems like a nice bloke".

The younger officer jumped at the opportunity and ran away, climbing the stairs and out of sight. We were now alone. He looked me up and down and then asked me, in an intimidating way:

"Why are you inside?"

"I don't even know myself!"

He looked me up and down once again. Then he untied a bunch of keys from his belt, picked the one for the handcuffs, opened them and took them off my hands.

"It doesn't do you any good for people to see you in handcuffs. Come on … move, and I'll be right behind you", I heard him say.

I was dumbstruck. My brain stopped working for a while. I had gotten used to the generous surprises life always had in store for me, but this time the universe had outdone itself. I was up against its most treacherous yet straight game. It was shamelessly testing my innermost soul, its essence. It was bringing me face-to-face with my inner conscious world. The man who, on Easter Day, after finishing his shift at four, instead of staying home and having dinner with his family, returns to the Transfer Division building to offer a prisoner some joy, is probably a good person. When, however, this same man risks his job so that people won't see the prisoner he is escorting in handcuffs, there's no doubt that he is a great person!

Did he deserve to pay for his kindness? And from me? The cuffs being gone, I felt free. The lieutenant escorting me was not particularly fit, not particularly strong either. If I suddenly broke into a run or if I attacked him to acquire his gun, he wouldn't stand a chance. I was prepared to escape, but the unlocking of the cuffs was an especially binding detail for me. As we walked and as we waited in the courthouse corridors, outside the offices, my feet waited for an order to run. And yet my conscience was fettered in chains.

The obvious reasonable counterpoint was that this policeman served the system, albeit doing it in his own way. And when it comes down to your own freedom, there's no place for sentimentalism.

What was at stake for me wasn't what the policeman stood for, but whether I would treat him the way he had, in a humane way. What my story would be in this wild world I now entered willingly, knowing there'd be no going back. Who I'd be and what I'd stand for. Whether my code of merit would allow me to cheat at dice, to achieve the desired result. Through such experiences, that pose extreme personal dilemmas which have to be answered with actions, on the spot, having no time to think them over, life taught me to walk on a tightrope concerning my own double nature. Being, at the same time, an attacker aiming to dismantle the System and a romantic rebel who refuses to dismantle his own character. In a battle between means and end, which justifies the other?

Life owed me and, after almost two months, it paid up. Or, perhaps, it was me who owed life, and I was the one doing the paying. Who knows?

Transferred to Chalcis

At the break of dawn they called the names of all the prisoners who were to be transferred that day over the loudspeaker. Among a handful of others they called my name and those of three other guys, with whom we were planning a breakout from the cellblock which served as solitary confinement for disobedient prisoners. Someone had snitched on us, and the potential snitches were many. Most likely, it was that "cell warrior" who I had approached a few days back, asking him to give me his bed, which he had been unable to refuse. His bed wasn't any better for sleeping in than mine, but it was strategically placed right underneath a window, one of the bars of which we'd have to saw off as part of our escape plan.

Even if there's no proof, suspicions linger, and now it didn't matter since we would shortly be leaving Patra. We packed our things, and half an hour later, we were on a prison bus. When we'd gotten far enough down the road they announced where each of us would go. One of the guys would be transferred to Corfu, another to Trikala, the third to Larissa and I would go to Chalcis. The snitch had done it. He had saved both the prison from a potential breakout and also his bed. What would the State apparatus do without its Ephialtes?*

Along with about ten other prisoners who we met on the new prison bus they had shoved us into at the Transfer Department, who I hadn't met before, Panagiotis (a lifer who had been in the same cellblock but had no part in our planned escape) and I reached Chalcis Prison.

We entered the reception booth, ready for the usual strip-search. After a handful of inmates had undergone body-checks, it was Panagiotis' turn to undress. He took off all his clothes, except for his underwear. The young employee, who had guaranteed a permanent job in the Greek public sector, thought it wise to enrich the humiliating ceremony with his baggage and his sexual complexes. When he had gone through all of Panagiotis' clothes, he turned to him with an attitude:

---

* Ephialtes betrayed Greece in its 480 BC war against Persia by informing Xerxes' army about a back route through the pass of Thermopylae, allowing them to outflank the Greeks and win the battle.

"Take off your panties as well!"

"You're the one wearing panties, you whore! You fucking tranny! You like being butt-fucked, don't you? Fuck you! And fuck your prison as well!"

He just wouldn't stop; he was enraged and, oh, he knew his fair share of four-letter words. The employee was scared stiff. It appeared that he had done this many times before, be it because of his unbridled masculinity or just to have a good laugh, yet now he had found himself in a pickle. His homophobic complexes, which he usually projected on the inmates' underwear, in an attempt to ward them off, now had come back to haunt him. Present in the strip-search procedure were two other employees, who did not intervene in the exchange, not knowing the intentions of the rest of us who were waiting in line to be examined. Some other guards hurried there, a sergeant came too, and I helped calm down Panagiotis, putting an end to the altercation. Because of the commotion, the rest of us didn't undergo strip-searches, entering the prison with all our belongings.

They gave me a bed in a tiny chamber on the first floor, where two elderly inmates and a third, around my age, lived. The prison was closed for leisure time. The young man helped me make my bed. I thanked him and laid down to get some rest. A sudden euphoric high surged through my body,like a strong feeling, a premonition, whispering in my ear that I'd leave this prison. Not when, nor how, only that it would happen. Holding on to this feeling and letting it wash over me, I drifted into a deep sleep. It was around the end of July or the beginning of August, 1991.

I woke up when leisure time was over, got up and went to have a look around. Climbing down the stairs leading to the courtyard, I realised I somehow knew this place. I tried to remember, yet I failed. Only when I turned to my past dreams did I figure out that this facility, just as I was now seeing and experiencing it, had registered in a dream of mine during my stay in Patra Prison. I was too rational to believe that some kind of mystical powers governed my destiny. So I carried on with my reconnaissance.

It was a small, two-floor, stone prison, with large halls and a disproportionate concrete courtyard that made the heat of that August evening even more unbearable. The facilities were old, so there was no interior dead zone, only a tall concrete wall, on top of which fork-shaped steel poles had been placed, along with many lines of barbed wire and above it, two lines of concertina razor wire.

There were three guard posts. The two corner ones were occupied by armed guards with MP5 submachine guns. The middle one remained unmanned, It appeared to be reserved for emergencies since the corner guard posts were located less than six yards away on each side, and therefore could cover it if the need arose. There was another concrete wall, fortified with similar barbed wires and about five feet shorter than the other, beginning at the prison's façade, which ran through the middle of the courtyard until it reached the outer cement wall, right underneath the middle guard post. Inmates used only part of the yard, to the left of the central guard post while other half remained, for reasons I'd never learn, vacant. The fact that the shorter wall led right underneath the middle guard post immediately caught my attention. It was five feet shorter and thus formed a natural step; an advantage to anyone who would take the risk and climb it. And I was prepared to take all sorts of risks to reclaim my freedom.

***

While I was passing these days inside, an armed bank robbery took place with several people getting injured, resulting in a lengthy car chase in the province of Kozani.* Aside from Nikos, who was a fugitive, I had also made the news as one of the robbers! Absolutely insane. What's even crazier is that more than twenty-five years later, they still accuse me of this robbery. A robbery recorded (along with five irrelevant others and a bunch of other falsities) as a historical fact in a book written by the "most renowned" investigative reporter in Greece.** This ultimate transcriptionist of organised crime ceremoniously presented his book to a packed house, with the lard-arses from the ruling left-wing party sitting in the front row.

How could I have taken part in a bank robbery in Kozani, and fifteen days later break out from Chalkis Prison? That goes beyond lack of basic research, that's lack of basic logic! They serve readers whatever the police and the judiciary give them without a second thought. Because when rightdoers write about wrongdoers, they have every right to brutally abuse the truth. It's the distinctive trait shared by all Greek crime and court reporters, to compete with policemen and judges in a competition of irresponsibility.

***

While still in Patra Prison, I had messaged Nikos to aid me in my breakout attempt. He dared not, lest I got in trouble — although I was already in trouble and in prison.

From the moment a man's head is out of his mother's vagina, he's already in trouble. Life itself is the ultimate trouble. This trouble is life's sweet fuel. Whoever can't take it, does not deserve to live. Blessed are those who enrich it with even more trouble from time to time. If and how you get out of it is one's own responsibility. Of course, you may ask for help to deal with that trouble, but not to forsake it. Nikos' refusal, instead of harrowing me, steeled me. I realised I could only count on myself and my own powers. My twenty-five years, my hundred and fifty trained pounds, my build that boosted my confidence in my abilities even more, and, first and foremost, my untamed will, would help me achieve my goal.

I wasn't convicted and yet I didn't wish to enter a fixed legal saga, although everything pointed to the trial going "well". My problem was entirely conscientious

---

*   The capital of West Macedonia, in northern Greece, about five hours' drive from Chalkis.
**   Most likely this is a reference to longtime crime reporter Sompolos Panos, who wrote *Stars of the Criminal Pantheon*.

and not judicial or penal. It was all about my freedom, which I never managed to separate from life itself. I wouldn't consent to a devious process, the goal of which was solely its stake. Nor would I countersign those limits set to freedom by the current system.

On the contrary, I had a sacred duty to follow my personal instinct concerning my own liberty, which was the cornerstone of my moral and conscientious existence. I wished to remain a free-willed human being, and I had no intention of negotiating or handing my right to do so to anyone without a fight. Especially not to "hands" holding bloody keys all day long before caressing their children's heads at night, just because they bring home the bacon. That is their "higher", their "useful" justice.

My first breakout

Every evening, around six, they rolled giant cauldrons containing our supper to the courtyard. Panagiotis was by my side already, still shocked by the incident when we arrived, telling me how much he disliked this particular prison. He wanted to cause a scene and force them to transfer him elsewhere. Suddenly, he stood up and walked to the spot where they were handing out the supper. He started cursing at the deputy warden and the cook for their shitty food etc.

"Why are you handing out the food outdoors? Why aren't you wearing gloves?"

Then they told him something, enraging him even more. He grabbed one of the cauldrons and turned it upside-down. The courtyard was filled with frozen beans, potatoes and indelible red sauce. A real environmental disaster. Backup arrived, they took him to the guardroom where he stayed for a week, and after he'd been beaten up pretty good, they sent him away to Corfu Prison. He had achieved his goal.

Now it was my turn.

I'd spend the next few days observing and collecting information on anything that could prove of use in my upcoming escape. Asking seemingly naïve questions, I learnt that there was a fence outside the wall of the courtyard so that nobody could get near. Another equally important detail was that on the outside, about ten yards away from the right guard post, was the office of the guards on duty. That was both a good and bad thing. It was good because the patrolling guard often walked down the exterior staircase to go there for a smoke, to drink some coffee or water, take a leak etc. And it was bad because I assumed the rest of the guards on duty would be in there too, ready to intervene the moment they got wind of the escape attempt.

On Sundays, the guards were absent for longer periods than usual.

The right-hand guard post had a disadvantage for the guard. The wall running through the courtyard obstructed him from seeing almost half the yard. If someone tried to climb to the unguarded middle guard post at the corner of the perpendicular and the horizontal wall, the guard wouldn't realise it before they reached the top of the wall.

I made my decision. I'd ambush them on Dormition Day when the bell would ring, signifying the closing of the courtyard. The Christian holiday was the most important one of the summer, so I hoped there would be a certain laxity concerning the exterior security measures. With any luck they'd throw a party in the guardroom, and the guard wouldn't be at his post. In the remaining days until the fifteenth of August I had to collect all the materials to make sure my attempted escape would be crowned with success.

First and foremost, I had to find the equipment to make a hook. It had to be heavy enough to reach thirteen feet in the air when I threw it, pulling with it another thirteen feet of makeshift rope, made from sheets. The only material that would do was steel, which isn't easy to find without raising suspicions.

In 'B' wing lived Stathis, a long-termer who was at the end of his sentence and had recently been granted his first furlough. He had been there for a long time. He had survived through harsh conditions, riots and solitary confinements, and so he was quite respected. I had first met him at the Prisoner Transfer Division at Piraeus, where I spent one night after my pre-trial detention concerning the Larissa case. He had shown great interest in me, clearly impressed by what I had attempted to do. So now I went and talked to him as an acquaintance. He was glad to see me, we had a coffee and talked. As we were chatting, I noticed a washing bucket under his bed, the handle of which was made of plasticised steel. I had seen the prison's cleaning crew use similar buckets, but they'd always lock them up in a storage room after they finished their work.

"Where did you find this bucket, my friend?"

"I can bring you one if you like. After my next furlough".

"I don't need the bucket, just its handle".

"What are you up to, kid?" he said, looking at me cheekily. "Be careful. The prison is full of snitches".

"I know, that's why I'm talking to you".

"Will you need many of these?"

"At least five. And the sooner I have them, the better".

"You're in a hurry, I see. Are you thinking of celebrating Dormition Day outside?"

"That's the plan. What do you say?"

"With luck, anything is possible".

"Could you get me some bandages?" I asked.

"Do you need many?"

"At least eight".

"Are you planning on dressing up as Lazarus?" he laughed. "I'll try and get you everything soon. Keep an eye out for snitches, this shithole's swarming with 'em".

"Don't worry, I will. Thank you anyway".

I left Stathis' cell confident he'd find what I'd asked him.

The riskiest thing during my escape would be the injuries. There was a big chance that the razor and barbed wire would seriously injure me, severing some tendon in my hand and making it impossible to continue with the attempt. For this reason, I had to diligently bandage my wrists and elbows.

Climbing to the middle unguarded guard post, I'd have to fall from a height of more than eighteen feet, outside the wall, not knowing whether the ground below was flat. If it wasn't, I ran the risk of hurting myself, and that's why bandaging my knees and ankles would also be necessary. As for the possibility of being wounded by a guard's bullet ... there were no solutions for that, so I left it to their own discretion and kindness.

* * *

The fifteenth of August was approaching fast, and everything was progressing smoothly. I had visited the prison pharmacy a handful of times in the previous days, using a supposed workout injury as an excuse, and I had extracted several bandages. After the prison bell rang, announcing afternoon leisure time, the countdown began for the final stage of my preparations. The young man sharing my cell was a good lad from some village in Agrinio, who was serving a sentence for growing pot (if I remember correctly). He was rather short, he had a spark about him, a shine in his eye, and his whole body was covered in tattoos. After the prison locked down and our two old cellmates fell asleep, I nodded at him, calling him to my bed.

"Can you keep a secret?" I asked him.

"To the grave", he replied.

I handed him a razor.

"Hold it and cut where I tell you".

We cut two bedsheets into thin strips, making sure not to wake up our cellmates or be seen by any guard who might come peering through our door's peephole. I placed the strips inside a washing bucket and hid it under my bed. At four, the courtyard opened once again. Stathis came himself to bring me six steel bucket handles and eight large bandages.

"Thankyou, brother. I owe you".

"You owe me nothing. I hope you know what you're doing. Be careful".

"Don't worry, I'll be fine. I hope we don't see each other again in a place like this".

"Amen", he replied as he walked away.

The regular evening uproar was coming from the courtyard. Shaking off their fate, the Earth's damned were wasting their time playing football in the small concrete courtyard-moat of the prison, under the blazing sun and the watchful eyes of the guards. I placed all the handles inside the bucket, along with the bandages and an uncut bed sheet. I covered the bucket with a towel; took a tracksuit and a pair of sneakers, and went to the bathroom.

The bathroom was divided into small chambers, each big enough to fit a single inmate at a time. Shy inmates could tie a bedsheet over the door. I did precisely that, hiding from the prying eyes of all the busybodies, and got down to work at once.

I turned on the tap to give the impression I was taking a shower and then I started to make the hook. I bent the handles into V shapes, curving their ends a bit, to make double hook shapes. I put them all together and tied them tight, turning them into one functional hook. I wasn't happy with its weight, but that's what I had, and it would have to do.

Next I tied three sheet-strips around the showerhead pipe and wove a pretty nice rope. I repeated the process once more, then I tied the strings together, placing the hook at their end. I coiled the rope, with the hook attached to it, and put that back inside the bucket. Finally I bandaged my ankles, my knees, then my elbows and my wrists. The tracksuit was out of season, yet there was no better way to cover all these bandages. I hoped I'd blend in with the fashion-show models that were always flaunting their new collections on the "look at me homegirls" courtyard runway (you have to hold on to something to survive in this forbidding place). I put the tracksuit and the sneakers back on, and exited to the courtyard, bucket in hand.

In this prison, washing buckets served multiple purposes. Prisoners would sit on them in the yard since there was nothing more suitable. The spot where I had to be when I made my attempt was occupied by three inmates sitting on their buckets. I approached them, turned my own bucket upside down nearby and sat on it to watch the end of the football match. The score was about twenty-three to seventeen. I saw Stathis and the young lad from my cell sitting on the steps leading to the prison building. They seemed to be casually smoking their cigarettes. I was sure they'd saved up their seats to watch a real-time escape. After all, they must have felt a bit privileged, since nobody else knew what was about to happen.

At half-past eight the bell rang, calling the prisoners to vacate the courtyard. The guard, as I'd predicted, wasn't at his post. The three inmates standing in my way however just wouldn't shove off. They were waiting for everyone else to leave but I couldn't wait for them. I took the rope out of my bucket and walked up to them.

"Stand aside. I'm breaking out!" I declared seriously.

They took their seats, eyes wide open, and hurried away.

They took their buckets, eyes wide open, and hurried away. I threw the hook with all my strength high above the corner of the two walls, aiming for the shorter one. The rope had gotten wet in the shower, and its weight prevented the hook from reaching as high as I wanted. It latched onto one of the concertina razor wires and pulling down, it reached my hands. Now was not the time for self-pity.

I grabbed it, and its razors slipped bone-deep in my palms. But who gives a damn about the details? I climbed up the short wall and then, with a leap, found myself outside the middle guard-post.

"Hey! Where are you going?" screamed the courtyard guard.

"You'll see!" I answered before jumping off the edge.

Landing outside the wall, I was shaken to the bone. The ground was cemented with an overlay of rubble; terrible for my feet. I wasn't hurting anywhere though; the bandages had done their job. At that precise moment, under the left guard post, a guard appeared from the corner of the wall, running towards me, a machine gun in hand, shouting repeatedly:

"Freeze! Freeze!"

I didn't pay him any attention. I jumped over the last easy barrier (a rudimentary exterior fence) and ran as fast as I could, heading right towards the sea. I reached a small cove, where four or five people were swimming and fishing. I passed them naturally, as though I were merely out for a jog. They didn't even notice me, nor did they spot my ripped tracksuit and my bloody hand. I ran a couple hundred yards more and, after making sure nobody had seen me, took cover in the undergrowth. I was away from any residential area, and soon darkness would fall. If they didn't locate me in the next fifteen to thirty minutes, the night would be my ally.

While counting my wounds I could hear police sirens in the distance. Apart from a deep cut on my elbow, which almost severed an artery, my other injuries weren't as serious. Night had fallen by the time I was done. I took off all the bandages and climbed down towards the sea, to wash my hands. The seawater's iodine would do them good.

About an hour later, I found myself sitting on a rock, high on the mountain above the city of Chalcis. The illuminated city, the sounds from fishing boats and sailboats which crossed the Gulf of Euboea like fireflies, imbued the night's scenery with a sense of deep serenity. Insatiably looking around myself and gazing at the moonlit horizon, I realised that, for a fugitive, freedom is not an abstract concept which invites philosophical contemplation. I had concrete evidence that freedom's limits should be set only by those who persistently, actively, and passionately seek it. Where would I have been that night if I hadn't taken a risk? In a small chamber reeking of death. So freedom requires virtue and daring.* Still, I knew well enough that nothing had been set in stone yet. This was the first, albeit defining, step towards achieving freedom. Now began the long struggle to maintain it.

That far above sea level it wasn't easy getting my bearings. I headed south towards Vasiliko, intending to reach the sea by the next evening and then use some boat to sail across the gulf to the Aulis beach. I was most concerned with obtaining new clothes and shoes since the ones I was wearing had been shredded to pieces by the razor wire. After hours of walking I found myself outside a detached house. I made sure there was no dog in the property and entered the yard. I found a pair of summer shoes on the landing. A decent pair of Bermuda shorts and a t-shirt were hanging on the clothesline as if waiting for me. I took them and left quietly, so as not to wake the residents. A bit further down, I threw away my old clothes and put on the new. They were all a size too big but freshly washed, smelling of soap. It was a nice feeling after all these hours I'd spent smelling of blood.

At first light I reached the coast. I located an abandoned factory on a forested hill, about a mile from the sea. It was an ideal place to spend the day, without

---

*   This is a homage to Andreas Kalvos' poem 'Lyrika, ode fourth, To Samos' (1826) which reads: "Let those who feel the heavy brazen hand of fear, bear slavery; freedom needs virtue and daring".

being noticed by anyone who might have heard about my escape. Euboea's entire police force would soon be out searching for me.

The abandoned factory was quite big and I remained inside it all day, drinking water from a bottle I had "stolen" from a wayside shrine the previous night. Fortunately, the water was fresh. Later, I climbed to the first floor, where the factory's offices were once housed. I found an old shabby leather armchair. I carried it to a small balcony and gazed at the Gulf of Euboea. From up there, I watched the most beautiful sunset I had ever seen in my life, which I simply can't put into words. It was magical; all existence had been dyed crimson. When darkness fell, I walked the remainder of the distance towards the shore.

Near a fishing village, I found a handful of fishing boats moored in a shoal. I picked one with paddles and a small engine. The waters were too shallow so I had to push it further into the sea before I turned on its engine, but less than ten minutes later, the boat reached the opposite shore. I didn't want to leave it there, because when they located it the next morning they'd suspect it was my doing and focus their searches in that area, so I tied a rope around the engine's throttle, turned it to face Euboea and let it disappear into the gulf.

Back on land I located the railroad tracks, and after a few hours had reached Avlon. I broke into a farmhouse whose residents were away and found some money, not much but enough for me to travel to Athens by train and take a cab if I had to. It was the first — and hopefully the last — time I entered someone's home uninvited out of necessity. I dreaded the feeling because I've always considered homes sacred places, a kind of personal asylum. Which is why I wrote a short letter to its owners, explaining that I really needed the money I took from them and begging them to empathise. Under no circumstances would I have done something similar if I had entered a villa in Ekali. But a humble shelter and a guarded palace are two different things.

From there I boarded the first train to Athens. In the city I was accommodated for a long time by a family, with which I shared no relation or common ideological stimuli as far as politics were concerned, and which expected nothing from me in return. Yet this family possessed a quality far superior. They showed solidarity with a hunted man. I hope they're well.

CHASED DOWN THE KALABAKA HIGHWAY

My first confrontation with the police, and the car chase that ensued, began from a traffic violation and had an unexpected, almost comedic, outcome.

It was the autumn of 1991, a while after I escaped from Chalcis Prison. Along with my partner Kostas (who had coincidentally also escaped), we were travelling from town to town, planning and executing armed bank robberies. That morning found us behind the wheel. Kostas was driving a Volkswagen Golf, and I was following close behind in a pretty weathered white Volkswagen van. We were rolling along the Kalabaka-Ioannina highway, on our way to Ioannina. This highway was an endless winding road, alternating between upward slopes and steep gradients, which the Golf enjoyed, being in its element. My van and I meanwhile were praying for this Golgotha to end as soon as possible.

Our prayers would soon be heard. A couple of miles before reaching the village of Panagia, on a left uphill curve, trying to maintain a decent speed, I drove the car right onto the wrong lane. It's common knowledge that the Hellenic Police are ubiquitous and never leave a crime such as the one I had just committed unpunished. The proof was right in front of me. The moment of the violation, a cop car with two policemen inside entered the curve on the opposite lane, in the direction of Kalabaka. We almost crashed.

They noticed, and before they were out of my sight I saw their car's lightbar begin to flash. I kept driving, certain they would make a U-turn to come and inspect the violator. I repeatedly turned my headlights on and off to alert Kostas of the upcoming confrontation. To my great surprise, he stepped on it and vanished around the next turn. It goes without saying that a leading car, which hasn't got the role of a herald and whose driver is armed, doesn't pick up speed and vanish when only a few seconds before it has come across an oncoming cop car. Let alone when a partner whose car is of lesser ability is trailing right behind it. When two or more drivers are on a mission road trip, they must maintain eye-contact and, if possible, constant communication via wireless.

Of course, from time to time, something unexpected comes up and so this is not always doable. Yet it is essential for both drivers to always keep in mind that they're not alone on this trip and that their partner might at any time require their assistance. A certain lack of vigilance on their part can only be justified when there's a co-driver in all participating vehicles, who won't hesitate to use a gun in a sudden, tough situation. And only in the instance that none of the said vehicles is carrying something of value that must not be lost. It's preferable not to have an assisting car at all, or to not consider one as such in case of a confrontation. Because otherwise, the driver and the other people (if there are any) onboard are trapped in futile expectation.

The van, apart from being weather-beaten, was also pretty loaded. Inside it was an Enduro motorcycle, guns, and lots of equipment, intended for future plans.

So it wasn't a car that would bear up to a car chase, especially on this particular highway. In the meantime, the cop car appeared in the van's wing mirrors. Mere seconds later it was right behind me, its siren screaming. They tried to overtake, stop me and inspect the vehicle. I thought this was quite rude. The issue at hand directly concerned me; they should have asked.

When people ignore my opinion, I occasionally get mad.

With a sudden turn of the steering wheel to the left I blocked them, forcing them to remain on my trail. This farce, them trying tooth and nail to overtake and me not allowing them, continued for more than a mile. At some point, in a stretch of the highway which was accompanied by a fairly wide overlook, they seized the opportunity and got out in front. That didn't radically change things. The problem wasn't solved for them; it just made the comedy unfolding right before my eyes that much more enjoyable. They were slamming on the brakes and swerving all around, trying to force the van to a halt, and I was right behind them, having no such intention, one moment driving on one lane and the next on the other, avoiding them.

Having the cop car in front of me was an advantage because, from my vantage point inside the taller van, I could see what was happening inside it. The driver was repeatedly checking the car's wing mirrors to keep track of what was happening, while the co-driver was peering at me behind the back seat of the vehicle. Suddenly, I became aware that the co-driver was holding a gun in his right hand. I concluded he was about to use it.

All right. I had to end it now, otherwise things would go south for me. Beside me, in the passenger seat, I had a black sawed-off shotgun with a pistol grip, looted from a provincial town's gun shop. I grabbed it and pressed it onto the van's windscreen. Then I put it back in the passenger seat and raised my right forefinger, motioning to them that guns wouldn't prove to be a wise choice on their part. They kept on staring at me, obviously bewildered now. They exchanged some words with each other, they turned off their lightbar and their siren, they stepped on it and vanished into thin air.

I never saw them again. As if they'd start a fight in the middle of nowhere with some stranger who had just shown them his shotgun, indicating he had no intention of changing direction. The nearest village was only a few miles away. It offered real tsipouro and delicious appetizers. Oh, how beautiful life is! As if they'd spoil their evening …

I kept on driving until, at an overlook, I came across the Golf. Kostas was waiting for me in the driver seat. It appeared that seeing the cop car drive past him, he'd had the decency to stop. After a small quarrel ("why did you leave", "I didn't see the cop car returning" etc.), we decided to head to Kalabaka. At some point, we changed direction, deciding to head to Grevena instead, because we didn't know if we were in the clear.

In this first car chase I ever took part in, I took advantage of the circumstances in the best possible way. I had to deal with two policemen, probably from one of the local police stations. That meant a lack of experience concerning such incidents.

They couldn't have assessed the gravity of the situation. The mountainous terrain hindered any communication via wireless. So they couldn't have been informed that the van was stolen. They also couldn't call others for backup.

All these things along with their lack of training — we're talking about 1991 — caused them unbearable stress, which gradually peaked during the car chase. So when I showed them my shotgun, they had already reason enough to get as far away as they could from this unexpected troublemaker. Now having the real and valid excuse that this unidentified male was heavily armed and that it wouldn't have been wise to have gotten involved in a firefight, they avoided the confrontation.

Of course, they weren't off for drinks, as I said tongue-in-cheek. Instead, they headed to the nearest police station to acquire bulletproof vests and MP5 submachines. After notifying their partners, who in turn notified the closest police stations, they were back on the road to search for the insolent armed man who had forced two officers of the law into a disorderly flight, all the while hoping and praying not to come across him again.

It goes without saying that how a car chase plays out is never a given. From the moment it began and throughout its twists and turns I was on full alert, ready for anything and everything, even an armed clash. I could have put an end to it before it even began, executing the two policemen, pretending I was willing to undergo a traffic stop. After all, the whole incident began with a traffic violation. Yet such a course of action was and still remains incompatible with my personality. Of course, if they'd started the shootout first, their drinks would be on me, and they would be drinking them in Saint Peter's company.

Another option would have been to abandon the van and vanish into the surrounding forests. But then they would have seized some handy equipment, which would tip them off about whom it belonged to and what these people were planning to do with it. Moreover, I was secretly hoping Kostas would be kind enough to stop and check whether I was all right. As if!

Another parameter of this car chase which I have to mention, and quite an important one, in my opinion, is that at that time cops and criminals rarely used guns; it was the last thing they thought to do. Not because they lacked bravery or courage, but because they were fully aware that guns take lives and they knew what life meant. That's why they exhausted every other option first, to reach the desired result for each side. It was an informal agreement between opposing armed sides, upheld by both, as a gentlemen's moral standard.

No big deal — they caught me eight years later!

EMPORIKI: MY FIRST BANK JOB

Bank robbers and robberies

Until 1991, armed bank robberies in provincial towns were extremely rare, non-existent even. The reasons were varied and quite complex. The main one was that there weren't many organised teams which could set armed bank robberies in motion. The ones that did acted mostly within the Attica basin. Some armed robberies took place in Thessaloniki as well, but nothing significant. These teams had no motive whatsoever to travel to a provincial town and attempt something in a place they didn't know well, where the tactics of organising and carrying out an armed robbery were very different than the city of Athens. They orchestrated and realised their plans in places they knew well. At that time, the congestion and decline of armed bank robberies hadn't taken place yet. Bank branches were much fewer than they are today, with lesser security measures and, of course, a lot more cash in their counters.

Even when an armed robbery took place in the Attica basin, it was treated by the media as a significant occurrence. They made extended reports on the subject because it wasn't something ordinary.

Also, more than two decades earlier, the only banks that had branches in provincial towns were the National Bank, Emporiki Bank, the Agricultural Bank and, rarely, private institutions. And they were all located in the main square of each town, with a cop car always parked nearby. That meant an inevitable confrontation with the police officers inside it, in case of a robbery. All these facts deterred any thoughts of decentralising armed bank robberies.

The robberies I have taken part in are too many, and there's no reason to mention all of them. So I'll pick two, based on their unique characteristics — which make these robberies stand out and go beyond the regular process of getting in, taking the money, and leaving. These two robberies unravelled into fully fletched adventures towards self-knowledge.

My first

Towards the end of the year we were thinking seriously about proceeding with an armed bank robbery in a provincial town, which would be our first. After exhaustive searches we located a branch of Emporiki bank in Ioannina, in a great spot near the city centre, right on the road to Arta. The branch was relatively small, so we wouldn't need a third person to stand guard outside. We found it ideal for the beginning of our new career.

On an operational level, our lack of relevant prior experience aside, we had almost everything we needed. We had guns, and already possessed two stolen cars, always able to get more if we needed them. All that remained was to plan our getaway, since we had no intention of staying in town or even in the region after the robbery. After careful consideration, we decided on a route that indirectly led to the prefecture of Kozani that didn't include any highways. Large parts of the country roads we selected were dirt paths which ran through mountainous areas, where abrupt weather changes are quite common. Therefore, we thought it wise for our second car, our getaway car, to be an off-road vehicle. A few nights later we travelled to Agrinio and picked up an almost brand-new Range Rover. Now we had three cars at our disposal. We would first use the Golf to rob the bank and then the Range Rover to escape. Still, we had to do something with the van, which had lots of useful equipment and quite a few fingerprints on its interior.

From the outset, I thought we should drive it to some nearby city, thinking that if it remained in Ioannina, it was highly likely that we wouldn't be able to retrieve it and that it would be located by the police (as it was). Yet Kostas was quite insecure. He wanted a third getaway car in case something went wrong.

"I'm like a fox. I want to have many options when it comes to escaping", he would say to me.

"We are not foxes but armed men attempting to rob a bank. If things go awry, we'll use our guns to seize the first passing vehicle that comes into view", I would answer, trying to encourage him. A complete waste of time. His insecurity was slowing us down, and I wanted to travel abroad, where Nikos was waiting for me. Unable to stand it any longer, I made it clear to him that if we didn't go through with the job the following day, he should count me out.

There was a strong military presence in Ioannina, as it is a border town, so we obtained camouflage clothing, on which we placed captain and lieutenant insignia respectively, plus camouflage caps with the national emblem. Our attire would help us blend in, both as we approached the bank and as we fled from it.

At eight sharp, Monday morning, we parked the black Golf outside the Emporiki bank's Ioannina branch. Everything seemed fine. We looked at each other, pulled up our hoods and, nodding, opened the doors in unison. Being towards the side of the bank, I ran up the stairs and opened the double glass door. The bank teller was right across from me; the vault behind him wide open. Perfect! I threw a sack in his direction and pointed my shotgun at him.

"Hey, champ! If you haven't already figured it out, this is a robbery. Put all the money in the sack, and you'll live!"

For a moment, the teller was dumbstruck. He stared at the bank manager, who was sitting across from him and to the left, waiting to be given a solution to this unexpected problem.

"Do as he says," suggested the prudent manager. So the teller began filling the sack, looking quite relieved. As it was early in the morning, there was only a single female customer in the hall. Kostas had taken position by the entrance of the bank, holding an Uzi. We had predicted everything, apart from the fact that we'd find the vault already open and full of money. Despite the teller's best efforts to fit more cash inside the sack, it soon became apparent that a lot would have to be left behind.

"I can't fit any more in", he said to me, visibly saddened.

"Don't worry, we're not greedy!"

I took the sack. We apologised for the inconvenience, bid them good morning, and left. The road was quiet. We jumped in the car, drove about five hundred yards down the main road and took a right. Following the narrow streets, we reached an apartment building's veranda, where we had parked the Range Rover. We drove inside the veranda, transferred the money and our equipment to the new vehicle, and were ready to drive away when we realised our four-legged partner had gotten off the SUV. No matter how hard we tried to convince him to follow us, he just wouldn't. Perhaps he didn't agree with what we had just done, or he may have been angry with us for not assigning him lookout duty during the robbery.

***

Kostas had found this large pup just outside the city of Serres while on his way to take a leak. He'd heard it whining inside the bushes, picked it up and brought it to my car.

"Do you want him to keep you company?"

"Yes, sure! The more, the merrier; throw him in the back ..."

He had furry white hair, with some black patches. He was quite big; a Greek shepherd for sure. In the following three months he had gotten even bigger and we had grown inseparable; he had adjusted entirely to life on the run. I have several stories to tell about him too — once he destroyed the whole interior of a stolen car, as a way to show his dissatisfaction for having been left alone for an entire night. Another time he jumped through the half-open car window and, following our scent, had reached the taverna where we were eating, making us buy him lamb chops. Another time, I had a fight with a friend of Kostas because he complained the shepherd was ruining his garden. A different time, some female students at the University of Ioannina had tried to "abduct" him ...

Yet now, as luck would have it, he wouldn't let us catch him.

***

We couldn't wait any longer; the cop cars' sirens were screaming very close to us. We decided to abandon our four-legged partner, the only Greek shepherd who has participated in an armed bank robbery, even if only as a standby, and who would now never get his share to spend on treats. I was devastated.

We left Ioannina behind us and took a byway to Kalpaki. For a few days, and that day even more so, there was thick fog covering the whole prefecture of Ioannina, and so we were driving slowly. Eventually a steel bridge, guarded by soldiers, emerged through the fog. They asked us where we were heading, as required. We had already taken off the military clothes and made sure we had quite a few cartons of cigarettes on hand.

I grabbed four Marlboro cartons: "We came to bring you cigarettes, lads ... take them!"

That was it. The soldiers took the cigarettes smiling, saluted us, and we crossed the bridge. We continued driving to Konitsa. A few miles later, we entered a dirt road to our right that led to Samarina and from there to Grevena. Surrounded by the fog, we drove through a thick beech and black pine forest on the foothills of Smolikas Mountain, following a slippery, wet, agricultural road. From time to time, we came across hunters driving their motors or farmers driving 4x4 pickup trucks. The local roads that cross most Greek mountains are impassable for an everyday car when wet. We had a 4.6 Range Rover and felt invincible. Though not for long ...

Kostas, feeling we were no longer in danger, since we had almost reached the county limits, wanted to test both his driving skills and the car's off-road capabilities. Things quickly went wrong. In a small plateau, on a stretch of the road, Kostas stepped on the gas a little harder than he should have. Next thing we knew, the SUV was stuck in thick mud to the right of the road.

At first, we thought we could get it unstuck ourselves. As if! The more we tried, the more the two-tonne beast sunk in the cloying mud. We now found ourselves fugitives, having committed an armed bank robbery in Ioannina just a few hours before, in a pastoral, autumn landscape between Ioannina, Grevena and Kozani. Our getaway car was stuck in the mud, full of guns and money, and we had no idea whatsoever as to what to do.

It was late in the afternoon when a Vitara appeared through the fog, its headlights lit. It belonged to two hunters from Athens. They pulled over and after giving us credit for our exploit, asked what brought us there. We pretended to be rich kids who had taken their dad's car for a little adventure but fucked it up. They offered to help the two rich kids yet, despite the Vitara's earnest efforts, the Range Rover refused to move. Then another two local hunters appeared, driving a 4x4 Nissan pickup truck. They also tried their luck but to no avail. It was them who suggested that we call an acquaintance of theirs who lived nearby, who owned a tractor and who could possibly get our Rover unstuck (for a price, of course, us being rich kids and all). They spoke to him on the wireless and assured us he'd be here in one, one-and-a-half hours tops because he had another job in a neighbouring village.

As they say, though, while the grass grows, the horse starves. We didn't have an option; we had to wait until dark.

We thanked the hunters for their efforts, and when they were out of sight, we decided that while we waited for the tractor we ought to count the bank loot —what a pleasant way to waste your time. It amounted to twenty-four million drachmas,* not bad for first-timers. We waited for the tractor in vain, until nightfall. We had to make a decision, which was simply to abandon the motor and walk to the nearest village. We gathered everything we had inside the SUV that was of no use to us anymore and set them on fire, pouring a whole tank of gas over them. We cleaned the van's interior in case there were any fingerprints

---

*   Approx £75,000 at 1991 exchange rates, worth roughly £165,000 in 2021.

left, we left its windows open so that its interior would soak in the mountain's moisture during the night, and began our night-time walk towards Eptahori village in Kozani.

We weren't stressing over the outcome of our attempt. We had reliable flashlights and maps of all the area's dirt roads and byways. After all, in situations like this I always have a very keen sense of direction, having been born and raised in similar mountains. The most pressing problem was the weight of the things we were carrying. The money was split in two and placed inside our backpacks. And although they too proved heavy enough for such a long distance, it was the excess firearms that truly made things difficult. Aside from our defensive weapons, which included a handgun and a sawed-off shotgun with plenty of cartridges, we had quite a few more sawed-off shotguns and a lot of ammo which were heavy and cumbersome to carry. And we couldn't just set them on fire like everything else.

We had no choice but to get rid of them. So, as we kept on walking, with the freezing drizzle soaking our bodies to the bone and the surrounding mountainous vegetation dipped in thick fog and darkness, we threw the excess firearms as far as we could to the left and to the right of the forest road. We filled the forest with sawed-off shotguns and cartridges. We kept on walking for hours until at the crack of dawn, exhausted, we saw the lights of Eptahori village. We waited until the first coffee shop opened its doors and phoned a taxi to pick us up. The driver took us to Larissa, and from there we used public transport to get to Athens.

It still wasn't over for Kostas. Without informing me, he phoned the Range Rover's owner and asked for a million drachmas* to give it back to him. Because the car hadn't got proper customs clearance documents and he didn't want to involve the police, the owner agreed.

He sent the money via the driver of the intercity bus doing the Agrinio — Athens route, which would arrive in Athens in a few hours. Kostas, absolutely delighted, told me the good news, asking me to get ready to go and pick up the money.

"Come on now, man. What did you do? You arranged to get money for a car that was used in a robbery without even bothering to ask me? Only yesterday we did our first armed bank robbery. We got a lot of money ..."

His answer hit me hard:

"So what? Would you mind having half a million more?"

I made it clear to him that I didn't agree with this action of his and that I was not in the mood to pick up the money. He left, only to return just after midnight, along with a mutual associate, to split the money in front of me. No one really knows what the souls of men incubate.

If I had been unsure whether to escape abroad or stay and continue with the armed robberies, this incident persuaded me, fifteen days later, to travel to Belgium.

---

*   About £7,000 in today's money.

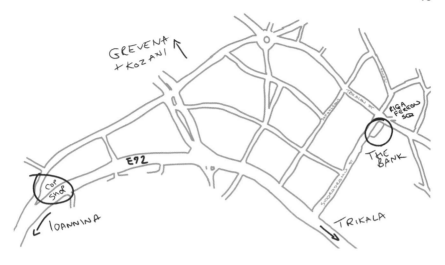

ROBBING THE NATIONAL BANK IN KALABAKA

The robbery

Ducked behind the wheel of a Nissan 4x4, penlight in his mouth and a small bolt-cutter in hand, Kostas stripped the wires off its lock. I was keeping watch, kneeling by the car's right door, holding a sawed-off shotgun and a tool of my own making for breaking steering wheel locks. Fifty yards further down the road, among other parked cars and sitting in the driver seat of his new crush, a brand new, all-red Opel two-litre (imported from Germany and stolen from Koufalia, a town in Pella), was Nikos, ready to intervene.

It was early June, at half past four in the morning, and we were trying to steal the Nissan, which was parked on a byway at a small town in Thessaly, as the full moon shone down on us, exposing our sin. There was dead silence, only a night-bird squawked mournfully, prompting the wireless into life.

"Hey man ... what's going on? Are you done?"

"It's going well".

"If you can't do it then leave it, I have a bad feeling. Don't you hear the fucking bird?"

"Don't worry. We'll take it. We're almost done".

"Come on. Give me the tool", I heard Kostas snigger. I chuckled too. We both knew how superstitious Nikos was.

The tool clipped onto the steering wheel. Crack! It was ready. We took the car and left. We headed to Kalabaka, where we had left a charcoal grey Audi 80. From there, driving the three vehicles along byways in Grevena and Kozani, we had to travel to Ptolemaida, where a branch of the National Bank awaited to be cleaned out. That was the plan, but we were running late and we wouldn't get there in time. Kostas agreed. Perhaps we ought to postpone the operation or change our target?

Before reaching Kalabaka I called Nikos, who was trailing us, on the wireless to share our concerns. He agreed, so we decided to find a quiet spot and make a collective decision. We parked the cars at a vantage point which wasn't visible from afar and began discussing things.

Kostas suggested that we postpone the job for the following day. Nikos pointed out the obvious. That day was the first working day of the month, and all branches of the National Bank would be loaded with cash because of all the payments. Aside from that, we'd also have to stay another day on the road, with three stolen cars, playing with fire. So he tabled the National Bank's branch in Kalabaka. We had considered it before, but had decided on the Ptolemaida branch thinking that, because of Kalabaka's location, they would surely pin any robbery on us, and so we dismissed it. Kostas expressed this same concern once again, requesting my own opinion.

"Fuck it, Kostas. As if they wouldn't pin the Ptolemaida branch's robbery on us as well. They pin every bank robbery that happens in the countryside on us!"

"Well, we can't really blame them, can we?" he said, smiling from ear to ear.

In the end he agreed to do it. The target had changed. We only had a few hours to carefully craft a plan of attack and our getaway. We knew the area well and Nikos and Kostas were familiar with the bank's interior, having visited it in the past as customers. We had cars, guns too. We had plenty of determination and experience. With any luck, everything would go well.

Reaching the town, we parked the pickup truck on a narrow street, and we all got in the Opel to locate the place where we would switch cars after the robbery. The idea of heading to Grevena or Ioannina was dismissed as the "Acropolis" rally was taking place, and their races would be on the dirt roads between these two regions. The races are usually broadcast live on TV, so there would be numerous TV helicopters flying in the surrounding area. If we found ourselves trapped by accident, they would probably help the police to capture us, if asked. We decided to pretend we were heading to Grevena and then, after switching cars, change direction towards Kalabaka and from there towards the Thessalian Plain. We found a suitable switching point about six miles further down the Kalabaka-Grevena highway. Just after the fork in the road, near the bridge in Mourgani village, we took a right turn onto a dirt road which, to our great surprise, crossed some old railway tracks. These tracks ran inside a dark, abandoned, railway tunnel to our right. It was the ideal place to hide our getaway car.

Wasting no time, we travelled to Kalabaka. Kostas took the Audi, and we drove back to the tunnel with the other two vehicles. So we left Nikos' beau to wait for us patiently there, hidden inside the railway tunnel. At five to eight, we found ourselves driving once again past the first houses of Kalabaka. Nikos parked behind the pick-up truck and we switched cars. I sat in the passenger seat, letting

Kostas take the wheel. We began driving, with Nikos following close behind, until we reached the local police station. A cop car was missing. Perhaps it was on patrol, but we had no intention of waiting for it. Kostas drove the van onto the sidewalk, vertically blocking the cops' parking lot. We locked the car, got in the Audi and the countdown began.

We had almost reached the bank when Kostas remembered he had left a makeshift silencer in his van, which he had made for the Uzi.— he demanded that we return to pick it up.

"Have you lost it? We're here, outside the bank, and you want us to go back into the belly of the beast?"

"Come on, Nikos. The silencer has my fingerprints on it".

"I don't give a damn. We've worked too hard to let a fucking silencer ruin everything!"

"Ok, fine! Let's go to the bank".

That was the short, lively debate among the two men. We drove around the central square and parked the Audi around the corner of the descending road, right outside the National Bank. I was sitting in the back seat and got out first. I was holding a large debris bag, inside which were two loaded, sawed-off, seven-round shotguns, and a big rucksack. Kostas, who was sitting in the passenger seat, got out second. He had an Uzi strapped under his coat. Nikos, the driver, got out last. In this order, we climbed the handful of steps separating us from the bank's entrance. We were all wearing sunglasses and jockey caps. Kostas stayed back to guard the door. I, being a step ahead of Nikos, got a sawed-off shotgun out of my bag and threw it at him. He grabbed it mid-air. I took out the other one as well, and the show began.

"If you haven't already figured it out, this is a robbery! We're here to take the bank's money, not your lives. Don't force us to do that. The bank will get its money back. Life can never be returned when lost. Behave, so that we can all go home ..."

I walked up to the teller and pressed the shotgun against his head.

"Open the vault or your math brain will be scattered all over this hall".

"I don't have the key, the manager has it", he snivelled.

I walked across the hall and into an office where the manager was sitting at his desk, pretending he didn't know what was happening, still scribbling down notes. He only raised his eyes and looked at me when he felt the gun pressed against his forehead.

"Hey there, boss. Stand up. Stop playing the fool! Do you want to see blood spilt inside your bank? Be assured it will be yours. So get your arse here and unlock the vault. Now!"

"Yes, child. Right away!"

We reached the counter, where the teller was waiting. The manager got a key out of his pocket and handed it to him, who, in turn, placed it inside the huge vault's lock and began turning it repetitively. Then he grabbed the big knob and pulled it hard downwards. The heavy steel door retreated, revealing the vault's contents.

Bingo! The vault was jam-packed with bundles of banknotes. It would be impossible to fit it all in the sacks we had brought. It was the second time we'd had to leave money behind due to miscalculating. I began filling the large sack with packs of cash as fast as I could, all the while listening to Nikos joking around with customers and employees, complementing the beautiful ladies. I filled up the debris bag, and yet there was still more money inside the vault.

"See if you can find me a bag behind the offices", I yelled at Kostas.

"I've already looked. There's nothing", he replied.

He walked up to me and handed me a sleeping bag sack which he got out of his coat (he was always thinking ahead).

"Fill it up, and let's go. We're running late. People are waiting outside".

I did as fast as I could. I handed Nikos the rucksack, I gave the sleeping bag sack to Kostas, I took the debris bag, and we were ready to flee.

During our five minute stay in the bank hall, Nikos' jokes had created a cheerful atmosphere. They were into it. Nikos was a past master at such stuff. After apologising for the morning disturbance, we bid them farewell. Smiling, thankful for the temporary escape from their dull daily routine which we had unexpectedly offered them, they open-heartedly wished for us to spend the money wisely.

Carefully watching the crowd, lest some cop was hiding among them, we exited the bank, guns in hand, ready for anything. We threw the money in the trunk and, covering each other, jumped in the Audi. The moment the engine started and we began rolling down the road, a "brave" plainclothes cop stood out from the crowd across the street. He pulled his gun and began shooting at us in the back without warning.

I used to run amok whenever someone shot at my back.

"Stop the car! Let me teach him a lesson!" I yelled at Nikos.

"Let him be. Why bother? He's worthless. He didn't even hit the car! Let's get out of here", he said with a familiar, condescending look on his face.

We reached the switching spot at full throttle. We transferred the money, got in the Opel and off we went. On Mourgani Bridge we saw the first oncoming cop car from Kalabaka, its emergency lights turned on. I lay in the back seat so it would appear the Opel had only two passengers. A few seconds after the two cars crossed paths, I heard Nikos say:

"Those fuckers pulled up by the side of the road, and they won't turn around. I think they're onto us ..."

"Are you sure?" I asked him.

"No, I'm not".

"Kostas, what do you make of this? When they passed by us, did they stare at you?"

"They stared at me as all cops stare. A bit more so since they're on the lookout for bank robbers. I can't possibly tell. They might have stopped at the fork to decide which way to go. What matters is what we'll do. Will we risk heading to Trikala or not?"

It wasn't an easy decision. Even if an alert hadn't gone out for the location and inspection of all Opel cars on the road, the bulk and weight of the money would force us to abandon it. My opinion was that securing the money at all costs should be our top priority. We shouldn't risk what we had obtained after working hard for such a long time, just to spare ourselves the hardship. I shared my thoughts with the guys, and they agreed with me. We were on the same page. What was the solution, though?

We knew that, for the time being, we shouldn't travel through Kalabaka, so we took a right turn at the football field, towards Diava. We saw another cop car with its siren blaring, and emergency lights turning, heading fast towards Mourgani Bridge. We assumed it hadn't seen our car and stuck to our course for about two more miles before turning left onto a gravel road that led to several small villages on the foothills of Koziakas Mountain. That's when Nikos made us a proposal.

"Dudes ... I just remembered a good place with many hiding spots to get rid of the money. After we hide it, we can sneak onto the mountain. We can steal a new car in the first village we come across and be off to our jobs. If we have strength enough to walk the mountain, I promise you they won't locate the Opel for days".

"Where the hell is this place we don't know of, Nikos?"

"Above the Monastery of Vitouma".

"If you're right about this, then we don't have a better option!"

"I'd never lie about something so serious. Will you trust me for once?"

He was persuasive ... we drove for fifteen more minutes up the dirt road until the monastery's stone wall came into view. Its enormous double gate, which reminded me of the doors in medieval castles, stood wide open. Two black-clad nuns, one holding a mattock and the other a water hose, were grooming the flowers planted at the sides of the monastery's entrance. Nikos, being a gentleman, slowed down so that the two benevolent old women, whose blessed eyes remained fixed on us from the moment we appeared to the moment we disappeared up the forested hill, wouldn't get dirty from the trail of dust left by our car. The car, carrying three robbers and their heavy loot, chugged along the abandoned rocky path. The Opel company hadn't intended this piece of art for the Greek boondocks.

I was happy that this creation of the descendants of the Axis* was persistently begging for mercy and we, being generous Greek souls, soon granted its wish. In a steep turn, we kept going straight, then took a right, and drove into a dead-end clearing, which you would either had to be shady, or searching for someone suspicious, to find. It was there we would leave the Opel to rest, until it was discovered by our pursuers. We counted the money which came to a hundred and twenty-five million drachmas.** The largest sum of money that had ever been obtained by armed robbers from a single bank branch in Greece. And yet we didn't feel satisfied; we had left a lot of money back in the bank. Lack of satisfaction leads to addiction; addiction leads to creation.

---

* A reference to the Axis powers in World War II. German-based (though owned by GM), Opel built parts, trucks and tanks for the German army during the war.

** More than £1 million in today's money

The late mountain thieves and talkative nuns

We split the loot in three, each of us stuffing his share wherever he could, and then we continued climbing until we reached the first mountaintop that came into view. Life in the mountains is a use it or lose it situation. With the heavy load we were carrying, and the scorching sun high in the sky, we were sweating pints, and our throats were parched. Hard times for brave men — thank goodness we hadn't managed to take all the money from the bank's vault!

As time went on, all three of us panting for breath, we reached a mountaintop at the eastern part of Koziakas. We hastily threw all the things that until recently had been necessary to us but which were now worthless on the ground, and lay down to rest. We had all put on about twenty pounds from living la dolce vita abroad, but on the other hand, this excess weight could allow us to stay on the mountain for days, drinking only water.

During that sweet intoxicating break, Nikos blurted it out.

"Dudes, you're not going to believe what I'm about to tell you".

"Try us!"

"Did you see those nuns outside the monastery?".

"We're not blind, are we?"

"Well, I saw those nuns two nights ago in my dream. They were washing my feet! Now tell me, isn't this a good omen?"

"I hope what we're going through here isn't the result of some dream, bro!"

"I swear I only remembered the dream when we saw them at the monastery. We're not children ..."

While we focused on Nikos' footbath from pious nuns, trying to make sense of the dream, they actually found something more creative and exciting to do, and decided to suck up to the cops. They called the police and told them that the robbers they were looking for had just passed in front of them with a red car, and had vanished inside the forested mountain. They probably heard the report about the robbery on the radio and ratted us out. The result: the cops came to check on it. So they first found the Opel and then, at night, located the Audi.

At that time we didn't know any of this, and it honestly didn't cross our minds that people who had dedicated their life to God would be capable of such a despicable deed (of course, sucking isn't a vile act; it's a heavenly gift but only when a dick is involved).

The interpretation of Nikos' dream changed radically when this adventure was over, and we found out the truth. Nikos took it pretty hard, and I just wouldn't quit teasing him about it ...

The chestnut forest

My gaze tracked down and to our right, lighting on a thick chestnut forest, which awakened memories from the past. It was like a dream, and we were once again children ...

***

It was five in the morning; acting like two eager fugitives, Pantelis and I ran away from our home. Tiptoeing, flashlights in hand, we headed to the barn where we kept our towering grey mule Rusa (we had named her ourselves). She had a bad reputation. When my father bought her, she already had a criminal record. She had been unanimously convicted by the neighbouring village for the premeditated murder of her previous owner, who died while ploughing his field, with Rusa as his beast of burden. From then on, the deceased man's family mistreated her, thinking her responsible for the death of her ploughman master. This didn't stop my father from buying her; something which is to his credit, though truth be told we were a bit scared of her.

After the usual affectations (stretching of ears, menacing display of teeth) she gave in to the superiority of our persistence. We bridled her, and I dragged her outside the barn, leading her towards a small rock. We climbed onto the rock to saddle her, stowing three empty sacks, our grandpa's hatchet, and a feedbag filled with barley for Rusa on the heavy saddle, then off we went. Where were we heading? To the chestnut forest of Vitoumas. Where was it? We didn't know. We had only heard stories about its giant chestnut trees and their endless chestnuts. Our young minds needed nothing more. We were heading north, figuring it out as we went; better to ask the way than to go astray. We were just two grade-schoolers, whose heads reached no higher than the mule's two front feet. And yet our souls rose high up in the sky; such was their force that they could tame the wildest among beasts.

It was mid-December so it was cold, yet when your blood is pumping, everything seems like paradise. We hit the road in the middle of the night, and after a mile or two, we changed direction, climbing the old path that led to the foothills of Koziakas. Stepping on red and black stone, we were making our way up a trail surrounded by mock privet, bushy cedars, kermes oaks, and, deep in the creeks, thick boxwood. By dawn, we were already far away from Kapsala, the bare mountain on the root of which our little house was built. From time to time, we stopped, allowing Rusa to rest and eat some barley. We never climbed on her saddle, something which she obviously respected. Having secretly left home, we had no supplies. Our joyous attempt and the water we could find everywhere around us were enough for us. Along the way, we'd come across shepherds, and we never missed the opportunity to ask them for directions to the chestnut tree forest of the Monastery of Vitoumas. They, surprised, would first ask us where our parents were, if they knew where we were heading. "Of course they do. They sent us there!" was our insolent yet convincing answer. The sincere shepherds took upon themselves to protect us. They saw themselves as part of some child protection mechanism. Their feet, hands, crook, facial expression, speech manner, as well as the contents of their betel bags, were at our disposal.

"You'll go along the mountain's foot, following the path underneath Lambros' sheepfold, you'll reach the col and then … and if anyone asks, you're my nephews. Come, take this piece of bread and some cheese and may God be with you!" they'd say, their accents as thick as they come.

With the aid of the pure mountain-bound shepherds, by midday, we had reached the chestnut tree forest of our dreams, which was very much real. As if long prepared for this, we climbed like cheetahs to the top of a gigantic chestnut tree and began shaking its branches as though we were possessed. Then we climbed down a bit. We shook the tree's branches one by one until there were none left. Chestnuts were falling on the ground beneath the humongous chestnut tree, like thick thorny hail. We loaded up the three empty sacks, making sure they were all of the same weight. We left behind an equal amount of chestnuts (history repeats itself). We bound the sacks tight, carried them to a place where the path had an opening and tied the first on Rusa's saddle. Holding the first sack, we turned the mule to face the other way. We temporarily placed a chestnut tree branch, carved with grandfather's hatchet into a stake, as a jack to keep the sack stable until we put the second sack on the opposite side of the saddle, balancing the load. Throwing the third and final sack vertically on Rusa's back, we tightened the ropes as much as we could, and headed homeward, quite proud of ourselves.

It was midnight when we saw our lonely, humble home in the distance. The storm lanterns' pale light was glimmering through the house's two windows. Although we had been gone with the mule for almost twenty-four hours, we were naïve enough to hope that, because of the late hour, our two parents along with our siblings would be asleep, and we would get away with it. Our two greyhounds smelled us from afar. They ran up to us and welcomed us by jumping on us and barking cries of joy and excitement. The dogs and the sound of Rusa's shoes on the stony pathway made our parents jump out of bed and run outside to see what was happening. We were sure of one thing: we were in for the tongue-lashing of our lives. Yet we were tough nuts to crack; it wasn't the first time we had been off on such an excursion. Adventure ran in our veins, it was second nature. Armed with a lot of courage and even more nerve, we attacked first.

"What are you staring at? Unsaddle the mule. Can't you see she's tired!"

It didn't work.

The shepherd, the mountaineers and some cans of coke

"Time to go, dudes", Nikos' voice woke me up.

We took our heavy backpacks and began climbing the hill. We kept going for a while until we reached the north-eastern side of the mountain. There, we found a place with natural hideouts, and we got rid of the money. Without the burden slowing us down, we began moving faster. The sun was in the middle of the sky; the heat was unbearable. Fatigue and sweat were exhausting us. We weren't prepared to climb a mountain, and since the decision was so sudden, we didn't have even the bare necessities, like water. A plastic bottle we had taken from the car had long been emptied. At the altitude we were hiking in early June, it would be hard to find water. Mountain waters were drained off at a much lower altitude this time of year. Following a trail, we came across a flock of sheep, stabled underneath the big shady firs. Suddenly, five or six sheepdogs ran up to us, barking relentlessly.

The shepherd heard the commotion. He arrived and scolded them, making them stop the attack. We barely managed to hide the shotguns under our t-shirts, lest the shepherd saw them. We headed downhill to bypass the flock, yet we didn't escape the man's curiosity-interrogation.

"Where are you from?" he shouted in his thick accent.

"From Athens ... we're from Athens" spoke Nikos.

"And what brought you up here at this time of day?"

"We're mountaineers, my fellow!"

"What are you?"

"Mountaineers. We thought we'd have a walk on the mountain. Get some clean air, you know ..."

"Oh! Yes, then, great. Good for you! Though you might get sunstroke".

"Don't worry, we have our hats, we're fine ..."

His eyes were hooked on us. His gaze sharp, searching, suspicious, as if clearly saying: I know who you are but whatever ... Just don't take me for a fool!

We walked away, listening to some news report resounding from the shepherd's radio. We all agreed that he posed no threat to us, and therefore we didn't change direction. Even if he decided to descend to the nearest village and report what he had seen, it would take him some time. Fortunately, there were no mobile phones back then! We kept on hiking, chitchatting and laughing about everything that had occurred during the robbery. Only then did we realise Kostas remembered barely anything about it! I had first come to know this aspect of him during our robbery at Yannena. He had confided in me, rather discontent, about many gaps in his memory concerning the main part of the robbery. I hadn't put much thought into it back then, thinking it was completely natural since it had been his first armed bank robbery. Yet, since then, and before the robbery in Kalabaka, he had participated in five armed supermarket robberies with some other associates of his (of course, when he got arrested, he pinned those on me as well, increasing my sentences by almost fifty years) and the memory problem seemed to persist, possibly getting even worse. Years later, I found myself reading some parts of his book relating to me. Aside from an attempt to present himself as a leading figure with strong moral fibre who had his partners under his guidance and control during every challenging venture, the segments of the book in question are rife with inaccuracies, or even outright lies. The description of events of which I was also part, including this particular robbery, couldn't be further from the truth. This poses the question of whether this was indeed an issue of blackouts, selective memory, or something more profound. In his book, he admits to experiencing blackouts, which he doesn't hesitate to overcompensate for with action-packed sequences, embellished with a bunch of believable dialogue, presenting them as actual events. When it comes to real events, to record them loosely is to some extent appropriate or sometimes even necessary, for example, when you must protect the identities of perpetrators or safeguard the tactics and strategies of operations. Also, when your goal is to accurately highlight the perpetrator's thought processes as the dominant guiding forces at the core of his struggle. Regardless, there is a difference between a loose record and wild fiction.

After hours of walking on rough trails and steep slopes, Kostas was exhausted. He couldn't keep up with us. Time and again, we tried to raise his spirits, but after a while, he just collapsed. His feet couldn't hold him, so he lay down in the shade of a big rock. He wouldn't stand, no matter what.

"You go. I'll stay here, and we'll see what happens ..."

"It's fine, Kostas. Take an hour to relax. We all need some rest, after all. We'll cross to the opposite hill, where the forest is thicker, and we'll hide there waiting for you", we said.

Then Kostas made me a proposal beyond belief.

"Vassilis, you're the youngest one and have more stamina than us. Go to Chrisomilia and bring me two coca colas and I'll give you half my share of the money!"

Had I heard him correctly?

"I assume you're joking, Kostas".

"Do you think I'm in a position to make jokes? Honestly, I'll give you half my share".

I tried to stop myself from making a scene. It was the last thing we needed right now.

"You know me well enough, Kostas. Don't you think that if I could go to the village and grab some cokes, I'd do it without asking for money?"

"I bet you wouldn't mind another twenty million!" he insisted.

"Listen, Kostas! As if it isn't enough that you're slowing us down when the police are after us, you're trying to tempt me with money to go into the lions' den to get you coca colas? Your request insults me as a human being, it is foul, and clearly showcases your innermost beliefs concerning money and companionship".

Nikos tried to put out the fire.

"Come on, Vassilis, you know how Kostas is. Leave him alone, he's just tired; he said something stupid, let's not make a big deal out of it. As for you Kostas, stop being an arsehole!"

We left him there and crossed to the opposite hillside to get some rest in the shade of the firs. Nikos and I adapted quickly enough, having grown in the mountains. While we had an abundance of stamina, the lack of water tormented us. Hunger flushes the wolf out; thirst flushes out the man in exactly the same way. We'd soon have to descend the mountain and find some water. It was already late in the afternoon; soon, it would be dark, and we had to take advantage of the situation. After an hour or so, Kostas arrived looking refreshed. He addressed the incident, trying to convince me that he never intended to question my ethics, arguing that the money prize would be an expression of his gratitude for the good I'd have done him! Bullshit ... Can you believe it? Coca colas after a robbery! At least ask me for beer, then we can talk about it! The tension was diffused; all was well for the time being.

It was already dusk when we began descending in search of water. Reaching the river, we came across an old water fountain, the water of which flowed inside wide animal feeding troughs. We quenched our thirst. We filled the plastic bottle we had on us, filled one more which we found nearby, and followed the old rural road that led us to the edge of Chrisomilia village.

It was dark. The streets were empty. All the women had returned to their homes to prepare dinner and in the village square's coffee shop imagination roamed free. Men, drinking tsipouro and eating local delicacies, concocted myths about robberies, money, cops, and robbers, then, now and for as long as there will be authority and injustice. And we were just outside! Don't bother with people who still know how to make up myths ... We thought it wasn't worth it to steal a vehicle from there, because we were still inside our pursuers' perimeter. Whichever road we chose, we would end up in one of their roadblocks. So we headed towards the villages of Pertouli and Elati, travelling on a rather well-maintained and rarely used dirt road. We could hear and see any oncoming cars from afar, and so had plenty of time to vanish from the dirt road.

The day was dawning when a miscalculation led us straight to one of the roadblocks that had been set up at the spot where the dirt road exited to the Elati-Pertouli freeway, in the fields of Pertouli. In a curve on the road, we saw them about a hundred yards away from us; they seemed rather energetic. We didn't know if they were aware of our whereabouts, yet we acted as though they did. We entered the thick forest and for more than ten minutes climbed the spine of Koziakas at the double. I was leading the way, Nikos was behind me, and Kostas followed last.

At some point, we realised that Kostas had fallen behind and disappeared. We didn't know where he was or for how long he hadn't been following us. Whistling, shouting, using our flashlights or trying to signal him in any way was out of the question. We waited for a while in case he showed up and then we resumed climbing the mountain. Kostas was a grown man; he could manage on his own. After all, it was not a guarantee that the fact we were moving all together was advisable. Perhaps Kostas had thought the exact same thing. This side of the mountain was easy to walk in. With the green vegetation hiding us from the waist down, we continued climbing as quickly as we could, and after a few hours, found ourselves overlooking the Thessalian Plain. Exhausted from having been climbing for so many hours, we sought refuge inside a huge hollow rock. We could be seen from neither land nor sky. There we lay down and contemplated the true meaning of life.

The incessant battle between robbers and authority

Koziakas was a strategic trump card. You must have sharp eyes and a healthy mind to guide yourself. Never leave any point of view offered by that fascinating chaos we arbitrarily name "life" unexploited. At this moment, the scenery imposed this very thought as an inner philosophical necessity. From up there, the clear sky afforded us a panoramic view of the unparalleled beauty of the Thessalian land. We allowed our souls to roam free, sweeping our gazes down and away, at Meteora and Theopetra then even further, to the den of the gods and the centaurs. They travelled together, following the rippling and whirling waters along Pineios River. Becoming one with the farmer's labour, who uncomplainingly ploughs the fertile soil of the always-supplying field. Then, as an act of eternal responsibility, they joined the heavy, calloused hand of this same farmer, to give a loud slap of rage to any cop-like, authority-addicted person, who pretends to be an embodiment of the law and hunts down bank robbers.

From this very mountain, on the top of which we were sitting, gazing down at the ancient land of Asclepius and the Thessalian riders, more recent memories surfaced. Memories of rogue dispatches hunting down a handful of robbers in a raging manhunt orchestrated by ruthless authorities against rebels who just wouldn't bow down to them. This relentless war was escalating into an unequal game of dominance. On the one hand, we had the lords; those who reaped the gains of the democratic fiction that they themselves had sowed to solidify their authority, usurping this land's, this country's, wealth. And on the other hand, we had the armed forces of the impoverished farmers who were left to their fate. Young men who refused to accept misery as a way of life and to tolerate authority's "boot" pressing on their necks. Men who, having decided to oppose the lords and their principals, took up arms, knowing at whom to point them. Against all those for whom the State's institutions are of value only when they operate in ways that serve their personal interests. They didn't have to study idealist rebels (after all, most of them were illiterate), because injustice and oppression were right there, in front of their own eyes. They had experienced them since birth. And they had to do something about it. When the unjust beast rises in front of you, threatening to squash you, there's no time to study rebel ideology and seek guidance. You have to take up arms. You must then and there take whatever your grandfather has hidden in his old trunk and fight the beast. All else is just an excuse; it is indefinite procrastination.

The deeds of these rebellious men were pure, honest, and heroic. These men enjoyed the country folks' acceptance because they aligned with the prevailing feeling. They were the peoples' children, and it was their accumulated rage they now expressed as violence against the callous squires. They didn't hide behind the anonymity that cities offer or behind cryptic names. Using their real names, with their faces uncovered, they directly fought the State, and they were proud of it. "It is us!" they would audaciously declare. "We're doing this for this reason. Come and have a chat!". And that was that. Absolute transparency.

Sitting high up there, we felt as though we were the link between these haughty and unhidden armed men of the past and the angry hooded men of the present, who resist the exact same authority, with the exact same ideals at stake, all in their own ways. Those enforced by the chaotic urban galleys. When the body remains chained, the soul can fly. Right behind where we stood, at the Pertouli fields in the late 1930s, the fearsome brigand Tzatzas along with his men set an elaborate ambush, trapping a large VIP entourage of vacationers and their muleteers. Amongst those, the families of the political, the business, and the scientific elite of Thessaly (and many more), who plundered the politics and the economics of the era (most of them still do until today). They had spent the summer at their vacation properties, cooling their plump (from sitting in their chairs of authority) arses inside the beautiful virgin fir forests of the area, away from the blazing south-westerly wind of the valley. While they were on their way home, Tzatzas and his men appeared like figureheads through the thick autumn fog and, heavily armed, blocked their way. They hand-picked some of them, based on their political and economic power, and held them hostage, asking for ransom from the government and their relatives.

Different people, different times, you might say. However, among the notable hostages that Tzatzas took was an ancestor of Chatzigakis, who until recently was a politician and who had, at some point, served as Minister of Justice for New Democracy. And guess what! He too was a politician (what a surprise). It must run in the family.

Times don't change for politicians, they just adapt to them, changing their tactics and their masks. They are the most versatile, devious and durable amongst the various types of criminals and crooks. The reaction of a single man can turn the whole world upside-down, be it only his. And may all people one day react the same way. Only then will the world truly become proper. Until then it will bow down, exalting the superiority of leeches.

Across from us, on top of a rock, a small roe doe appeared. It stayed still for a while, staring at us; its eyes sad. With our pursuers on our trail, we almost forgot we were in an ecosystem of unparalleled beauty, where these little creatures too laid claim to the land that belonged to them. When we saw Kostas again, he told us he had come across a bear! Fate has different things in store for each of us. The little roe doe's eyes seemed fixed on us. I wondered if it had seen another human being from that close up before. What could it have been thinking? Was someone expecting it? Could it have known about the robbery? One thing was for sure: at that very moment it was playing on our hunger while at the same time pressing its luck. Yet how could we point a gun against this living miracle of nature? We preferred to starve. We were two cowards, incapable of committing such an easy and unpunished crime. Only law-abiding citizens showcase such bravery. With the State's blessing, of course. They need its permission to pull the trigger, pointing at the souls of their children. Premeditated crimes against nature and life. The bloodthirsty criminals of this world rest under the shadow of the laws, dreaming of poisonous arrows. Nature is always so generous and man is nothing but a problematic child who stubbornly refuses to detach itself from its wounded breasts.

Deciding it had stared at us for long enough, the little roe doe raised its ears and tail and, after swaying its slender body for us (the ugly-ass representatives of the most ridiculous being on Earth), so that we could memorise the real beauty of life, vanished into the forest quietly, with a series of little hops. As if we never crossed paths … our souls at peace and our bodies haggard, we fell asleep. There, inside the hollow rock.

The escape, the chief and the breach

Late in the afternoon, we began descending towards Kori. We had reached a cultivated area when at some point, we came across a cherry-tree orchard. The cherries were ripe, and boy did we appreciate it, all the while knowing what would follow. We hadn't eaten in two days, we couldn't restrain ourselves. Night had fallen by the time we reached the first houses of the first village we came across. We located a small pickup truck, stole it, switched it with something better when we reached northern Greece and off we went. The job, however, wasn't finished. Kostas and our share of the money were still in that mountain. We waited until the following afternoon, on the off-chance that he'd contact us somehow. He didn't. So we conceived and began executing a deceptive plan to save him.

Nikos phoned the Trikala police department. He asked to speak to the chief. The officer who probably picked up the phone requested to know who was asking for him.

"The chief is busy at the moment!"

"Tell him Palaiokostas is asking for him. Nikos Palaiokostas!"

For a few moments, there was no response.

"Could you hold on for a minute?"

"No ... I won't hold on! Put him on now! Right now! Or else ..."

"Yes? Who is this?"

"Mr grab-it-all".

"Who?"

"It's me. Nikos. Nikos Palaiokostas".

"Oh, hello Nikos ... is that really you?"

"Look, I can't talk for long. I phoned to tell you to call off your people. Don't bother. We took the pickup, end of story".

"But why, Nikos? Why did you do that?" He was referring to the robbery.

"I don't imagine you want to discuss this now ... I'm hanging up. Get your people off the mountain; you've fucked them over enough already. Bye".

"Bye!"

Our plan worked. The officers abandoned the roadblocks. Kostas came down the mountain two days later, exhausted, and the first thing he did was phone some well-known journalist from Trikala to give him an interview about the robbery, saying a bunch of things that didn't make any sense. Almost two weeks after our adventure, we came together again to climb back on the mountain and retrieve the money. We approached the spot by car, reaching as far as the dirt road we had chosen on the north-eastern side of the mountain allowed us. Kostas and I were tasked with carrying the money. Nikos would leave and return in a few hours to pick us up. Everything went well. We were already on our way to Athens with the money in the car's trunk when Nikos directly addressed the issue of the interview.

"Now tell me, Kostas. Who authorised you to give this interview and admit we were the ones who committed the robbery? Do you realise that now they'll surely build a case?"

"Come on, Nikos! We had barely gotten a mile away from the bank, and news reports were already mentioning our names [it was true]. They found fingerprints from all three of us in the Opel, and you think they'll build a case against us based on my interview?"

"No, Kostas. I'm saying something even more serious. That you acted on your own in a case that involves all three of us".

"So? You called the chief! Did you ask for my permission?" he demanded, impudently.

"I contacted the chief after discussing it with Vassilis. And with a good reason too. So that you could get off the mountain. But you thought we were trying to steal your thunder. Oh, you're so obsessed with fame and glory, that's why you ran to that reporter".

"I didn't ask you to save me. You should have left me there to be caught!"

Nikos wasn't one to mince his words.

"I won't speak on behalf of Vassilis, who doesn't know you as well as I do, but as far as I'm concerned, I didn't do it just to save your sorry arse. Because, as it appears, you don't wish to be saved. I just didn't want to lose our money, knowing well enough that if they caught you, you'd tell them where we'd hidden it".

What Nikos was saying was a sad truth. This flaw of Kostas overshadowed all his many virtues. In the world of bank robbers, this was an unforgivable issue. Kostas knew it, and that's why he was reacting this way. He believed that his partners ought to understand his weakness and accept him as he was. Of course, inviting him to join in the operation meant that we accepted his flaw since we had prior knowledge of it. We had sent him the wrong message ... oh boy.

Kostas wasn't the common sort of willing and targeting snitch who cooperates with the police but was one that does so out of need, and repeatedly for that matter. Every time he got arrested, his partners had to vanish from the face of the Earth. Sometime in the past, I had directly and considerably naively (given my lack of experience, and thinking it was something transient that wouldn't happen again) asked him about this flaw. He had answered honestly and in total self-awareness: "When they arrest me, my defences go down. I can't handle it. It's something I can't control. I wish I could, but I can't. It's impossible to do anything about it."

His answer had shocked me. It had awakened me from the romantic lethargy that the excitement of my youth kept me in. It was then that I realised, in the most painful way, that the most challenging part in armed struggle is the human factor. It was a valuable lesson that I would much later include in the "training program for promising new armed men" who wanted to be part of this world and accompanied me, some longer than others, at a later point in my career. If you don't surpass me, I'm worth nothing! A teacher gains value from the students that absorb the bud of his knowledge and transform it into a seed but don't copy his character and, especially, his weaknesses. Only by detecting their teachers' flaws can students become better, forming a personal balance between skills and morals; a necessary ability on the tough track of armed struggle. Their attack skills must be in complete harmony with their defensive ones. Otherwise, there is an imbalance, corruption of character. That's what I'd tell them, among many other things.

Approaching one of Athens' entrances, we pulled over so that Kostas could grab a cab. There, he asked me to give him his radio transmitter. When I explained to him that after we parted ways on the mountain, I thought it was an unnecessary burden (along with mine and many other things) and I got rid of it to be more flexible, he demanded that I pay for it!

Nikos was enraged.

"Have you got no shame? We had such a successful operation, we've just come through such an adventure emerging victors, and now you're asking for compensation for a transmitter? How do you expect us to work with you again when you behave like this? You're lucky, you fool. If it was someone else, you wouldn't be alive to add insult to injury. But it's our fault that we allow you to act this way ..."

Kostas then did something unfathomable. He exited the car and walked away with his backpack.

We would never collaborate with him again; it was the last time we ever saw him.

Such a pity for a man with so many unique skills (a pure genius) not to be able to contribute to a partnership, because of a "faulty gene". After years, when I was imprisoned, he sent me a letter from Corfu to welcome me, which began precisely like this:

"I'm not sure whether I should be sorry or glad for your arrest ..."

He couldn't have possibly fitted more viciousness in so few words. It was sad. And I had learnt so much from him.*

The irony of this particular robbery is that both Nikos' and my shares of the money (eighty million) would slowly be deposited back into the National Bank's Kalabaka branch. In conclusion: no matter how many banks one robs, the money they extort will at some point return back to them. They're the only ones that never lose! Just like the sea, they wait patiently for the rivers.

Money always rolls into them ...

---

* Author's note: long after the robbery, Kostas was arrested at the port of Patra as he was boarding a ship bound for Ancona. In 1996, he escaped from Patra Prison. He was arrested after a few months and served the rest of his sentence. He is now "free".

CAR CHASE IN KATERINI

It was early May in 1995. Nikos and I were travelling in a dark brown Opel. Nikos was driving, and I was in the passenger seat, with a CZ under my thigh and a Kalashnikov in front of my feet. We were calm, still always on the watch, as we entered Katerini coming from Elassona. Like most rural cities, Katerini already had a severe traffic problem. Heading to the city centre, we got stuck in a traffic jam. We saw a bunch of beautiful girls walking beside us on the pavement. They looked at us, smiled shyly, and that was it. Nikos spoke to them, they responded, and we began chatting. After all, we didn't have anything better to do, moving at a snail's pace. The jam was becoming worse by the minute.

Suddenly, we got wind of a motor officer about fifty yards behind us, heading to the city centre. As far as we knew, being stuck in traffic and flirting with girls didn't constitute a traffic violation, so we kept on flirting. The officer was moving along the immobilised cars, approaching fast. When he reached us he looked at the girls and, obviously realising the imminent danger they were in, sternly demanded that we pull over for inspection (if only he had known).

He was about twenty five to thirty years old, tall, wearing leather attire and Robocop-style boots, guns hanging over his hips along with a baton, a flashlight and many other gadgets. A proper terminator. The guy was a real badass. Judging from his appearance and his vibe, it was apparent that he was a real terror for all the area's criminals. But he had just decided to add chick-guardian duties to his job description.

"We'll get into trouble with this mother fucker", whispered Nikos.

At once, he made a U-turn and began driving on the opposite lane, which led straight out of the city. The motor officer initially thought we were doing this to facilitate his inspection. Seeing, however, that we had other plans, picking up speed instead of stopping, he jumped on his bike and began chasing us while informing headquarters about the ongoing event. I was ready to take action. My window was already down from our chat with the girls, I had unfastened my seatbelt, and my finger was already on the Kalashnikov's trigger, ready to fire.

For as long as the motor officer was driving, we didn't run the risk of him using his guns, yet police headquarters was now informed that two guys travelling in a stolen vehicle had resisted inspection. It was only a matter of time before the first cop cars appeared to assist the officer, their crews ready for action. This only made our goal to evade the otherworldly creature as fast as possible and drive away from the city even more pressing.

Nikos drove the Opel inside the first alley we came across to our right. After six yards or so, he suddenly slowed down, to force the officer to approach our car as much as possible. He did just that, reaching at full throttle just mere inches away from the rear bumper on my side of the vehicle. I was already half crawled outside the window, pointing the Kalashnikov against this human scarecrow who had gotten used to scaring away the local outlaws.

"Stay right where you are, you moron, or I'll blow your brains out", I screamed. Still pointing the gun at him, we sped up again, and having built up a safe distance between us, I returned to my seat, sure we had seen the last of him. I was wrong. After staying stock-still for a few moments, the officer revved up, catching up with the Opel. He had obviously concluded that the gun I had pointed against him was merely a water pistol. Being irreligious, I crossed myself. Only in the face of such events did I find faith in some superior force guiding stupid people.

"This lobber must be on drugs! He neither hears nor sees, I wonder how he's able to drive", I spoke my thoughts out loud.

"Don't bother with him. He's just another arsehole; let's not kill him. It'd be a shame. I'll try to lose him", said Nikos, knowing I was ready to book the officer an appointment with Beelzebub.

I trusted Nikos' driving skills. He was fast, careful, always in control, and able to make on-the-spot decisions. Yet, with the moron motor cop on our trail, I doubted whether he could pull it off this time. We were driving past the last houses of Katerini, travelling along the local road towards Elassona, with the officer still on our heels. Nikos still hoped we could evade him. I, on the other hand, believed that the elfish creature had never laid eyes on a Kalashnikov before and needed to hear its fire to really grasp the situation he had gotten himself into. For a handful of miles, nothing changed — until I made up my mind to confront the beast.

Reaching a straight part of the road, which ran up a hill before vanishing behind it, I fired the Kalashnikov, aiming right over the officer's head. He stayed there. Stock-still. After all, he could hear well enough; he was just blind. This piece of information was of no use to us anymore the damage was already done. Knowing our direction of travel, the police had irresponsibly, criminally you could say, contacted all villages through which the local road ran. As a result, the villagers expected our arrival. Some of them tried to stop our car, not knowing who was driving it, why we were being chased, or that we were heavily armed.

We were now driving through Fotina village. About fifteen miles ahead of us was the Livadi police station, which we were sure had already been informed, just as the Elassona police station had, and which could afford to send a lot of manpower after us. As things were turning out, our best option was to abandon the road. We checked the map and finally decided to head to the town of Servia in Kozani, following a dirt road that crossed the Pierian Mountains. We had driven a few miles on the dirt road when it began raining hard. As we drove uphill, the way became gradually worse. The Opel started to make strange noises. About two hundred yards before we reached the mountain ridge, it got stuck in the mud.

Mountains have their own god. It was three in the afternoon, it was snowing, and fog had rolled in. We got out of the car to find ourselves, after such a long time, right in our element — on the mountain. How else would we have seen snow in Pieria, in early May? We put on raincoats, grabbed our backpacks and like two forgotten rebels, with the Kalashnikovs in our hands, entered the primeval forest, swallowed by its thick fog. And the snow was falling heavily. Only nature knows how to welcome wild, unbowed souls with open arms. Kiss my ass, Robocop.

ESCAPE FROM PATRA

It was midsummer in 1995, and Nikos decided to abandon Greece for a while. Taking everything into consideration, we concluded that his best way out was the port of Patra, so we drove there and bought a ticket to Ancona. The ferry was expected to depart at eight o'clock in the evening. Validation of the ticket and passport control required the traveller's physical presence in the port's waiting area, one hour before departure. We drove around the port a few times, without spotting anything alarming. The coast seemed clear; no clouds on the horizon. About seven o'clock, we parked the car on the road heading to Patra's beach, fifty or so yards away from the port's gate.

Our plan was simple enough. I'd accompany Nikos while he validated his ticket, then I'd wait outside the port's offices in case something happened to go wrong during the validation process. If everything went well, I'd leave the port and then Patra altogether.

We got out of the car and, after locking it, walked steadily towards the gate of the port. Nikos was carrying a pretty large travelbag but had no guns on him as he'd be travelling soon. I had a loaded CZ on my belt, as well as an extra magazine. I also had a bag hanging over my right shoulder, inside which I had hidden a Scorpion, its safety released, ready to be used, along with four back-up magazines. I also had two defensive grenades in the bag's interior pocket.

The port of Patra was swarming with people, that much became clear as soon as we reached its entrance. To our left, we saw a large mass of tourists, who formed a queue beginning from passport control and ending near the port's entrance. At the end of this queue, a black Alfa Romeo was parked; its windows down. Two men with sunglasses were inside it, scanning the passengers. Plain-clothes, obviously.

At that time Greece wasn't a member of the Schengen Area, so there was a separate passport control for Greek citizens. Calmly, yet wary, we proceeded towards passport control, which was about fifty to seventy yards ahead. Around us, tourists and Greek passengers were milling around purposelessly, waiting to board the ferries. We were fifteen yards away from the port administration building when we spotted the first two harbour patrol officers standing to the right of its entrance. They were dressed in camouflage uniforms, had berets on their heads and MP5s strapped to their backs; they were chatting, glancing about them, looking serious.

In front of us were five or six steps, about ten yards wide, that led to the administration building's entrance. A handful of tired tourists were sitting on them. Among them were two men and a woman with backpacks, sitting like all the other travellers. For some reason, an alarm went off inside me concerning these three. I slowed down. When Nikos was already on the third step, I was just about to climb the first one. That particular group were sitting in the middle of the stairs, two yards to the right from the spot where we were climbing.

The moment I climbed on the first step, they casually began to rise from their seats. I remained still.

The girl and one of the men proceeded to inspect Nikos. The other man approached me swiftly. He opened his mouth, but he didn't get the chance to say a word. My Scorpion was already pressed against his chest.

"Don't say a word, motherfucker, or I'll execute you here and now".

He panicked. He put his hands up and began telling me how many kids he had etc. I wasn't in the mood, and I had no time to listen to his family drama, so I called for Nikos who, along with the two plain-clothes searching him, hadn't gotten wind of what was taking place behind them. All three turned their heads and saw us. The two plain-clothes ran away, screaming. Their screams frightened the two harbour patrol officers who joined them on their run, and all of them hid inside the administration building. Nikos was already behind me. Still pressing the Scorpion against the plain-clothes' chest, I grabbed him by his shirt and, as he was, hands still in the air, dragged him with me until we got far enough away. I left him there and, always pointing the gun at him, we backed away until we reached the gate of the port.

The two plain-clothes sitting inside the black Alfa Romeo, near the gate, had seen nothing until this moment. The female tourists' tanned bodies had done the trick. They had stultified them. By the time they realised what was going on, we had already entered the parked car, ready to leave. The Alfa Romeo backed up and exited through the gate. It was now coming towards us, ready to crash into us; a very ambitious plan on their part. A few yards before they hit us, I fired a hail of about twelve bullets at them, trying my best to target the Alfa Romeo's grille. The driver, seeing the first bullets flying against him, lost his cool. He made a right turn, as both he and his partner ducked down seeking cover. As a result, the Alfa Romeo ran past us and crashed into a wall. We were still outside the port's entrance and panic was spreading throughout the harbour. People were running to and from every direction, drivers had immobilised their vehicles in the middle of the road, without even knowing why. Manoeuvring around them, we drove away from the port. The coastal road was bustling. Not long afterwards, we heard police sirens. I dropped the Scorpion and grabbed one of the two Kalashnikovs. Come now if you dare, lads ...

I didn't have to use it after all. Nikos switched on the car's hazard lights and then began switching its headlights on and off. This, as well as his repeated honking, allowed us to move past the other cars, pretending to be plain-clothes. The drivers of the vehicles in front of us, hearing the sirens, thought that we were with the police. After all, our hand gestures gave this exact impression. We drove for a few more miles until we couldn't hear the sirens any more. We exited the main highway, changed direction, and we were gone.

After this terrible shock and the emotional distress we suffered, it was now necessary to visit some places of worship. We purged ourselves by invading a handful of modern temples while heavily armed. And by modern temples, I mean banks.

Vassilis and Nikos in their youth

KIDNAPPING HAITOGLOU

Kidnappings and ethics

After robbing the National Bank's Kalabaka branch, the idea of kidnapping a businessman or a member of a businessman's family to ask for ransom drifted through my mind for quite some time. It seemed ideal to get such amounts of cash. In time, as I put more thought into it, I realised that there were many aspects that had to be taken into consideration by all those that would get involved in such an operation. It now seemed to me as the most complex, multidimensional and unpredictable venture we had ever attempted.

In an operation that is based solely on extortion, a question of paramount importance is whether we would be adequately prepared to go through with our threat and whether we completely understood what this would entail. You can't hope to carry out such an operation if you're not prepared to go through with your threat; because then you can easily go from doing the extortion to being extorted yourself. When everybody involved has given an affirmative reply to this dilemma, the next preparatory stage is to carefully examine all the steps that have to be taken to minimise, and if possible eliminate, any chance that you would actually have to — and that if it comes to it, any shooting would be initiated by the other side. That they would decide whether to pull the trigger or not. That they would be the ones to kill for their money, and not us. They, who'd do it in a heartbeat when it comes to other people's money and lives ... we'd have to let them decide how precious or not their expensive life was and allow them to act accordingly. (After two kidnappings, I'm still not buying their value system or their vague kindness — perhaps I should give it another go!)

All these things attested that to achieve our goal, the selection of the person to be kidnapped had to fit three essential criteria: firstly, that he could deliver our ransom demands without being completely destroyed. Secondly, that he would have a coherent family environment (parents, wife, children, etc.) to ensure that negotiations would run smoothly and that we would get our money. Thirdly, that he would be healthy enough to endure the ordeal.

For me, kidnapping a boy younger than twenty-two years of age or a woman of any age was out of the question. My reasons weren't sentimental or driven by some light moral ideology. They were, first and foremost, practical. Because no one could guarantee that a kidnapping would have the desired outcome. No matter how carefully planned and orchestrated it was, unforeseen circumstances could always arise.

Given that we'd be ready to go through with our threat if something unexpected were to occur, being left with a hostage, for example, we wouldn't want them to be a child or a woman. We couldn't hold a child responsible for having a wealthy father, so how could we kill it? And even if things worked out as planned, how could we scar it for life? There is no deed more barbaric and obscene than the killing of a child, no matter how you justify it, and especially when money is the reason. Even if the side which is being extorted is willing to sacrifice that very same child for the sake of money. These doubts become allayed when you're dealing with an immoral, corrupted businessman who, one way or the other, knowingly affects the lives of a group of people, possibly yours too.

An adult woman could be chosen if we had the proper infrastructure to keep her hostage for as long as it took for her family to stop resisting and pay the ransom. Naturally, a defender of gender equality would wonder why a woman who owns or manages a group of companies with a high turnover, possibly a bad employer or involved in crony capitalism, shouldn't share the same fate as a male hostage. I can't offer a convincing answer to that. The train of thought towards rationalising this weakness is labyrinthine; so I'll just say this: just because we love them. That's why they always get away ... at least from me!

Throughout the process of selecting a "victim" I would face many similar — and equally serious — ethical dilemmas. In two consecutive instances, by the time I had reached the final stages of surveillance, both the potential "victims" coincidentally lost someone from their immediate families (the first in a traffic accident, the second in sudden death). Taking another blow, being kidnapped, for example, would undoubtedly finish them. Of course, the two families were, for the time being, crossed off our list of potential victims ... so we were back at square one!

Many others would be crossed off my list when I realised they weren't ruthless businessmen. When I found out they possessed an earthly-human way of doing business, something that didn't leave me unmoved. I randomly mention G. Boutaris. Reading many of his interviews and learning that he was the founder of Arcturos,* I realised that he had his own unique way of seeing things and life in general. Even when it came to contributing to society, he didn't operate as most reputed business families that seek absolution of their sins by awarding each other — and always in front of the cameras — their self-inspired philanthropy awards (he who pays the piper calls the tune). So he was out of the picture. I hope I didn't make a mistake.

Repatriation with a view to kidnapping

It was the spring of 1995. Nikos and I returned to Greece with the sole purpose of kidnapping a businessman. While in central Europe I had studied many Greek business magazines and newspapers and created a decent list of potential targets, which would prove useful in the final selection process. A good friend of ours had provided us with all necessary weaponry, which originated from the Yugoslav Wars:** CZ pistols, Scorpion submachine guns, Kalashnikov rifles, grenades, and sufficient ammunition. We kept anything that suited us, and we buried the rest. Armed to the teeth, and iron-willed, we set off to find a suitable victim. During this process we suffered a few setbacks, which resulted in a slight delay, because it was already the middle of summer and we were way over budget. So getting our hands on some money was our top priority. How would we accomplish that? By robbing a bank, of course!

"Good day. Your money, please. Thank you, farewell!"

When money withdrawal is bureaucracy-free, life becomes that much simpler. We managed to get enough to replenish our stock and bought ourselves some time to pursue our initial goal.

Nikos and I made a hell of a team. We could mess with the district police stations doing robberies, escaping from roadblocks and long car chases, some of which would end in an exchange of fire, yet they never managed to corner us, let alone catch us. We were so sure of ourselves that many times we would joke around while being chased, amused by the terror their actions showed. Yet we were their opponents only as far as our right to freedom was concerned. We knew they'd always stand in our way. They were doing their job. We were doing ours. We didn't consider them enemies; just gate-crashers! An invention of civilised

---

* Arcturos is a non-profit, non-governmental, environmental organisation (NGO) founded in 1992, focusing on the protection of wildlife fauna and natural habitat, in Greece and abroad (arcturos.gr)
** A series of conflicts in the Balkans directly north of Greece from 1991-2001, sparked by the collapse of Yugoslavia. At the time the Croatian War of Independence and Bosnian Wars were drawing to a close. The US and Pakistan had engaged in arms smuggling operations backing different factions throughout, while a number of Orthodox Greeks were directly involved supporting the Bosnian Serbs.

human beings to trammel their own potential. The witless beast of burden that time after time carries the brutality hidden within them.

Nikos was always behind the wheel. Fast and collected, he knew all the country's freeways, roads, dirt tracks and paths like the back of his hand (Google Earth was planted in his mind before even being invented). I, on the other hand, was one badass passenger. A Kalashnikov always on my lap, ready to be used if and when the need arose for guns to do the talking. It was like we were in sync. A single nod, a glance or a gesture were enough to get the party started. It must have been because the same blood of generations of defiant highlanders ran in our veins. And it was that same blood that never let us rest, never let us surrender.

Yes, we cooperated perfectly during all operations. The same cannot be said concerning strategic planning. Nikos was a "let's get what we can, as fast as we can, and get out of here" type of person. I, on the other hand, was more of a "we should carefully examine, target, plan, and attack" kind of person. Nikos was unpredictable, temperamental, with a strong intuition and an overdeveloped survival instinct. I, on the contrary, was stable, perseverant, even stubborn when it came to achieving goals, and talked hard to the point of often being misunderstood.

Nikos' instability would once again do its trick when, after the robbery, he began to grumble.

"We shouldn't have come back to Greece. They're going to catch us. We'll rot in prison … let's get out of here. We could use this money to start something new somewhere far away".

"We made this trip for a reason. We have a goal. The problem is not solved. It will come back to haunt us. When you run away from a battle, you'll have to fight it again and again. You're free to do as you see fit. I'll stay here until I do what I came here to do", I would respond.

And so it happened. One morning, I dropped him at the border, waited until he crossed it, then returned to move forward with my plan, alone.

Seeking the rats of ethics

I flung myself into collecting data concerning mostly, but not exclusively, the economic regime. I began patiently and methodically collecting whatever economy-related data I could get my hands on from the daily press (political, financial), financial magazines, company annual balance sheets, tabloids — anything could give me useful insights. I still can't get my head around what I discovered. The stench from the rotten economic and political systems invaded my nostrils, threatening to shut down my brain. These shameless initiates were rolling in dirty money. These were the years of the decline of PASOK,* when socialists were having a feast at the expense of the rabble, plundering

---

* The Panhellenic Socialist Movement, known mostly by its acronym PASOK, is a social-democratic political party in Greece. Until 2015, it was one of the two major electoral forces in the country, along with New Democracy, its main political rival.

the Greek peoples' savings and future. Machinations, scandals, political favours, transactions; those were only a few of the parliament's occupants' great weaknesses. Affluent families, both old and nouveau-riche, knew well enough how to give bean-feasts,* as long as the voracious politicians took legislative measures to protect them. The right-wing opposition wasn't left out, making sure to take its cut. After all, it has always been the upper class's favourite and thus always holds the heavy golden keys of venality.

My future target, Alexandros Haitoglou, was financially aiding the conservative Political Spring party and its leader — subsequently Prime Minister — Antonis Samaras.** They were friends. Every time Samaras travelled to Thessaloniki for some political rally he would stay over at his house. Haitoglou himself told us this, among many other things concerning the interplay between capital and politics, when we held him captive.

Of course, the Left was reaching out to get some treats too. When you control the servants, you're bound to snatch something. You won't let the big predators have all your earnings. If you're a trade unionist you'll find a way to lay your dirty hands on some nice well-cooked chicken legs. After all, you're entitled to them. And if they protest your discourtesy, you can threaten them with a strike in the kitchen. It always works. They're willing to make you their convive, after appointing you a member of Parliament of course, lest their fat bellies get hungry. If you're a total prick they might even appoint you a minister; so now you have a permanent place at the big feasts, which you won fair and square. Still, there's a problem. These big meals attract various hungry wildlings like us, who'd be willing to use their weapons just to get their hands on a slice of bread — which back then was used for decorative purposes only — from Haitoglou's plate. Even if they knew they'd be chased away by his banqueters, his servants, and all the dogs, on or off the leash.

When you're having a celebration and some terrible rifle-holding men spoil it, you take firm measures. So they'd dig deep to put a two hundred fifty million drachma bounty on each of our heads. How generous! This realisation did not come as a surprise to me. Due to my temperament, I didn't merely have suspicions, but was entirely sure about what was actually happening; yet I wanted proof. When the evidence is in a cesspool, you have to stir it. And you know what they say: stir a cesspool, and a foul stench arises ...

As a simple example of their venality consider this: at the time, and due to our peculiar profession, we knew all the Greek mainland's freeways and country roads and had reached the conclusion that they were all destroyed, dangerous to drive

---

* Formerly common as a Twelfth Night custom, party, or when a patron would take their underlings on an outing. It's also the root of "going on a beano".
** Political Spring was a largely single-issue party formed to push the government rightwards during a nationalist moral panic over whether Macedonia should be allowed to call itself "Macedonia" (after a two decade argument it's now called North Macedonia). Think Ukip, except the Farage character was smarter, more pragmatic, and leveraged his popularity with the hard right to take over New Democracy, eventually running the country from 2012-15.

along. Yet still, the alternating governments would regularly post construction bids for the maintenance of highways and country roads or for the construction of new ones, awarding them primarily to Bobolas' company AKTOR, Triantafillou's AEGEK etc. They, in turn, would place some trucks, unloaders, and a handful of workers there for the sake of appearances, declaring that the project was under construction. During the pre-election period, they'd pick up the slack — possibly with extra funding — to make a part of the road. Then the Prime Minister would pay them a visit, flaunting his new creation via a TV channel that happened to be owned by the very same constructors who had been awarded the bid. And life went on ... downhill. Such practices were becoming increasingly common, deeply corrupting municipalities and communities. They'd sloppily pave a dirt road using cheap materials, which two months later would be full of potholes.

Two weeks before the robbery mentioned above, we had decided on an escape route, which included a freshly paved six-mile road. At the time, knowing it had until recently been a dirt track, we joked around saying that the local mayor had rolled out the carpet for us. During the robbery itself however we would curse the mayor for setting us up, because we found the road to be full of potholes. The car couldn't go more than fifteen miles per hour. The mayor had surely pocketed more money than we did that day! And still, we were the ones being hunted. Such are the works of those in power.

Outsider businessmen, worshipped by the media dedicating front pages to detailed reports glorifying their cleverness for having reached the top — always honourably — despite being self-made, were, after a while, found to be involved in scandals. This corrupted rabble was followed closely, just like Dionysus, by the Satyrs: reporters, judges, lawyers, doctors and, of course, those raving clergy, thuribles in hand, blessing plundered loot and exonerating thieves. This democracy of rats makes me sick.

I continued broadening my knowledge, investigating all levels and aspects of the so-called economic-political system. By chance, I discovered a tome by the Union of the Greek Chambers of Commerce and Industry in some Thessaloniki bookstore. It included a list of almost all large Greek private sector companies (whether public or not), along with exhaustive financial data and their owner's private information (date of birth, spouses, offspring, residential addresses etc.). This would come very handy in the next few weeks, allowing me to locate even more industrialists' homes in Thessaloniki and, later, Athens.

Among them was the Haitoglou family, with the homonymous Macedonian halvah. The two brothers were somewhat known in Thessaloniki due to their business and contributions to local society but also because of their involvement with sports. Kostas, you see, was chairman of the Iraklis Football Club. While inexperienced, Alexandros seemed to be the man at the helm of the family business, being the one to promote the brand through constant interviews and intensive socialising. The family's patriarch, his elderly father, had founded founder the company. Their factory was located in the industrial area of Kalochori, Thessaloniki.

Their villas in Oraiokastro were built on a vast tree-lined property, surrounded by a large stone wall. It seemed that they were good potential kidnapping victims, owning a medium-sized enterprise. Aiming to kidnap someone wealthier to extract more money seemed unwise under the circumstances. To even hope to achieve something like that I'd first have to move to Attica, where the big sharks of the economy dwelled, yet I didn't know my way around there well.

I was willing to overcome this obstacle if some local partners were willing to accommodate me and aid me in the mission. Back then however Greek bank robbers (the best fits for the job) had neither the patience nor maturity to work as hard as such a kidnapping operation required. Or at least, if there were any, I never got to know them. So the Greek big-shots, undisturbed, without any enemies, would continue gnawing at people's wealth.

I had stayed in touch with some robbers who had broken out of prison. They, in turn, could find some others who knew the Attica basin like the back of their hands, offsetting my weakness. When, however, I mentioned that a carefully orchestrated kidnapping of some millionaire could easily yield ten to twenty billion drachmas (thirty to sixty million euros), they'd eye me suspiciously, as if wanting to say: "You're crazy. You're trying to get us into something impossible".

It was apparent they were resting on their laurels, doing what they knew best: armed bank robberies the pickings of which were five or, in a best-case scenario, a hundred million drachmas. So that ambitious personal project would have to be indefinitely postponed.

Fugitives and fugitives

Around that time, I got in touch with a friend of ours from Attica who, being a fugitive himself, had just returned from a hiding spot in Europe. He was interested in joining in anything I was planning, along with a friend of his, who was also on the run. Fugitives stand united.

"Come here, and we'll come up with something. Thank God, the country is full of banks!"

My ultimate goal was to discuss a potential kidnapping after the robbery. We made an appointment in the Vale of Tempe. They would drive there from Athens, and so I wouldn't have to take my car, we'd use theirs to travel. I arrived at our meeting point first, armed to the teeth. I waited for five minutes, where the road was a bit wider, until a black Golf stopped in front of me. I hadn't even managed to greet them, when behind us came a black BMW with its hazard lights turned on. Three men were in it, sporting short haircuts and sunglasses. I was alarmed.

"Who are those motherfuckers behind us?"

"Relax, they're with me. They're the guys who broke out of Trikala Prison last week".

I was dumbstruck.

"And why are they here?"

"They came with me. They're broke, and they're looking for work".

I was infuriated by his recklessness, but by then the guys were already standing nearby, ready to greet me. They were three of the seven men who had broken out of Trikala Prison, and who had been given shelter by Kimon ever since. They greeted me warmly, introducing themselves one by one. Among them were Kasapakis (a pure bank robber) and Keremidis (self-styled), who were both killed a few months later in different confrontations with the police, in Athens. I was a role model for them, having been a fugitive since 1991 and regularly making the headlines because of my operations. I didn't want, and it wouldn't be right, to let them down, by showing I didn't fancy them being there. After all, they were in no way responsible for being invited to this meeting. So I controlled my temper and wished for them to enjoy their newfound freedom.

I tried to handle the change. I had found myself in the Vale of Tempe, "stuck" with five armed fugitives. I didn't know how they'd react in a potential confrontation with the police, and I had to display real solidarity. I had to make a decision.

"Ok guys. Follow us. Don't lose eye contact with our vehicle".

I entered Kimon's car and, driving along familiar roads, we headed south. Simply getting there was our primary goal. Performing an ordinary bank robbery along with five other people is at best ridiculous, so we changed our plans. We'd split up into two groups and target two banks in the same city. A scheme was forming in my mind, but we still needed two more cars. So we'd go out at night, again split into two groups, heading in opposite directions to find and steal two cars.

We waited in a remote location until nightfall. Then, after rendezvousing at the same spot, Kimon, his friend, and I set off first. Around five in the morning, we returned with a decent second vehicle in our possession. The other three men were already there, loudly snoring. They'd never left the spot, having fallen asleep. Prison habits die hard.

After this, I told them I'd go. We agreed that I should take one of the cars they'd brought from Athens and they would use the one we'd stolen the previous night. In the glove compartment I found an ID card, belonging to someone who looked very like me; we were even around the same age. I asked Kimon whether it belonged to the owner of the car, and he corroborated my theory.

"If you intend to use the cars in some operation, you should clean them well first because I might have touched them. They might have my fingerprints", I said to them, and they promised to do so.

It was pointless to talk to Kimon about a kidnapping. I bid them farewell and made my way homeward. I cleaned the car diligently before abandoning it in some small town, yet I kept the owner's ID. It proved useful in the future, when I decided to get a mobile phone.

The abduction

It was not long before Nikos, just as I had predicted, expressed an interest in returning, determined not to leave again before we had carried out the kidnapping. Once he'd arrived we got down to business, and began surveilling

Haitoglou's house, trying to determine what time he left for the factory where his office was located.

He'd set off each morning, just before eight, along with his two children (the boy was a bit older than ten; the girl about seven or eight years old). After dropping them off at school, near the freeway's exit in the direction of Oraiokastro, he'd head towards Kalohori, using a byway which was perfect for an ambush. We made sure that his daily routine was regular and began orchestrating the next stage of our plan, which of course was the most difficult. Our fool-proof and straightforward strategy was tailor-made for the two of us. Taking advantage of the rugged Greek countryside terrain and our years of experience as drive-by armed rangers in each area's maze-like road networks, we'd make our hostage vanish off the face of the earth until we got our money. We rejected the idea of keeping him in some house, finding it highly problematic. It was just the two of us after all, and we had to watch the hostage, enter negotiations, pick up the money etc. Even more so, the thought of being locked indoors with a hostage simply didn't appeal to us.

So what else did we need? Just two cars for the abduction and a mobile phone to contact the victim's family.

In 1995, you needed a complete financial statement to buy a mobile phone. Another way to get one was to pay part of the price beforehand as collateral. Confident that money makes the world go round, I visited a mobile phone store in Thessaloniki, part-paid in advance and bought a mobile using the stolen ID that the guys from Athens had given me the previous summer.

We had one car to get around in, but we needed another. It was winter, meaning it'd have to be an off-roader as the areas where we'd be driving were rugged. So one of the following nights, we drove to Grevena and picked up a brand-new RAV 4x4. We had reached Elassona by dawn, Nikos driving the RAV while I was following close behind in a Ford Mondeo.

Unfortunately it was raining, and on a sharp curve I was blindsided by a semi-truck that had entered half into my lane. In a matter of moments, the car flipped.

Nikos, despite being ahead of me, got wind of what had happened. He backed the RAV up until he reached me. I had already climbed out of the car and handed him the sack with our guns. I opened the car's gas cap, and as the Mondeo was flipped, the gas began to spill. I warned the drivers who had stopped on both sides of the road to stay away because the car was about to go up in flames! They were startled as I grabbed a paper towel roll, set it on fire and threw it towards the Mondeo. The fire spread at once. With its tank full and a ten-litre gas can inside, it would burn to ashes. The burning car was right in the middle of the road, immobilising all other vehicles. I entered the RAV, and we drove away, leaving the dumbstruck drivers wondering what the hell they had just witnessed.

To my surprise, Nikos regarded it as a good omen.

"Since you got out unharmed, it must have been for the best … no more bad luck for us!"

I found his view interesting and undoubtedly convenient, even though I didn't understand it completely.

"So what do we do now?"

We looked at each other, but we had already made a decision.

"Screw this. Enough splitting hairs. Let's go grab him and be done with it ..."

Truth be told, a second car wasn't absolutely necessary. If we lost the RAV as well, then yes, we'd be in trouble. For now though, and after a few adjustments, our plan seemed better than before, given that we wouldn't have to leave a vehicle behind. Over the next few days we focused on rehearsing our operation until one morning, the countdown began.

***

Haitoglou, after dropping off his kids at school, would turn onto a narrow, one-mile gravel road, passing through an intersection, then continuing straight until he reached another stretch of tarmac. Nikos dropped me off at that intersection, before driving uphill towards the school.

It was mid-December, so rather chilly. I was wearing gloves, fake glasses, a knit cap that covered my forehead and ears, and I had a Browning hidden in my trousers along with two backup magazines, ready to be used. In my backpack, among other things, I had a Scorpion with a handful of magazines, plus two grenades. The streets around the intersection were relatively quiet. Barring any unforeseen circumstances, no one would get wind of anything.

It hadn't even been ten minutes when I saw the RAV coming down the hill, followed close behind by Haitoglou's red Opel coupe. Nikos, being a good and law-abiding driver, stopped at the intersection to ascertain whether the way was clear. Haitoglou, a law-abiding citizen himself, stayed behind the RAV. Nikos had done an excellent job. The Opel's passenger door was in my reach. I opened it casually, and sat in the passenger seat. I already had the Browning in my right hand. I pressed it against Haitoglou's chest.

"Do as I say or I'll blow you to pieces!"

He panicked and tried to take off his seatbelt. I slapped his chest with my left hand. Grabbing his coat and his shirt's lapel, I pressed them hard against his throat.

"Don't even think about it, you little twerp! I'm gonna rip you in half!"

He surrendered. I shifted into first gear and asked him to follow the RAV. We turned left at the intersection and then, a hundred yards later, turned left again into an empty alley which led to a grove. We parked the cars, side by side, in a clearing. Nikos came over and opened Haitoglou's door.

"Get out. Get in the back of the SUV" he ordered, sternly.

Haitoglou got out of the car and made his way towards the RAV, but just before reaching it, he froze.

"There's a briefcase that might interest you in the truck,", he said.

I took the briefcase, opened it, checked its contents, shut it again, and gave it to him.

"You can have it. Maybe it'll help you sleep better".

I saw disappointment in his eyes. The briefcase was his last hope. But we couldn't be satisfied by the two million drachmas (six thousand euros) it contained. He got into the RAV's trunk (we had modified it, making it fairly comfortable), we put a hood over his head, handcuffed him with his hands in front of him and set off. For the time being, we were confident of two things. no one had gotten wind of what had happened, and it would be a long time before they located his car. That bought us precious time to put some distance between us and the scene of the kidnapping, and plan our next steps.

We made contact with Alekos' family when we reached Katerini. First, we allowed him to speak with his brother Kostas. He told him he was being held by kidnappers, and that they shouldn't involve the police but do whatever he could to guarantee his release, following the kidnappers' instructions to the letter. Kostas, on the other end of the phone, naïve enough to think we weren't listening, began asking his brother how many kidnappers there were etc. Nikos took the mobile phone.

"Listen, dude, cut the questions and gather three million Deutsche Marks as soon as you can. When you're ready, you'll receive all necessary instructions".

Haitoglou's brother told Nikos he'd comply as long as we guaranteed his brother's safety. When we assured him of that, he decided to become overly friendly.

"You know, being chairman of the Iraklis Football Club I know many crime bosses ..."

"You big-headed prick, we're our own bosses! You're not dealing with henchmen or sports fans; you're dealing with professionals. So act accordingly", said Nikos before hanging up.

Proletarian ignorance

There's a short yet quite revealing story behind our decision about how much money we'd demand. When I began my research on the Haitoglou family, all indications were that it was old, and wealthy. The annual company balance sheets testified to that, reaching a high point during the previous year when their net profit amounted to nearly a billion drachmas (three million euros — not taking into account unreported income, given that we're talking about Greek family businesses). Given the target's financial state, our own roots, our future needs, and the effort required for the operation etc. I estimated that two billion drachmas was quite a reasonable amount of money to demand.

Greek outlaws (and others as well), being proletarians, often display creeping servility. That, paired with their ignorance concerning the flow of money, how much, where it ends, and also the roles they themselves assumed by taking up arms, turned them into carpetbaggers. In a supposed dilemma between kidnapping a corrupted tycoon and kidnapping a non-corrupt, less wealthy businessman who contributes to society, they'd thoughtlessly choose the second. Even if they were sure that the risk (sentence-wise, effort-wise, risk of arrest etc.) was the same.

Unfortunately, this bitter realisation partially stood for Nikos as well. So it appears that apart from knowledge and virtue, both of which determine our choices (taking into account the quality of each person's individual righteousness), another equally decisive factor is how soberly we perceive the role of our struggle and all its parameters.

Money had value to us only with respect to bearing the costs of maintaining our freedom (which was more than one would think). Such expenses could be taken care of with a single bank robbery each year if we didn't intend to leave Greece. The choice to kidnap a businessman was made precisely because we had made up our minds to leave the country once and for all. Since its people were not perceptive or courageous enough to revolt and force all the dirty dynasty rodents infesting this land onto a cruise ship (they have many after all) and, if not shipwreck it (let's not pollute our oceans), at least drive them out of the country, but instead attempted to mimic their treacherous ways, the rodents were forcing us to emigrate. And since they were driving us off our land for good, one of them had to pay from their loot which, either way, wouldn't have returned to the Greek people.

Right after robbing the National Bank's branch in Kalabaka we travelled abroad. We visited many countries, some of which we wanted, and could live in for the rest of our lives. What we realised, however, was that to stay there permanently, not having to return a few years later, we needed a lot of money. Not to live large, but because, no matter which country we chose, nothing would change. We'd still remain wanted men. When you're a most wanted man, it is hard to begin anew, building a new life from scratch in a foreign country. So having some money was absolutely necessary. The more, the better.

Given that this would be the first such kidnapping in Greece, success was almost guaranteed. I believe we should have gone after an even fatter, dirtier rodent than Haitoglou. Knowing Nikos' reaction, I didn't even suggest it. Taking all this into account and being fully aware of the whole situation, I suggested that we demanded a billion drachmas. Nikos once again disagreed.

"It's a lot of money, they'll never pay. They'll set us up to capture us, or kill us or ..."

Fearing he'd once again walk out on me, we reached a deal. Three million Deutsche Marks. No more. No less. We had a deal.

Deliberate amateurism

In the meantime, Alekos decided to lift up his hood and enjoy the ride.

"Come on, Alekos ... we didn't hood you to keep your head warm but so that you wouldn't be able to see! Do yourself a favour", Nikos yelled at him.

"It's hard to breathe, you guys. That's why I took it off", he said.

We took a slight detour. We got Alekos out of the car and realised he indeed had trouble breathing. He was experiencing something like angina; the poor guy was in shock. His system was not responding. Realising what was happening to him and fearing the worst caused him discomfort.

"Whatever happens next, whether we get our money or not, you'll return home", we assured him.

"Why are you doing this, guys? You seem like educated men".

"How dare you, Alekos", Nikos yelled at him.

He laughed. So did we. This encouraged him.

We decided to allow him to sit in the back of the car, like a regular passenger. The RAV's rear doors' windows were tinted and, along with the rear doors, had been modified not to open from the inside, so he sat in the back seat — without a hood on this time. The situation was becoming surreal, and we were always open to new challenges.

An ignorant person would reasonably wonder whether our attitude towards the hostage was advisable in a kidnapping operation. If we'd been talking about someone else, my answer would be no. For us, however, it was a perfectly normal and controllable situation. We weren't two plain outlaws carrying out a kidnapping. Our future wouldn't be determined or defined by this one operation. We were escaped convicts, hunted down by the Hellenic Police, convicted of every felony listed in the criminal code. So whether or not they pinned Haitoglou's kidnapping on us — if we ever got arrested — it would make little difference. We weren't (consciously) interested in the penal side of our actions, so we felt free and blithe when it came to making decisions that seemed unusual for professional outlaws. After all, we considered ourselves neither professional nor outlaws, not even fugitives. We thought professional outlaws and fugitives were only those who do not follow their conscience. Those who, day after day, dance to the rhythm dictated by the rules. Looking back, I would say we were armed men outside the norm. Whenever we thought of something as being more urgent, more meaningful, we never hesitated to improvise, going beyond the methods and highroads aped by local outlaws.

In this case, we were humans before anything else. Kindness was our last bastion of resistance. We'd never abandon this stronghold, no matter where life took us.

When you consciously decide to permanently shrug off oppressive State laws, you're left naked and vulnerable. At first, you feel like a turtle without its shell. A readymade shell we didn't want. It was too heavy, too tight, for us. It didn't fit us, and so we wouldn't serve it; in this life, we weren't turtles or beggars, but challengers.

Nobody knows their real individual legal boundaries until they have struggled to get rid of the common human and divine laws, without then latching onto others, ready, promising, progressive, thus entering a new, more modern shell, which would provide them with all necessary security. This crossroads of struggle is no easy matter. It is painful. It is man's greatest fear. In the face of such fears, you have to discover your own way of protecting yourself. The options are as follows: you either get rid of them once and for all or you serve them for the rest of your life; you either grow wings to climb to the sky or a thick skin to crawl into the mud.

As for myself, I never showed disdain towards the value of human life; yet I found the act of taking a life perfectly legitimate and acceptable, under certain circumstances and with good reason, as when "wider" freedom was concerned. Because death is the inescapable consequence of life. On the contrary, causing pain by torturing is something horrible, something heinous. Leaving Haitoglou tied and hooded in the trunk for days would have been torture. And we had no intention of committing such a crime.

Alekos the outlaw

Having taken our seats back in the RAV, we continued our journey south. Alekos adapted rather quickly, to the point where one might say he began enjoying himself. Nikos, being more extroverted, started chatting him up, about metaphysical stuff.

"Tell me, Alekos! Did you feel something was going to happen? Did you see any strange dreams? Inexplicable anxiety perhaps?"

"No! Absolutely nothing! I was completely taken aback this morning. I was afraid you were going to kill me when you took me to that grove. I thought you wanted the money in the briefcase".

"Oh! Since you mentioned it … give it to me for a second".

I opened it, took a hundred seventy thousand drachmas and replaced it with one of the ten one thousand Deutsche Mark banknotes I had on me. Then I told him, handing him back the briefcase:

"It'll prove useful, after all, as a portable currency exchange".

He was surprised.

"What are you doing? You can take it all! I don't mind if you do!"

"We do, though. You'll go back right the way we took you, along with the briefcase and its contents".

"As you wish … but so you know, if I were in your position, and you were in mine, I'd take it all!"

We laughed. As it turned out, he was a cool guy with a sense of humour and a positive mindset. I was sure the next few days, until we got our money, would prove interesting enough. Way out of the ordinary, even for us. We were already becoming pals and if someone were to peek inside the car they would never guess what was actually happening. Apart from trying to build trust in the RAV, our eyes, and even more so our minds, were focused on the outside. Our eyes, sharp from years of training, proved very useful in situations like this. Two pairs were scanning and processing all incoming data during the whole journey. Everything was being sieved. We wouldn't let anything go by unnoticed, and we did it so naturally that it couldn't possibly be perceived by any third parties.

As the day went on, everything seemed to be going even better than expected. Alekos was now "one of us". He shared our worries; he offered solutions to our problems and was willing to help in any arising obstacle. And why wouldn't he; it was his own life on the line after all.

"In a few days we'll give you your own gun!" we'd tease him, and he'd laugh.

He told us not to worry. That the money's there. And that we'd get it because his father wouldn't put his son at risk for the sake of the cops. He even advised us to be careful while on the road lest the police stopped us for some random inspection.

"Handcuffed back here I'll take all the bullets. I won't be able to react! If anything happens, you should untie me and give me a Kalashnikov!"

We hoped he was joking. But you never know ...

"You better hope the police have set up some roadblocks, Alekos. It'll be something you'll never forget! A once in a lifetime experience. After all, you're paying a lot of money, you should enjoy some action", it was our turn to tease him.

Fugitives and entrepreneurship

We spent that first night on a plateau among the snowy mountains. We folded the RAV's back seat and made room for Alekos to lie down. We gave him a sleeping mat, a sleeping bag too — we treated him like royalty! We'd take shifts for the night. It was winter, the night was long; there was plenty of time for both of us to get enough sleep. I took the first watch. I woke up in the morning with Alekos standing over me, wide-eyed with worry. When Nikos had replaced me at about one in the morning, I had laid a groundsheet on the snow and crawled inside my sleeping bag. By morning, however, it was thick with frost. That's why Alekos was surprised.

"Are you alive?" he asked me.

"The only one in danger of dying on this mountain is you, Alekos, if you keep on bothering me. I'm alive and hungry, and I see you're in a good mood, so let's grab a bite".

We had taken plenty of food with us for this expedition: canned tuna, cold meat, graviera cheese, toast, olives, tomatoes, bread, and plenty of nuts. We had some of everything for breakfast. Alekos did not forget what he'd seen that morning.

"Have you served in the Special Forces?" he asked me.

"I've never served anyone or anything, and I don't intend to. I went to the armoured warfare training division, and I was constantly punished for being disobedient, so I had to stay for two-and-a-half more months than the four I originally had to!"

"I don't get it. Why can't the State make use of talented people like you?" he wondered out loud.

In turn, I wondered how an industrialist, having his breakfast along with two heavily armed kidnappers on a RAV's hood set against the snowy plateau of some beautiful Greek mountain, could be concerned about how others could make use of those kidnappers. It seemed that nothing, not even weightlessness, could change a businessman's way of thinking. Alekos finally admitted that his questions concerning the military weren't random but stemmed from a personal interest in the subject. At first we thought we were dealing with some military-obsessed fascist, soon however we came to realise that for him it was just a hobby.* His interest was focused on a scientific approach of defensive doctrines etc. If I remember correctly, at some point, he wrote articles on the subject for publications of that sort.

When we had finished our simple breakfast, we got in the RAV and drove to a different area to contact his brother, Kostas. We needed an update concerning his effort to collect the money. Having been informed that everything was going well we had the rest of Saturday to ourselves, so we decided to have a day-long crash course in the real market economy.

Alekos was our teacher. And we two fugitives, bank robbers and his kidnappers, were his students. It doesn't get more surreal than that. He showed us no mercy while teaching us the whole process, from primary production to recycling. He was blunt and straightforward. When your raw materials are sesame and sugar, it goes without saying that you know their production, sale and purchasing processes as well as their harvesting, standardisation and packaging methods. And, of course, the process of circulation of the products you process until they reach the shelves of retailers, enter the shopping basket and then, through the natural route of modern consumerist societies, end up in landfills, in the ocean or in biological waste treatment facilities. You can't even imagine what stories about schemes, bad checks and all kinds of blackmail we listened to that Saturday, vividly revealing to us the capitalist market paradise!

What I remember most vividly from that free lesson is the blunt blackmail attempted by large supermarket chains. For a prepacked product with a new label Alekos wished to circulate through a large supermarket chain, he'd have to give its owner large sums of dirty money just for the product to reach the shelves. The specific amount required depended on the place (display) inside the shops. If the new product wasn't well-received by consumers within a reasonable period — depending on the deal — he'd take it down as uneconomic, because there were a lot of new products waiting in line to try their luck on the supermarket displays, and always more underhand dirty money deals. Half his company's expenses were for the promotion of products through such means, or through similar deals with TV stations to advertise them etc. And who pays for all this? Those who usually do.

At the end of the day we ceremoniously received our graduate degrees. I, not intending to take advantage of it soon, but just in case, framed it in the corner of my mind, adding a footnote: kidnappings, my arse. The money is elsewhere! Being so occupied, we never noticed when darkness fell. We searched and found a safe place to spend the night, far from the previous night's plateau. With our minds exhausted from being bombarded with financial information the whole day, they took advantage of the night's silence to calm a bit. Alekos, however, wasn't finished yet. Dessert included a personal story.

---

*   His military hobbyism got a bit out of hand in later years — an entire room full of vehicle and gun replicas fills 'Alexandros Haitoglou Hall' at the Museum of Macedonian Struggle in Thessaloniki.

"Two years ago, someone used to work in my factory", he told us. "One day, he came to my office and happily announced to me that he had won eighty million in the lottery, and so he'd give up work. Six months ago he returned to my office. He asked me to hire him again because he'd spent all his luck money. Now he's working in the exact same position he had before quitting!"

And he went on boldly:

"I'm only saying this, because the money you're going to get isn't much, so if you don't manage it properly, you'll soon run out".

"Stop playing with fire Alekos", I said to him, subconsciously looking at Nikos as if wanting to say: "You should listen to this!"

It was impossible to sleep after that.

The kidnapper, the kidnapped and their unspoken prayers

I'll only mention Sunday for one reason. We had dinner right outside a chapel, built on the top of a fir-covered hill. When we felt full, my companions stood up and, without saying a word, as if having already planned it, opened the door and entered the chapel. Nikos, who was following Alekos, was still armed. Five minutes later, they appeared again. They stood on the chapel's landing and said to me: "Our candles are burning side by side in the chapel!"

Now, it seemed, this abduction was turning fast into something much bigger, an agonising inward journey in search of deeper metaphysical and existential issues of predator and prey. My faithlessness was shaken! I was frozen, with the Kalashnikov still in my hands. I was staring at them; a handful of questions swarming in my mind. What was it that had led each of them to do this? What had they been thinking? How had they been feeling? What had they said to each other? What had each of them wished for? What were they expecting after this? Did they actually believe in a god? I've never been indiscrete and, always being a supporter of personal information protection, I never asked them any of this and so I never learnt. Yet this scene is the first that vividly returns to my mind, whenever I try to recall this kidnapping.

Final negotiations and tension

Monday was the day we would finally get our ransom money, but also a day of high tension between Nikos and I. From the beginning of this operation, each of us was aware of their role and responsibilities. Nikos, among other things, had taken on the task of communicating with the family. We had agreed that the ransom was non-negotiable. We had asked for three million Deutsche Marks, and that's what we'd get. We were only willing to make some concessions if they had trouble finding foreign money. Irrespective of the currency, however, the price remained the same. We estimated the time he'd need to get from Thessaloniki to Lamia and phoned Kostas an hour earlier to tell him to get ready. Alekos spoke to him first. He said to his brother that we were heavily armed and methodical and that we knew what we were doing. He also told him that if he intended to bring the cops to the meeting, it would be best if he didn't come at all because he'd put his own life in danger too. He said all these things without being forced by us. Kostas asked Alekos if he was sure we'd set him free if he handed us the money. He said he was.

Lately, Nikos had been walking away from the car whenever we contacted Alekos' family because we had realised he got stressed. That's what he did then; moving away from us, but on his return he dropped the bomb: they hadn't managed to gather the money, and he had accepted an offer to bring us two hundred and seventy million.

I was infuriated.

"Why didn't you insist on the sum we had agreed? We've gone through all this trouble, Alekos has reassured us that they have the money and that we'll get it and you back down at the first sign of trouble. Those people are businessmen, they know exchanges and blackmail, it would be no trouble at all for them to try and save half their money!"

Nikos was trying to explain himself, saying his piece.

"What's done is done, let's not argue. We still have to pick up the money, and it's still a lot. It's not worth ..." and he concluded: "Don't you see the poor man's condition? No one can guarantee us that tomorrow ..."

"In our condition, Nikos, no one can guarantee us anything, not of tomorrow and not of the next hundred years. So whether we have this man with us or not, you and I are the only ones who can make guarantees for ourselves. When we were planning this job, we both agreed to keep him at least for a week, and now you're wavering in the face of a false dilemma".

It is risky to say with certainty what is right and what is wrong in situations like this. It is purely a matter of assessing ongoing events, something which ought to be done by all those who participate in them and, consequently, define them to a great extent. Nikos assessed the situation based on his own criteria and acted as he saw fit. My objection had to do with the fact that he did not consult with me, to make the assessment of this turn of events together and make a joint decision, whatever that might have been. Instead, on a whim he took responsibility for the outcome of the kidnapping. It was pointless hollering, the damage was done, and nothing could be done to undo it. We had just set our future plans in stone. I buried my anger and entered the required mental state as we approached the finish line.

Picking up the ransom and setting Alekos free

Night fell between half-past five and six. Kostas arrived in Lamia at about nine. The instructions were straightforward: "Turn right and take the road that leads to Amfissa. After the first gas station you come across, enter the first dirt road you see on your right. About fifteen yards further down you'll come across a small bridge. Leave the money there, back up to the main road and return home".

He came, he dropped off the money, and he left. We went, we picked it up, and we left.

We drove to the valley of Lamia and, following a predetermined route, headed towards Karditsa. As soon as we were back on the road I began scrutinising the bundled cash, searching for any suspicious items while counting them at the same time. It amounted to a hundred and fifty million drachmas in crisp ten thousand drachma notes and less than a million in Deutsche Marks.

We entered Karditsa and dropped Alekos near the town's long-distance bus terminal. He was obviously happy. He bid us farewell by saying the most outrageous thing in the world:

"Guys, If it didn't cost that much, I'd very much like to have another adventure with you!"

"Don't worry. We'll give you a discount ..."*

In the wake of the kidnapping, the bounty and being Greece's most wanted

We grew to like Alekos. We found him to be good-natured. He proved this the following day when he spoke to the media, saying, among other things:

"They treated me well, given the circumstances. They seemed like educated people. If they get arrested, I wouldn't want violence to be used against them. The State should show more interest in the correctional system ..."

Yet the ruling class does not forgive such actions. They mercilessly derided him. They diagnosed him with Stockholm syndrome and other nonsense. They didn't want the public to think that his kidnappers were human beings and had proven so. Their goal was, and still is, to scare the public. His brother was the worst of them all, furiously inveighing against us. In the following year's balance sheet, he deducted the money we had taken from Alekos' dividend. Alekos once again proved he was a cool guy many years later when he was asked in court whether he recognised me. He said no, telling them he was hooded throughout his captivity. Over the next few days, we learnt a lot from newspaper reports. Among other things, we learnt that Haitoglou (not specifying who, but probably the father) had won two hundred fifty million in the lottery a year earlier! An extra reason for me to be angry.

We also learnt that the police had always known my involvement in the kidnapping, because of a devilish coincidence. After everything, the ID I had used to buy the phone used in the abduction didn't belong to the owner of the car I thought it did, as the guys from Athens had reassured me. Instead, it belonged to the second car with which some of them — without bothering to clean it — had used to commit an armed bank robbery in Athens the very same day we parted ways. The cops found fingerprints belonging both to Keramidis and me,

---

*   Haitoglou was the first industrialist to be kidnapped in Greece for ransom. After his release, he continued working in his family business until his death in 2016.

something of which I was unaware until then. Needless to say that I was convicted for that robbery as well as two others in which the same car had been used!

And so came the bounty*. Greece is not so far from the West, after all. And the Far West for that matter. That piece of work, the then-Minister of Public Order Sifis Valirakis**, announced the issuing of bounties for me, Nikos and Keramidis (whose fingerprints just happened to have been found along with mine inside a car, and that was reason enough). It wasn't the first time Volirakis had done something similar. Almost a year earlier, he had issued a decree stipulating that every citizen who aids in the prevention — or singlehandedly prevents — a bank robbery would be awarded a million drachmas (three thousand euros). There have been more than a few citizens who, going after that million, got hurt or killed.

***

A year or so after the issuing of the bounty, I came face to face with my colleague, the former fugitive Sifis. I was with a companion — who wasn't involved in any illegal activities — walking down a central street in Athens lined with bookstores; while he was walking in the opposite direction, talking on the phone, accompanied by a donkey and a cow. If I remember correctly, he was still Minister of Public Order. I recognised him from afar. In my bag I had, among other things, a Scorpion ready for use. Yet, taking advantage of the narrow pavement, I settled for prodding him, hoping he'd lose his balance and realise that there's space for only one of us in this world. He didn't feel a thing, and neither did his pets. He kept on talking on his phone, possibly with some snitch who identified Palaiokostas and had to be informed on how to collect the bounty. And that miserable little man wants me to believe he escaped from Corfu Prison!

It is common knowledge that after the fall of the Greek military Junta***, many of today's politicians modified or enlarged their records, as they deemed fit, presenting themselves as former insurgents and dissidents. Now for real, if there is anyone who actually believes that Sifis used to plant bombs during the Junta, they should really be deprived of their civil rights. Because they would be as useful to democracy as Sifis was dangerous for the colonels. Unfortunately, this country's history has been and continues to be written in secret or in plain sight by dark, manipulative mechanisms.

---

*   Author's note: for the State to place a bounty on the head of a member of society is an insult to all Greek citizens, indicating that the State treats each individual citizen as an immoral, venal being.

**   Iosif Valrakis (1943-2021) better-known as Sifis, is written up in official histories as a leading figure of the anti-Junta resistance. The story goes he was convicted over a number of bombings and jailed by the regime in 1971, later performing a spectacular jailbreak from Corfu Prison in which he swam to Albania. When the Junta fell he became a senior member of the new PASOK government.

***   The Junta was a military dictatorship which dominated Greek life from 1967-74 in the wake of a coup against the weakened democratic State. It was overthrown following the Athens Polytechnic Uprising of 1973, ushering in the PASOK/New Democracy period of two-party politics.

Because this book is being written by someone who at least knows a lot about breaking out of prison, I'll make some arbitrary interpretations and let the readers judge me. First of all, a man who in the past has reacted this particular way when deprived of his freedom would never have accepted becoming Minister of Public Order for moral reasons. And as good-humoured as I may be, I still can't justify the use of such obscene methods as prompting unrestrained ratting for money.

It was quite rare for a single man, or two men, to escape from Corfu Prison. My experience, my (extensive) knowledge and his later, dishonest, life persuade me that this man simply walked away one night, through the main door, after someone from the inside had opened it for him. Let him tell us why and with what purpose. The rest is history; he became Minister of Public Order issuing bounties. And then he became chairman of the enquiry committee investigating scandals. Good grief. We're hopeless.

***

In 1996 the Atlanta Olympics took place, and it was the first time Greece had won so many medals (some of them Gold). It was then that I realised the money provided by the Greek State to thank all these people was slightly over a hundred million drachmas.

My critical thinking skills often operate illustratively, so an image was forged in my mind: all these Olympic champions gathered in front of a bank counter, getting their share of the money; and in front of a different counter, a hooded snitch, with his sneaky gaze and smile, cashing out even bigger sums of money from the Greek State for having committed such a treacherous deed. A State like this, which generously awards treacherous men, granting them asylum and offering social recognition to their mentors, will never set sail to a brighter future.

After the favourable outcome of Haitoglou's kidnapping, Nikos' and my common path in illegal struggle came to an end. Right after the kidnapping he abandoned Greece, and I've not seen him since.* **

---

*   Author's note: after sixteen years of being mercilessly hunted down, with many armed bank robberies in the countryside and countless car-chases, Nikos was arrested in September 2006, near Mount Parnassus Ski Resort. During another car-chase his car overturned and Nikos got caught. He's been in prison since then. He has never taken a human life, he has never injured a human being, and he has never fired against people. The Greek justice system sentenced him to life in prison. He is still a hostage of the State's corrupted authorities.

**   Editors' note: Nikos was released into house arrest on health grounds as this book was being readied for print. He is to serve the rest of his sentence in the village of Moschofyto, where he grew up. He had spent sixteen years in prison.

ROADBLOCK AND CAR CHASE IN PARGA

The night's torrential rain had stopped for less than five minutes, and they'd already managed to set up a roadblock. There were ten or so guards, wearing military clothing and heavily armed, with four vehicles at their disposal, one of which was an unmarked Alfa Romeo. We saw them as soon as we made the last turn before the intersection towards Parga. We were coming from Igoumenitsa. They were about seventy yards ahead of us, their powerful flashlights in hand, and signalled us to pull over so that they could perform an inspection.

"Here we go again. Let's get this party started!"

It was my own instinctive way of mocking the otherwise quite dangerous situation we were about to get into. I turned on our hazard lights and kept driving at full throttle. How can you slow down when you're driving a Lada Niva on a wet highway, and there's a deadly roadblock in front of you? Obviously, the Bolsheviks had never imagined car chases in Parga, Epirus when they revolted. The Lada, Soviet feat that it was, was not made for such dangerous missions. After all, in the ideal communist world, nobody pursues anybody, because they're all already caught. I drove past the roadblock going almost seventy-five miles per hour, splashing water all over them and getting them even more soaked. If natural fluid is interpreted as a hostile act against authority, then the Lada's passengers (certainly communists) need to be immediately apprehended and given an exemplary punishment.

I looked at the Niva's side-view mirrors (yes, you clueless reader, it has mirrors) and saw the faster and braver four among them jump in the Alfa Romeo. Weaving between cars they joined the rally with the self-assurance of men in possession of superior technology. There's no way the Lada could outdrive them …

Yet communism, apart from the Lada, also manufactured the Kalashnikov and the Scorpion to balance the gross injustice of Western imperialism's technological leadership. I always had one on me, along with many magazines and a handful of bullets.

Our aspiring pursuers placed a portable emergency light on top of the Alfa Romeo, which approached us fast, its hazard lights turned on, as well as its high beam headlights. I had found myself in a tight spot: about two hundred yards behind me were four cops holding G3 battle rifles, with the rest of them certainly following close behind. I was driving a Lada which couldn't go faster than seventy-five miles per hour and which I could feel skidding on the wet road; the car chase was taking place in an area I didn't know well and, as if all that wasn't enough, Thomas didn't want anything to do with illegality (though oddly enough was in the Lada's passenger seat). He was a good friend from Athens, who had wanted to participate, for the sake of experience, in one of my tours of Epirus' prefectures.

It was a tough call deciding what to do to get us out of this challenging situation. And yet I made it. There was no other option as things had turned out.

Thomas had to use a gun, but not the Kalashnikov. He lacked the experience for such a weapon. It was my responsibility to guide him concerning the use of it. So I spoke to him in an authoritative, austere manner.

"Thomas, open the map. Find the first exit we'll come across to our left".

Never before having been caught up in that sort of business, Thomas panicked. He dropped the flashlight, he dropped the map. He lost it. It is one thing imagining the beast and another coming face to face with it. It is even worse when that beast comes after you.

"Forget it, Thomas. Grab the Scorpion, get it ready, open your window and be ready to shoot when I tell you to ..."

I took stock of the situation and commanded him:"Get out and shoot!"

Holding the weapon with both hands, he crawled half out of the Lada's window and fired a hail of five or six bullets in our pursuers' direction. They didn't seem to notice anything. Thomas returned to his seat all flouncy, thinking that his mission was over.

"Come on Thomas ... get back out there and dump the whole magazine into them!"

He did it. And he managed reasonably well, given that he lacked practice in such matters. I looked in the Niva's mirrors and saw the Alfa Romeo's lights getting smaller in the distance. They'd gotten the message.

About a hundred and fifty yards ahead was a narrow overpass, but thirty yards before that was the exit of a country road. It appeared to go downhill and then under the bridge, leading to the opposite side of the highway.

I barely even thought about it. As long as we remained on the highway, the odds were against us. I slowed down, turned onto the narrow road, which indeed crossed under the overpass, and kept on driving through an abandoned hamlet. Past that, the road climbed the mountain through countless steep hairpin turns and soon, from on high, we could clearly see the cops.

All the cars that were at the roadblock had arrived just outside the abandoned settlement, their emergency lights turned on. From then on the environment became hostile and they dared not proceed. They didn't know what they would encounter if they did so, in the middle of the night. Fear of the unknown held them back.

We pulled over to catch our breath. I checked the map to see where we were exactly and which was the safest road out of Epirus. We had a long night ahead of us. Yet I couldn't help but feel satisfied with the outcome, especially for Thomas. If things hadn't worked out as they did his life would have changed forever, and he was in no sense ready for something like that. He had, however, his own distinct sense of humour, which was always a pleasant surprise. He looked at me, and said quite convincingly: "Man, there's something wrong with me".

"What? What is it?" I entreated him.

"I believe I grew some major balls after shooting at the cops!"

We laughed our arses off. Car chases can become, in a sense, pleasant in the company of friends with a good sense of humour. Even if they're not outlaws.

Adventure in Corfu

It was the beginning of August in 1996, and I was in Igoumenitsa, boarding a ferry to Corfu. Having arranged to flee abroad, I'd chosen to go to Italy from Corfu, rather than any other port, for several reasons.

In 1996, passport controls for passengers heading to Europe were conducted in only three big ports: Patra, Igoumenitsa, and Corfu. I'd dismissed Patra due to the previous summer's incident. So I had to choose between the other two.

We had taken the passport I was going to use for my escape, along with eighty others and the equipment to make more one night, from a safe in Kilkis. Having blank passports and official embossed seals, we could make our own documentation. Yet we ran a high risk in doing so: we didn't know whether the seals' serial numbers had been made known to all the country's points of exit or whether they could be cross-checked. The only thing that put my mind at rest was the fact that a few months before I attempted to flee the country, Nikos had gone through passport control with a passport from that same batch. With that in mind, I chose Corfu as the most remote of the three ports, lest someone happened to recognise me while waiting or when boarding the ship out.

The ferry from Igoumenitsa arrived at Corfu around five in the afternoon. I disembarked and set off to buy a ticket for Italy. The ship was expected to depart at ten that evening. It was the first time I had visited the island and it was a great opportunity to at least get to know the city. Having had a cup of coffee at one of the central square's coffee shops, I began wandering Corfu's endless alleys, admiring their beauty. I had dinner at one of its many restaurants and then headed towards the port, since the ferry's departure time was drawing near.

I crossed the gate and entered. The ferry to Ancona was at the jetty, and the first passengers were already embarking while all kinds of vehicles were being loaded. I spotted three armed harbour patrol officers, wandering around lazily, waiting for another boring shift to end. Straight ahead and to my left there was a group of about twenty tourists waiting by the passport control. I got in line to wait for my turn. That's when a policeman appeared inside passport control holding the tourists' passports, asking them to follow him. He was obviously going to inspect them and hand them back their passports on embarkation. So, suddenly, I was on my own.

I walked towards passport control and stood in front of the counter. Inside were three cops. One was facing the other way, doing something on his desk. The second was right in front of me. He took my passport, and without even looking, handed it to the third officer, who was the youngest of the three and sat in front of a computer in the corner to my right. After thumbing through the document, he began typing in the personal information written on it. At the same time the policeman who had earlier escorted the tourist group to the ferry came and stood next to me, placing his elbows on the counter. He began telling us how stupid all tourists are, especially British ones, with compelling evidence and arguments which he started reciting to me.

After a while, the young policeman rose slightly from his chair. He stretched out his hand to hand me back the passport, unable to get his eyes off the computer. Suddenly, he froze. He sat again in his chair, bringing the passport close to his face. From where I stood, I could barely see the computer's monitor. Still, I made out some red letters. I needed nothing more. I knew what would follow. I didn't react. Without them noticing, an alarm had gone off inside me, readying me for an impending confrontation. I had but a few seconds to plan my next moves. My small suitcase, apart from a printer's daisy-wheel, some books (Nietzsche, Heraclitus, Epicurus etc.) and two changes of clothes, contained nothing of value, so I had to get rid of it. Either way, it would be impossible to get the passport back from them. They'd soon know to whom it belonged.

As it happened my backpack contained everything I was going to need: a map of Corfu, a hat, and a shaving machine, among other things. In my bum bag I had a Zastava pistol, which didn't have a trigger reset, but worked fine if you cocked it each time. I had decided to take it with me mainly as a deterrent, and not to weather a possible confrontation. Either way, I had intended to drop it in the ocean after we set sail, or hide it somewhere in Italy just in case I ever had to return. So I had no intention of getting it out there and then. Even though I had a two-hundred-fifty million drachma bounty on my head and was on top of the most-wanted list, they couldn't possibly recognise me. They didn't suspect whom they were up against. The odds were against me, yet I still had the element of surprise. I had to take advantage of it as best I could. Things would stay as they were for a few seconds. The three policemen on the other side of the counter continued with their tasks, with the one standing next to me still trying his best to persuade me of the validity of his "progressive" beliefs concerning tourists.*

The young policeman turned and looked at me. Then he asked me politely:

"Was your passport stolen recently, Mr Divanis?"

"No, I stole it", I answered him, equally politely.

Dropping my suitcase on the floor, I turned my back to them and broke into a run, heading to the port's gate. I never looked back, but I was under the impression nobody had followed me. I could only hear the voices of bewildered men. I exited onto the main road which runs through the whole island and was immediately faced with a dilemma: enter the city and find somewhere to hide, or hijack an incoming car and drive to the northern or the southern part of the island? I decided on the latter. To my left, by the roadside, there was a taxi stand, which was full of drivers. If I attempted to get a car by force they'd realise and follow me. I crossed the road. Heading north, I entered the first alley I came across on my left. After walking about fifty yards, I found myself at a dead-end. In front of me was an archaeological site, which was enclosed by a ten feet high fence. Right in front of it, at the end of the narrow street, was a vacant lot with a handful of parked cars. I saw a woman sitting inside a Fiat Punto, listening to music. She was about forty years old. I walked up to her and told her quite sternly:

---

*   The surname written on the passport.

"Get out of the car, madam ... just a routine inspection ... I'm a drug enforcement agent".

"Yes, officer, right away", she said, getting out of the car.

I got in and started the car.

"What? You're taking my car?" she asked, starting to suspect something was off.

"Don't worry. I'll return it soon enough!" I said, backing it up.

She didn't need to hear anything more. She ran towards the exit of the alley, screaming that someone was stealing her car. I was trapped in the middle of the alley. In front of me was another car and behind it a huge truck, which was obviously having trouble entering the main road due to the traffic. There were pubs on both sides of the alley. Their customers, hearing the woman's screams, came to her rescue. About ten people surrounded the Punto. Some lad, full of himself. kicked my door after discovering he couldn't open it, since I had locked it.

During the trial, which took place some years later, the lad who had kicked my car boasted about this exploit of his during his testimony, making the car's owner lose her temper. She told him off.

"Oh, so you're the one who destroyed my car? Shame on you. And boasting about it too! Do you know how much money it cost me to fix it? The guy didn't even touch the car, he left it just as he found it ..."

Everyone in the courtroom had a good laugh. For this incident alone, the hijacking of the car exactly as I'm narrating it, the island's blind whore* sentenced me to thirteen years in prison! A combined sentence. What a judicial fury ...

In the meantime, having all those hopeful heroes around me, I had to take immediate action. I turned onto the main road, in the direction of the port. The police were nowhere to be seen. A little way down the road, I saw an opening in the road barriers, so I made a U-turn and headed north. I covered several miles before abandoning the main road, down an adjacent track that led to several neighbouring villages. I decided to leave the car in an olive grove, making sure it wouldn't be visible from the road. The longer it took them to locate it, the better for me. I was completely aware of what was about to follow. The very same night the police would realise who the man who had escaped from the port was. The incident with the car would allow them to draw some conclusions. The next day, backup would arrive from the neighbouring prefectures, certainly followed by the Special Anti-Terrorist Unit along with helicopters ready to intervene in case they located me. They wouldn't let such an opportunity go to waste. And they didn't.

For the time being, darkness had fallen. I began walking, heading south, and by sunrise I had travelled about two-thirds of the way across the island. What I had realised the previous night was that I was going to have trouble finding fresh water. My fast pace, along with August's unbearable heat, made me thirsty. Clean water was of vital importance. I was forced to enter residential areas and into houses' yards to get it.

---

*   Lady justice.

Corfu had thick vegetation. I didn't have trouble locating a shady spot to spend the day without being noticed. I slept for many hours. In the afternoon, I shaved. I had a pair of sunglasses in my backpack in case I needed them. Yet, carefully examining it, I realised something awful had happened: the bag's outer pocket was open. The map and hat were missing. They'd probably fallen somewhere along the way without me realising it. The confrontation with my pursuers had indeed caught me entirely by surprise, otherwise I'd have had some food packed in my backpack, along with water, a small radio for information on the other side, and a mobile phone.

Things were about to get even worse in the next few days, but I didn't know it yet. I had weathered quite a few storms in the past; this was just another challenge. I had to pull through and once again come out victorious. Since the moment I had abandoned the car in that olive grove, an idea had been stuck in my head: get to the southern part of the island, find someone with a boat, hold them hostage at gunpoint and make them transport me to Igoumenitsa. When it got dark again, I resumed walking. A little after midnight, dark clouds formed on the horizon — a storm was coming. The heavens opened and for an hour kept spitting water and fire. And I kept on walking. Although I was soaked to the bone, this sudden rainstorm was welcome. The temperature dropped.

When morning came, I estimated I was now near the western side of Lefkimmi. The area was packed with tourists. I thought it wise to pretend to be a tourist to try and locate some anchored sailboats and yachts. It was Sunday, about ten in the morning when I walked into a corner shop to buy a phone-card and a bottle of water. I was shaved, wearing Bermuda shorts, a t-shirt, sunglasses, and a hat which I had found the previous night on some beach. Inside the corner shop were a few tourists doing some shopping, two women, and a man along with four children. The latter three seemed to know each other; the man was behind the counter. I spoke English while paying and left.

I was trying to find a phone booth. I spotted one about a hundred yards down the road, got to it and began dialling a number. The four children I had seen inside the corner shop appeared next to me, talking in whispers and staring at me. They obviously hadn't come there on their own volition but were sent by the grownups, to eavesdrop on what I was going to say during my call. I didn't like that at all; it was a bad sign. Speaking in broken Portuguese, I was informed that the media of the country had yet to mention the incident. I told my interlocutor that I would have to hang up and that I'd contact them at the earliest opportunity. Once I'd done so, the children ran back to the corner shop. I headed to the beach. The street I was on was uphill and extremely narrow, barely fitting a car. I kept on walking for about two or three minutes when a big vehicle appeared in front of me; I can't recall its model or brand. Reaching me, the driver, who was alone, suddenly stopped the car. He grabbed an MP5 and pointed it at me through the car's open window.

"Where are you off to, dude? Police! Don't move! Stay right where you are", he yelled at me.

I remained perfectly calm.

"What's happening? I don't understand. What's going on?" I said in English.

"Police ... police ... passport ... passport", he kept on yelling.

"Ok, no problem", I said, almost sweetly, always in English.

The pistol in my bum bag had been useless since the first night of my journey when, in an attempt to ease my feet, I had walked for hours along the strand. It had somehow got wet, and its breechblock was clogged with salt. It was too high a risk to bluff with a useless gun. I was also too close to the car, and the MP5's barrel was less than three feet away from my chest. I lowered my right hand to the bum bag, pretending I was getting my passport. I made a conscious step forward and to the right to get out of the gun's bead and then, without any warning, punched him in the carotid, while at the same time choking him with my left hand. I tried to open his door with my right hand. It was locked. It appears that he had accidentally locked it as he placed his elbow over the open window to aim his submachine gun against me. There was no time to wonder how I could unlock it; the cop was already getting over the shock of my sudden attack. He was trying to escape from my grip, crawling towards the passenger seat. He was still holding on to the MP5, but he was unable to use it. He just held it tight so I couldn't take it. He was strong; his neck was thick as a boar's. I couldn't hold him much longer with only one hand. After all, it would have been stupid and pointless to pursue a hand-to-hand combat. I'd tried to blindside him to take his gun and his car, and it hadn't worked; so now it was time to go. Just as unexpectedly as I had attacked him, I let him go and broke into a run, headed in the direction from which the car had come. A few yards down the road, I jumped into a large yard which I came across to my right, from there to a field, and then to a vineyard; not once did I look back.

At this point, it seems appropriate to explain some incidents that sound unbelievable but which still can be logically explained. My many years of experience living as a wanted man allowed me to be positively sure that I couldn't be recognised at that stage. The policeman's reaction, who was completely taken aback by my attack, testified to that.

Still, what I started to suspect after the incident at the corner store was that the locals had been informed by the local media concerning the bounty on my head and were going out of their way to find the buried treasure. Two hundred and fifty million drachmas was a lot of money back in 1996. A lottery ticket was on the move on their island. They all hoped to be the lucky ones, as long as they kept their eyes and ears open and had no decency. So the local police stations were constantly receiving calls from ambitious opportunists. The head of police had given strict orders that all incoming calls and information ought to be checked, in case they happened to prove lucky. Given the local stations' shortage of staff, in order to investigate all reports they often sent just one officer for an on-the-spot inspection of suspects the locals pointed at. The officer who came to examine me had probably received many similar calls concerning possible suspects in the last couple of days and thought it was just another one of those.

After I was eventually arrested in the late '90s, a seemingly endless series of transfers for the purposes of hearings and trials began. During these transfers, and in the courtrooms, a dispatch from the Special Anti-Terrorist Unit was always present. Since they were part of all operations related to my capture, they were curious and had questions so we'd get into conversations concerning my cases. That's how I learned that as early as the morning after my incident at the port, the whole Special Anti-Terrorist Unit flew to Corfu by helicopter and were barracked in a beachside hotel. They actually thanked me for the exciting fifteen days they had spent there, staying undercover since it was high season. They'd spent the whole time chilling on the beach, sunbathing their balls, waiting for orders to intervene which never arrived.

Related to this, I mentioned the incident with the police officer. They had never heard anything about it and made it clear that if such an incident had been reported, they'd have immediately intervened, aided by the helicopters.

Still, at the time I was in no position to assume the chastened officer would stay quiet about how I outsmarted him. I planned and operated based on the most logical and probable scenario, which included the area being cordoned off by armed police forces, helicopters, etc. I was in a sparsely populated area with no prospects of getting out of there soon.

Whichever plan or future scenario might happen, I was in a tough situation since I was on an island. For the time being, my goal had to be to walk as far away as possible from where the incident took place and hide in some forested area until nightfall.

Making sure I was always moving under cover of the trees, always on the double to avoid getting heatstroke, I'd soon covered a handful of miles, heading west. I spotted a forested mount over a secluded beach and decided to spend the rest of the day there. So much for my plan to take hostages on some watercraft. At least for the time being.

It was well into the night when I began searching for any working boats I could use to escape the island. I located and inspected quite a few during the night; waste of time. I could swim, yes, but otherwise I was completely sea-illiterate. Even if I got some inflatable boat to work, it was highly likely that instead of Igoumenitsa I would end up in the Samoan Islands — which wouldn't be that bad a destination!

At about five in the morning I reached a secluded fishing port, just in time to see a fisherman getting ready to set sail on his boat. I had decided to force someone into getting me to Igoumenitsa so as soon as the fisherman started his engine up I appeared in front of him, holding the pistol. He froze, staring at me.

"I need you to take me somewhere", I said to him, straight from the shoulder.

"Where?" he asked me, puzzled.

"To Igoumenitsa".

"This old thing can't get there. It'd take us a week" he said to me quite convincingly, explaining to me what kind of boat I had just boarded (a seiner, a caïque, or something like that; I am unable to remember his exact phrasing).

What mattered was that my maritime-illiteracy had done the trick. What was I thinking, coming to an island? The fisherman wasn't finished yet. After explaining why his boat wasn't suitable for the job, he offered a solution to my problem. He pointed at another fisherman who in the meantime had arrived and was now casting off his inflatable boat.

"See, his boat could get you to Igoumenitsa. It has two outboard motors, of such and such constant velocity etc".

He straight sold him out.

It seemed like an excellent opportunity. I knew that inflatable boats are the fastest. The fishing port was tiny. I jumped in the knee-dip water and reached the inflatable boat, the motors of which were now started up. I jumped on it. My newly nominated transporter stared at me as if a great white shark had invaded the fishing port.

"You'll take me to Igoumenitsa", I said to him.

"I'm not going anywhere", he yelled, bursting into tears.

It was unbelievable! How could I possibly handle this … I slapped him twice and tried to inflame his male ego.

"Shame on you. A grown man crying like a wuss? You'll be safe. And I'll reward you handsomely once we get there".

Things got even worse. He fell on his knees, sobbing, begging me not to kill him because he had a wife and children to look after. I couldn't believe what was happening. What else did the island have in store for me? The inflated boat's motors were started up. For a split second, I thought I could govern it by myself and reach Igoumenitsa. I dropped the idea when I heard the first fisherman talking with the coast guard on the boat's radio. The people of Corfu were all proving to be quite the tattletales! Indignant — and after slapping the bald beseecher's head twice more — I got off the inflated boat. I moved north-west along the coastline until sunrise.

I was at a critical stage. I had to make a wise decision, taking into account the recent incident. And that's what I did. I located a spot where I could find both food and water, armed myself with patience, and remained there for about a month, making sure nobody saw me. Afterwards, I exited and called Dimitris, giving him my coordinates. He came, having plenty of food hidden in his car, thinking I would be starving. He was surprised to find me only a bit thinner, sculpted, and tanned, without having spent any money! In thin disguise, we left the island by ship, since security had loosened.

Just like that.

A CHILDHOOD JOURNEY

The Seventies had just ended, I was eight or nine years old, and spring was ending. Deep in sleep, the sounds of goat bells reached my ears, mingled with human speech and the hoofing of horses. I awoke with a start, pushing the heavy rug away. I had gone to bed with my clothes and shoes on, to be ready. I ran outside to participate in what I already knew was taking place.

The stars were still glimmering in the sky. In the front yard, our gangly grey mule was waiting patiently as my father, Leonidas, and my brother, Pantelis, who was older than me by two years, were loading the last of the things on its back. My mother, Georgia, who had four other children, was holding a gas lamp and being bossy, making constant remarks because, according to her, the two of them never did anything right. The poor woman had stayed awake the whole night baking bread and pies. She wanted them properly placed on the mule, lest they be spoiled by the sun, and we had nothing to eat on our journey.

Uncle Demos and his wife Sofia had already arrived along with their laden mule. Their flock, about one hundred sheep and goats, merged with our own and now amounted to about three hundred head of livestock. Sensing what was to follow, the animals began trotting downhill. My father hurriedly locked our little house, which was made out of cinder blocks, and we all began chasing after the flock, flashlights in hand. We could hear no bleats, just ringing bells and pounding hooves. It was as though the flock didn't want to wake up the land that had been feeding it for nine months. Instead, it was slipping away silently, in the dead of night, lest it be hurt.

At the age of nine, my unripe mind and guileless soul understood this as the beginning of a bucolic three-day ceremony, which would end in the heart of Pindus. It was the first time I'd be part of this ceremony; which was why I felt so excited. And just in time, may I add, since there were talks for the flock to be either transported by truck from the following year, or sold outright. My father wasn't keen on taking me with them, fearing that I wouldn't make it and that he'd have to put me on the mule. Our whole family loved our animals; we didn't want to mistreat them. Loading fifty-five pounds or more on an already laden mule was abuse if not torture. After getting a lot of pressure he'd agreed, and now I had to make right by him and by myself.

My childhood journey began from a sparsely populated pastoral village in the base of Koziakas, windswept and snowed in during winter, unsheltered from the Thessalian Plain's libeccio* during summer. We'd spend the whole year, except for the hottest months, in this windswept land, along with our flock. When the nights were cold we'd gather around the woodstove, roasting chestnuts and listening to our father's stories about a thick forest with enormous trees; a forest which the Greek State handed to unsupervised lumberjacks after the land swaps with

---

*   A hot wind which drives in from the south-west.

Turkey, resulting in its deforestation. Its inhabitants hadn't even bothered to give it a name, so it remained exchangeable.

Around the time of the fall of the Junta, a-mile-and-a-half from our house, in an abandoned warehouse located between two rivers, they opened a cold one-chamber school to educate the wild offspring of the stock breeders; to initiate them into the vastness of grown-up knowledge. began and finished my primary education in this school, along with twelve other wildlings. It was a one-teacher school, and what a teacher he was! The embodiment of that passage from the Junta into a (so-called) democracy. He was a goodhearted man and had the patience of Job, something we regularly took advantage of.

Whenever it rained, and the streams swelled, we would demolish the wooden bridge so that he couldn't get across and teach us. We acquired a clock, and when it struck eight sharp we would get up and leave because he wasn't punctual — our clock was purposely adjusted ten minutes later As if we were taking all our childish rage against authority out on him, one of the times we cut school, we pushed his small green Fiat down the hill. Yet he only reprimanded us, always calm and collected. He knew that for children to accept your knowledge, they first have to trust you. Assembled green sheets of metal have no worth when children's trust is at stake; children who have a natural and irresistible duty to test people's endurance. Life itself places inside their tiny hands its secret hammer and orders them to hit hard, until they shatter the shell of human hypocrisy. Just so that they can look at it bare. And laugh heartily out loud, like only children know how.

More than forty years later, I still don't have a clear answer as to why, at the end of that school year, he gave me a leather-bound book about the life of the rebellious Greek klepht Katsandonis.* He never had, and he would never again make a personal gift to one of his wildlings. Was it a random act? Insight? Who knows. He never asked me if I liked his gift or if I ever actually read it. Which I did. I read the whole book in just three days, and then I left it there, confident that the starved mice would gnaw at it. Nothing lasts forever.

But let's continue on our journey.

A mile further down, inside a creek full of plane trees, we met my mother's brother (who was my namesake), his wife Olga, and two of my four cousins. They were accompanied by a laden mule, a donkey, two hundred and fifty sheep, a hundred goats, thirty cows, and a handful of dogs. Something like a multinational corporation of the time. After greeting them and having a chat, we decided to merge the flocks. Ours would go first, having a true unanimous leader: a ewe that had made this seven-day hiking journey seven years in a row as leader of the flock and had never lost her way. It goes without saying that we were very proud to own the most intelligent ewe in the world, with an undeniable leader's temperament.

---

*   Antonis Katsantonis (1777-1808) was a famously fearsome mountain raider (klepht) who rebelled against Greece's then-rulers, the Ottoman empire. After Greece gained independence in 1822 Katsantonis became popular as a symbol of its long fight for freedom.

Sunrise was still two hours away. We had to take advantage of that because the flocks would need to find a shady spot to rest when the sun rose in the sky. By dawn we had reached Genesi, and by sunrise, Prodromos village. The villagers, who had flocks of their own, were running in alarm to keep them away in case they got mixed with ours. Because our caravan was like a small fast-flowing river which enveloped whatever it met along the way, never to be found again. We made our first afternoon stop in a shady creek full of plane trees, over Filira village. My uncle slaughtered a young goat. It couldn't keep up with the flock because of an injury. He skinned it, took its skin and its intestines, walked to the nearest houses of the village and returned with a spit to roast the carcass. Back then, things were that simple.

We spent our first night on a plateau with dense undergrowth, located between St Vissarionas and Pili. We unloaded the mules and allowed them to graze free. Then, we gathered some wood and built a big fire. Next to it, we children placed a rug on the ground. We lay down side by side and dragged another rug over ourselves. The sky was clear, full of stars. The only sound was made by the bells of the sheep, which were seizing the chance to satiate their hunger after a hard day. The grown-ups, sitting around the fire, began telling stories; stories that we overheard. Stories that worked like a balm for our young souls and imaginations. I closed my eyes and fell asleep, listening to the old, brave, fearless guardians of the flock: Leventis and Karaoulis. Grandpa's two massive sheepdogs could prey on bloodthirsty wolves and fight with enormous bears ...

The following day we once again woke up before sunrise. At dawn we crossed the stone arch bridge of Pili and kept walking along the Portaikos River. Moving deeper inside the mountain complex, lush vegetation welcomed us with a festival of colour, natural sounds, and scents. Nature was celebrating, and so were our senses, which were fully awakened. The warm reception this rough land had in store for us was an eternal promise of resistance to the ravages of time. A new visual show with every step we made; a new olfactory discovery with every breath we took; every sound a melody crafted by skilful nature.

Once in a while, our path took us through some small stone-built village, whose streets were covered with vines, blooming rose bushes, marjoram, carnations, and basil. Poor yet goodhearted people stepped out of their homes to watch the flocks pass by. For them, the flocks' passage was summer's harbinger. They generously offered us some water, a cup of coffee, walnuts, a handful of cherries, and we repaid them with what we had: fresh milk.

At noon we made a stop at the famous inn at Kapsalis. As with all inns, Kapsalis' place was located in a strategic spot. The inns were leftovers from the Ottoman State, when their owners reported on who and what passed through. Some were double agents: giving food to the lads and reporting back to the pasha. Before any highways were opened, all those who attempted to follow the ancient path linking the villages of central Pindus with the Thessalian plain had to go past this spot. My grandpa's stories drew in my mind images of countless beasts of burden following the rough mountain trail, transporting the highlanders' products from and to the Pindus. Despite its decline, the inn offered tired passers-by warm food and a place to sleep. At this crossroads we met many other flocks, heading to the inner Pindus to spend the summer. At nightfall, we camped on a plateau at Gropa. An alpine landscape of wild, virgin beauty. Underneath the old firs, which were vibrating from the chilly mountain breeze, and with sheep's milk boiling in a pot on top of a big roaring fire, it was once again time for some night stories. This time, they were all about rebels and their battles against pursuing forces, that had taken place right there, where we had camped.

The next day we crossed Gropa's Saddle and moved downhill, entering the thick ancient beech forest, where no sunrays were allowed to penetrate and caress the earth. Walking a few more miles following the leftovers of an old path carved on the rocks on the one side of a gorge, we reached the spot where the two rivers merged into one. Picking our way around Vathirema village, we climbed the tall mountain behind it, and after some painful hours of hiking along its ridge, we at last saw our stone summer home, waiting for us on the other side of the valley. The surrounding landscape was smiling at us. The cool breeze smelled of oregano, fir, and grass. Flocks and men, we all began running faster to reach it sooner. The flocks knew they would live free in the surrounding verdant mountains; the mules would be unbridled since there would be no work during the summer; and we children would run wild for three whole months: swimming, fishing for trout on tributaries of Achelous river, raiding fruit-bearing trees only to be chased by their owners, going head-to-head with children from the neighbouring villages, and sleeping out of the house most summer nights ... plain happiness.

Some tea and him

We were running and screaming. After catching our breaths, we ran back up the uphill trail. We screamed our lungs out once again. And it blatantly ignored us. Circling twice over our heads, getting ready for its impending attack, it took the shape of a black rocket and ripped the morning sky in half. Then, just before it crashed into the rocks, it suddenly opened its enormous wings and stretched its strong legs, ready to grab the little goat it had spotted in the rocky cliff.

The goat, unable to react in any other way, fell about ten to twenty yards further down the cliff with each attempted attack, before managing to get back on its feet, scared. By the time we managed to climb the hard uphill trail and reached the bottom of the cliff, we'd watched the same attack routine unfold six times already. Our arrival coincided with that future prey's last fall down the enormous vertical rock. It was limping, and must have suffered abrasions from the predator's sharp claws. It ran as far as it could, given its condition, towards the scattered flock of about two hundred goats that were grazing on the rugged hillside. The livestock had become one with the landscape; real wild beasts!

They didn't seek mercy from anyone. Especially from someone they didn't know. It didn't even let us get close to it, let alone take care of it. Such was its pride. Equal to the predator.

Five or six angry, threatening screams penetrated our ears, reaching the bottoms of our souls. They sent chills down our spines. They turned our stomachs. We looked at the sky and saw its imposing figure. We stood there for some time, watching it fly away haughtily, just over the mountain tops. Something inside us broke. It was our spontaneous sense of justice, which the grown-ups had taught us through their own actions. What was it that had urged us to take a stand in something that didn't concern us? What if the bird had its nest in one of the surrounding mountaintops and its hungry children were waiting for it to feed them? Why was it that the flock had to always be right and of more value, and we had to favour it? We soon cast away any guilty thoughts to focus on our goal.

We had already been hiking for four or five hours. It was the middle of August, and the surrounding sheer mountaintops promised us the starry sky. Yet we were after some flavoured tea; we had prepared just for that. Each having a folded sack tucked under our arms and holding a Swiss blade, we continued our reconnaissance on the surrounding mountaintops, on which there were no trees at all yet there was a lush green, with all kinds of herbs.

"Up there! That's certainly tea! Let's go!"

We climbed the craggy peaks, cut, filled and continued.

Evening came, and we had just managed to fill our two sacks. Time to go.

"But where to? Which way did we come from?"

"There ... past that mountaintop ..."

Following a goat trail which climbed up the mountain, we finally reached its summit. We looked around and realised that the landscape looked completely unfamiliar. Full of mountaintops, none of which we recognised. We turned to one of our other strengths: instinct.

"There, on that vantage point. We're bound to see something familiar from there. Let's go!"

We reached that spot ... nothing. We tried a few more. Again nothing. We were utterly disoriented. We felt disorganised. We couldn't think logically. We thought we had lost our minds! Wherever we looked, we only saw foreign, hostile landscapes. Our fears consumed us.

Young children, wearing shorts and t-shirts, we had set forth at the crack of dawn to pick some mountain tea, and now we found ourselves at nightfall, exhausted and dehydrated, in a foreign, unwelcoming land. We hadn't drunk any water all day; we hadn't saved our strength, thinking that we'd be home by sunset. Walking in sun-kissed gorges all day long, the burning August sun had dried our bodies. Our mouths were dry as well; our lips chapped, bleeding ...

At an altitude of more than six thousand feet, the mountain climate reigned supreme. And night was falling. The cold evening breeze slowly began to penetrate our weak, dehydrated bodies. But we were tough lads, we knew what it took to survive, and we wouldn't give up that easily. For the time being, we focused on getting through the night. We searched for and found a small cavern on the leeward side of the mountain to spend the night in. We emptied the two sacks to make a comfortable mattress. We put one sack inside the other, turning them into a makeshift linen sleeping bag; then we crawled inside it and lay down on the soft tea-leaf mattress to enjoy the most fragrant sleep we'd have in our whole lives.

We were awakened by the blazing and ruthless arch-enemy of darkness, which is always a punctual and integral enchanter of life. The dawn's first golden rays on the surrounding hillsides made the cold morning dewdrops sparkle, reflecting a thousand colours. We got out of our makeshift sleeping bag, ready to confront it head-on. To take it on for the second day in a row. The good night's sleep had given us strength, and so we could think more clearly, something we couldn't do the previous day. We filled the sacks once again and began searching for the nearest natural viewpoint so that we could look afresh at the surrounding area. When we found it, we sat on our sacks and activated all our senses. Our eyes flooded with barren steep ridges, our nostrils with the velvet scent of musk, and our ears with the sweet song of rock partridges. Indeed, it was quite an accomplishment to feel lost in paradise.

While we were orchestrating our complicated plan of salvation (which basically was: head downhill and see where we end up), we thought we heard a prolonged scream coming from afar. Our hearts skipped a beat. We turned to face the clear morning sky, impatiently scanning it from end to end ... and there it was! A small black dot in the horizon. Slowly roaming around the sky. As if it was taking its morning stroll. We didn't speak. We just began our fight for survival. Our eyes locked on its black silhouette, we ran. Every so often we would stumble. Down steep inclines, we first let our sacks drop, and followed right after them. We didn't care how. We just did. Not once did we think to stop. Such was our self-will.

Exhausted, and with our legs covered in blood, we reached a spot from where we could see a spring down below us. A spring, the cold waters of which, according to legend, made the teeth fall out of anyone who drank from it. The bird was still high in the sky. Proud. Majestic. Superior. Circling high above our heads, screaming indifferently. Absolved from petty laws and petty justice. Its mere existence an unwritten, absolute law. An eternal buoy of justice. A bright celestial lighthouse for all disoriented souls. But how could we even dare to thank it, to humbly apologise, without insulting it? We, two young children ... and it, so proud.

Mavrorema

It got dark in the middle of the day. The sky above our heads seemed merciless. Violently spitting fire on the earth, rocking the surrounding mountains to the core. The rain was getting heavier ... fat, massive drops crashing onto my young body as I struggled along the flat, narrow, man-made trail on the bottom of the cliff. I was in a hurry. I wanted to get to Mavrorema as soon as possible. The stream connects to the Acheloos River at the base of two mountains, sculpted by nature and time, opening up a narrow mile-long chasm. A violent autumn storm had broken out when fifty of our goats were inside that gulf. I had to get them out of there; they were in danger from falling rocks. These mountains were unstable; each summer we would lose five to ten animals because of landslides.

Reaching the spot where they were grazing, carefree, I continued downhill and stopped near the verge of the gorge. Most of the goats were down there. I couldn't see them, except for three or four enjoying the green grass on the opposite side of the river. There, right in front of me, one of them climbed on a huge rock. The rock, as if having waited for this precise moment for centuries, collapsed. The animal barely managed to jump off it, avoiding getting swept away, and the massive boulder rolled for a few feet down the steep slope before falling from a height of twenty yards right into the gorge, making a loud crashing sound. The goats ran in the opposite direction. A hundred yards further, following the trail, they arrived on my side of the river looking quite shaken up. After counting them, I realised one was missing.

I followed the slippery crevasse trail from where they had appeared, getting down to the riverbed in case the missing goat had been hurt and needed help. The rock had fallen on the opposite bank, and the stream had already begun to swell. I crossed the river, stepping on protruding stones, and circled the fallen rock. From underneath it protruded the head of a familiar goat. Two horns broken at their base, an eye frozen, looking at the mercilessly raining sky, and a chestnut tree twig stuck in its bloody mouth. That farewell meal before it shuffled off this mortal coil was the only thing that escaped the natural catapult that had crushed its body. Over it, like a holy shrine, a soaked living statue stood still. It was the usual annual gift of the goat, which always gave birth during summer when the livestock was free to roam the mountains; a gift which the goat proudly presented to us each year at the beginning of fall. This time it wouldn't … the kid was almost touching its snout on its mother's deformed head, lest it hear a silent lament, then stood back up, ready to run back up the gorge and join the rest of the herd.

I stayed there, frozen, for quite some time, unable to take my eyes away from what I was seeing. Vast volumes of muddy water flowed into the creek, dangerously raising its level by the minute. The waters' rushing sound and the incessant thundering wove together into a menacing roar which shook Mavrorema, a claustrophobic scene from a horror film. Five or six more rocks loudly crashed down, only a few feet away from me. Nature's fury was testing the limits of my courage, making it quite clear who's the boss in this world.

The poor little goat had never before seen a human being, yet my presence didn't seem to upset it. I bent over, opened my arms, and took the kid away. As if tamely following a fate dictated by its dead mother, it didn't resist. Now heavier, I crossed the river, once again stepping on the protruding stones. I climbed up the hill, seeking shelter inside a small crevice in the rock. Gasping for breath, I sat there, placing my elbows on my knees and made a shelter for the shocked little animal. My empty gaze wandered down the cliff, landing on the voracious torrent. I didn't care about anything that was happening around me, because now a storm had broken out deep inside me. Burning questions swarmed my young mind. Questions about chaos and order, life and death, chance and destiny, right and wrong, good and evil, the business of gods and demons in all these and many other things. No godsent prophet or crier of the modern societies has the courage or the ability to bluntly pose such questions to a young child, and yet a goat on the mountains of Pindus had just done that very thing.

As a grown-up man, whenever I heard people say that "their fate was in their hands," I'd laugh on the inside, imagining the surprise of these arrogant men, when at some point they'd realise they were holding nothing more than the macabre shroud of their mummified lives. As for me, protected from nature's fury inside that cave, as water kept on mercilessly whipping the earth and lightning tore the dull landscape apart, I didn't wish to give definite answers to the accumulated questions that this — and many other — naturally violent, experiential stories of my childhood gave birth to. I didn't want to allow fear to take the reign of my soul. I wanted to be able to keep my head high in the face of any threat.

Questions open doors; answers close them. It was in my nature to find closed doors suspicious. I always fought to open them and then leave them gaping wide. Given answers, you stop producing questions. You're forced to become their guard. Enforcing order gives shape to a servant who has to serve that order. When you give shape to a god, you stop searching for him, depriving your imagination of the possibility of creating one or more that could be better, rendering yourself this one god's eternal servant. The same stands for any regime made by people, and the laws that govern it. No matter how revolutionary they may seem.

Such vivid memories overwhelmed me, making me emotional and nostalgic for my innocent childhood, on an evening in May as I was driving through the villages of Karditsa at Pili, Trikala. These are the memories and emotions that are carved so deep in the mind and soul of a child that become part of their chemical knowledge, part of its DNA, bound to follow them for the rest of their life.*

---

*   The author of this book is the fourth of the five children of a family of seven. Until the age of thirteen he led a nomadic life, as do all shepherds in the Greek countryside, given that his parents were stock-farmers and therefore seasonal nomads.

ROADBLOCKS AND GUNFIRE IN PYLI

Confrontation

The landscape was colourful from nature's Spring rebirth. I opened the black Vitara's windows, letting a cool evening breeze into the cabin, and with it the scents of the world. The day was coming to an end and its bright yellow sun had just disappeared behind the iconic Karava Mountain, leaving a golden beam wavering on the horizon. Koziakas, like a vast unconquerable castle wall, towered high in the sky, casting its heavy shadow over the Thessalian Plain.* An impenetrable border for prying eyes. Only imagination was allowed to wander free in its hidden depths.

My aim and destination that afternoon was the following: to get past Pili and, after hiding a handful of weapons and ammunition which I had packed, to drive through the picturesque villages of Agrafa until I reached Arta. I had wanted to make that road trip for a long time, to bring my childhood memories back to life by seeing these places once again, and I was looking forward to it. A little earlier, while still in Karditsa, I had bid farewell to a new partner, as he was spending a few days with his family in southern Greece.

As I exited the last village before Pili there were two cars in front of me, both with local plates. My Vitara had fake license plates which matched those of an identical model.

I saw the cops' checkpoint after about a mile or so, stopped about a hundred and fifty yards straight ahead of me, two of them.

"For God's sake, here we go again!" I said out loud, annoyed.

I had a feeling in my gut that they were going to pull me over. And I was right. They didn't have any other vehicles pulled over for inspection, but let the first two vehicles continue on their way before one of the pair jumped in front of my car. His right hand raised and the other one pointing to the side of the road, he made his fortune for the afternoon, and possibly for his whole life.

"Oh! Okay! You wanted this! I have something better for you ... surprise!"

I turned on my hazard lights to confuse them and slowed down because the arsehole just wouldn't get out of my way. The last possible moment, he got off the road. A second more and the SUV would have squashed him. I shouted something at them, quite angrily, trying to crush their authoritative arrogance. Out of the corner of my eye I saw a Xsara, hidden behind some thorny bushes by the right side of the road (the stealthy talents of Hellenic police officers at their best). The officers ran fast towards the Xsara, as if they had been waiting for this specific moment their whole lives, to feel complete as human beings and worthy servants of authority.

---

*	Karava and, to its north, the Koziakas ridge are part of the Pindus range in Trikala prefecture. The chase takes place along the eastern edge of the mountains, on roads to the south of Trikala city.

Soon they were after me, their emergency lights and siren turned on. I assumed that a third person was driving the car, having already been in the driver's seat. This realisation made me wary. — maybe it wasn't just a regular traffic stop. I was about two hundred yards ahead, not so safe a distance given the vehicle I was driving, and the possibilities of escape from a place which I knew well were few. The car chase had already begun, and I would determine its outcome to an extent. I knew who I was, what I wanted, and how to achieve it.

On the contrary, the men after me didn't know who they were, what they wanted, and who the man they were so passionately pursuing was. As in every similar situation, I felt obliged to guarantee the safety of all those involved. What a lousy habit!

My co-passenger on this scheduled trip down memory lane, (which had just been postponed because of these idiots) was a Kalashnikov AK 47S, with one round already in its chamber and nine more in its magazine. It had been sleeping for quite some time, covered by a towel on the passenger seat. Time for it to swing into action and do justice to its reputation. I removed the towel hiding it and set the selector switch to rapid-fire mode. In the meantime, the men had gotten closer, down for anything.

The car chase began a mile away from the entrance to Pili, and as we passed its threshold I put into action an old trick of mine, which had proved successful whenever I had tried it in the past. I made an abrupt turn right into an alley, then right again, and then right once more until I got back on the road where the car chase had been unfolding. The Vitara wasn't a quick turner, and so my pursuers didn't buy the trick. Their mistake. I was trying my best for their own sake, and they didn't show any appreciation.

I turned the vehicle again and drove the opposite way, in the direction of Paliomonastiro,* with the leeches still after me; their unselfishness was inspiring although they were making a hell lot of noise. In situations like this, I can't help but think of the worst-case scenario. In this case, it was that my pursuers knew who they were after, had already called in the surrounding police stations which were now on the lookout, and had at least an MP5 in their Xsara, ready to be unloaded on me when they got within firing distance. Years later, when I got arrested in Livadeia, I learnt from a colleague of theirs who personally knew them that they'd had a few drinks in a local bar just before the chase, gotten all high on tsipouro and were feeling macho or something. Yet, back at that moment, I knew I had to end this, and pretty soon before things got out of hand. Despite my honest attempts to make them rethink their decision, it was apparent that the cheerful fellow had no intention of ceasing the chase if some iron didn't rain. And everyone knows I'm not one to spoil a party.

Half a mile before Paliomonastiro, going a hundred and sixty kilometres per hour, I slammed on the brakes. The Vitara's tires shrieked, smoke coming out of them as they rubbed against the hot road. The Xsara slowed down and drove left

---

*   A village south-west of Trikala

to get past me. As if! First gear, full throttle, a left turn and they found themselves immobilised right behind the Vitara. I had the Kalashnikov already in my hands. I turned to my left, I climbed from the driver seat and began firing, aiming at the Vitara's rear windscreen. The Kalashnikov's rattle was deafening. The first shots shattered my windscreen, and the Xsara appeared almost up against my Vitara. I emptied the entire magazine into its hood. I swapped out to a full mag and cocked the rifle again just in case. The cabin smelled of fragrant smoke and gunpowder. The atmosphere was heavy, suffocating, warlike.

Through a cloud of smoke, I saw the Xsara's passenger door open, and someone rolled out onto the green grass. I hoped it was out of excitement. I had seen enough. What was done was done. First gear, second gear, third gear, full throttle, and off I went. I turned right after Paliomonastiro, in the direction of Mouzaki. After half an hour of driving fast — as though I was still being chased — I reached Lake Plastiras. There I made a stop to call my partner, who was on his way to the Peloponnese. Thimios had almost reached Athens and was already aware of the incident. He informed me that all radio newscasts were mentioning that two policemen were severely injured and had been taken to the hospital, one in critical condition. They were identifying me as the culprit (that was fast!). Thessaly's whole police force, as well as those of neighbouring areas, was out and about trying to locate me.

Short Kalashnikov rifles are hard to operate. The strong recoil, created by the gun's short barrel, makes them dangerous in the hands of ignorant people, especially when it comes to blind shots on rapid-fire mode. But I knew how to properly handle such a gun. It seemed like a bit of a stretch to me that two policemen were injured in this confrontation, let alone severely. I was sure I had aimed straight for the police car's hood. Yet you can never be sure when it comes to guns. What was certain was that this would fire up their colleagues, so that when they located me, they wouldn't think twice before shooting to kill.

Shots in the back, convoy, and escape

Thimios, to his credit, was willing to return and help me. I didn't want him in the police's grip, so I told him to get to Lamia and wait for my call. My plan was as follows: I'd use a bewildering route (which I knew well), to approach the outskirts of Tymfristos by car. It was an excellent spot to temporarily hide the guns, set fire to the Vitara, and be picked up by Thimios. This route had one weakness: the necessity of going through Fournas village, which had a police station. I was determined to take that risk, hoping that in case they were on the alert, they'd have set a roadblock on some main intersection outside the village.

Late that night, I drove past the first houses of Fournas. I drove uphill on a narrow serpentine road that runs through the village's main square. A while later, I found myself underneath the circular wall of the elevated village square. Fifteen yards ahead of me, on the exact spot where the uphill road reached the square's height, the Vitara's headlights illuminated a police Land Rover.

It had been parked in the middle of the road. I stopped and, not knowing why, looked up to my right, at the square's wall. I saw countless heads appearing and disappearing — many times, very fast. Then I spotted a handgun and a machine gun, though whoever was holding them remained unseen. A puppet show of sorts. I allowed the Vitara to slide down the narrow road. Hearing sporadic fire (depending on the direction of the wind), at the first opportunity I turned the car and exited the village following the exact same road.

I was trapped between the mountains of Evrytania, but I was too stubborn to give up. The lads from Fournas didn't chase after me (no suckers them) but still, they must have contacted the inhabitants of the neighbouring villages to keep an eye out and inform them of my whereabouts. And boy did they want to. For years they must have been dreaming of seeing themselves on some news program, even a morning one.

I put a risky plan into action. I turned off the headlights of my car and drove using only the handbrake for almost six miles, until I reached Vraha village. This particular village was amphitheatrically built on the slopes to the back of Tymfristos. Its inhabitants, having been notified, had gathered in the village square, their gazes scanning the riverside for any sign of car lights heading uphill towards their village. I couldn't help but laugh at their reaction when I drove into their square, turning on my high beam headlights.

"Theeeere! Theeeere! It's him!" they all screamed, jumping and running back and forth as I sped past.

After the village there were only unpaved tracks ahead. I drove along a dirt road and kept on for a few miles into the forest. According to the map, the path connected to the Fournas-Karpenissi main road on Tymfristos' eastern hillsides. The Vitara proved to be a war dog, gulping down the rugged dirt road mile after mile. It was under strain since I had been driving on the rough roads of Agrafa for many hours already — I was scared it might break down.

I drove through the gap in the mountain and then down. Just before I exited the main road, however, after a sharp turn, a police car had blocked the way twenty to thirty yards ahead. no one was inside, they were in skirmish formation. I slammed on the brakes and dropped it into reverse. They began firing, hidden in the darkness. I was only a few yards away from the turn. Backing up, I turned the SUV round as it came under fire from sub-machine guns. I was driving back uphill, with the cops following close behind, when I realised the bullets had slashed my tires. It was time to abandon the car. I drove it off the dirt road entirely and up a small hill, but they were on to me. The police car stopped at about the spot where I had exited the track, headlights on the Vitara. They got into firing positions and, cursing gods and demons, opened fire against the now-abandoned SUV. By then I had already got to their side of their hill, holding the Kalashnikov, having released its safety. I was about twenty yards away from them, under cover of darkness, admiring their antics.

Once I had seen enough of their pathetic show, I left them shooting and cursing at the mountain.

I followed the road where, just a few minutes ago, they had stopped me, and when I was a safe distance away from them, temporarily hid the backpack with the guns. By sunrise I had reached St George's Bridge.

There, finally, I got a signal. Thimios had stayed awake the whole night waiting for my call. I gave him my coordinates, and sat on the riverfront to wait for him. I had barely hung up the phone when the road leading to Fournas, on the opposite side of the river, filled with vans from the Special Anti-Terrorist Unit and the Special Police Force, many police cars, unmarked vehicles, and a prisoner transport carrying dogs ... actual dogs! They were driving in convoy, and they had stopped right across from me. For a moment I thought I was done for. I thought they had located me. I stood no chance; there were too many of them.

Observing their movements, I understood they were heading to the forested mountains of Evrytania to arrest Palaiokostas and had just stopped there to coordinate. It was apparent they hadn't come for me; I was wrong to worry. Happy hunting, lads! Thimios soon arrived and off we went ...

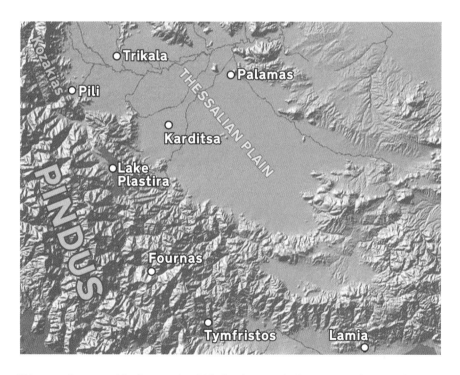

This map shows roughly the area in which the chase took place, over a distance of 100km or so. The region is ruggedly mountainous with tight, winding roads overlooking long drops into the valleys below. Small hamlets and villages cling to the hillsides, looking down over the Thessalian plain, which has historically been the breadbasket of Greece. Vassilis' route takes him from Thessaly across the administrative border to Central Greece.

ARRESTED IN LIVADEIA

Prison under construction

It was mid-December of 1999 when, while having a discussion with some friends from Athens who were involved in social struggles, I learned that a new maximum-security prison was under construction someplace in Phocis. Immediately, I thought of a construction site I had seen some time ago near Lake Mornos. At the time I had thought some factory was being built there. I hadn't put much thought into it since it was very common for factories to be built in remote locations. Funded by the European Union and the Greek State, many crooks would start on a project until they got their money and then let them rot away. I decided to return to the area and make sure whether a prison was actually being constructed there, hoping that if things worked out, I'd plant a bomb and cancel their humble plans. One of the following days, I made my way back there.

Just outside Malandrino village, I saw huge cranes in the far distance to my left. I drove onto the dirt road that passed in front of the construction site, where a giant billboard notified passersby what exactly was being built there (project budget, construction company, etc.). Among other things, the guys had informed me that this company belonged to the Ministry of Justice and had been set up for the construction of new prisons throughout Greece. Blessed and noble were its works.

It was a Sunday, there was a deadness everywhere I looked, no one around. The construction work was at an advanced stage. The wall had already been built to half its intended height. Except for some of the first buildings, which were being constructed of brick, the rest of the prison — meaning the wings, where the inmates would be buried, and the exterior wall — was being built of concrete blocks, transported and placed by the towering cranes. That was a huge problem. Where and how would I plant explosives, since I was dealing not with a single facility but with many unfinished buildings made of cement and iron, scattered around the site? No matter how many explosives I had at my disposal, they'd be wasted there. What I was left to hope for was that an explosion could make the area's residents rethink their decision, and react against the plans of the Ministry of Justice to get rid of its shame in their own backyards.

I had no explosives at the time, but a good friend of mine had about twelve pounds of TNT and he was willing to give it to me without knowing or asking why I needed it. The quantity was sufficient to destroy the administration's building compound. With any luck, it would also destroy the cranes which were placed on the front of the building site.

Aside from a sheep farm, about five hundred yards away from the building site, there was no one else around. The nightwatchman's container-turned-house was outside the construction site and at a safe distance in the event of an explosion.

And I was sure he'd be gone by nightfall, like a true Greek man. It was late in the evening. Since I'd come that far, I decided to stay there through the night and observe what was going on. South-west of the construction site was a line of low mountains. I found a way to its top and drove there to get good all-round visibility. The construction site was about one to two miles away, and illuminated at night, so with binoculars I'd have a perfect view of it.

For now, I had plenty of time to enjoy the twilight in the natural cover offered by my vantage point. To my left, the beautiful green Vardousia Mountain in the north, and a bit to its right, the eternally snow-capped Mount Giona. Enormous black clouds rested on their peaks, transfusing them with a spiritual grandiosity; a truly awe-inspiring sight. Haughty mountains, untracked, storied in countless local legends. Having become lairs for so many bandits and rebels of the past.

From their guts stemmed Mornos, a fast-flowing, labyrinthine vein that transported its liquid abundance to their base, creating a peaceful silver lake. A result of nature's generosity, these freshwaters quench the thirst of the whole population of Attica, including those twisted-minded men who conceived and set to implement the idea of creating a soul cemetery in this remote place of untamed beauty.

Back then, insurgent left-socialist Giannopoulos* was the Minister for Justice. More than a few times I had heard him brag on his TV show that he'd had the historic privilege of shaking captain Aris Velouchiotis by the hand when they were both fighting on the mountain. Observing the hellhole under construction through my binoculars, I imagined that this was the spot where the two men had shaken hands. Minister Giannopoulos was honouring the captain and his struggles by building this monument dedicated to true resistance and freedom. He'd gotten too big for his boots, as Aris might have said.

In the meantime, night gently and quietly spread its black winter veil over the surrounding massifs. For some reason, I felt as though my heart was sinking, suddenly cold. It was an omen for what fate had in store for me. The following day, I'd run out of luck, putting an end to this eight-and-a-half-years long, relentless manhunt. And three years after that, I'd be transferred to this very same prison, the construction of which I had been hoping to halt.

Around midnight, having seen everything I needed to see, I fell asleep in the driver seat.

A show of hares, the accident and the arrest

I was awakened by a sudden noise. Instinctively, I grabbed the Kalashnikov. It was the crack of dawn. I looked through the steamed-up windows, and soon I located the source of the noise. The culprits were two hares which had transformed my mountainous mini parking lot into an acrobatics stage, hopping on and off the car.

---

*   Evangelos Giannopoulos (1918-2003) was a participant in the Greek Resistance during World War II, a lead prosecutor of the generals of the Junta after 1974, and as a PASOK minister covering various briefs under two administrations between 1981-89 and 1993-2000.

Triple, quadruple flips. Pirouettes! The incredible little creatures were gifting me with a free morning show of wild chasing around and all kinds of tricks. It appeared that the small clearing I had arbitrarily occupied was their meeting spot for some morning games after a night of grazing and the two of them were using it to the fullest. After all, they knew they might never meet again, their species being always at the top of the most wanted list. In a while, it would be morning, and the inhuman posses would come after them, armed with pump shotguns and trained dogs.

It's in moments like this one that you feel painful shame for belonging to the human species. Only the thought that I was myself hunted by my species soothed my personal embarrassment.

Opening the door of a car on the hills of Lidoriki at six in the morning could constitute a barbaric disturbance of ecological balance. Yet life has its rules, its own emergencies. One of them being morning urination. Sorry fellow hares. Time for you to find a hiding place while the sun is still down, and time for me to head home.

I made a pit stop at Arahova to grab something to eat and get some newspapers. At about ten in the morning, I entered the ring road around Livadeia. The traffic was a little heavy. A light drizzle had been falling since early in the morning. The road was slippery, and vehicles were only going about fifty to sixty miles per hour. I was driving a Hyundai and a truck was rolling in front of me. I was about twenty yards behind it when I realised it had suddenly started to slow down. The Hyundai wasn't fit for emergencies, and I wasn't the best driver in the world. I instinctively hit the brakes, but it was already too late. In a split second, I would crash into the back of the truck. I saw an oncoming police car, its emergency lights turned on. Just my luck. I twisted the wheel right, hoping to avoid the collision, but instead, I lost control. The car rolled down the cliff, and I found myself inside an old concrete irrigation canal.

My first thought was to make sure I wasn't severely injured. My second was that, although I wasn't hurt, I'd have to deal with the cops who witnessed the accident and would have certainly turned around to investigate. My whole body was numb and weakened from the shock of the collision. Still, for the time being, I had no visible injuries. The doors on the right side of the car were at the bottom of the canal. The driver side was stuck. With great effort, I managed to open the left rear door. Grabbing my survival backpack and a briefcase, I got out of the car. I had to climb fifteen yards up the steep slope to reach the road where two cops and several onlookers, who had stopped to either have a gander or help, were waiting for me. I knew they couldn't recognise me.

Reaching the road, the two police officers, looking truly worried, asked me whether I was injured. I told them that thank God, I was fine! For a second, I thought about pretending to be injured so that they would transport me to the hospital, from where I could walk out without being bothered by anyone, but concluded it would be an unnecessary delay. You never know what might happen next. More could arrive and make things worse, or they could run a search on my car's plates and realise it was stolen etc. What I had to do right there and then was walk away.

And there were only two ways I could achieve that: hijacking either the police car or that of one of the onlookers. The police car would be ideal. Its engine was running, but it wasn't close enough. I couldn't anticipate how they'd react in the time that would take me to get to it and jump in. Taking a policeman hostage to escape seemed irrational given the situation.

The onlookers' cars were parked on the right side of the ring road. The one nearest to me was a maroon Avensis. Through its rear window, past the car's two front seats, I saw its keys still in the ignition. Walking fast, I got to it and sat in the driver seat. In the passenger seat was a slightly plump woman. She was terrified when she saw me. She opened her door, let out a cry and got out, leaving the passenger door open.

I threw the survival backpack and the briefcase, which contained an MP5 with four full magazines, an automatic pistol, two defensive grenades, and thirty-five thousand Deutsche Marks, in the back seat of the car. I was so sure I was going to escape that I didn't even bother to grab the pistol — big mistake.

I turned the key in the ignition. Nothing. I turned it again, this time pushing the clutch. Nothing. For a moment I thought the car might be already running and I just could hear it because of the noise. I shifted in first gear and stepped on it. Again nothing. Suddenly, I felt two hands grabbing my right arm. It was the hand I would have used to pull the Glock out of my belt. At the same time — and before I could even react — they opened the driver door, grabbing my left arm as well. It was futile to resist. I was in the driver seat, they were many more, and I hadn't fully recovered my strength since the accident. Citizens and cops, united like a fist, pulled me out and handcuffed me. So it was over. Just like that. Out of the blue.

They searched me …

When they found the Glock and the grenade, they understood they had someone important in their hands. They demanded to know who I was, while calling for backup. The station was near so it would arrive soon enough. I wasn't a sore loser and that time I had lost. I had to admit defeat. I had no reason to hide any more. I answered their question.

"You lads are in luck. You've caught Palaiokostas!"

They didn't believe me. The contacted headquarters and mentioned my name

"Which one?" I heard one of them ask headquarters.

"I'm Vassilis".

"Control, it's Vassilis" he conveyed.

"Follow all safety protocols. He's dangerous. Make sure he doesn't get away" someone was yelling from the other side of the phone, rattling orders off fast, like a machine gun.

The road was packed with police cars now, and cops were warding off the crowd of nosy onlookers, which was growing by the minute. They shoved me in a police car and transported me to the police station in convoy. They didn't take my handcuffs off when they put me in the holding cell and, surprisingly, two unarmed cops stayed with me to make sure I didn't go anywhere. Two others, holding machine guns, remained outside the cell, their eyes locked on me.

Such was their panic that this continued for as long as I stayed in the station. Once every hour they'd change shifts and two new cops would enter the holding cell. The same for the ones outside the cell. I was like a caged beast. And all of it because of my rotten luck ...

I was trying to piece all events in order, to conclude whether I had done my best given the snag I had hit. From the swapping policemen-cellmates, I learnt that the truck in front of me had intended to change lanes and enter the gas station across the road. The road had a dual carriageway, and something like that was forbidden. The truck driver, seeing the oncoming police car, didn't use his signal, waiting for the police car to drive away before he committed the offence. He tapped the brakes, something which I never saw. His lights were either muddied, or they didn't work at all.

I also learnt that the Avensis, on which I tried to escape, had a strange immobiliser and that was why it wouldn't start. It was as though the whole world's bad luck had fallen on me that morning.

What put my mind at rest and cleared my conscience to an extent was that none of the police officers who spent an hour with me inside the holding cell ever said that I had another choice. At that point, I really just got a bad break.

"Police cars cross the ring road once every hour at the most, and it happened to cross your path right when the accident occurred". they'd tell me quite convincingly.

There was plenty of teasing as well, always in a thick country accent.

"Come on, Vassilis! The whole Hellenic police force was searching for you, and you got caught by traffic police? And you fell into the ditch as well!"

Some others, who were intellectually superior, urged me to place a wayside shrine by the spot of the accident, since I hadn't been killed or suffered any severe injuries. I have to admit they had a point about the latter. Even though I had lost my freedom, I still had my physical health and with a bit of luck, I could claim my freedom back.

A few hours later, two officers entered the holding cell, bringing a small table and two chairs. They had come to take my statement.

"I'm not saying anything", I said. "Take what you found in the car, what is in the briefcase, and what you took off me, and that's it. Use that".

They looked at each other for a while.

"You mentioned something about a briefcase. To which briefcase are you referring?" one of them asked me.

"The one with the MP5, the pistol, and the grenades".

They gawped at me.

"Where is this briefcase?"

"You're asking me? I threw it in the back seat of the Avensis ..."

They took the chairs, the table, and they left quite panic-stricken.

It was ridiculous. Had none of them noticed I was holding a briefcase?

Aside from anything else, if it fell into the hands of young children, it could prove quite dangerous. The two guns were armed. Let alone the grenades.

About an hour later they informed me that the owner of the Avensis had been located and that the briefcase had been found in the car's back seat. They were waiting for some police car to bring it in any hour now. Who knows? Perhaps the briefcase had reached Athens by then. Or, maybe, the thirty-five thousand Deutsche Marks had postponed its retrieval.

Incidentally it was the owner of the Avensis who got rewarded by the Hellenic Police for my capture. Because it had been him, who had first grabbed my hand, who saved the world from the worst ...

Oh, they know how to sell their kindness really well.

Hopeful shouting, a trip to Korydallos Prison and the sound of The Bounty

The fierce chief of the Special Anti-Terrorist Unit arrived that same evening. He forcefully informed me that the police station was packed with his men, and warned me to forget any escape plans with or without the help of my partners — Greek exaggeration at its best. Taking into account the arrival of new shifts hour after hour, for two consecutive days, the whole Central Greece's police force must have come through my holding cell. Those who made the worst impression to me were a handful of young guys who had arrived from Athens. They were straight out of the academy, and the Hellenic Police had obviously seen it fit for their budding youngsters to spend an hour with a criminal of my magnitude as part of their training. I don't know if it was a coincidence, but they were all little fascists. They had a hog's ignorant expression planted on their faces. Being sure I was the criminal and not them, men hired for a fee to be trained as modern social janissaries* who would enforce the State's iniquities, they tried their best to proselytise to me about their admittedly original ideologies. Fatherland, religion, family ... and, above all else, security.

They were barely in their twenties, with no hope of salvation.

When they didn't achieve their goal, as if all having swallowed the same tape, they'd say: "You know what? We enrolled in the police force because we don't like the system and we want to attack it from the inside!"

My answer remained the same: "The system is a voracious beast and whoever ends up inside it will soon find out that there's only one path towards the sewage, and it's a quite painful one. You'll serve like bacteria for its digestion".

Almost twenty years later, putting these events on paper, I wonder: where are those young lads? Do they still fight the system "from the inside", with their fascist bellowing? If I judge the way things are now, then probably yes; and quite efficiently. I underestimated them back then. This, as a good lesson for all democrats who believe little hogs can take orders — absolutely not. Aside from ozone depletion, they could prove to be the biggest threat to the harmonious cohabitation of human societies.

---

*   Originally an elite standing army of the Ottoman empire trained from child slaves, which later became a byword for reactionary, self-serving military pomposity. The force drew heavily from Greece.

Nevertheless, it would be Christmas in three days, and they were pressed for time, so the following afternoon they transported me first to the district attorney and then to the examining magistrate, a young and beautiful woman.

I made it clear to her that I wouldn't enter a plea.

"Whatever I have to say, I'll say it in court".

"It's a pity, Mr Palaiokostas. I was hoping we could have a little chat".

"I still hope you'll let me free", I replied.

She laughed.

"You know it's not up to me".

"If you decided to take control of your life, it would become much more interesting. For both you and I. Let alone for everyone else ..."

She was smiling as she detained me pending trial. Let's say I got something out of it.

By six o'clock in the morning I was already on my way to Korydallos Prison in the back of the prison bus, in the company of a handful of heavily-armed cops. There were three more in the driver's cabin, who was driving like the devil. The motorcade was equivalent to that of a visiting US president. Two of the Special Unit's Cherokees were leading the bus, while four others were tailing us. In addition, there were many police cars and as many unmarked police vehicles, which were often joined by the traffic police of each district. It was pouring down outside, the convoy was moving fast as hell. For a moment, I thought that even though I had survived my car accident, I wouldn't be so lucky if something similar were to happen now. I shared my thoughts with my uniformed co-passengers, and they told me the ministry was anxious — too simplistic an answer to take.

I begged to differ. The crazy cop-caravan, driving fast as hell on the freeway while the rain hammered down, was part of the promotion for this new product they unexpectedly got their hands on. The emotionally constipated and incapable heads of ministries didn't give a damn about the sufferings of the public or their subordinates, as long as they could sell their prey to public opinion at the highest possible price. This march of the ill-fated thus had it all: swearing, bullying, cornering, cars being pulled over and their passengers getting inspected.

"That's why people hate us!" I heard someone's audible self-criticism. The same guy confided to me that he was part of a special unit of officers and sergeants that had been set up by the Ministry of Public Order with the sole purpose of capturing Nikos and me. They often held intensive seminars to memorise our modus operandi and prepare for a possible confrontation with us.

"From what they'd been teaching us before I saw you, I thought I'd see a beast. Now I believe that none of our teachers knows you or has ever seen you from up close. You exist only in their imagination", he said to me.

You must indeed have a messed-up imagination to make a beast out of a man, and even more cynicism to use this phantom to squander — secret or not — State funding, whether by holding seminars or by paying for supposed information that comes from imaginary inside informants.

These innermost thoughts were rudely disrupted when the window of the partition between the cabin and the back of the prison bus suddenly opened and someone announced: "Right now so-and-so (he mentioned one of the many tele-skinners and rawhide valuators) suggested on his morning show that the Minister of Public Order should give that bounty of two hundred and fifty million drachmas to the Livadeia police station!"

A triumph! Rejoicing inside the prison bus! On the outside (obviously, the piece of news came through) all the accompanying police vehicles turned on their sirens. The soaked police band's concerto (*The Bounty*) echoed down the freeway. Who said that the service staff of the Hellenic Police lacked musical education? But the day was only beginning. Even more painful surprises were in store for me. Like authority taking out all its rage on my body …

INCARCERATION

Hypocrisy, the stuff of prisons

The prison bus entered the grounds of Korydallos Prison and parked in front of the steps leading to the command centre. A little over thirty years old, I was now leaving behind nearly a decade of intense, continuous struggle. A new, dark and uncertain chapter had just opened for me. I was fully aware of my dismal situation. My only solace was my self-awareness. My will and my abilities left the door open for some wishful thinking that sooner or later, the odds would shift in my favour.

We climbed the steps and then headed to an office, where delivery of the old yet fresh product took place. Some officers and some men from the special task force shook my hand, saying (insinuating my eventual escape):

"We bet you'll be out of here in less than six months".

They got the "six" right. But it would be years, not months.

A team of prison officers led me to a chamber which all inmates went through to undergo body cavity searches before being escorted to the wings. They left me in an oblong, fairly spacious room, closing the door behind them and saying I'd have to wait for the warden. He wished to talk to me before I was escorted to my wing. This came as a surprise. If the warden wanted to speak to me he could have summoned me at his office, any time of the day. I didn't understand why he had to do it right then. I didn't put much thought into it however, thinking he'd arrive soon and my questions would be answered. I'd just have to wait.

I was left alone, listening to the sounds of prison for quite some time. They were metallic, otherworldly, creepy, full of terror, incompatible with human life. As though they were echoing up from Hades. Foreshadowing death. Death of the senses, of desire, of dignity, of hope, and of the very human soul. What collective hopes, what dreams legitimise the construction, the existence, the operation of such places? What kinds of citizens, of what society, accept the continuous torturing of their fellow humans as a natural consequence and compete for a paid job in these experimental hellholes so that they can sleep tight knowing they have job security? It is in such moments that you realise how repulsive even the right to work can become.

The most extreme form of exploitation of human behaviour in the Western world is deservedly exhibited in the land of the free, the Promised Land. It's a role model for the majority of Western countries; which have adopted versions of its frameworks. The most populous, powerful, and politically influential country, the US of A, belongs to its gatekeepers. Coordinated, methodical, ruthless; they possess all the qualities society requests of them. Society, in turn, is willing to set up all kinds of funding for them to guarantee its continuation.

I lost my train of thought when I realised I was freezing cold. We'd left the Livadeia police station in such a hurry that morning that I'd forgotten to ask for my coat. I was wearing only a jumper, trapped in a damp chamber at the end of December, I hadn't eaten anything, and I had barely slept since my arrest. My body and mind were exhausted; they were protesting. I knocked on the hatch of the iron door. I waited for a while until an arsehole appeared through the opening. "Can you tell me how much longer I'll have to wait? The cold is unbearable". "I don't know. I'm just following orders", he replied, shutting the hatch.

I follow, you follow, we follow ... orders. I had no choice; I had to arm myself with patience. I had to wait for Korydallos Prison's chief gatekeeper, Aravantinos,* whom I knew by sight from the countless TV shows which he appeared on thanks to his profession. The topics of these broadcasts were always hot and topical, the most burning being the critical question of how drugs find their way inside prisons. To shed some light into this unsolvable mystery they enlisted television crews and, in the role of Hercule Poirot, got ex-convicts, drug addicts or not, to speak out, their backs turned to the camera, a hood on their heads, their voices altered. The anchorman of the show, along with his genuinely concerned guests, would listen to the hooded men swear that drugs find their way inside prison from the top, from the bottom, from the front or, more pleasurably, from behind. The guests were always professional psychiatrists, criminologists, big-shot lawyers and, often enough, politicians, who extensively analysed the new discoveries, babbling incessantly and trying to impress the public by sheer force of verbiage starting with Aravantinos. I never heard anyone wonder, even fleetingly, from where and why drug addicts enter prisons in the first place.

A translation of the late-night eulogy delivered by the celebrity anchorman would be as follows: dear dumb viewer, the fact that you're watching our shit at this late hour just goes to show that our experiments to get you addicted to stupidity are working. The whole journalistic community, which is working hard, day and night, to establish the network presidents' feudal fiefdoms, beginning with their endless stolen money and abetted by political power and the whole legal establishment, will steadily continue to offer you massive daily doses of stupefaction so that you never have to feel any painful withdrawal symptoms, as common drug addicts do. The road towards absolute stupidity is long and agonising so we urge you to be patient, understanding, and trusting. The blessed day will soon come when, incapable and bereft of any thoughts of resistance, you'll be able to enjoy the nirvana of supreme happiness — the happiness of an idiot. Then, having thanked the cream of the crop, that omnipresent "scientific" rabble

---

* Born in 1960, Antonis Aravantinos began work in the Greek prison system in 1982, later becoming one of its most public and controversial figures as the warden at Korydallos Prison as well as a leading member of the prison officers' union. By the late 1990s he was a hugely influential figure, half-jokingly referred to as being more powerful than the justice ministers he supposedly served — he forced the resignation of one, Georgios Kouvelakis, in a 1995 showdown where the then-minister accused him of belonging to a criminal gang. He continued in post despite several scandals and a number of accusations of brutality against prisoners (and even officers) until 2020, when stories emerged of sleazy parties being thrown on prison grounds. He has since been busted down to work as a guard in the women's section of the jail.

who assist our masterplan with their presence in our exciting discussions, I will bid you goodnight. You have to go to work tomorrow. And remember, the life of an unproductive idiot has no worth whatsoever, let alone if they don't participate, even passively, in the globalised media fair that oversees the disintegration of the human brain. So good night, for now, dear idiot.

Welcoming torture

Three hours had passed sitting in that chamber when the door opened, and Aravantinos appeared with his squad. He stepped inside the room, a handful of fucking flunkies following behind, some holding batons. I didn't like that. I didn't have a reason to worry yet however, because there hadn't been any sign of hostility against me until then. This was a mistake on my part. I didn't take into account the self-important ruler's insecurity that my arrival might change the status quo in his dominion.

"What'd you think you're doing, huh?"

"Aside from having been locked in this freezing room for three whole hours, I'm fine", I replied.

"Where am I going to put you now?"

"You're asking me? You're in charge here!"

"Look, prisons aren't what you remember. They've changed a lot".

"There's nothing I can do about that".

"Someone tells me you've some scores to settle with some other inmates".

"Me? I have no enemies, in or out of prison!"

"That's what I've been told", he insisted.

"Then put me where they told you my enemies are and find out if it's true".

He came really close to me. His breath reeked of alcohol. He raised both his hands, clenched into fists, and hit my shoulders, while at the same time saying:

"I left my child at the hospital ..."

I grabbed the lapels of his leather jacket and, pressing my hands against his throat, I backed him against the wall.

"What'd you think you're doing, you worthless piece of shit?" I said to him, looking him right in the eye.

He lost it. He stayed there, still and scared. He hadn't expected such a reaction. His lackeys jumped me from behind. There was a scuffle. I took one of their batons. More of them entered the chamber.

They were too many and too strong for me — It was a lopsided battle. They put my hands behind my back and handcuffed me. One of them grabbed the handcuffs and held my hands up in the air, forcing me to remain bowed and making things easy for the others. They began to physically assault me. In their hatred, they didn't even care where they got me. Kicking, kneeing and punching. My face, my head, my ribs. Everywhere. That coward stepped in from time to time and joined them. When they got tired, they dragged me out of the chamber to transport me to the command centre.

On the way from the command centre to the guardhouse, there was a big garden. In it were a handful of working inmates and some prison employees. To justify what they were now seeing (probably some of his employees didn't agree with his practices) he put on a cheap act in the middle of the garden. He stopped, turned to face me and began yelling:

"See what happens when you curse my child! Laying a hand on me, you scumbag! And calling me worthless! Arsehole ... you got your hands on some guns, and you think you're someone now!"

I focused on his face and spat blood at him. He was standing far enough from me that I missed him, but he was afraid of me, even when I was handcuffed. Shame on you, coward. Fuck your authority, you fucking bastard. That mad glow, of a crowned man whose coronet has been desecrated in front of his subordinates, returned to his face. He nodded at his baton-holding flunkies who seized the opportunity to resume doing what they knew best, while at the same time dragging me inside the guardhouse corridor. He entered his office and called to one of his cohorts. The door was left open, so I overheard their conversation.

"Give him new clothes, put him in such and such cell in 'A' wing, and check on him often. If he needs to go to a hospital let me know".

The motherfucker didn't know where to put me, but he already had a cell picked out. Then I heard one of his flunkeys pose a question.

"Sir, he's too tough. He got his arse kicked pretty bad, and he didn't even make a sound".

It seemed that this particular flunkey found pleasure in the cries of pain of their defenceless victims and he hadn't enjoyed himself as much as he would have liked this time.

"Did you think he'd be just another wuss? Of course he's tough!" responded the expert on human toughness.

They gave me new clothes (mine were covered in blood), and escorted me to cell ninety-three, 'A' wing.

Every man for himself, and all for the gatekeeper

None of my three cellmates minded my swollen face and my limping. They didn't even bother giving me one of the bottom bunks because of my situation. And why should they? One of them was in prison because of troubles with his girlfriend, the other for drugs, and the third for a catering business that went belly-up. We didn't believe in the same god, we didn't share the same value system, and there was no prisoner solidarity. To them, all laws were reasonably good ("perhaps they ought to be a bit stricter"), except, of course, for those that kept them in prison. Those ought to change for the better, or be abolished altogether. I doubted whether they even knew who they were dealing with or what he stood for. So every man was for himself — and all for Aravantinos.

That disgusting piece of work knew well who he was dealing with. A decade earlier, such behaviour on his part would have been received as an insult by all the inmates — it would have caused uprisings. Aravantinos knew what he was talking about when he said that "prisons had changed". His phrasing had been misleading. He wasn't talking about the buildings with their barred gates, their wire nets, and their state-of-the-art security and surveillance systems. He was talking about the living human material that our virtuous and unpolluted society so eagerly attempts to get rid of, assigning this mission to the guardians of the rule of "law" and the repressive State apparatus. The latter willingly take on the task of hiding that material inside the concrete boxes of the formidable Greek correctional system.

And because no one is born inside a prison, all these inmates must have come from somewhere, carrying with them the beliefs of a society that had been in a state of total moral decline for several decades. Moral decay, when in a state of duress, grows stronger, takes shape. It turns men into opportunists, rats, schemers, snitches. Proud of its flabbiness, it undresses right in front of you, free of inhibition. Whole generations have added to it, accumulating subcutaneous fat on it.

All kinds of transactions with the one in power, with the persecutor, with the handler, were acceptable. From time to time, such transactions were considered smart or viewed as some kind of personal skill, expecting something in return, recognition at the very least. The eventual recipient and administrator of these dealings in human degeneracy was a corrupted PASOK henchman who had managed to convince the dotard Minister of Justice Evangelos Giannopoulos* to appoint him consultant in matters concerning the correctional system. What a joke! But one couldn't possibly expect anything better from a Minister of Justice lawyer, who appeared on television to publicly share his view that inmates need beating from time to time, as TV stars laughed along with his witty remark. Abysmal hypocrisy is required on the part of the preachers of democracy, as well as their many willing, giggling courtiers with empty heads, for the serpent's egg to hatch. They've arguably done pretty well. Its head has already emerged.

These thoughts rattled around in my mind as I lay inside my blankets in the days following. I couldn't even get myself to eat to gain strength. My nose and jaw were broken, as probably were some of my ribs, because I was in terrible pain. If there was no internal bleeding, I'd be fine. I needed great patience to get through those hours, and I had plenty. What I couldn't handle was my pride. I felt a strong urge to find a knife, or make one of my own when I got better and, after tricking him into summoning me at his office, kill him right there and then. There was nothing I wanted more than to see the terror in his eyes or to hear his squealing death rattle.

On New Year's Eve, my family travelled from Trikala to visit me. Aravantinos didn't allow them past the gate, saying it wasn't 'A' wing's visiting day. The truth was that he didn't want them to see me beaten up. He didn't even allow them to

---

*   Giannopoulos (1918-2003) was active against the Junta and helped prosecute the colonels after they were deposed. He took over the Justice Ministry aged 78, serving until 2000.

give me the clothes and the food they had brought from far away. At the same time his favourite temporary shareholders in the prison's protection were carrying huge bags, a gift for services of theirs towards the maintenance of the smooth coexistence of State and lawlessness. There's no shame in doing favours, as long as they're fruitful ...

A few days later a beefy guard, who had been among the most willing and artful during my beating, came by to check on me. My cellmates would later inform me that his name was Galimanis. He was Aravantinos' henchman and admirer, and always front row in the torturing of inmates.

It's no coincidence that when we want to harm someone, we aim for the head. It's because all decisions flow from there. That's why I had targeted Aravantinos. I wanted him to account for his crimes. Yet I wouldn't have minded planting a bullet in that bulldog's empty skull. Years later, when I was out of prison, I learnt that he had been in a car accident and was in a wheelchair. I didn't bother with him any longer. I was surprised when he got strafed by a Kalashnikov outside his house in a village near Lamia and even more surprised when I learnt he had become warden of Domokos Prison. I was pretty bummed that I wasn't the one to have taken his life, but at the same time, I thought: "Bless your hands".

This case clearly showcases how this pitiful State rewards and shelters its torturers. I'm certain that just like him, all the others who participated in my beating have by now been appointed to key posts in various prisons throughout the country.

Dancing with the State and the deep State

At that time, 'A' wing housed inmates who were convicted of all kinds of crimes. Drugs, rapes, paedophilia, honour crimes, crimes of passion, economic crimes, and many others listed in the Criminal Code. Many needed the authorities' protection because they had ratted out their partners. Some were as young as twenty two years old, others as old as ninety. The ward was entirely controlled by Aravantinos through his hulking pets. Bouncers — beyond their phonebooks, in which one could find high-ranking officers' private numbers — who had a peculiar relationship with power, whether they exercised it or served it. Outside prison they had their own hierarchies, inside they served whoever was the top dog. They professed themselves apolitical, with some far-right beliefs and behaviour, and lacked neither muscle nor courage. I'd go as far as to say they were good guys when you got to know them individually, and off duty. They did, however, exhibit a severe lack of morality, due to their profession. And that was precisely what Aravantinos was looking for.

Most were from Attica, and that alone was reason enough for them to want to remain in Korydallos Prison because it guaranteed them easy visits, contact with lawyers, connection with their work outside the prison and much more. They secured all these privileges by offering their services to Aravantinos, who wasn't a simple warden but also a member of the then-government, close to the Minister of Justice, president of the prison officers association, while also having a hotline with the chief of the Hellenic Police, the NSA etc. Drunk on the power that exercising authority brings, he used these bouncers to scare inmates into obedience. He extracted useful information from them, which he then echoed back to the Hellenic Police. He also secured himself front-row seats at whichever nightclub he wished, to blow off steam with his friends, everything being on the house of course. If, on the other hand, he was having trouble with someone outside the prison's gates, there'd always be some willing muscle to take care of it or plant a bomb inside their car. No kidding. A man in power with any self-respect leaves no opportunity unexploited. The prison didn't have a public prosecutor, a manager or a social worker, so everything was under his control: prison furloughs, transfers, visitations, work, cells, and anything else that had to do with life — legal or illegal — inside the prison. Such a basket of gifts worked like a lure for all inmates, let alone for those who had loose morals.

After about a year, they brought a scumbag of a cop into 'A' wing, convicted for abuse of power, after his colleagues arrested him with many polybagged shots of heroin. He had been using these shots to arrest hundreds of people (not only drug addicts) playing this simple little trick. He (along with his gang) picked whoever looked like a drug addict off the street and accused them of carrying the said shots of heroin, which was enough to book them on a felony charge. Then, lo and behold, the heroin remained in his hands to be used for his next victims. His clearing initiative had filled Korydallos Prison's cells. Aravantinos ordered his shameful pet henchmen to protect this scumbag, although some of them confessed to me that he had strip-searched them in the middle of the street!

A few days after his arrival in the ward, a Romanian boy visited my cell. Only my two cellmates were there at the time. The boy, after telling them his story, asked whether he had my permission to attack the cop. The guys, without thinking twice and without saying anything to me to plan things better, gave him a go. The boy, having gotten the all-clear and knowing that the cop was taking a shower, got down to the shower room. Rebar in hand, he began drawing the showers' curtains one by one, until he located his monstrous victim. Unluckily for him, he found the cop in the last shower and began beating him while in the meantime all the inmates who had been showering, insulted by the audacious intruder who had drawn their curtains, jumped outside.

Along with those who had been waiting in line to take a shower, they saved the cop and began beating the boy. A real mob. Afterwards, Aravantinos and his zealots took on the task of squashing him and, after a week in solitary confinement, he was transferred to Corfu.

The short story the young lad had told my cellmates before heading to the showers was as follows: in the past, he and his girlfriend had fallen victim to the cop's schemes (without either of them being involved with drugs). When he locked them in a holding cell, accused of plenty of felonies, the honoured combat boot of the Hellenic Police which the uniformed scumbag wore, landed on the belly of the boy's six months pregnant girlfriend, causing her to miscarriage right there, in the holding cell.

The public will never know this. Ingenious crime reporters, who appear very talkative when it comes to revealing the crimes of a civilian offender, never break police omertà, condemning to eternal darkness all those crimes that take place in the depths of police stations. They know they'll be handsomely rewarded for their silence. They'll be given information to write extensive articles, cannibalising the accused-victims and finish them off by pillorying them on national television, securing (exclusive) private conversations and videos (most of which have nothing to do with the charges).

Machiavellian practices

Shortly after this, my lawyer paid me a visit and instructed me to file a lawsuit for aggravated assault etc. I had so many court hearings in my future that I didn't want any more — after all, Aravantinos' conviction at court would mean nothing to me. I also suspected however that his warm welcome wasn't as innocent as it appeared, but had been ordered from much higher in the chain of command. My suspicions weren't without grounds, because inside the briefcase with the guns they had found in the car I attempted to escape in was a folder with data (marital status, houses, cars etc.) on the country's ten most influential businessmen. That sort of bastard, used to obedience and being in such a key position, is capable of anything as long as he serves those who keep him there. Anything; even killing me, if he got, or I gave him, the opportunity.

Based on these suspicions, making the incident known would prevent any future plans against me and trick him into thinking the consequences for his actions would only be legal. So I agreed to file a lawsuit against him (which I dropped later on). This move unexpectedly helped me in another domain as well. It helped me sort those whom I could trust from those I couldn't. He had both employees and inmates convey to me his displeasure that an inmate with my record and history had resorted to lawsuits for a random incident (that's how he called it). He loved using the principles of outlaws, as though he too was one of us, just because he had adopted them.

An inmate, being a good friend of mine, suggested that he should set up a meeting between us to talk things over. Under one condition. That I'd apologise to him because I had attacked him first.

"Are you serious? This is like adding insult to injury. If I see him, I plan on punching him in the face. I've deeply regretted not doing it then when I had the chance, still, I didn't know yet how far he was willing to take it".

"Come on, Vassilis. Let it slide. If you're thinking about beating him, I want nothing to do with it. I offered to help so that we could move on with our business".

He was suggesting a future escape.

"I don't know what your business is, but I know mine well, and I can do it well enough on my own".

The next day, Spyros, who was present during the previous conversation, came to my cell to talk to me.

"Look, Vassilis. You have a clear soul, so you should be careful. The walls in here have ears. I'm referring to what you said yesterday. That you want to beat him up".

"Well, you'd be surprised with what I'm really thinking," I replied.

"I can understand. I don't blame you. If I were in your shoes, I'd feel the same way. But remember you're on his turf now and the guy has proved how ruthless he is. Everyone knows he was the one who held Matei's nose closed when he was sedated on the stretcher. The big-shot cops instructed him to do so. To shut him up before he managed to talk about what happened on Niovis Street".*

"Are you absolutely sure?"

"The whole prison knows it".

"And what reason did he have to do something like this?"

"He was doing a favour to the cops who were responsible for the operation to arrest Matei. He was also involved and partly responsible himself. It was him that got the leader of the Albanians from 'D' wing out of prison and escorted him to the house where Matei held his hostages, to persuade him to release them. You do understand what I'm getting at. Because you're well known and Greek, he won't try something similar, but he's unpredictable and a coward. Who would have expected that he'd attack you as soon as you got here? What's best for you is to figure out a way to get out of here. When you're out, you can deal with him as you see fit".

I had to admit he was right. Spyros, although taking part in the dealings with the prison's authority, was a naturally forthright person. He didn't like the rotten state of the prison. In time, he'd come over to my side and later on we'd even become friends.

Once Aravantinos' initial tactics proved fruitless, as my stance slowly but steadily brought me more and more inmates, he put an even more sinister scheme into action. He began telling people how impressed he was by the way I was handling our rivalry after the incident and other similar bullshit.

"Never before has an inmate like him entered Korydallos. I'm left speechless by his attitude. I owe him an apology, and I'll apologise to him the first chance I get", he'd say to anyone he knew would come tell me. He had used this Machiavellian style tactic with many "high profile" inmates. And it always worked. More than a few of the bouncers he had beaten up became his bosom friends in exchange for more privileges than other inmates had. This way he succeeded in their double humiliation.

In the meantime, I had fully recovered. I began training extensively, yet I couldn't always keep to it because the court hearings had begun. Almost once every fifteen days, I'd leave for one of Greece's cities.

---

* Sorin Matei died in Korydallos Prison hospital on September 26th 1998, having been seriously wounded during a botched hostage rescue attempt by police. A hand grenade went off during the raid injuring Matei, the hostages and several officers, leading to the resignation of the head of police. The coroner's report found that Matei's death was caused by a combination of head injuries and heavy sedation.

Returning to Korydallos Prison, after one of these transfers, I was informed at the gatehouse that I'd have to switch cells, for some reason I now cannot remember. My new cellmates were Peter, a Lebanese American lifer who after a while escaped with the aid of the prison's psychologist (he was one of the warden's many pets), and Yorgos, who had been convicted for score-settling between crime bosses. Peter, as a lifer and having been there longer, gave me information about the prison, while at the same time trying to learn whether I had something planned. I didn't trust him, and so I never told him anything.

A glass of whiskey, an apology, and the warden's heart and soul

One night, after the inmates were counted and the doors of all cells were locked, we heard a key turning in our lock. Two guards told us that the warden wished to see us. All three of us.

All three of us … all three of us. What could I say? How to decline his invitation without hurting him? We put on our shoes, and we followed the guards until we reached the guardhouse. The door of his office was open. When we entered, he was talking on the phone with some journalist, arranging a future appearance on some show to talk about crime and correction, so he didn't pay us any attention. He was sitting behind a reasonably big desk, on the right side of the chamber. On our left, there was a big sofa and a handful of chairs. There was a window wall right across us, allowing an almost full view of the garden, which was now lit up. I had been told that Aravantinos had overseen its construction and upkeep. He had even built a mini zoo with small cages which "housed" several birds and little animals. He'd once owned a monkey (according to some spiteful comments it looked a lot like him), which often escaped from its cage to climb on the garden's trees. He'd throw rocks at it to make it get down until one day it ran away for good and he never saw it again. Probably just malicious rumours!

After he'd finished negotiating his appearance on the TV show, as an experienced and learned man, he got up and shook the hands of my cellmates. To me, he simply said: "What's up, Vassilis?"

"Sit", he urged us.

I sat in a chair while the other two sat on the sofa. He seemed to be in a good mood. He had a lengthy chat with my cellmates, avoiding looking at me directly. It seemed logical and expected. He felt closer to them. Peter was under his protection and Yorgos was his friend, although he had beaten him in the past. At some point, he leaned under his desk, and when he got back up, he was holding four glasses. He leaned under once again, and this time he got out a sealed bottle of whiskey. He placed it on the desk.

"Let's blow off some steam, all right gentlemen!" he exclaimed, shooting us a conspiratorial look.

He opened the bottle, filled the glasses to the middle and sat on his throne.

"Come on, grab your glasses. Let's empty this bottle tonight!" he said.

Peter and Yorgos took their glasses and returned to the sofa.

"What about you, Vassilis? Don't you drink?", he asked casually.

"No. Alcohol doesn't suit me". I lied.

"Oh, I chug a whole bottle of this every night", he said, pointing at the bottle.

He looked at me, then he looked at Peter, and then he facetiously said:

"Every single day, ten or more inmates come to tell me you're planning to leave. I'm not lying, every single day ... isn't it terrible?"

"And yet every single day we remain here", Peter responded.

"You're right. Once I had two rats in each wing, yet all their information was accurate. Now I have two hundred and fifty, yet all their information proves false. You can't work like that", he concluded in feigned bitterness.

The message he was indirectly sending me was clear. Don't even think of trying anything because two hundred and fifty pairs of eyes are always fixed on you. I pretended not to understand and asked:

"What do you believe is these peoples' motive for passing on information — real or not, it doesn't matter — from inside the prison to you personally?"

"Trust me, Vassilis, I wonder about that myself as well. I've never made anyone a rat or a drug addict, whoever tells you otherwise is a liar. I assume you understand that to manage the biggest, hardest, and most dangerous prison in the whole country, I need allies. Even you, for example. If you decided to help me, it would be a great honour and joy".

"If you ever decide to demolish it, then count me in".

He always had a quick wit; he wouldn't waste an opportunity to get the conversation going.

"You don't need to demolish it, because I'm giving you its keys right here and now. Do you want to be responsible for all the murders, the robberies, and the rapes that will result from you setting free inmates convicted for every felony listed in the criminal code and others awaiting trial for heinous crimes?"

"It's not up to me to decide whether to set the inmates free since I'm not the one who put them in here. I helped build no prison. Of one thing, I'm sure. That those who preserve this disgusting system are guilty; those who put you in this position even more so, but I don't see any of them in prison. Just a word of advice, if I may. Throw the keys you're offering me to the inmates and then run. If someone needs to escape and fast, it's you".

Surprisingly, my words didn't upset him. On the contrary, he seemed to be enjoying himself. The topic of our conversation was one he knew well and, given his sense of humour, he felt safe.

"How many inmates do you think will try to escape if I throw the keys in your wing? Not one. I'm sure of it. They'll lock the doors and hand the keys to the gatehouse. Do you think I'm holding them here?" he asked me.

Without waiting for my response, and being under the false impression that across him stood a well-read and ideologically learned person, he attempted to showcase his erudition by babbling social, political and correctional analyses, combining social philosophers, rebels, Machiavelli, and others.

When he'd finished, he used his swivel director's chair to turn so that he was facing the wall behind him.

"Do you see all these? I've written them. Take a look if you like" he said in a slightly boastful manner, pointing at a collection of framed missives.

Indeed, a handful of frames (some bigger than others) were hanging on the wall above his head. I felt an irresistible curiosity to read their contents. Thinking, however, that this way I'd attach importance to the stains resulting from the arrogant warden's profound mental masturbation, I didn't allow myself to. The booze was flowing, and he was in the mood for a chat. He suddenly became apologetic.

"Vassilis, I understand what you're trying to say; I'm but a pawn of the system myself. I've never claimed that I can change the world, yet in the specific territory entrusted to me by the State, I've done more than anyone else, and I'm very proud of that. I'll give you an example. Five years ago, here, we had an attempted breakout every two months. It was the time when Albanians entered Greece by the thousands, and many of them ended up here. Greek long-termers, who wanted to escape, used them as shields, after planning mass breakouts. I've seen with my own two eyes two hundred inmates attempting to climb the interior and the exterior wall of the prison at the same time, using makeshift ladders while being fired upon, and not even thinking of giving up. They were so full of themselves, so sure they were going to make it, that they were carrying sacks with their clothes. Some of them, usually those who orchestrated the escape, actually did it. The rest got trapped in the dead zone. A handful got tangled up in the wire netting, hanging up there like goats, until the prison crew untangled them. We lived through many situations like this, until I decided to have a meeting with all the staff and discuss how we could deal with it. I told them to be patient and that in a few years, everything would change. You can see it for yourself. Nothing of this sort is happening now. Everything is under my control. To you, perhaps, all this is of no importance, but to me, it wasn't just a job. I put my heart and soul into it!"

I called bullshit on that. What happened could be easily explained. When a State functions poorly, unable to offer solutions, relinquishing its role and responsibilities towards its citizens, it invariably pulls some rabbits out of its hat. It produces Aravantinos and his ilk to stand in for it. It presents them as an ideal solution. And when it ought to be ensuring its citizens' constitutional rights, it instead covers for the crimes of men like Aravantinos, making sure they get away with it each time.

***

In this same State, which never takes to heart its role and responsibilities, fugitive-turned-Minister of Justice Valirakis had issued another obscene decree, based on which policemen were to be awarded a few thousand drachmas (a double daily wage back then) for every Albanian they arrested. So, even when they were off duty, policemen flung themselves into an unprecedented hunt for Albanians to supplement their wages.

Once, while I was still free and driving along the Konitsa-Samarina road, near Samarina, around two hundred yards ahead of me I saw a police Land Rover. Its emergency lights were switched on, and it was almost blocking the dirt road. My first and most natural reaction was to slow down and cock my Kalashnikov, but as I approached I realised there was no one inside. After scanning the surrounding area, lest they had entrenched themselves somewhere nearby, I located a group of people down in a gorge.

Wasting no time, I got out my binoculars. Two cops, obviously feeling the need to spread the word about the famous Greek hospitality, had trapped a group of men, women, and children, and were aiming at them with guns, threatening to push them off the cliff.

Although it would have been an excellent opportunity for me to take the Land Rover's keys, burn it, drive it off the cliff, or strafe it with my Kalashnikov, I realised that all such courses of action would work to those people's disadvantage. Newspaper headlines ("A heavily armed group supporting illegal immigrants attacked defenceless police officers who were putting their life on the line while trying to do their job under extreme adversity") would sow hatred among the "indigenous" population against the supposed ruthless and organised intruders, whose sole aim is to take over the country.

Another time, someone we knew asked us to meet with him, and we agreed. He confessed that he was cooperating with some cops, transferring Albanians from the border to Thessaly using vans and taxis, for money. When he dropped them off at a prearranged spot, the police would intervene as agreed and arrest only the illegal immigrants. The fat profits from transferring these men, as well as the financial rewards offered by the State for the capture of each of them, were split among all those who participated in this orgy of abuse and cruelty. Our acquaintance, fully confident that he was now part of the elite of the Greek crime world, asked us for a gun, to give it to a friend of his who was a cop. When we asked him the obvious, meaning what did the cop intend to do with the gun, he gave us an obvious and logical — at least from his point of view — answer. He'd use it instead of his service pistol, in case he needed to kill any Albanians. Tell me, now, how can I feel proud of being human? He was lucky I knew his parents and they were good people. Most Greeks get away with their crimes because they have an in with somebody.

They'd put these people in prison busses and drop them off at the borders. There they'd arrest some of them, mostly the younger ones, pin on them all kinds of unsolved theft cases and send them to the district attorney. The attorney, without even bothering to examine their cases, would send them to prison. Humiliated by the police force of a country to which they had come hoping to find a solution to their problems, and instead finding themselves imprisoned for crimes they hadn't committed with nobody to stand up for them, escaping inevitably became their only ray of hope.

***

The insulting warden, who likened those long-suffering men to goats hanging on the fence of the prison, since he had no intention of going against the political decisions of his superiors, operated like any other true man in power who respects and serves the power structure. He'd use his dirty schemes to press downwards. He'd find among the Albanians those who wished to build an in-prison career and, most importantly, those who had no scruples (like himself), and he'd make them leaders, granting them total control over the wing's management. He only asked that there wouldn't be any complaints about the living conditions, no uprisings and, most importantly, no escapes! All the humanoid-clones of his, would, in turn, surround themselves with a handful of knifemen to keep things under control in their wings, awarding them the best work posts and having all remaining posts to give to anyone they liked (making suggestions directly to Aravantinos) just as agreed. If anyone needed a job, a certificate of good conduct for the court, a change of cell, unsupervised visits, a furlough, or the essentials, they only had to ask these clones. And they'd convey the request to the prototype.

At that time, I estimated that about sixty to seventy per cent of the inmates used heroin. About thirty to forty per cent began using inside the prison. A prison plagued by drug use was the exploit he boasted he'd put his heart and soul into. Unless he was referring to a different feat aside from the dealings mentioned above.

"I don't believe you called us here to talk to us about all this", I said.

"You're right. I strayed a bit. From time to time I need to talk about all that's been eating me on the inside. I called you here, Vassilis, because one day soon you'll be transferred to a different prison. And because we had a misunderstanding, I wanted us to talk, to sort things out.

"Then it would be best that the guys, who have nothing to do with our misunderstanding, not be present", I suggested.

He seemed puzzled by my suggestion. He remained looking awkwardly at me for a few seconds.

"No. I called the guys precisely because I wanted to apologise to you and I wanted my apology to be public".

I didn't quite get whether he was honest or whether he was simply afraid to be alone with me.

"As you wish".

"Look, Vassilis. I'm really sorry. I think I got out of line. That day, I left my sick child at the hospital just to come and see you. It doesn't matter if the timing was bad or if it was your reaction, but the damage was done. I can't turn back time and fix things. The only thing I can do is apologise to you, and that's what I'm doing right now".

"Aravantinos".

"Call me Antonis, Goddamn it! Antonis!"

"All right, Antonis. Can you tell me why you wanted to talk to me before they put me in my cell?"

"I've already told you. Someone told me you had troubles with some Albanian inmates".

"When I broke out in 1991, there was no sign of Albanians inside prisons. It's 2000 now. I'd never met any Albanians until now, how could I have rivalries with them? Can you tell me who told you such a lie?"

"Your former partner, Kostas. He called me from Corfu Prison and told me just that".

I was dumbstruck. Aravantinos wouldn't have dared lie to me about this, because I could have easily found out the truth. Why would Kostas have called him? Why would he have his phone number and be close enough with him to ask favours? Later, I'd ask and learn that my former partner had ended up ratting out his fellow inmates while in prison, and to protect himself he had taken Aravantinos as his patron. Perhaps Aravantinos had thought I'd be just like him, and therefore easy to manipulate. Right then, however, I knew none of this. I was suddenly confronted with hundreds of questions. I didn't want to jump to conclusions; still, I kept the conversation going.

"Why didn't you come alone, or with just one or two of your men, but instead arrived with a legion of bruisers? What were you afraid of?" I asked him.

"Some of the guys were already with me. The rest came out of curiosity because of who you are. They wanted to see you".

"And what about the batons? Were they just beauty accessories? In fact, those who entered with you already had them in their hands".

"Most employees have batons," he replied.

It was useless to insist.

"Look, Antonis ... let's wrap this one up. If there was the slightest possibility of me accepting your apology, it'd be if you were man enough to admit that you came with your henchmen to terrorise me, to take me down a peg, and things got out of hand, and we all know what happened next. Inserting your child into our personal dispute seems like the cheap excuse of a cheap man. Even the cops — many of whom I've wounded — treated me better. If it was a one-time thing, I'd let it slide. But you've attacked people before, and you keep on doing it. So how can you ask me to accept your apology when you don't even mean it, and you're doing it just because you're afraid?

A moment of silence. He served the rest of the whiskey in the three glasses, obviously trying to control his annoyance at my refusing to accept his apology.

"Vassilis, you're not ready to accept my apology. That doesn't mean it's less important, because I truly mean it. I want you to understand one thing. It is the first time I've done something like this because I believe — and you have proven so — that you're a proud man; you more than deserve the name you've built for yourself. I don't know what they've told you about me, but all these people I've beaten up and you're now defending were and continue to be my men. They help me do my job, and I preserve their names. It's a scratch my back and I'll scratch yours situation. I'm writing a book right now. I hope I'll have finished it in about six months. Then you'll see. They'll have nowhere to hide".

Go figure. I'm still waiting for that book. I waited for the guys to finish their whiskeys (when would they get the chance of drinking whiskey again in prison) and after we bid him goodnight, we were escorted back to our cells. There I was in for some more grumbling. By Peter this time.

"The only thing you achieved was for him to become even more afraid of you. Security will tighten. It was a mistake not to accept his apology. You'd have the most privileges of anyone in here ..."

Blah blah blah. Nothing to be done. It's wise nature's masterplan. Between a crocodile and an eagle lies the abyss. Both are predators, yet songs aren't written about crocodiles. It's a matter of aesthetics and grace. How can a poet be inspired by a carnivore that lies in murky waters in wait for its prey?*

Collector of fretsaw blades

I'd see Aravantinos three or four more times. One afternoon, they opened our cell and turned the place inside out, finding a handful of metal-cutting blades, a cutter knife, handcuff keys, a phone charger, and some other things. He came to join his men, knocking some metal broomsticks together just in case we had something hidden inside them. As expected, after the inspection, they escorted us to the guardhouse. While we were walking, I made it clear to my cellmates (one of whom was Greek and the other Albanian) that I'd take responsibility for all the other things except for the phone charger. One of them would have to explain its existence. I didn't want Aravantinos to know I had a mobile phone. Aravantinos was already there, waiting for us with Thomopoulos, who was his right-hand man. On one side of the table he had laid the wares he had discovered in my cell.

"I didn't find what I was looking for, but I found something else!" he said, looking at my two cellmates.

"And what is that, warden?" I asked him.

"Drugs!"

"Drugs in my cell?"

"You don't live in this cell alone", he said, still looking at my two cellmates, who had their heads down.

"Antonis, you're unfair to them. They've sworn to me that they don't do drugs".

"And you believed them? Don't trust men who swear. They're unfair to you! Why aren't you saying anything, huh? Cat got your tongues? Swear it to me then. Swear that you don't do drugs!"

They kept mum. They looked guilty.

"Whose is all this?" he asked, showing the rest of the things on the table.

"Everything's mine, except for the charger".

"Why don't you own the charger as well and be done with it?"

---

* Peter had received two consecutive life sentences for murdering women. Taking advantage of his personal relationship with Aravantinos, he got romantically involved with the prison's psychologist and with her help managed to escape in 2002. About two years later the couple were found dead in Colombia.

"It's not mine. Who knows, it might be filled with drugs!"

"What the hell did you need all these fretsaw blades for? And where did you find them? I'm impressed!"

"Oh ... well, everyone in this prison knows I'm a collector of all tools for cutting metal. So anyone that gets his hands on one comes to me to sell it. I'm just doing them a favour".

My two cellmates and Thomopoulos were wheezing, trying in vain to keep from laughing. Aravantinos, for some inexplicable reason, wasn't upset. He answered humorously as ever.

"Never before have I met a collector of fretsaw blades in this prison. It appears that the visual arts are gaining ground here and I should feel very proud of this surprising turn of events".

He turned to face my two cellmates, ready to scold them.

"Go back to your fucking cell. Trying to convince me you're not doing drugs. You fucking little sneaks ..."

They got up and ran out of the office, relieved by how easy they got off, leaving me behind to deal with the "beast".

"What am I going to do with all these things, huh?"

"Whatever the law says, warden".

"If I waited for the law to tell me what to do, we'd both be locked up in your cell", he said.

He turned to Thomopoulos and ordered him:

"Bring me a garbage bag!"

He got out and returned moments later, holding a big garbage bin. He placed it under the table, right where the confiscated items were. He reached over the table and with a sudden sweeping movement, pushed everything inside the bin.

"That was it, we're done! As you understand, I'm trying to make up for past mistakes. I hope I'll repay you someday".

I left without responding. I was indeed flattered by his earnest efforts. But ...

The drug-dump method

We met again the same night that Passaris used the "drug-dump" method to get a gun that he'd later use to escape.*

'D' wing's yard didn't communicate with the outer wall of the prison and, as a result, 'A' wing's drug-addicted inmates acted as delivery men, grabbing whatever weed packages were dumped in their yard. At once, they'd throw it inside 'D' wing's yard, settling their fee later. This happened daily, in the blink of an eye,

---

* Kostas Passaris escaped in February 2001 from the Gennimatas Hospital, killing two police officers who were escorting him. After being tracked down by the Special Anti-Terrorist Unit at an apartment in central Athens that June he was shot in the leg but escaped again, heading to Romania. He was finally arrested in November by Romanian police after he and his accomplice robbed an exchange bureau, killing two employees. He was jailed in 2003 and held in Romanian prisons until 2019, when he was extradited to Greece and sentenced to four life sentences.

right in front of the interior guards, who'd pointlessly run to grab all the things dropping from the sky. The inmates were trained, fit and, most importantly, much more motivated. They wanted to get stoned. They also had the advantage of expecting the drop-off. They knew when and where the drugs would fall and were able to grab it mid-air.

Such comedic incidents often take place inside prisons, where the State dumps drug-addicted convicts with no regard for them. It only remembers them when their sentence ends and even then, just to unlock the door, letting them temporarily walk free, only to arrest them again shortly after in their known hotspots. And they have every right to try and survive, whichever way they can, in such arenas where survival of the fittest becomes a daily routine.

One evening, as soon as the prison yard was locked, an inmate knocked on the door of my cell. I was inside with my two cellmates (Simos, an anarchist they'd pinned a bank robbery on, and Vangelis, a drug addict and diamond in the rough).

"Come inside".

Nothing.

"Go on, Vangelis. Open the door ..."

He opened the door for him.

"How are you, Vassilis?" he said hesitantly, keeping his voice down as though the walls had ears.

"Who's asking?"

"I wished to talk to you alone if that's possible. There's a good reason why I'm asking", he said, still keeping his voice down.

The guys looked at me and, after making sure everything was all right, they left smirking (they knew how politely I treated sudden intruders in our cell).

"I hope I didn't make the guys leave for some unheard of bullshit ..."

"No, Vassilis, I have a good reason for being here. First of all, don't you remember me? I'm Dimitris! The guy who came with Yorgos, when we met you outside the store with the wooden boats on Kavalas Street in Peristeri. You were holding a violin case with a machine gun inside. You talked about Thanasis' case".

"It's been such a long time. How could I remember you? But I'm sure you're not lying. How else would you know all these details? So yes, you were present at that meeting. Tell me now, what do you want?"

"If I might be so bold, I thought it was my duty to inform you that the guys in 'D' wing have gotten their hands on a gun!"

"What do you mean? What sort of gun, what guys and how do you know about this?"

"I grabbed a weed package and threw it over to 'D' wing. I grab most of the weed packages dropped in 'A' wing's yard. This one was too heavy to be anything else. I've done this a million times now. I'm not wrong. I can weigh them mid-air before I even catch them. This one was so heavy that I almost fell down".

Well then ... I had the honour of standing in front of a "drug-dump" expert! He just didn't know he was talking to a "pet" expert.

"How long have you been in this wing?" I asked him.

"Eight months".

"Eight months and you only came to talk to me now, although you knew me from before?"

"Uh, how could I have come, Vassilis? I've become a drug addict. I was ashamed".

"Aren't you ashamed now?"

"At least now I've come to bring you some good news that might be of interest to you".

"It might be of more interest to Aravantinos. Run along and tell him. And also tell him that I don't follow others".

He left; his head down. Pretending to be embarrassed.

I was fully aware that Passaris was going to get a gun one of those days, but I didn't know when and how. I only hoped he'd use it well to achieve his goal. Every man like Aravantinos has some key people like Dimitris, master of drug-dumps, as his pets. A collector of dropped drugs is such a key person. When he's one of your men, you know at all times the trajectory, the speed, the weight and the spot where the dumped goods fall, their eventual destination, their possible recipients, and perhaps even the sender; and you act accordingly. You always draw attention to their mass and weight. When it's large but light, it's probably just pot, and nobody gives a damn ... When it's smaller and a bit heavier, it must be heroin, in other words, some godsend sedation. When, however, it is heavy, too large, too hard, and ready to spit fire and death, let it stay as far away from us. Because nobody had signed a contract with fear, as he'd tell me later the same night.

When bedtime came, from my cell (which was then on the second floor and allowed a view of one of the front sides of 'D' wing) we got wind of some action over there. I, knowing more than the others, paid more attention. For a while, we watched as hands appeared through barred windows, dropping whatever illegal things the inmates may have had inside their cells. It was pretty clear that an inspection was underway in 'D' wing. While we were watching the poor guys from 'D' wing, we heard the key turning inside the lock of our door. An inspection ... they were after the unspeakable package, fearing it might have ended up in my cell. The mere thought of the possibility made the warden ill. They didn't find it and left disappointed. Not five minutes had gone by however when they unlocked the door of our cell once more.

"Vassilis, the warden wishes to see you".

Here we go again.

They unlocked two more cells and got out two more inmates whom I knew, so as not to raise suspicion.

On the guardhouse's couch were three inmates whose faces looked crumpled. They'd had their daily beating, to confess what more they knew concerning the dropped package, apart from what the "drop" expert already knew and had told Aravantinos. He cut me off before I got the chance to complain about what I was seeing.

"Don't look at them like that, Vassilis. They're the ones who have fucked up my whole prison with their drugs. And all this time I thought you and the guys were responsible! That's why I called you. To apologise and to show you who is responsible for the inspections in your cells!" he said.

Then, he called two of his employees, and they carried the beaten inmates out of the chamber.

"Did you see them?" he asked as soon as they were gone. "These guys have filled this prison with heroin in the last few months. Today I was informed that a gun was dumped inside the prison. If this is true, I'm going to find it at all costs. I hope that if you ever get your hands on a gun, you won't use it inside the prison but during some transfer, because nobody has signed a contract with fear; we're all afraid because of our job!"

That was it. We left without even having to talk. And what can be said about Aravantinos' erratic decision to summon us to his office ...

Easter, the crucified, and Christodoulos of Athens

On Easter Sunday of 2001, we'd see each other for the last time, and Aravantinos would make one final attempt to reconcile with me. During noon count, the employee in charge of locking up the cells told me I was wanted at the gatehouse. What a surprise! On Easter Sunday? Accompanied by an employee, I got to the gatehouse. There were many guards there who, as soon as they saw me, told me that the warden was waiting for me in the prison garden. They unlocked the door, I went through and stood on the landing. Before me stretched a narrow stone pathway, about sixteen yards long, cutting through the lush garden and ending up in front of some steps, leading to the second, lower level of the garden. There, down these steps, with their backs to me, I saw my former partner Kostas and another inmate, who had been convicted for political militancy and hunted for many years until being caught a few days after my own arrest. Now decommissioned, he had decided to get in with the prison's authorities, and enjoy himself on such a holiday.

They were chatting with Aravantinos, who was facing them, standing next to me. About ten yards to their right (as I was looking at them) was a big gazebo. Underneath it was a huge wooden table, at which a dozen inmates were sitting, drinking beer and nibbling at festive delicacies. Most of them were workers from "E" wing. A bit further away from the gazebo, in front of a long pit filled with burning coals, six or seven other inmates were sitting on short stools, holding their beers and rhythmically turning the skewer, roasting some more lamb. The festive atmosphere was completed by folk songs playing through the garden's speakers.

Such banquets were always held on Christmas, New Year's Day, and Easter Sunday. After the midday count, they'd unlock the cells and call the names of all the prison stars, Greek or not, to attend their social event and celebrate with the people who locked them up in their cells each night. The select guests dressed festively and strutted their way to the feast. If there's one thing for which I take my hat off to Aravantinos, it was precisely this. His ability to tactfully humiliate people, ridiculing whichever inmate he wanted while they were as proud as punch that they had been invited. The inmates weren't as sharp as him; they simply couldn't compete. It was child's play sedating them with recognition in the small world of the prison.

With these celebrations, which he himself established, he could make it abundantly clear who his chosen ones were, who helped him maintain control of the prison, calling their names through the loudspeakers and making sure there was absolutely no sense of community and solidarity among the inmates. The anonymous pariahs, having the pantheon of confined criminals who they admired — and in a sense wanted to be like — showing them through their actions the way towards such a status, had no reason to keep up appearances. They'd kill each other just to get the chance to have any sort of dealing with the Boss, adopting and reproducing dehumanising behaviours destructive of human morality. This grovelling, witnessed throughout the prison, made imprisonment even more unbearable to men with a sceptical temperament.

Since the previous December there had been five grand celebrations to which I had not been invited, not in person nor through the loudspeakers, because he knew I wouldn't do him the honour of attending. This time he did it before the doors of the cells were unlocked, and his favourites were there. The reason was that if I declined to join the feast, he didn't want his chosen ones to see that I was snubbing him. He was a master conniver when it came to such things; he left nothing to chance. Just as he was doing now, waiting for me, his eyes hooked on me and the two unsuspecting wild cards — the bait. I descended the steps of the gatehouse and walked along the stone pathway. I had almost reached its middle when he shouted at me:

"Here you are, Vassilis!"

My two acquaintances turned my way and were quite surprised to see me. Reaching them, I shook their hands while we exchanged the usual nonsense Easter wishes: Christ is Risen; indeed, He is Risen etc.

I cut to the chase:

"What did you want from me, Antonis?"

"We're having a little celebration for our Jesus Christ, so I thought I'd invite you to join us!"

I snapped.

"Stop for a moment and think how Jesus lived in a cave hunted by the authorities. He had twelve companions with him, there was a thirty -pieces-of-silver bounty on his head and, when one of his companions betrayed him to collect the sacred ransom, he was crucified, regarded as a criminal. Perhaps he was a social robber or an anti-authoritarian of his time. What he has been reduced to, two thousand years later by overexploitation and the distortion of historical reality, is a whole different story. There are many Christs in every era, and they're always crucified. If there was one now, you'd have him here, locking away his soul every single night. With that in mind, I should be grieving and not celebrating this day".

The wild cards joined in the conversation about Christs and unworthy men and, half in earnest, half in jest, we rapidly talked things over,

"Relax, Vassilis, even just for today. Sit with us and have some beer or some wine. If, on the other hand, you don't want to sit with us, grab a carton of beers to drink with your friends in your cell!" he suggested.

Right then, his priest approached us. Aravantinos introduced him to me as a former rebel (vaguely) and me to him as a bank robber. He was a decent-looking old man. He greeted me warmly, saying: "Nice to meet you, Palaiokostas".

How did a rebel give birth to a warden? A sign of the times. All this time, the inmates who were sitting under the gazebo were calling me to join them, clink glasses, and have a drink together for the sake of the day. But I knew well enough that if I did them the favour, I'd lose the match. So I bid them goodbye, thinking about how masterfully humanity's imagination turned guilt for a heinous historical crime into a celebration, by coming up with the Resurrection. Their Truth is as real as that latter event (ie. non-existent), and yet they presume to guide people.

They were equally sure when they crucified Jesus, and yet they found themselves carrying him on their shoulders for eternity. His blood is still dripping hot down their sweaty backs. Many centuries of obscurantism and the heavy, permanent burden in the soul of the Western world was Jesus' revenge. All crimes have to be paid for at some point. Some select few pay them in cash, right here and now, as befits the dwellers of fleeting human life. The masses postpone payment indefinitely. Instead, they put their money in history's holocausts and in new atrocities. With their iniquities they weave the red carpet which they will later lay reverently before their children's feet, to guide them to the steps of another hell, from which it will be much harder to escape this time. Miracles only happen once. Especially that of Resurrection. Because at some point even lies are bound to run out.

The previous Christmas, the Archbishop of Athens and All Greece, Christodoulos,* had visited 'A' wing. Surrounded by a legion of the church's young robed henchmen and as many prison officers, with Aravantinos serving as his guide, he'd entered our wing to be welcomed with applause and cheers by all inmates! An uncontrollable wave of incarcerated warm believers, led by those who'd fucked and killed their mothers, surrounded God's representative and, one by one, kneeled before him, religiously kissing one of his extended hands. At the same time, he laid his other hand on their heads, blessing them!

This ritual went on for a few more minutes, as the Archbishop moved towards the staircase that led to the upper floors, followed by his guard. Reaching the first floor, he headed towards the bridge that connected the cells' aisles. He stood in the middle of the bridge and, looking at the open interior of the prison that was swarming with impatient inmates, began handing out wishes. Then he began preaching the word of God to the lost souls, who held their breath lest they miss a single word from his fiery Godly speech.

---

*   Of the Orthodox church, which was and remains very powerful in Greece, with 90% of citizens identifying as followers. A right-wing hardliner, Christodolous died in 2008.

After about ten minutes, as his babbling was coming to an end, the whole wing was shaken by a prolonged round of loud applause. Then the ecstatic inmates' clapping became rhythmical, accompanied by an also rhythmical slogan-request to the Archbishop. "A-nec-dote ... a-nec-dote ... a-nec-dote ..." their voices echoed inside the wing. The head of the Church and God's representative smiled and, amidst a deep din of giggles, began telling anecdotes about a female goat and several male suitors.

I've never felt more ashamed about the degradation of men and inmates. Despite my curiosity, I couldn't stand watching this nauseating show a second more, so I entered my cell, swearing. A young inmate living in the cell next to mine heard me and ran inside my cell, breathless and upset.

"What did you do?" I asked him.

"I threw three eggs at Christodoulos and his entourage, as they were exiting the wing!"

"And why did you come to my cell you little fucker?"

"Some believers got wind of it, and I was afraid they were going to lynch me!"

"You did well! I wish all the inmates would do the same ... did you get one of them at least?"

"I got a guard, right on his bald head!"

"Who'd you expect to get? Christodoulos is protected by God!"

The spitfire young man had once been an Orthodox Christian until he came face to face with harsh reality. About three years before, he had been working as an inmate in one of the prison's offices. There he could watch the daily beatings of inmates by prison officers. What shocked him however, and became the reason he apostatised, also giving up his post at the offices, was when he saw the prison's chaplain participating in one of those routine beatings.

The gruesome image he described to me was as so: curled up on the concrete hallway outside the guardhouse, with his hands tied behind his back, an inmate was being brutally beaten up by a rampaging Aravantinos and his henchmen. The inmates' guardian angel guest-starred on the show, holding his robes to the height of his knees while he repeatedly raised his one foot like a ram, driving it down onto the head of the helpless inmate. Again, and again, and again, and again ... until the floor was dyed red with his victim's blood, as was the chaplain's black patent shoe. That kind of fascism is hidden behind the robes. The torturing old git retired that year. The media, singing his praises for his divine work, drew his icon using the blood he spilled. Such lies, such deception and such hypocrisy, hidden in the media.

So as not to be accused of one-sidedness, I'll mention the benefits of the Archbishop's visit. Because he didn't come empty-handed. A few minutes after he was gone, a handful of prison guards arrived at our cells and handed each inmate a small paper bag, with the familiar red ribbon. You'll wonder now, dear reader, what was inside the bag — a vast array of soaps and perfumes. Obviously the clergy, aside from their faith in God, believe in other tall tales as well, like the one about inmates dropping the soap.

That's why they made sure to provide us with so many … if there's one chance for those who call upon God to escape his fury, it is for them to pray day and night that he doesn't exist. Because if he does, woe for them …

Honestly now: I'd light a candle in a church, where the priest takes his flock after Sunday Mass to a beach, a river, or a forest to clean the garbage that the religious leave there. Who, the following day, might visit a burnt wood, planting one, two, a thousand trees to replace those that the religious burned. And who, the day after, would hit the streets with the men and women of God to give food and nurse the needy, who have fallen victims of religious people … the sins of the men and women of God are too many to list here.

I'd become a strong supporter of any religion where the teachings would bring people together for a common cause, urging them: "Let's make this planet the paradise in which God will live!" Its priests would be the loyal warriors of God and not his bearded, robed wailers. Warriors who would use His strength to fight the same war. Who would destroy weapons of mass destruction. Who would abolish borders. Who would fight hard daily battles against rulers, economic feudalism, injustice, famine, and environmental destruction. Who would kill the dark side of the men and women of God … and those men and women themselves!

They'd be activists and guardians of life on Earth; they'd be able to look God in the eye, innocent like children, without fear and servility.

Are the people of our era rich and clean enough for God to live inside them? No wonder only naked devils dance on this land.

Revenge

Perhaps — my extensive references to Aravantinos may appear obsessive and to an extent, vindictive. They're nothing of the sort. I'd never allow myself to stray down that road. After all, all references to events that involve other people are not intended to criticise or victimise these people, but to confer and record as distinctly as possible my own truth, as I lived it, being at the centre of these events. Keeping to a straightforward recording of events, something like this would be impossible.

After all, this book is written first and foremost for people who react and act, by someone who wilfully chose armed struggle. A targeted, ethical, rules-governed struggle with a cause. It doesn't point to a specific direction or target. It stems from a more profound need to offer, as selectively as possible, the events of this journey, the treatment of which I believe better sums up and reflects my way of thinking. I think that Aravantinos' case includes several elements that record and illuminate some characteristics of this way of thinking. And the people of struggle will always come across men like Aravantinos, each time in a different guise.

The narration of real incidents from the mandatory cohabitation of a — in all respects — power-obsessed warden, who is part of the rotten and deeply corrupted regime and a caricature of representative democracy, and a defiant, self-governed convict, who does not stoop to wallow in the trash that's been offered to him, is an excellent opportunity to shed some light into two radically conflicting moral worlds that collide. One of the thousand such encounters, where our contemporaries hide their shame.

To be fair, Aravantinos wasn't but a sucker on one of the many giant tentacles of the monster of corruption that is twisted around the Greek people, passionately and tenderly constricting them, threatening to strangle them. All boasting, self-obsessed suckers do whatever they can to carry out the task that has been assigned to them.

At the time, in other prisons, there were other wardens, directors, even public prosecutors, who were the definition of inmate torturers. Compared to them, Aravantinos was a saint.

And as for my desire to get revenge, when I broke out six-and-a-half years after my beating, it had subsided. But I had promised myself to do him over, taking responsibility for my action, and I wanted to remain faithful to my promise. I looked for him, but something always happened to make me stop. I, who nosed foxes out of dark mazes, couldn't locate Aravantinos. One reason for this was that I wanted it to be me who did it because I thought this was the right thing to do. It wasn't in my nature, assigning jobs for a fee.

Having broken out for the second time, Alket and I did at one point come across him by chance: he was exiting the combat vehicles military camp in Avlonas, driving a forest-green Hyundai. His son was in the passenger seat; the same son he had once used to justify his dirty doings had now grown up and was serving in the armoured warfare division of the army. He obviously had some time off, and his father was picking him up. In that random meeting of ours, and in contrast to him, I showed respect for his son and didn't get him involved in our conflict (remember the two conflicting moral worlds we were talking about?). In time, I grew to believe that he had a lucky star protecting him, and one day I shared this belief with a friend of mine. His response took me by surprise.

"Vassilis, it's you who has a lucky star that doesn't let you stoop to getting revenge. You're not destined to take a human life. At least not like this. Stop bothering with him. Don't give his life more importance than it deserves".

A very convenient belief ... but still, not a fair one!

A TOUR OF GREEK HELLHOLES

The snitch

At the break of dawn, in the middle of the summer of 2001, they put me in a prison bus. I didn't know where they were taking me. I didn't have any pending court cases so it was a one-way journey. At the time, I didn't know the reason I was being transferred; only later would I learn. A nightmare …

Over the previous few months I had begun planning an external attack on the prison, with the aid of partners who wished to be part of my liberation. Among them, having a secondary role, was Ben (of Albanian origin) with whom I had lived for a long time in Korydallos' 'A' wing. Spending time with him over several months, I got the impression he was a nice guy. That is why I kept in touch with him after he was released. And also because, as he was leaving, he told me to count him in if I ever planned to break out. When my partners needed another person, for a secondary role in the plan, I pointed them to Ben, who at the time was robbing banks in Athens. Additionally, I was told he was quite competent in all kinds of operations. As it turned out, he was good at other things too.

Well, this nice young lad had some hidden talents which he had kept to himself. One of these was that, aside from bank robberies, he also sold and did coke. When they caught him with his merchandise on him, and he was convicted of the bank robberies he had done, he made a deal with them. He offered to show them Passaris' hideout and reveal my future plans if they stopped the prosecution and set him free. The heads of the Hellenic Police, as was expected, agreed to it at once. Two weeks after I was transferred, a failed operation to capture Passaris at his hideout took place. He managed to escape, yet they arrested Dimitris, the owner of the house, whom I coincidentally knew and was in almost daily contact with.

About a year later, this holy child, Ben, returned to 'A' wing of Korydallos Prison, where we had first met. Coincidentally, because of a court hearing, I had been transferred from Diavata Prison where I was, to Korydallos' "E" wing.

The reason he had once again found himself in 'A' wing is very telling of dealings between the police, the judiciary, and snitches, all of who take advantage of legislative monstrosities to legitimise their impunity, in the name of crime-fighting. Ben's frequent meetings with the Hellenic Police, informing them on bank robberies, among other things, and allowing them to award many gold stars and credits to whoever their leaders wished, made him feel invincible. He got overconfident, beginning to rob a different bank branch every fortnight.

His protectors couldn't tolerate his antics any longer, as it made them accomplices. They sorrowfully watched their own child on CCTV footage, gun in hand, robbing banks in Attica, knowing they'd have to cover for him if they wished to have any more successful operations against crime. But this was overstepping the bounds of tolerance. Having had enough, and fearing that their naughty chosen one might cause worse mayhem than even Passaris had, they picked him up and dropped him at the border (nobody is irreplaceable). Who cares about the twenty-five or so armed bank robberies he did in the country? They'd find someone else to pin them on.

"Don't ever return, because we'll be forced to lock you up and we wouldn't want that", they told him. In other words, "you're the kind of person who can get us into trouble". They hugged, they French-kissed, and they reluctantly said goodbye. They bawled their eyes out! What can I say? A passionate love affair between the Hellenic Police and a brutal foreigner. The police do have a soft spot for foreign lovers. So many instances to recall ... all of them tearjerkers!

But this romance wasn't over yet.

Ben couldn't bear his lovers' rejection. A month later he was back in Athens, determined to win them back, even if that meant going to prison. He kept sending them sizzling-hot love notes through the surveillance cameras of banks. They pretended to be flattered by the way he was expressing his passion and his love for them, and asked him to meet, discuss, and, if possible, live together forever. So, without him realising it, he found himself deep in a pit full of snakes; the same snakes he'd so eagerly been feeding his insatiable lovers, while he was free. When, however, you play games with big snakes, they might wrap around your neck, form a noose, and strangle you.

It must have been the evening after the day he arrived in 'A' wing when an inmate opened the door of cell number ninety-eight. Aghast, he saw Ben hanging from the radiator's pipes, a deadly noose around his neck. Two fearful green eyes and a slimy forked tongue, hanging out of his mouth, led this final whirling aerial dance which was the apex of his dishonourable life. That's how secret affairs with the honourable Hellenic Police end. Many men love treason, yet nobody has ever loved a traitor.

When such a detestable creature gains your trust, it means disaster. This is the most cunning, arrogant, capable-of-anything kind of human being, and the hardest to unmask. You simply can't accept that there's such a species until it unveils itself right in front of you, and by then it is already too late. Damage is already done, in some cases with tragic consequences.

Treason has a thousand faces. I came across so many that to mention them all I would need more than one book. So I choose to mention only some of the worst. All of us who feel disgusted about treason are vertebrates, yet we still have a long way to go. I leave it up to all those for whom the subject hits close to home to self-identify, yet I don't really believe they'll ever manage to get back on their feet, because snakes simply don't have any.

Corfu Prison

I won't describe the medieval hellhole of Corfu; better authors have already done that. Never before had I been to that prison. The only things I knew, I had been told by other inmates. What was burned into my mind was when there was an uprising there (circa 1996, when I was a fugitive).* The prison was burnt to the ground and the ministry had decided to shut it down for good. It sent prison busses to transfer the inmates to other prisons, yet the guards, most of whom were from — and lived on — the island, had other plans. They locked the doors, refusing to hand over the inmates, whom they had already beaten hard after the uprising because they feared they'd lose their jobs. More police arrived at the scene, finally managing to open the door of the prison. TV crews were recording and broadcasting the charming scenes that were taking place at the main entrance of the correctional institution. Exhausted from the lengthy uprising and the subsequent beatings, the inmates were being dragged around by the prison officers who were trying to get them back inside and the cops who were trying to get them out. This contest of who would manage to pull inmates the longest was won by the prison officers (one has to fight to win) and their medieval principality is still operating to this day.

I was thinking about all this when I entered their miserable stone dungeon. As I was searched, some prison officers found the opportunity to remind me where I was.

"This is not Korydallos Prison, Palaiokostas. This is Corfu Prison" they announced to me, with chauvinist magniloquence.

"You don't say! Give me some time, and we'll see", I thought. Yet I didn't say anything. I never started a conversation with the living obstacles I came across; that's life, that's how they make a living. Only when you perceive them as such, as living obstacles, do they gain some value; it's to them that we owe our victories and our experiences. What would life be without some obstacles? A dead-silent cardiograph. I had just begun to get used to living there when they loaded me on a prison bus and, accompanied by many police vehicles, sent me to another new residence, Diavata Prison.

Diavata: torturers and fascism

Diavata was known for torturing its inmates, but it wasn't the first time I'd been there. While at Korydallos Prison, I had been transferred many times to Thessaloniki to be present at court hearings. The prisoner transfer division thought I was too dangerous to be kept in house so this prison "accommodated" me. At the time it was being run by a vicious trio: a warden, a director, and a state attorney, all of whom were the epitome of fascism. They had beaten up a lot of people. Torturing and beating inmates as a means of correction was a daily routine, and there had been many complaints, but none ever got beyond the prison walls. After all, these people stood no chance; the prison's public

---

*   Mostly in Greek of course. The prison is a 19th century relic of British construction, based on Jeremy Bentham's "panopticon" design — five wings jutting out from a central rotunda with an inspection house at the centre giving views of the entire facility. HMP Pentonville is of a similar type. The 1996 riot was perhaps the most infamous in modern Greek history, with 44 prisoners escaping.

prosecutor was said to participate in the beatings (literally) and force female inmates to do him sexual favours in return for granting them furloughs, which they were entitled to by law (there were complaints by female inmates, but they were never brought before the court).

While visiting the prison, they'd illegally keep me in solitary confinement. They'd open the door of my cell each morning, allowing me to walk down a relatively long hallway; the same thing would happen each afternoon. One night, way past midnight, and while I was asleep, the door opened. Nitsos entered, obviously drunk, accompanied by three or four other people.

"What's up, Palaiokostas? Have you heard about me?"

"Oh, I've heard about you ..."

"Nice things or bad?"

"It depends on how one perceives those two notions".

His mental world, trapped within the prison walls, didn't allow him to engage in such a conversation. After all, he had been drinking. The cogs stuck, he gave up. He stared at me for a while, as though looking at a species utterly foreign to him, having no clue how to handle it. Trying to cope with his mental defeat, he gave a stupid smile to his entourage of admirers.

"I told you! He's heard about me", he stuttered loudly. "You should know that nobody has broken out of this prison, and for as long as I'll be warden here, it is not going to happen" he continued, determined to defend the underworld of which he had been given charge.

Without waiting for my response, he exited the cell, followed by his entourage. This guy, who was paid (I think he still is) by Greek citizens, would send inmates to the guardroom with little or no reason at all. He'd beat the crap out of them until they spat and peed blood, throwing them a rope noose and urging them to hang themselves during the night, because the next day would be even worse. Then he would lock them up, leaving them alone to decide their own fate. All this in cooperation with the warden, the state attorney and, ultimately, the ministry itself. The horrible nightmares of inmates guaranteed the blissful sleep of peaceful citizens.

But if you pee in the sea, you'll find it on your plate ...

Democracy was indeed restored, but the methods used by the Junta still prove useful from time to time. God forbid we allow our experience to go to waste. No knowledge is without use. So don't think that in this faux democracy torturers are dead. No. They're throwing a party in democracy's own backyard, and everything's on the house. They always reign supreme, just as those in power desire, looking shocked only when (very rarely), such incidents become known.

Human beings' deep-seated need to torture their fellow people is not eradicated with pompous announcements about the arrival of democratic ideals and other bullshit. We all harbour a torturer in a dark secret corner of our soul; a torturer who never misses an opportunity to discreetly show: in one's gaze, expression, speech, sorrow, joy, bliss, deprivation ... always omnipresent, always with a bat in hand. And this perverse human being doesn't distinguish between a political activist, a bank robber, a thief, a drug addict, a homosexual, a prostitute, a wife, a child, an elderly person, a worker etc. To such people, what's most important is staying true to their perverse nature. Being torturers. A fixed universal value that can take the form of a State and lead whole generations into bankruptcy when it gets out of hand and grows out of proportion. Poverty is the worst form of violence, as Gandhi would say. All kinds of poverty, I would add to that.

That's why no torturer has ever been punished in this land. Because the State itself is the cruellest torturer of its citizens. All those who dared punish torturers are still in prison. The shameless guardians of makeshift, decadent political systems must learn that democracies can't be imposed. And they can't operate with deprived, deceived, marginalised, and scared citizens either. True democracies don't force people to become addicted to their lowest instincts, turning them into subhumans because they prove easier to control. Instead, they recognise and accept their uniqueness. They give them social standing, securing their dignity, their freedom, their self-direction, all of which are essential factors towards their active participation in democratic life. No society can operate democratically when it's being hunted by the blood-thirsty vampire of an everyday life that deifies lies, money, and deep stupor. Neither can its citizens ever feel free, surrounded by hungry packs of fears ...

There has never been a remotely real democracy in the history of modern Greece that would justify the use of the term "restoration". The handling of Greek people's votes by all sorts of charlatans was named democracy. A fraud that has mostly managed to keep citizens passive inside this fallacy. This way, a species of hyper-deceitful politician and a species of feckless, naïve citizen were formed, giving this relationship of interdependence the archaistic name "democracy". This is no different from the sign of a Greek restaurant, named "PERIKLIS"* by its crafty owner to attract more customers. Sacred symbols sacrificed in the name of get-rich-quick schemes.

The State's harshness against a significant portion of its citizens, which is expressed through the way justice is served, and the utter disinterest in, the consent even, of law-abiding citizens to the maintenance of a medieval imprisonment system based on the torturing of their fellow people, are inextricably linked to everything Greek people live through today. I dare say that they're some of their leading causes. I will only mention one of the many consequences, which is deeply rooted in these behaviours and methods, in the neo-fascism that knocks on the door of Greek people and soon will break it down, bursting into people's everyday lives.

If in times of "peace" you leave even one inmate at the mercy of the unaccountable State suppression system, one day a shouting order of bewildered humanoids will jump in front of you and you will wonder where the heck they came from. Inevitably, you will re-enter a war against them, which will bring you back to a primitive state. Even if you win the battle, you'll feel defeated because

---

*   An intentional misspelling of the name "Pericles"

you allowed this war to be fought again. Fascism was only recently acknowledged by the State, when it began walking the streets with its hood off, a Swiss knife in hand; when the State's convenience and its interests began to be threatened. The State is unable to look any further than that.

Listen, scribes and Pharisees,* fascism didn't suddenly emerge like a charming mermaid out of the Aegean Sea. It incubated and jumped like a repulsive zombie out of the manure you've been accumulating unblushingly in Greek society for more than fifty years now. Fascism lived inside you, in your guts; it's your perverted, deformed child, which none of you wants to recognise, hypocritically dumping its paternity on society.

"They're corrupt, they have a short memory, they live in oblivion, they didn't learn from the past, they don't stand up for themselves ..." people hear you criticising them! When it was your unwholesome and vile caste who spent half a century building a democracy of fools. You were keeping people sedated and muzzled, making sure that they have a short memory, that they live in oblivion, that they don't recognise their past, and that they don't stand up for themselves. The only thing you allowed them was to excel at bootlicking and dirty tricks. That's what you want the people to be, you bloodthirsty leeches: blood-donating backs, on which you can throw your leech parties and then add insult to injury. The many years I have spent in prison, often visiting police stations and courtrooms, are an undeniable testimony to all the things I'm saying.

Blood! On the floor, the walls, the dirty blankets; blood everywhere. Faces swollen, bruised, and deformed from severe injuries. Tortured bodies, curled up inside sheets for weeks, unable to even use the bathroom on their own — stacked up souls, abandoned in chambers, cells, holding cells. Being transferred in trucks, treated worse than animals, with no future, with no hope. The legislator is harsh, the judge inhuman. Both convinced that human hope can't bloom without fear and pain in one's soul, they'd brandish the cold, steel axe of justice over peoples' heads, getting so much pleasure out of it that it makes you detest human civilisation and its accomplishments.

It was 1986 or 1987, under the government of Andreas Papandreou. In a military camp at Sérres, where I stayed for part of my military conscription, behind the camp commander's office (I visited him often because of my insubordination) there was a large, well-maintained framed photo of the Greek dictator Papadopoulos. There was another smaller framed photo of the well-polished cock on the 21st of April.** Along with the captain and several lieutenants, all of whom were consumed with the same dictatorial emotions (all of them openly voted for the far-right political party National Political Union), they formed a fascist military set. All serving soldiers who were proven to have the same beliefs were awarded military conscription exemptions, daily permission to leave the camp, many days off etc.

---

*   A religious reference: in the New Testament Jesus criticises the Pharisees and their scribes for hypocrisy and perjury.
**   The Junta was formed when a Brigadier-General and two colonels, including Papadopoulos who became de facto dictator, mounted their military coup on April 21st, 1967.

Having finished my mandatory army service, I visited many police stations. And there, I'd always hear words of praise for that seven-year period, accompanied by the usual nostalgic sigh: "Oh, where is a man like Papadopoulos when you need one!" Since then, I'd always come across the fascist gaze of the dictator in laws voted by the parliament, in the way politicians exercised their power, in the fiery speech of the paid rabble-rousing journalists, in the judges' verdicts, in the guns of the police, in the prison officers' batons. I saw the swastika symbol drawn with the journalist's ink, and the Junta's bird symbol jumping out of the journalists' mouths. I saw it fluttering and twittering happily, following the flow of their speech as they used their tele-fascist whips to mercilessly slash the Greek viewer's tormented thoughts.

The State is a continuum, so is masked fascism. Because the transitional government never bothered to stamp it out. On the contrary, they operated as though they were conquerors, having invaded and occupied a foreign country. Seizing power, they pinned up a bright sign that said "democracy", and everything else remained the same. They used to their advantage the finely tuned repressive network set up by the Junta to control the citizens and isolate all truly progressive fighters (those who really fought against the Junta and fascism), because they saw them as adversaries, as obstacles to their plans.

In a democracy that cites the constitution but uses it as a weapon of repression on the same terms and with the same motives as a Junta, and where society's problems are solved with the extremely conservative and corrupt judges' choppers as well as the whip of the sadistic repressive apparatus, fascism itself isn't at the gates but already inside, because it never actually left. Maintaining secret schools of fascism inside the judiciary, the police, the military, and the correctional bodies, as well as in the whole citizen-repression apparatus, fascism was also preserved in the hearts of a large portion of the public. It is a devious, extremely infectious, and highly contagious virus which infects people's psyches. It feeds on hatred and, under certain circumstances, it replicates at an alarming rate, infecting the whole population. The accumulated, though justified, contempt in the souls of the citizens for the way the elected politicians of the country manage the parliamentary system, was the best and warmest nest for it to lay its fascist eggs. Eggs from which hatred hatches in the shape of a snake. That very same snake has found a way to express itself, intending to seize power. To govern with much hate.

A soul governed by hate is just a sick soul; many souls governed by the same hatred generate the danger of fascism. The most inappropriate reaction of the people against the unjust, indifferent, corrupt, arrogant, and authoritarian administrators of the State is to become themselves full of fascist hate. This is coming from the mouth of a man who has every reason to hate everything and everyone.

Many are to be held responsible for maintaining, breeding, and spreading neo-fascism. First and foremost, all those who managed the political landscape after the Junta and until today. They are the same people who sidelined the phenomenon with the same weapon: their own constitutional fascism. The colonels had military laws. The democrats have antiterrorist laws. The dictators had the Greek Military Police (EAT-ESA). The democrats have the Units for the Reinstatement of Order (MAT), the Special Anti-Terrorist Unit (EKAM), the Rapid Reaction Force (DELTA), the Motorcycle Police (DIAS) and the Crime Prevention and Suppression Unit (OPKE). During the Junta we had the events of Athens Polytechnic University. Democracy has had cases such as those of Alexandros Grigoropoulos, Avgoustinos Dimitriou, the beaten-up robbers of the Velvento robbery, torturing inmates to death, Iakovos Koumis, Stamatina Kanellopoulou, Michalis Kaltezas. So many to recall.* The two sides fight violent, daily battles to claim supremacy in the war of attrition. All this with the same arguments and the same goal: order and security as a means of guarding democracy.

Yet now that genuine fascism is snowballing,** threatening to overpower the faux one, they fight against it by adopting its ideas! It's more convenient for them to transform into real fascists, as long as they control the distribution of power and secure their interests! After all, they don't know — nor do they have — a different way; their faux democracy is, in any case, a bankrupt sham. It doesn't have solid foundations. Their only choice is to solemnly re-serve their reheated shit on a luxurious porcelain plate. Lest the nagging people starve and cause them any inconvenience.

What saddens me is the parliamentary left-wing party's attitude, which has (or so they say) first-hand knowledge of what fascism means. Throughout my detainment in Greek prisons I never saw a delegation of left-wing parties visiting detention facilities to discover the real problems of the inmates and how they experience their incarceration. The executives of the formerly revolutionary left-wing parties that now rest on their laurels don't care about today's prisons. Accompanied by TV crews and great hypocrisy, they often visit places of exile where fighters had been imprisoned and tortured (if they were alive, they'd spit right in their faces), to reminisce about past glories.

"We fought, and we keep on fighting for a sacred, noble cause", they scream. Ah, diddums.

If this political approach isn't their indirect assent to the torturing of all those who don't fight for "sacred causes", then what is it? Since the inmate doesn't

---

*   The Athens Polytechnic Uprising was the catalyst for the collapse of the Junta, and the university retains an iconic reputation for resisting police incursion. The police murder of 15-year-old Grigoropoulos sparked the 2008 Greek riots which remain a high point in 21st century anarchist street resistance. Dimitriou was a famous police brutality case where two officers were jailed and six cleared of beating a student. The 2013 Velvento case saw police torture eight anarchist bank robbers so badly that Amnesty International got involved. Koumis, Kanellopoulou and Kaltezas were workers and protesters beaten and shot by the MAT in 1980 and 1985, dying of their injuries — they are held up as martyrs by the Greek anarchist movement.
**   At the time of writing Greek fascist party Golden Dawn was making significant gains — it had seats in parliament from 2012 to 2019. Its vote collapsed following both New Democracy's political resurgence and shift rightwards and a five-year trial which convicted 37 of Golden Dawn's leading members as being part of a criminal organisation.

espouse left-wing beliefs, it serves them right. They deserve a good beating. Left-wing parties don't bother with heathens!

I know, I know ... the two eras and their respective stakes can't be compared. Of course they can't be compared, because today they're not the ones being hunted and imprisoned. Some other people are. After all, I've never heard a leftist talk about abolishing prisons. Prisons don't interest them at all if the prisoners aren't leftists or communists! I don't know if you get it, left-wing gentlemen, having entered parliament and making yourselves and your flocks comfortable. You were and still are members of the parliament. You had, and still have responsibilities. Even more so because you're leftists. Many of you are now even governing the country. Who would have thought this would happen! Make sure that you don't go down in history as the leftist cleaners who eagerly took on the task of cleaning the piles of garbage resulting from half a century of wild partying, because of which Greek citizens became impoverished, and then hand the keys back to the worst revellers. Those happy-go-lucky ones, who will revive their dictatorial feast in that famous entertainment venue known as the Hellenic Parliament, where the drums and the violins of the constitution of Greece will play enthusiastic democratic tunes. Oh, fellow Greeks ... though you're sharp when it comes to inessential matters, you're really thick when it comes to those things that actually matter.

To those inquiring minds who can take the pressure and suspect that whatever I can't clearly express here flows underneath my words, clear as water, I say this: the detestable dictator pardoned his would-be assassin. At the same time, he himself died in prison without asking for mercy. The pillars of the constitutional State under the rule of law only pardon their own crimes, which serve the earthly interests of their clan and assure themselves posthumous recognition. Their blood-stained rhomphaia* awaits all the rest.

Who's who.

Improved squalor is still squalor

"Life" inside the Diavata tomb continued on. An overcrowded prison where no newspapers or other print media were allowed; where you couldn't order fruit and groceries, nor was your family allowed to bring some to you when they came to visit, although not even starved pigs could eat the prison food. Where they allowed only one phonecard per week per inmate, for them to communicate with the outside world using the only two payphones in a prison with a hundred and fifty inmates. These and other innovative methods meant to improve the inmates' living conditions were left behind by the aforementioned fascist trio, with the full knowledge and support of the Ministry of Justice, even if, pressed by constant complaints and to clear themselves, they did eventually decide to replace them.

---

*   The rhomphaia was a close-combat blade used by the Thracians. Slightly curved, it attaches to a short pole, placing it somewhere between a sword and a spear.

This time around however I met a new trio of worthies. The public prosecutor, the warden, and the director were mild-mannered and understanding. I stayed in that prison for almost a year and not once did I notice an inmate being mistreated. Still, what's the point when the previously enforced conditions still existed? Those conditions were themselves torture, not just mistreatment. And yet, when judges announce their verdicts, they don't mention that the prison sentences they so lavishly hand out would be accompanied by constant torture. I'm not exaggerating; my family guaranteed better living conditions for the livestock in our village during the 1970s. Even more so, we loved them, and we cared for them.

I had no intention of obsessing about the prison and our living conditions there, something that would move me away from my goal. I didn't care whether the coffin I was forced to live in was built of fibre boards or of rosewood. This information proved useful only when viewed as a means of achieving my goal. On the other hand, I felt shame as I watched the species to which I belong, humans. Perpetrators and victims, both being the same kind of zombie. The victims, dragging themselves around in dead rooms hoping they'd get a second chance in their already messed up life and the perpetrators, twisting the rusty knife in the festering wound of the formers' ridicule. A solution, I think, would be for the victims to cut the perpetrators' long arms and escape from these dead rooms. They owe their own human dignity as much, even if a judge would later convict them (which he would). Man's hope is a miserable oppressor, worse than the most bloodthirsty jailer who holds it in his hand as bait. And only those special ones can stand up, cut off its head and drink its blood in a wine glass.

There was no way I would capitulate as long as this shameful situation was still going on. For me it wasn't a simple reaction — driven by personal aesthetics — against everything I saw happening around me; I fundamentally differed with it, as I had a more profound need to protect human existence from its own abasement. That's why I postponed my plans for a while, to attend to the affairs of the living dead. I asked to see the director and the warden. They agreed to see me at once. I was upfront with them.

"You either improve our living conditions or transfer me to a different prison immediately. Or else there'll be trouble", I said to them.

They replied that it wasn't up to them to send me away. And that they were trying their best to improve the living conditions and yet they didn't get any funding from the ministry etc.

"Who's paying those crews that have been working day and night, not letting us get any sleep?" (Since I had arrived, the prison's interior had been turned into a construction site by crews of blacksmiths and electricians fortifying it with electric barred gates and surveillance cameras).

"You know the answer, Vassilis! You know the only thing they care about is that you don't break out. When they fear you, they put their hand in their pocket, but when anything else is concerned, other troubles both employees and inmates face, they don't give a damn. Be patient, we intend to try and make things better".

"If you indeed have such intentions, call the Hellenic Telecommunications Organisation right now and ask them to place ten payphones in each ward. Allow inmates to have more phonecards so that they're able to contact their relatives and lawyers. This way they'll stop hanging about at the queue for hours, beating each other over who will get to use the phone first. You should also lift the ban on newspapers and groceries and open a canteen. You need no money for all this, they're all immediately feasible. It's just a matter of will".

In two weeks, my requests were met. The living conditions became a bit more bearable. Most inmates didn't benefit from them however — because of their financial hardships, the only food they could get was that given for free at the prison. Under pressure, the catering manager and the cook were fired, and thus the food became a bit better.

Upheaval and a food strike

It was the end of the summer of 2002. There was an intense heatwave — a real inferno. The inmates, crammed between sizzling concrete walls, were moaning because of the unbearable heat. The minors, who were housed in the middle floor, in a separate wing, sent me a letter in which they described the muggy conditions in their cells, due to overpopulation and the heatwave, since they didn't even have a fan. They wrote to me that they were willing to go on a hunger strike within the day and they wanted to learn what the grown-ups' intentions were. The children were willing to do what the adults ought to have done first.

When children ask for your help, there is no excuse to refuse it. I sent them a letter telling them to leave it to me; that I would take care of it, that they shouldn't inform the prison's administration of their intentions before they hear back from me, and that they should trust me. At once, I swung into action. I gathered in my cell all those who had the most influence with the inmates to read them the letter I had received, telling them: "It would be a shame if young children go on a hunger strike for problems that mostly affect us, while we look the other way. Either way, we're going to have to follow suit. So, to avoid being dragged into a situation we can't control, we should decide the details of this attempt of ours and make our requests to the administration of the prison".

They all agreed that we shouldn't hunker down and do nothing. Assessing the morale of the inmates (which was weak), we decided that our requests had to be relevant to our living conditions. We'd set off a chain reaction. For starters, we'd begin an abstention from prison food, and then we'd refuse to enter our cells. Within an hour, all the wings were ready to go. In each wing, three men were put in charge, one Pontic, one Albanian, and one Greek, to guarantee better coordination and cohesion between the inmates.

We drafted a text, summarising our most essential requests; I took it and walked to the wing's barred gate. I asked to see the guard on duty. He came, and I gave it to him, telling him:

"Don't bother bringing food, because no one will take it".

He panicked. He accused us of targeting him, and that was why we were beginning the abstention on his watch. Everyone has their own problems!

"I'll bring the food, I have to", he said in despair.

"I know. I just thought I'd inform you".

Not an hour had gone by, and they summoned me to the gate. It was the warden.

"What happened, Palaiokostas? Who wrote these requests?"

"I did, but none of them really concern me. I only have one grand request ..."

He tried to smooth talk me out of it, saying that all requests would soon be met etc. Seeing there was no use, he changed his tune.

"I was born in this prison; I know it better than anyone else. It's a prison for those awaiting trial. Everyone is waiting for their trial hoping they'll be released. Every day we have about ten to fifteen releases, you hear them yourself from the loudspeakers. This won't get you anywhere, you're trying in vain. You'll figure that out on your own when the food arrives. Most of them will go to grab a bite".

Although I had ordered all those responsible for coordinating the wings to not obstruct but instead urge the elder and the suffering inmates to get food, not a single inmate went to get any, something that truly surprised me. The next day, early in the morning, the prison's state attorney arrived at the barred gate, holding a microphone. With an air of absolute authority, he pretended to address all inmates, saying:

"Those responsible for the upheaval must put an end to it right now, or else they will be prosecuted to the fullest extent of the law. The administration will not allow anyone to disrupt the state of normalcy within the prison ... blah ... blah ..."

Well, well, look what great things this holy State is teaching us. Normalcy is the torturing of inmates; disruption is the attempt to open a skylight so that ray of sunshine can reach your soul and you can get some clear air in your lungs.

As it happened, most ground floor inmates were in the corridor of the wing, discussing the events; I was among them. Hearing the arrogant public prosecutor's threats, they all turned to look at me and see how I'd react. Without thinking I made a conductor's gesture, and suddenly all inmates joined in a harmonious, loud booing, which resounded throughout the whole prison. Like a lousy dog scolded by its owner, with his tail between his legs, the public prosecutor was quick to return to his fowled nest. They had no intention to let up on us though. After a while, as I was reading my newspaper sitting on the white plastic table in front of my bed, a guard entered my cell.

"Vassilis ... the director and the warden want to know if it's safe for them to enter the wing and talk to the inmates".

"And why are they asking me?"

"Who should they ask?"

"Fine ... tell them that tourists are allowed to enter the prison. No one will harm them".

It was true that the warden at least had had no conflicts with inmates. He was free to enter the wings whenever there was a reason. During a period of unrest, however, no one can be sure. About ten minutes later, the warden and the director were standing outside my cell, ready to lecture the crowd of inmates who had gathered around them, prepared to listen to the great things they had to tell us. Every so often, some inmate would come to let me know how the conversation was progressing until the prison officer who had come before returned to my cell.

"Won't you come out and talk?" he asked me quite puzzled.

"Why should I? There are already so many inmates out there".

"Who? The junkies?"

"See? They're doing fine! Junkies can become quite vocal when they feel they can trust someone. Don't underestimate anyone in this life, especially junkies. They're just strayed fighters, whose enemy had been hidden from them and they end up fighting their own selves".

"They came for you. They're waiting to talk to you, to end this", he said and left.

Just in time two guys I trusted entered my cell.

"Vassilis, come outside because those fuckers are seconding the administration and they're influencing the inmates".

"Those fuckers" were none other than dealer-junkies collaborating with the administration. The dirty right-hand men every administration has at their disposal in prisons where drug usage is off the charts. More than a few times, inmates' rebellions were ended because of them. Because, in any case, the intense needs of the body are a priority. A thirsty man will deify anyone who'd give him a drop of happiness, not giving a damn about universal morals. They're of no practical use in arid areas. They wouldn't even care about their incarcerated comrades' struggles. The moment I got out, they ran away, back to their lair.

After an hour of fierce debating with the "tourists", we agreed that two other inmates should accompany me, as representatives of the largest foreign communities, to visit the other wings. We would establish a committee that would represent all inmates and their requests at an impending meeting with the administration. We also agreed that the warden would come with us to open the wings' doors, but he'd stay outside until each session had finished.

First we visited the minors' wing. We weren't allowed to enter, and I had no reason to insist. The young lads were excited to see us. They were proud that all this had started from them; especially now that they were seeing the warden, his head low and keys in hand, accompanying us, a mere extra in all this. They jumped on the barred gate and began talking to me, all at once. I couldn't understand any of them. They had never seen me before, yet they somehow knew it was me. I gestured to them to be quiet.

"Is someone collaborating with the administration?" I asked them playfully.

No response.

"Who isn't collaborating with the administration?"

They all raised their hands, laughing and cheering.

"Do you have a leader?"

They all turned and looked at a young lad, who didn't seem at all like a leader. Yet armed with the courage and the conviction of a young man who desires to seize back control of his life from those who dominate him, he stepped forward.

"Open it for him, Ilias ..."

"I can't do that. It's prohibited by regulation. A minor in an adult wing? That's unheard of!"

"Come on, we all grew up being around adults. You're an adult too, and you enter their wing. I don't think he's in more danger with us than he was with you. After all, I'll look after him".

He opened the door, and the young lad proudly joined us. In about an hour, we visited all the wings. All the inmates believed that we'd started our strike quite abruptly. There was no time to organise properly for a longer struggle. Some inmates had a few supplies, but they had already handed them out, and they wouldn't last for more than a couple of days. The protest would inevitably turn into a hunger strike. I had many reasons to disagree with this way of making demands. I prefer for the lives of those on the other side to be at stake and not mine.

Thinking that the administration would agree to most of our requests, asking for time to see them through so that the uprising would stop, we decided it would be wiser to play along. That way we'd have enough time to organise better and come back stronger and with greater conviction, with the administration now fully responsible for not delivering on their promises. We'd discuss everything again after the meeting, to make a final decision.

The meeting was planned for that same afternoon. After sitting around a large table in the guardhouse, the state attorney addressed me directly, obviously targeting me.

"Palaiokostas, a wet man does not fear the rain, yet I'd be careful if I were you. Stay soaked for long, and you'll catch a cold!"

"Oh, how poetic, sir! You're scaring me! I got the chills!"

"Your sentence and your name may allow you to joke around, but you don't have the right to drag the other inmates down with you", he said.

"We didn't come here to listen to your divisive rhetoric. We came to discuss our requests. If you have no intention to hear us out and try to work things out, then we'll return to our wings and continue what we started ..."

"That's why we called you here. To solve any problems that might exist. But that can't happen if we're being threatened. The administration has every intention to ..."

In this spirit, we sat there for about an hour-and-a-half, bargaining. In the end, they told us that the next day the secretary-general of the ministry would visit the prison and that he had expressed an interest in doing us the honour of meeting with our committee. Progress! That was altering our plans. We'd wait for that meeting before deciding on our next steps. The ministry delegate did indeed come the following day, but he made a mistake. Instead of meeting with the inmates' committee, he met with the dealer-junkies working with the administration. What a family. The ministry's firm determination ripped out the cancer. They solved the problem once and for all with a single transfer order. At the break of dawn, the day after that, the whole committee was loaded on a prison bus, to be scattered in different prisons.

Malandrino Prison

Next stop ... Malandrino! The ministry's brand new pride and joy.* It had been operating for some months, and the ministry aspired to make it a place all outcasts feared. It was the beginning of an ambitious project for the correctional system's future over the next fifty to a hundred years. Their only real concerns were to line their pockets by overpricing projects, secure more votes among the inhabitants of the surrounding areas (presenting the construction of prisons as development projects that would provide employment opportunities, boosting local economies) and to seclude all those who had broken laws at the corners of Greece, as though they had the plague.

This genius plan of the progressive minds of the Ministry of Justice resulted in inmates just waiting for their release, drowning their unbearable daily tedium in drugs, as well as in uncontrollably barbaric administration-cliques, whose responsibilities began and ended with maintaining the security of the prison, in exchange for money and a few favours ... real humanity would have to wait. This is such a small country for such great barbarism.

I, being naïve, wonder how those in charge, instead of spending taxpayers' money filling small prisons, haven't thought of building two large complexes near the two biggest cities. Two complexes that would house a health centre, a rehab, and classrooms, all staffed with trained personnel (doctors, psychologists, social workers, teachers etc.). That would offer activities and technical training to ensure the vocational rehabilitation of inmates, as well as facilities for the inmates to work out and let off steam. Complexes that would be easily accessible by car for the inmates' lawyers and families, and staff supervised by public prosecutors for any misconduct, torturing of inmates etc. And all the rest could become open working prisons, primarily of an agricultural type. There, inmates could serve the rest of their sentences in a state of day-to-day temporary release and actively participate in special agricultural programs, focusing on environmental awareness, the balance between human and nature etc. Their dirty argument is that the European Union allows (it doesn't dictate) that a prison may be constructed in any geographic region that has an appeal court. They couldn't let such an opportunity go to waste! They filled the country with human dumps. For them, these humans are plain rubbish outside their house's front door which they have to throw somewhere ... and we have life sentences coming out of our ears.

It's an oxymoron, Palaiokostas making suggestions as to where and how prisons should be constructed.

My former honest life does not leave any room for misinterpretation. The whole repressive system knows my opinion on the denial of a human's freedom. They've had first-hand experience of it. These are not suggestions but ironic, rhetorical questions based on their own ideals, not mine. My intention is to demonstrate

---

* Nicknamed The Alcatraz of Greece and built high in the mountains, Malandrino is a high-security prison completed in 2001. Touted as the most advanced facility in the Greek justice system with advanced anti-riot design, both Nikos and Alket have previously escaped.

the sadistic face of a State that emphasises its democratic ideals every chance they get, yet when faced with a dilemma between freedom, humanity and hope, and inhumanity, repression and submission, its legislative body hypocritically prefers the latter. They stand firm when it comes to egalitarianism, all the "ideals", and warn about the danger those face from anyone who shows disbelief, doubts them verbally in public or most importantly, acts rebelliously. Yet the kind and the quality of a regime isn't defined by the legislative process, but by the legislation itself. By their aims and what they bring upon society as a whole. Terrorism, organised crime, hooded men, destabilisation, fighting enemies of democracy ... that's their rhetoric for justifying horrible deeds.

There is no more blunt an example of the mentality of the majority of those gaining power from the Greek people's votes than that of Tsochatzopoulos*. This socialist jellyfish, incarcerated in 2013, repeatedly decried the wretched conditions of his detention. He denounced the system that he himself had nourished for decades when he felt its stinking breath down his own neck. He was protesting about the best version of detention the Greek correctional system offered and in which he lived, and about the best legal treatment which might be enjoyed from his own State. He didn't even say "we" — such was his sense of socialist solidarity — lest he be thought of as one of the incarcerated pariahs. This chosen man! This superior man! This politician! He, who passed every repressive, terrorist, deadly, sickening bill discussed in the "temple of democracy" for his inferiors with his left hand, while he used his right hand to get whatever bribe he was offered by those who sell military equipment. The Zeybeks** are still rolling over in their graves over his crass dancing on the backs of the debilitated Greek people. This is but a small example of how professional crooks were — and still are — taking advantage of citizens' votes. Treating them like a valuable key towards personal fortune and a reliable tool which they will use to legally guarantee them impunity for their crimes against the people.

My arrival at Malandrino Prison coincided with the arrests of members of revolutionary organisation 17 November.*** My predictions about what kind of people were hiding behind the organisation's name were one hundred per cent right. Conversely, my predictions about the way they would handle their arrest were one hundred per cent wrong! It was sad ... and the worst among snitches got the chance to be vindicated. At least they didn't claim that their actions were for the citizens' greater good. Like many Greeks, I had been studying the organisation's every proclamation. I expected something more dignified from

---

* Akis Tsochatzopoulos was a co-founder and vice president of PASOK. He served as minister in various departments, including the Ministry of National Defence. He was accused of corruption scandals and got 20 years for money laundering. He was let out of prison in 2018 due to failing health and died in August 2021.
** Zeybecks were irregular fighters living in the Aegean Region during the Ottoman Empire. There is a debate over their origin, with the Greeks claiming they were Islamised Greeks while the Turks claim they were Turks. There is a dance that gets its name from them, the Zeybek dance.
*** A Marxist guerilla group, active from 1975 until shut down by police raids in 2002.

a group of armed rebels whose struggle and speech could be engraved in the consciousness of people. You wouldn't expect the defensive system of men who force ministers to the ground in the middle of Athens to collapse when they are arrested (because their offensive system was unparalleled). Koufontinas* saved the day. He alone still fights to this day to make sure the world remembers the masterpiece and not its ruin. A worthy man.

What was even sadder was that all these people who up until then had been applauding the organisation's actions, exalting it as a formidable adversary to the corrupted regime, now abandoned these men, showing them no support whatsoever. They were left to be preyed upon by the cynical and relentless repressive mechanisms, with the help of the well-fed yet always hungry and willing journalist-dogs of the system. Anyone who prays for others to do something for him deserves his fate. And when his prayers are heard, but those who are willing to do something for him meet unfortunate ends, he recedes deeper into his couch exclaiming: "Oh … those fuckers weren't careful at all. I know better, that's why I hang back!" Wait, you poor fellow, and see how safe it is to hang back. You can already feel something lurking behind you …

Women with keys and deadly marks

So I was in Malandrino Prison … and there were women there! Yes, yes, there were women, and beautiful! No, no, it's not what you think, just one of the State's novelties. Equality in repression, complicity, and stupidity, nothing more and nothing less. Women in uniform, with bunches of keys. They'd lock the doors of the cells of men twice, causing as many orgasms in the process. Female sensibility is a myth — the twists and turns of cursed fate. Right at that moment, some inmate with an Aristophanic sense of humour would always come out of the shower, and his towel would always drop by "accident".

My fellow inmates hated me. Two weeks after my arrival, a new warden arrived at the prison, and he forbade any female prison officers from entering 'A' wing. Not a single female was seen in or outside the wing. The guards must have known something. Better to be safe than sorry.

One night, no more than an hour after lights out, a crowd of employees arrived at the wing, led by Tsironis. He was a deputy warden, who had been one of Aravantinos' lackeys back at Korydallos. The reason for their after-dark invasion was to turn off a tap! Some inmate had left it turned on in the wing's laundry room. Mitsos, who was staying alone in the second cell next to the laundry room, couldn't let such an opportunity slip by. He began moaning orgasmically, as though he was having gay sex. That injured the manly pride of one of the intruders, and he started knocking on the small door of the shaft located between Mitsos' cell and the one next to it, demanding to know who was making all the noise.

---

* Dimitris Koufontina, 17N chief of operations. In 2021 he nearly died while on a 65-day hunger strike demanding a transfer to Korydallos.

Mitsos was an honourable lifer. His sentence would end sometime in 2015. During a bank robbery, the one or two million promised by Valirakis to anyone who stopped a robbery persuaded a sixteen-year-old boy to run and jump on Mitsos, who shot him and killed him (in the heat of armed robbery you don't do face control, nor do you ask for a birth certificate).

Mitsos got a life sentence, and so did the brother of the deceased. These are the results of the legal jiggery-pokery of a State which, on top of everything else, makes provisions for the vocational rehabilitation of a relative of someone who fell in battle against armed robberies. The complicit banking system applauded and accepted this law. Perhaps it even enforced it ... citizens have to know how to sacrifice themselves to safeguard the banks' profits. So the young deceased man's brother was hired by the National Bank of Greece as a guard and after a few years being on the inside, stole six and a half million euros from one of the bank's branches. Divine retribution-condemnation! Whatever the crime, whoever the criminal, the accomplice is always the same.

Mitsos couldn't let such an insult go unanswered. They dared knock on the door next to his cell, asking who did it. "I did it, you arseholes! I did it! Get on your knees so that I can fuck you! Come on, you whores! Let me fuck you! Open the door, you motherfuckers ..."

He had lost it. He was kicking the door of his cell, provoking them and swearing at them. Some of the things he said ... I'd never heard them before, nor do I dare write them down. The officers didn't dare enter — Mitsos wasn't one to be messed with. His rage could turn him into a savage beast, able to take down five or six men on his own. Tsironis, fearing the worst, bent over, stuck his head in the narrow window of the door and glowered at me, without speaking. With a single abrupt hand gesture, I made my point.

"Better go now. Take your men and leave at once!"

He followed my advice without arguing. He took his men out to the fully lit yard, in a spot where all the inmates of 'A' wing could see them. Mitsos got wind of them and unleashed a new wave of swearing at them. Tsironis once again turned to look at me. I repeated the same "get out of here" hand gesture and he at last left, humiliated. Next morning, as always, I got down to the so-called exercise room (it had no exercise equipment) first. This was, like every other part of the prison, always under the watchful eye of the guards working inside a big-brother type room, located in the main administration building. I had totally forgotten about last night's incident. Tsironis reminded me, barging into the room.

"What's up, Palaiokostas? Aren't you quite the early bird!"

"Are you watching me?"

"Whether I want to or not!"

"How come you're awake so early?"

"I wanted to discuss last night's incident!"

"What more is there to discuss aside from the fact you fucked up?"

"Was I the one who fucked up, or Mitsos who began swearing at us?"

"That served you right!"

"Is that so? I thought you were a serious inmate. I never thought you'd applaud such behaviour".

"Why did you enter the wing last night, Tsironis?"

"I won't report to anyone about my actions ... because the tap had been left running. I had to come and check what was happening".

"You don't need all these men to turn off a tap! If you can't control them, you must assume responsibility for their actions".

"You're right. But still, what if it was a trap?"

"All ifs are based on imaginary data that might lead to a fiasco, just like last night".

"Vassilis, I didn't leave Korydallos to come to Malandrino Prison for fun. I want to leave my mark on this prison".

"Tsironis, leave as many marks as you want, just make sure you don't lose your life in the process" I said, prophetically as it turned out.

Such incidents took place daily in the prison. Yet I forgot about them as soon as they were over. This little story would also have no worth whatsoever if after some years, as a fugitive once again, I didn't learn from the media that an inmate had gutted Tsironis. He had died there, inside the concrete halls of Malandrino Prison. His fellow prison officers avenged his death. They tortured his killer to death, making Tsironis' dream come true, albeit posthumously. He managed to leave his mark in human pain. All nightmares begin as dreams.

Malandrino Prison was new, and therefore one had to search to locate its weak spots. With an ingenious young man from Romania, we started looking. We had reached a satisfying stage of a risky and difficult-to-accomplish escape plan, yet they got to us first. Perhaps they got wind of something, or someone ratted us out; maybe it was just a coincidence. Either way, it was for naught and I found myself back in Corfu.

TRIALS AND JUSTICE

Leisure trips

I must mention that before my arrest in December 1999, I held a somewhat unique record. Despite being a fugitive, having a bounty on my head, having broken out of prison, convicted many times in absentia and facing all kinds of charges (bank robberies, car chases and firefights, injuring police officers, abducting a businessman to get ransom etc.) I'd never attended a court hearing, neither as a defendant nor as a mere spectator. To be more specific, I'd never stepped foot inside a court. Now, a barrage of writs of summons was being issued throughout the country, permanently threatening my personal freedom (for the time being my freedom had already been mortgaged and, as Greeks say, there's nothing more permanent than the temporary).

While I remained free, my persecutors declared me the most wanted man in the country. After being arrested and imprisoned, they proclaimed me the most likely to attempt an escape (that's what was written with big red letters on the large white folder that the officer in charge of each of my transfers received and handed from prison to prison). A trial for the most likely inmate in the whole country to attempt an escape wasn't a simple task. No, it was a great big hassle. For security reasons, all transfers were kept secret until the very last moment. Except for the officer in charge of the transfer and the warden on duty, no one else knew a thing. I realised that when, during the transfers, the escorting cops received phone calls from their relatives, asking them where they were, and they couldn't answer them.

"They haven't told us. I'll know when we get there", they'd always reply.

At five in the morning, several prison officers would unlock the door of my cell.

"Pack your things, Palaiokostas. You're being transferred".

That was it. They wouldn't tell me how, when or why. They'd stand by the open door waiting until I had packed my things, closely monitoring my every move. From the writ of summons, I could calculate where I was being transferred. I'd put the barest necessities inside a bag, and then I'd be accompanied to the gatehouse to be recorded and then searched. Afterwards, I'd board a prison bus and, in the company of several police officers and men from the Special Anti-Terrorist Unit, I'd be off to my destination, sometimes Thessaloniki, other times Yannena, or Patra, or Larissa etc. Reaching my destination, I'd be handed to the officers of the prison, they'd search me, take me inside the new prison, and place me in a cell or a chamber.

The day of the trial, the process was the same. Early wake-up, search, prison bus, police escorts, a court full of heavily armed cops etc. When the trial was over, the reverse process would begin, until I found myself back in Korydallos or whichever other prison I was living in at the time. For a single trial, I had to suffer not one but six body cavity searches. More than once there was a fight while these went on, because some weak-minded prison officer followed the fucking law to the letter, claiming he wouldn't discriminate between inmates. One time when I refused to bend over for the body search, a prison officer dropped his trousers and bent over to prove to me that what he was asking me to do wasn't that big of a deal. When inmates' arseholes are under thorough investigation as the main reason for the destabilisation of the correctional system and the system in general, society is ailing. I genuinely feel sorry for all those who envision the world's future from this perspective. Especially for those before whom many windows to this "world" are opened every day. Shame. This is a correcti-anal absurdity! This State is only consistent when it comes to such searches because it is but a mirror of the body part under investigation. They are very alike indeed ...

Predators of Justice

The duration of my sentence had already been determined from the first two or three trials and, as a result, I had no interest in all ongoing ones, making the whole back-and-forth process physically tiring, soul-crushing, and utterly pointless. This is also the reason behind my generalizing when I list sentences and trials.

Indeed, I only physically attended these trials because I was forced to. When you're enfettered continuously, attacked by flocks of insatiable, flesh-eating crows, you stop counting pecks. Preserving your mental and psychic balance comes first. During every trial, I'd simply wait patiently for the final croak of the master-crow. Guilty for that many crimes, that many misdemeanours, a total sentence of fifty-five years, adding up to a concurrent sentence of twenty years! That's how my suffering ended each time.

At some point, so as not to be utterly bored, I decided to also mentally participate in some of the trials which concerned me, and I thought were interesting from a judicial angle. I also started attending the hearings of other inmates set for the same day, trying to form an opinion on how Greek courts give justice. Not that I didn't already know or suspect.

I gained the "privilege" of attending and observing other trials because I was considered dangerous. Most times, those in charge of guarding me thought it safer for me to remain inside the courtroom until all other trials were over. So the rest of the trials also took place with the courtroom surrounded by heavily armed men from the Special Anti-Terrorist Unit. I was surprised at how shamelessly these trials took place. The judiciary, acting as a corpse cleaner, was patently and blatantly trying to bury our crumbling society's reeking hopes, murdered by the democratically elected bellwethers of institutions, pinning the murder on all kinds of offenders of its laws. Behold those to blame! They conspire against the happiness and the wellbeing of the people. They should be immediately escorted to social-waste landfill sites. The old, sound, and efficient tactics of any corrupt regime.

The courtrooms were real sacrifice chambers, with the judges assuming the role of slaughtermen, showing no mercy to their victims. Cold and indifferent, they never deviated from or questioned police charges. Their judicial monstrosities made courtrooms branches of the police, for the formal processing of pre-judged verdicts and pre-imposed sentences.

All my sentences, imposed by about twenty courts, added up to three hundred years, a hundred of which were just hot air. Meaning they gave me a hundred or a hundred and fifty more years for cases I had nothing to do with, and the remaining two hundred were the result of unconsidered verdicts and the maximum possible sentences. Accordingly, one-third of all sentenced men are innocent, the rest simply mistried. It's not a coincidence that in none of the trials I unintentionally attended did I hear the word "leniency". On the other hand, the retributive justice, the classism, the racism, and the crushing intent of their indictments were glaringly apparent. The judges' racist comments, their insults in the form of smart-ass jokes and verbal bullying of the defendants were the norm. As were the ignorant public prosecutors who, embodying the unrepentant nature of the Greek justice system, brought down a macabre curtain on every human sacrifice with pompous, sanctimonious lectures on good and evil, moral and immoral, that verged on being a tragicomedy. From experience, and now with evidence too, I can speak confidently about the criminal nature of justice. The whole justice-serving system is dipped head-high in shit.

I cite one of the many regular exchanges between the presiding judge of a court in Thessaloniki and me, when I was on trial for three armed robberies in supermarkets, in which I had no involvement whatsoever.

"Your honour, you're a jurist; you know that except for the case of a life sentence, the maximum penalty that can be served is twenty-five years. To date my sentence adds up to a hundred and fifty years (that's approximately what it added up to back then). Adding fifty more years to it won't make a change. It does, however, give me freedom to speak the truth, since you certainly won't believe that a robber can be honest, and I'm telling you I was not involved in these robberies.

"But, Mr Palaiokostas, your own partner implicates you. He has confessed you both orchestrated these three robberies. Do you admit that your co-defendant Kostas S. was, at some point, your partner?"

"I've never renounced my past yet, apart from this confession, there's no other evidence attesting to the truth of his statement".

"What reason would your partner have to implicate you?"

"I don't know that, and neither do you. Since the one implicating me isn't present, his motives for this testimony remain unknown. Tell me, really, why do you attach importance to the testimony of a disreputable man, who so blatantly falsely accuses one of his former partners?"

"I don't believe your partner, but this is a piece of evidence incriminating you and the court can't disregard it!"

"Your honour, aside from the holy bible that you consider my casefile to be, and the letter of the law, there's also common reason, to which I'm trying to wake you up. So I say again: whichever penalty your court may impose against me, it doesn't really change anything for me. My conviction will save someone else from many years in prison; I'd be doing a good deed. Why would I try to be acquitted?"

"The court is wondering the same thing, Mr Palaiokostas!"

"I don't want to be convicted of a robbery in a supermarket. To me, it's a matter of principles. I'd only enter a supermarket to buy groceries".

"So you agree that armed robberies are reprehensible acts, but you disagree only when they involve a supermarket?"

We were talking at cross purposes ... I was obviously dealing with an arsehole.

"Fine, fine, announce your verdict and be done with it".

They gave me about thirty years for the two robberies, while they acquitted me of the third, despite having the same incriminating evidence for all three of them: the same co-defendant's testimony. No logical consequence, just a simple merger. We convict you of two, we acquit you of the third, and you should be happy with that.

An all-purpose Public Prosecutor

Later, the prosecutor from this trial took up duties in Diavata Prison. Two years after that, when I was transferred there, he came to welcome me at an inappropriate moment. Every afternoon, I had a compulsive habit of walking in the prison yard, headphones on, until it closed. I always did that alone. It allowed me (escaping for a while from the daily routine of imprisonment) to meditate for a couple of hours while listening to music. Everybody knew I got riled up whenever someone came and bothered me during my walk. They'd have to have an excellent excuse to do so.

One evening, while I was strolling, lost in my musically-adorned thoughts, I felt someone tapping on my shoulder, softly but repeatedly. felt as though being woken at midnight for a graveyard shift! That was it! I felt a surge of anger race through my body!

"What the hell do you want?" I screamed, turning to face whoever was insolent enough to have overstepped the eleventh commandment. I saw a man in a suit, with grey hair, about fifty years old, with his right hand extended, awaiting a handshake, mouthing something. Behind him were the director and the warden, both also mouthing something.

I took off my headphones and returned to reality.

"Palaiokostas! I'm the prison's public prosecutor! I had served as the public prosecutor in two of your trials, here in Thessaloniki. Don't you remember me?"

"Yes, yes, he's the public prosecutor!" cried as one the other two members of this holy trinity.

I grabbed his still extended arm.

"Welcome, public prosecutor. So what brings you here?"

"I was notified that you arrived at our prison. I thought it best to come and meet you here instead of summoning you to my office".

"That was kind of you, and somewhat of a novelty, I have to admit. In which of my trials were you a prosecutor?"

"In the trial for those supermarket robberies and in one for a bank robbery near Veria".

"Oh, great! I've just met one of the men who erased thirty years off my life with two verdicts".

In the meantime, all the inmates who had been in the yard gathered around us, listening to our conversation with great interest.

"You're exaggerating. You're making things sound more tragic than they were!"

"Do you want to know what's tragic? Perfunctory trials and frivolous verdicts that destroy defendants. They are tragic! I admit that I wasn't affected by these sentences, yet if someone else was in my position, someone with no prior convictions, someone innocent, who would have the right to erase such a big part of their life? You're the ones who in cases of manslaughter assert the sanctity of human life, but you don't think twice before butchering it and throwing it to the dogs in the name of justice".

"I would be lying if I said I don't agree with you. If it was up to me, I'd let you free at once. I'm sure you pose no threat to the public. Your attitude during your trials that I attended as a prosecutor gives me the right to have a personal opinion on you. You're righteous, honest, and humanitarian. You have a strong, fully-developed personality which, in relation to your broad perspective on life, cannot be subject to any kind of correction".

"Wait a second! This sounds familiar. I've heard all this before".

"That's how my summation ended in one of your trials! You don't have to believe me, but in both trials, I suggested that you be acquitted. The others shared my thoughts on you, yet they voted guilty".

"The distance between what we believe and how we act is the tragedy of the human species. What you just said is an indirect confession that people are held in prisons, with the sole purpose of their physical extinction, something that didn't affect your conscience at all when it came to taking up your current position. And since you failed as a public prosecutor, apologise now to the inmates for the horrible conditions of their detention".

I reached my point at the right moment. He began being bombarded with questions and complaints by the dozens of impatient inmates who had long waited for this moment. I put my headphones back on and walked away, to continue what Mr Prosecutor had interrupted. The man who diagnosed that I didn't call for, nor could be subject to, correction. Perhaps it is society that needs to be corrected, to be able to accept me.

Justice on demand

Throughout human history, never did the judiciary stand by the side of rebellious and revolting people, groups, or nations that attempted (and still attempt) to establish true justice; it instead applied laws. In antiquity, it used the laws written by tyrants and emperors. In the dark Middle Ages the same. In recent history it supported totalitarian, Nazi, military, and theocratic regimes. Today, even more deeply corrupted, it applies the laws of venal politicians, working on behalf of multinational corporations, facilitating the global economy on its way towards economic totalitarianism.

A rotten political system, which bluntly disrespects the constitution and reeks of corruption, needs allies, or accomplices, to better conceal and fortify itself. It searches for and quickly finds the first and most necessary ones in the judiciary, then in law enforcement (men who are willing to kill and be killed) and so on and so forth. Slowly but steadily, it channels its rot throughout society. Citizens, without even realising it, find themselves complicit in a state of decay, lawlessness, and corruption, given that their votes are considered as a conferral of authority. This way, representative democracy becomes a weapon in the hands of clans that aim at controlling authority and how it is shared, transforming State structures into a stronghold of (officially elected) organised criminals.

Their guilt now a nose ring, and their votes a heavy chain held and controlled by this socio-political cluster's long dirty hand, the sovereign people transform into a docile Cyclops, in thrall to a globalised stupidity, artfully served as the supreme, universal commodity of the future. This way, the gigantic yet dumb mass of people, bowed and silent, are being dragged into a bleak future, because they feel and understand what is happening to them as simply their fate, rendering them unable to react.

White doves

It was February. A thick veil of snow shrouded the land of Macedonia. Because of this, I thought I couldn't be transported and my trial would be rescheduled. After all, having so many convictions already, there was no real hurry. Yet the State is all-weather; always operating. I'd forgotten that. They came at the break of dawn to remind me, with their usual underlying spite. "Palaiokostas ... you're being transferred".

A convoy of ten vehicles filled with policemen and, between them, a prison bus also swarming with heavily armed men in uniform, waited for me outside Diavata Prison destined for some town in West Macedonia. All the convoy's vehicles had chains on their tires since the snow was almost one and a half foot high. Only the main roads remained open. There was thick fog, and it was freezing. Even if they opened the truck's door for me, I couldn't possibly go anywhere with all that snow. Why so many security measures? The State works in mysterious ways ...

Inside the bus, I was surprised to find another inmate from a different wing, who told me he had a court hearing the same day in the same town. He was reasonably talkative. Willing to narrate this whole illegal struggle to me, thinking it was thrilling at the very least. Yet snitches put a stop to his emerging brilliant career, locking him up in prison. He was furious at them. He hated them. He said it again and again. Thinking that he had either been assigned to get me to talk, or was a cop pretending to be an inmate, I put on my headphones to escape his incessant babbling.

At noon we arrived at our destination. There was no prison in the area, so one of the police station's floors was configured as a prisoner transfer division, with four spacious cells to accommodate prisoners. They placed my talkative fellow traveller and me in an empty cell. After a while, a prison bus arrived from Yannena, bringing about fifteen inmates. They split them into two cells from which they couldn't see into ours. Not long after their arrival, the officer serving as chief arrived at my cell.

"What's up Palaiokostas? I hope you're not thinking of doing anything stupid while you're here! We've taken precautions".

"Don't worry officer. I haven't got anything planned. There's nowhere to go with all that snow and cold. I'll leave it for a better day".

"When I say we've taken precautions, I mean it!" he said, laughing, before continuing. "I have a man from Albania who just arrived from Yannena and is hell-bent on coming to your cell. His name is Tony. You don't happen to know him, do you? Do you want to see him?"

"I can't say for sure. Bring him here so that I can decide".

Two cops brought him before my cell. I didn't know him. He told me his name and that he brought greetings from so-and-so (he mentioned the names of five men who were highly respected among Albanian and other prisoners). I understood that these guys had sent him to me so that I'd help him with something. I didn't know what exactly, and he had no intention of telling me in front of the officers.

I took the initiative at once.

"We're ok, officer. You can put him in the cell, there won't be any problems".

"There's no way I'm doing that Vassilis. He won't come inside. If you want me to leave him here for ten minutes so that you can talk, I'll do that".

Allowing this was very human of him and he wasn't obliged to do it, so I thanked him. As soon as the officer left the first surprise came. A raging Tony began to verbally attack my snitch-stricken fellow traveller, who up until that moment hadn't uttered a single word.

"Why did you do this to me, Argiris? I trusted you, I dined at your house, I made all these gifts to your children, I knew and respected your wife, and you ratted me out at the first sign of trouble? You're a common snitch!"

I had a feeling things were about to get really interesting. I was very excited.

"Calm down Tony ... tell me what's going on".

"This traitor and I have known each other for four years, Vassilis. The last two of them we were partners in drug trafficking. I'd bring it, and he'd sell it. The last time I handed him a hundred and fifty pounds of pot, seven pounds of heroin, and about two pounds of coke.

I'd gone to Athens to buy some things I needed, and as I was returning to Albania, I was pulled over and arrested by the police, at the direction of Argiris. While I was in Athens, they had searched his house, found the drugs, and he told them that I supplied them to him. This guy is pathetic. He didn't just give them my name. He also told them where to find me, what the model of my car was. He called me himself, asking me to stop near his house on my way back, saying he wanted to talk to me about some major development. They beat me up hard, and I wouldn't confess anything. They tortured me. A year has gone by, and I've still got medical issues".

"How did you, Tony, know I'd be here for my trial?" I asked him.

"My lawyer, who's from the city, told me so. He learnt that your case is being tried on the same day. I phoned some guys from other prisons in case you could help me".

"Speak fast. How can I help you?"

"My lawyer rigs trials. If I'm acquitted, the public prosecutor and the judge will get twenty thousand euros each, and my lawyer will get as much. The only condition is that Argiris changes his testimony during his plea hearing so that the court's verdict would be justified. If you manage to convince him to state in his plea that the testimony he gave to the police was the result of physical and psychological coercion, I'll definitely be acquitted. Do whatever you can because it was his fault the cops caught him, not mine".

"Tony, I promise you nothing. All this is too sudden for me; I have to think about it before picking sides. Know, however, that I will do what I think is fair".

"Vassilis, I'd never have asked for your help if I knew you were an unjust person. I'll respect your decision, whatever it may be".

Tony shared some more information with me. He told me that apart from his trial, there was to be another, rigged for the exact same fee. It was the trial of two compatriots of his, facing similar charges. They were the first two cases for the day. Shortly, the cops came to take him away. He thanked me, bade me farewell, and I was left to think over all this information while a snitch was in my cell.

In the world of illegality, things are pretty simple when it comes to such cases. No matter what the crimes of those involved are, a snitch is always considered an abomination. They have to pay. There will be leniency only if they manage to make things right. For me, the dilemmas arising were first and foremost ethical. I was finding it hard to pick a side in a legal dispute between drug dealers given that, in any case, I disapproved of their immoral actions. What was even worse was that my involvement would facilitate a cash transaction between a drug dealer and judicial staff.

The guys who advised Tony to come to me were leaders among the Albanians in most Greek prisons. I had met them during my various tours through the country's correctional facilities. Their behaviour and their respect towards me had left me speechless. Whichever prison I was transferred to, everything was on them, as long as I was in a wing under Albanian supervision. It was the first time they had asked for a favour, and that was why it was so hard for me to turn them down. It was even harder, though, resisting the temptation to watch in real-time as "blind" lady justice threw away her balance and her sword.

Argyris, like a beaten dog, had curled up on the mattress of the concrete bed. I had no intention of going after him. I just wanted to talk to him.

"Come on, lad. Stand up and confess. You know the drill well enough. Tell me everything".

He stood up and began narrating.

"Vassilis, I was ratted out by some other guy who was like a brother to me but who ... blah, blah, blah ... who ... blah, blah, blah ..."

"Do you know how disgusting a man who hides behind his wife's skirt and invokes his children to justify his actions is? Have you ever considered what kinds of danger you are exposing them to just to save your ass? Do you think that Tony and his friends will ever let you off the hook if you don't retract? Why don't you take responsibility for your actions? Prison sentences end at some point, yet the stigma never fades. No child is proud of having a snitch as a father. No wife is either.

I told him many similar things. In the end, I promised that if he decided to retract, I'd pressure Tony into promising that he'd help his family financially. He seemed very puzzled. If there was an ounce of shame left in him, he'd make the right decision. He lay awake all night. In the morning, he announced he'd do the right thing.

The first to be transported to the courthouse were those who had arranged for their trials to be rigged. They returned after about three or four hours. The judicial staff had to make sure everything was going as agreed. The cases began being tried in their regular order and, after the witnesses for the two rigged cases had testified, the court adjourned claiming there was some kind of problem, rescheduling these two cases for the end of the day and releasing the witnesses (all of who where cops) so that they could return to their homes or posts. When, late in the night, the verdict was announced, nobody would realise what had happened because nobody would be inside the courtroom. And if some people happened to still be there, they'd be so tired that they wouldn't give a damn about the sentences.

Next it was my turn. Men from the Special Anti-Terrorist Unit and the Crime Prevention and Suppression Unit holding machine guns, bulletproof vests, full-face masks, sunglasses, and smug looks, showed up with SUVs, emergency lights, sirens — and off we went! Reaching the house of justice, cameras, reporters, plainclothes, busybodies, and runners were waiting for us. They were all mingling around on the frozen snow, and before we got inside, a handful of cops found themselves flat on their backs, holding their machine guns in their arms. A truly gut-wrenching sight. Horror in the snow! I just hoped they were insured. The whole State mechanism was trying its best to aid the judicial staff's struggle to make a living. The court resumed, and I had the privilege to watch, from up close, the innocent white doves of Themis. Radiant inside their costumes, freshly-shaved, calm, serious, above all suspicion. Only twisted minds would even dare think that these pillars of the justice institution could be dishonest. Every rational mind would feel shame at the mere thought. These decent men were unaware that I knew they'd been paid off under the table (or so I want to believe unless I'm that hopelessly innocent).

As soon as the trial process began, I asked for the TV crews to be escorted out of the courtroom. They didn't like that at all. I was spoiling their plans. They had something else in mind. They didn't go through all the trouble of throwing that welcome party out in the cold for their viewers to not see how harshly high-calibre criminals like myself were judged. They chatted silently for a while and the presiding judge, having no choice, granted my wish. Then the court designated a lawyer to represent me (because I'd never had one).

Do you want to know who that lawyer was, dear reader? The one who rigged trials, of course! That's right! So that no mistrustful fellow would think that the court favours anyone. The "kind" lawyer wanted a two-hour break so he could study the case (the longer his two cases were postponed, the better for him). I spoke before he managed to make a request.

"Relax, man. Don't take everything to heart. We improvise. Whatever you hear, whatever your process; make an oration if you like, then that's it!"

"Fine then. As you wish. You're the boss!"

"That's my boy!"

The specific case concerned a bank robbery (what else) in a small town in central Macedonia, involving four robbers. The bank's employees couldn't identify me. The clerk pointed at a different robber. The manager couldn't identify me, but he was confident it was me, forcefully adding: "Who else could it have been!" The cops' witness from the local police station, consciously lying, testified that he had seen me lurking around the bank in the days before the robbery, yet he hadn't thought of arresting me. Themis' instruments didn't think the witnesses' statements were deplorable at all, and didn't bother to pose even a single question. At the end of the day they'd score twenty grand each from Tony's case. Their minds were too occupied with that to ask any questions …

The presiding judge asked me to take the stand and enter a plea. I didn't move an inch.

"I won't apologise for anything. I'm here because I'm fettered, and I don't have a choice, but I won't participate in this process. I'm not interested in trials, cases, and your sentences. Make your decision and be done with it; we can't sit here all day!"

The rigid public prosecutor was offended. He put on a sour face and said: "Mr Palaiokostas, this is a court of law. You can't mock the trial process. You're obligated to enter a plea. The court has to listen to you and learn some things from you so that it can reach some conclusions! If you don't wish to enter a plea, at least tell us who the other three were!"

Corrupted men have got a lot of nerve! He wanted to know who the other three were. I felt a strong urge to rat out my dick and my balls as my accomplices and ask him to order their immediate arrest. To make them take the stand. I stood up, and I almost swore at him. The men from the Special Anti-Terrorist Unit formed a circle around me, lest I decided to attack him. He got scared and withdrew into his shell. He didn't address me again. They sped up the procedure, imposing the maximum possible sentences for all charges.

Their Pool of Siloam* was twenty years imprisonment for me. What infuriated me was that these decent scumbags had me to thank for the forty grand they would receive from Tony's case (perhaps I should have been convicted as an intermediary). I was transported back at the station, and they picked up those next in line. Tony and Argiris were the last to return, at about seven. Everything had gone well, for everyone. Tony was acquitted, Argiris got a bit more than ten years in prison, and the money found its way into "blind" lady justice's pocket.

Screaming hyenas and low-flying vultures

Being a valued member of the world of illegality granted me the privilege of seeing the whole profitable business that is the maze-like control and management system for unlawful human conduct. The incident above, concerning the perversion of a court judgment in exchange for money, wasn't an isolated incident, only an example of the extensive para-institutional behaviour that judicial staff displayed throughout the country, and even more so in Athens. The reason why I mention this incident is that it unravelled right before my eyes. It answers many of the questions of good men who think of the judiciary as a firm, untainted pillar of democracy.

Naturally, someone can imagine the scope of the transaction, free from the pressure and the commotion caused by my presence. Behind the scenes, nobody was stopping them.

Since 1997, prisons have been filled with guys like Tony and Argiris. Albanians had begun cultivating pot back in their country. Alone or as part of organised rings, they'd bring it into Greece, letting Greeks store it and traffick it. The majority of those involved were first-time offenders, and so they had no experience with the basic rules of crime. Their motives were economic in nature and nothing more, that's why they so easily fell in the hands of the police. From then on, the position they chose to adopt was dictated by their character and their life experiences. Most of them decided to speak, and the devil took the hindmost. The devil is always followed by his scavenging friends. In this case, the system's putrefaction-addicted vultures and the hyenas took over the role of devil's courtiers.

With the aid of legislative and executive powers, judges of all ranks, lawyers of all price-ranges, and, in essence, all those who are part of the prison system went on a spree of unprecedented violations against defendants' rights, bleeding them dry in the process. The sworn protectors of institutions, under a banner of crime prevention and suppression and having the strict, albeit vague, legal framework as their ally, raided and plundered the offenders' pockets as well as those of their families. The vagueness of the gap between minimum and maximum sentencing, is transformed into a space of financial negotiation.

---

* The Pool of Siloam is sited in Jerusalem and was historically a starting point for pilgrims to the Temple Mount, used for ritual purification. In Biblical canon, it's where Jesus healed the blind man.

When the minimum prescribed penalty for a crime is five years and the maximum is a life sentence, and that choice is left in the discretion of a corrupt judge, then it all comes down to the price one can afford. If someone is broke, that's his fault. He has guaranteed himself a life sentence! This is why over-packed briefcases are passed under the table, and dirty money becomes clean.

It's not a coincidence that the stakeholders within the criminal justice sector are the first to react to the prospect of easing sentences, because they stand to lose a blackmailing instrument, and a bargaining chip against defendants. Twice, one time in Diavata Prison and again in Korydallos Prison, during inmate uprisings to secure better living conditions, I asked the two most prominent bar associations to take a stand. They didn't. They never have. Especially the one in Athens. They always go along with the Ministry of Justice. They stand by it, become its crutch, complicit in its criminal legislation. They know they stand to profit from the unaccountability of the justice system.

Owners of financially sound law-firms, pitiful creatures, would arrive at Korydallos Prison during visiting hours, accompanied by several attractive law-school prodigies (both female and male) as bait, to buy clients! Their credentials were unimpeachable: their many victories in prominent court cases receiving broad and lasting coverage from the always impartial media.

Lavish, high-profile, well-fed, select, and beloved suitors of blind lady justice, who like her have never seen or heard any of what happens behind the closed doors of the hell-holes they threw their victims in after every trial. They never spared a few seconds from the endless screen time lavishly offered to them by the objective and independent channels which they use to promote themselves, boasting about their work which is undoubtedly a jewel on Greece's legal civilization. And then again, when inmates' struggles were taking place to secure a more humane criminal and correctional treatment from the State, they were nowhere to be seen.

Dead silence. Themis' miserable crutches would drop off the face of the earth, lest the revolting inmates win, something which would be a mere inconvenience to them. When your wallet is full, and you have guaranteed recognition for your brand, two standard factors towards social climbing and acceptance in this vain world, then of course everything around you seems like paradise. Now, if some choose to live in hell, that's their problem, their choice, and their responsibility. The State understands them and tries its best not to let them down as they go downhill!

It's not a coincidence that half the parliament is composed of speech-obsessed lawyers who, while practising their profession, follow the doctrine that "just is whatever is decided in courtrooms by independent judges". And, while they're active members of parliament, that "democracy is whatever the legislative body votes for" tailor-made to serve financial and other kinds of interests.

And poor citizens wonder why they can't get justice when they have to prove they're right not with their own arguments but with the politicians'. The arguments they have been taught in schools they pay for, longing to see their own progenies graduate from them summa cumme laude. These willing citizens, always ready to serve for a noble goal, confident they're helping humanity reach a higher level. And all this, only to realise to their horror that on this higher level the insolence of men like Kougias and all other carpetbaggers is left bare.

These are the men who honour justice, attacking the weak and defenceless, roaring like lions. But when it comes to the powerful, their lion-like behaviour turns to kittenish giggles, and they become nymphs, dressed in spidery wedding dresses ready to be joined in happy matrimony, with the overexcited crowd cheering them on ...

Nikos' arrest and sentencing

It was an autumn afternoon in 2006 when, after sixteen years of investigation, and after a car chase outside Arachova, they managed to arrest Nikos. The following day, the Minister for public order, Vyron Polydoras, along with several highly decorated dogfaced police officers, gave a performance for the press, raving about their accomplishment. They were audacious enough to apologise to the citizens of Greece, assuming responsibility for allowing Nikos to remain free for sixteen years. How touching! As if Greek citizens cared whether he was arrested or not ...

When will the Hellenic Police feel the need to show the same concern and apologise to the Greek citizens for the crimes committed against them during the Junta and the political transition? Never! When will the narrow-minded politicians, hiding away inside the parliament like modern Quasimodos, leave their posts as an act of apology for all the damage they have caused to this land? For the global defamation, for squashing the dignity and pride of the people, for throwing them to the global loan sharks?

Never, of course! The consciences of the powerful are paper-thin. Even now, they extend their hands like beggars, trying to secure peoples' votes, only to transform them into paring knives which they then stick in the people's flanks, the moment they unsuspectingly turn their backs. And as for the murder, they know what to do: find some man like me to pin it on. The lost shame of institutional officials. This would have been the most fitting title for the history of modern Greece.

One of the most blatant instances of a miscarriage of justice took place in a courtroom in Kastoria, while Nikos was being tried. There, justice showed its real, hideous face. The court of appeal upheld the decision of the court of first instance, which was a life sentence, pulling the wool over the eyes of all suspecting citizens.

Let me explain: Kastoria regional unit, bordering Albania, was a natural passage for drug trafficking, which flourished at the time. Such activity became an unexpected jackpot for local judges.

Money rolled in under the table, straight into their pockets. Encouraged by the Hellenic Police's senior officers, the corrupt judges of Kastoria took advantage of an outdated and extremely vague law that mandated life-sentences for gang-leaders who carry out a bank robbery in a "particularly cruel" way. Thus, they imposed the maximum penalty on a man who has never taken a human life or injured anyone. According to the judges, cruelty came when one of the robbers' guns went off by accident, due to mishandling, slightly injuring a customer. This way, the judges washed their dirty hands of it in a "particularly cruel" way, and the officers of the Hellenic Police took their revenge for having been ridiculed for fifteen whole years.

So it appears that matters that pertain to the behaviour of a citizen against society as a whole are reduced to a personal dispute (with strong elements of a personal vendetta) between the "law-breaking citizen" and those in charge of the repressive apparatus. For them, it is a matter of "honour". How many times have we heard about this "honour"! Honest, big words uttered by small, dishonest people. Honour should be the least of your problems! You ruthless abusers of speech and its meanings ...

All those behind this travesty of justice must know that it was Nikos who, while being chased by that motor officer in Katerini said: "Let's not kill him. It'd be a shame". It was Nikos who told me not to empty my Kalashnikov into three plainclothes we cornered during a car chase outside Edessa. Countless are the stories that testify to the good nature of a man who never used the power endowed to him by his gun as a means to control anyone, let alone kill. Because the quality of each human is determined by how they manage the authority bestowed on them. On the prospect of killing or simply injuring a human-looking serpent, Nikos would say "Let's not kill it. It'd be a shame!".

They've never been taught shame. These cold-blooded bastards will never even understand what it means. They should know that the senior positions they hold reflect neither their kindness nor their morality. We all know that in human societies those who crawl are the best climbers. And sometimes they're even poisonous.

After twelve years in prison, this man hasn't been granted a single furlough, while all the system's leeches that find themselves entangled with the law are released from jail within mere months of their sentencing. The fanatic supporter of New Democracy, who crushed a teacher's skull with a crowbar, stayed in prison for only seven years, because the supposedly democratic party had his back. At the same time, other inmates have to serve their life-sentences to the very last day for possessing one or two grams of heroin! Seven years inside a Greek prison is too long no matter the crime. It's utterly inhumane. Whoever gambles with peoples' lives, uncritically imposing sentences to them, finds his soul scrabbling in fascism's disgusting mucus.

But thus I counsel you, my friends: mistrust all in whom the impulse to punish is powerful. They are people of a low sort and stock; the hangmen and the bloodhound look out of their faces. Mistrust all who talk much of their justice! Verily, their souls lack more than honey.

~ Friedrich Nietzsche

The Pyli case

I think it would be interesting for me to talk about my trial concerning the Pyli, Trikala case. To be more specific, there were two. The Greek justice system decided to treat the random (as it proved to be) road-side inspection one evening at Pyli, Trikala, which ended up in a car chase and the exchange of fire, concluding on the ridge of Tymfristos at midnight, as two separate cases to be tried in two different cities. Their justification was that the first firefight took place inside the Trikala regional unit while the other two inside the Evrytania regional unit. I wonder what would have happened if the car chase had gone on throughout the night, concluding in the Peloponnese, with fire being exchanged in every regional unit along the way. It would have been funny if one of the fire exchanges had taken place right on the boundary between two regional units. It is evident that the Greek justice system not only recognises borders inside the country, but enforces them, handing out titles and positions throughout Greece at will.

The first trial was held in Lamia. It concerned the roadblock the cops set for me on Evrytania's mountains, before opening fire on me. The whole case file was a travesty. It included a detailed description of the cops injured at Pyli, Trikala, as though it was that case being tried, while the roadblock at Fournas wasn't mentioned at all. The cop witnesses claimed it was I who opened fire, aiming to kill them. The poor guys never shot back, only firing some shots to scare me. As proof, they presented the shells that had fallen inside the car's cabin from when I had used the Kalashnikov against them, during the Pyli car chase. The indictment was equal to the mood of those who issued it: attempted murder without regard for human life, and it only got better.

The police directors of Central Greece, Lamia, and Evrytania attended the trial along with several other highly decorated good lads. Both the presiding judge and the prosecutor were women. As soon as the trial process began, I made myself clear, as I always did. After the charges were read, I took the floor and addressed the presiding judge directly, telling her pretty much this:

"Your honour, I've already given up. You know that this trial, or any trial for that matter, won't change anything for me. I only care about the truth. I hope this court will help uncover it. Senior police officers are already in this courtroom. You must be troubled by the fact that police officers lie in order to influence this court's verdict for no apparent reason. It's a crime when officers act this carelessly and vengefully in cases that might result in severe penalties. Let me say something to the liars; something they don't know. They'll hear it from me now, in this courtroom. I had the chance to kill them when I found myself twenty yards away from them, in the darkness, with a loaded Kalashnikov in my hands. They'd have died with their boots on if I had decided so. I wish they would find the courage to tell the truth, even now".

The presiding judge, after assuring me that the court's intention was to uncover the truth, called them one by one to testify. What followed was tragicomic.

The inconsistencies of their accounts and their different answers to the same questions revealed their lies. The court wasn't brave enough to reduce the charges of attempted manslaughter to misdemeanours. The presiding judge, however, imposed the minimum prescribed sentence. That was a first. The presiding judge wished me good luck, expecting the charges to be reviewed by the Court of Appeal, which I never attended.

Already from the beginning of my long judicial odyssey, I felt the subtle sympathy of women in legal positions. This liking was surprisingly extensive, yet I won't be tempted to go into further detail. So, in mixed courts, when I had the right to reject jurors, the ones I rejected were always male. Many officers who attended my trials or whom I met in police stations also seemed to like and respect me.

During the trial mentioned above and my two-day stay in Lamia police station, many young officers from the Crime Prevention and Suppression Unit, who were tasked with guarding me, would get into a conversation with me about all kinds of subjects. One of them (a lower-ranking officer) was impressed by me. He couldn't fathom how a man like me could not believe in God!

"If I were in your shoes and I didn't believe in God nothing would stop me, I'd commit all crimes listed in the book!" he said to me at some point.

"See? I don't believe in God, yet I don't commit all kinds of crimes", I replied.

"That's what strikes me about you. What is it that stops you? Perhaps you're a better human being than I am". He silenced me.

After a month or so, I received a package in Korydallos from him. In it, I found two large volumes: the Old and New Testaments. Although I would have preferred one of Thucydides' books, I appreciated his gesture, because it's the thought that always counts. It's a privilege to be liked by your pursuers.

Mixed court of Volos

The second case was tried by the mixed court of Volos. Most of the judges and the jurors were male. Too bad for me! The hearing had barely begun when my first confrontation with the presiding judge occurred. He was a real lizard. The reason for our fight was his mention of my arrest in Livadeia. Wanting to impress the jury and the audience, he mentioned the firepower that had been found back then, stressing that all guns had a round in their chambers. Something that was strong evidence of my intentions and of how dangerous I was. I stopped him.

"Your honour, my arrest in Livadeia has nothing to do with today's trial. I believe you're deliberately mentioning this to influence the jurors and the court's verdict in general. Guns are part of my job. Just like you don't have only one pen in your office, I possess many firearms. The fact that there were rounds in their chambers is my way of handling my personal firepower, and in no case does it prove my intention to use them. That can be proved by the fact that the guns you mentioned have taken nobody's life. Anyway, have you never heard that unloaded guns kill people?"

There's none so deaf as those who don't want to hear. So the presiding judge went on summing up the charges as though I hadn't even spoken. Among other things, he mentioned that an officer took three bullets from a Kalashnikov, while another officer took seven. All of them creating entry but no exit wounds! All this was certified by a doctor at the Trikala hospital, where the injured officers had been taken after the confrontation. When I received the case file at Korydallos Prison, these medical reports weren't in it. The only thing mentioned was that two police officers had been injured by my shots. Nothing more.

The hidden Xsara on the Trikala-Pyli country road, the medical report by the police-obsessed doctor who had taken the Hippocratic Oath, the intentional withholding of substantial evidence concerning the defendant, the court that uncritically adopted such practices ... I imagined that all these were part of a bigger plan of surprises and twists the State had in store for its citizens; a way of keeping the collective social justice's reflexes alive and fully awake. The presiding judge addressed me directly, asking if I accepted the allegations made against me. I wasn't prepared and so I decided to buy myself some time to think.

"I don't accept any accusation that is the result of a conspiracy. I will talk about everything during my plea", I replied.

The two "injured" officers' testimonies couldn't be further apart. The one who had taken seven bullets was furious with me, serving the presiding judge's intentions well enough, whose questions allowed the officer's vindictiveness to come through at every opportunity.

"He wanted to kill us, your honour! He unloaded the entire magazine not caring about our lives. We're lucky to be alive. I'm still struggling with mental health issues after the incident. I've been seeing a therapist. I haven't been able to get back on duty. I'm on extended leave".

If he needed a therapist, what the hell should I say? After so many confrontations and car chases, I ought to be confined to some psychiatric ward! The other witness, the one who had taken three bullets, told a whole different story. He spoke highly of me.

"He didn't want to kill us, your honour! He just wanted to immobilise our car. The bullets, all of them in the car's hood, prove that. We weren't injured by the bullets but by car engine fragments. They entered the cabin and injured us. I wasn't even hospitalised. My colleague was released from the hospital the following day".

"What are you talking about? Has he bribed you? Is he threatening you? Are you afraid? The court will protect you. Speak the truth!"

"This is the truth, your honour. Vassilis is from our hometown. We know him well. He isn't a bad guy. He has helped a lot of people. Everyone from Trikala can testify to that. He has never hurt a human being. This whole incident was just a big accident. If he wanted to kill us, he could have gotten out of the car and done it".

Both the presiding judge and the prosecutor were tearing their hair out. They wished they could disappear. This was not how they had planned things.

The time for my plea came. I usually avoided entering a plea, but in this case, I had decided to do so because of the two injured officers, only because it was the right thing to do. I took the floor saying pretty much the following:

"I don't imagine there's someone in this courtroom who believes I participate willingly in this process. It is my right to try to beat back anyone who threatens my freedom, which I consider equal to life. I have never taken a human life, yet I wouldn't hesitate to do it if I was at risk of losing my freedom, which is of supreme value to me. But always as a last resort and always having first made my intentions clear. In the case for which I'm being tried now, I did nothing more and nothing less than that. My goal was to stop the car chase before any more police vehicles showed up. Then, yes, we'd be talking about deaths. If those two policemen had been my targets, it would have been much easier to execute them when they tried to inspect my car. I gave them plenty of opportunities to stop during the two-mile long car chase. I understand the police's revanchism, but it's unethical on their part to be using a medical report forged by an immoral doctor to achieve their goal. I'm one hundred percent sure that the two police officers weren't injured directly by my fire".

"What are you talking about, defendant? There are documents, the police vehicle is riddled with bullets, and you're saying you had no intention to harm them?" The presiding judge interrupted me, pulling an A4-size photo of the bullet-riddled Xsara (another instance of withholding evidence, but which in this case would come around and bite them in the arse) as an ace up his sleeve.

The photo was taken from the exact same perspective I had during the incident. It was perfectly sharp. The bullet holes were clearly visible. I asked the presiding judge to count them. There was one on the corner of the windscreen over the passenger seat, seventeen on the car's hood and one on the lower left side of the driver's door going downward. It all became clear. Six to seven bullets had been used until the SUV's rear window shattered, some were wasted as I had lowered the Kalashnikov and some had hit the Xsara's front tire. Add to them the nineteen bullets we had counted with the presiding judge, and you get a thirty-round magazine! The origin of the ten bullets said to have been found inside the officers' bodies was to be investigated.

"Your honour, you're obviously not familiar with guns, or you wouldn't be presenting this photo as proof of intent. Don't worry, though, because as it happens the best gunmen are here in this courtroom; the officers from the Special Anti-Terrorist Unit. If you suspect that any of the things I am about to say are lies, feel free to ask them. The Kalashnikov is a powerful assault rifle with an effective firing range of about seven hundred yards, meaning it can kill a human being from that distance. From a hundred and fifty yards it can penetrate a double bulletproof vest; from thirty yards it can amputate someone. However, because we're talking about a short-barrel version, these numbers are divided in half. These people are claiming — and the court is following that view — that they were shot at five yards. One had taken seven direct shots and the other one three, with no exit wounds! If it were true, at best, they wouldn't have been able to come to this hearing on their own. At best. I don't know if I have the right to request they show us their scars, but even if I do, I wouldn't want to subject them to this torment. You, your honour, wouldn't either. Because you know what you're going to see. Nothing! Now, how you managed to turn nothing into multiple criminal charges ..."

The court adjourned so that the judges could deliberate on my sentence. Several police officers and detectives came up to me and congratulated me for the way I handled the whole trial process and for my attitude towards their injured colleagues. It was then that a young female reporter charmed her way through the cops and approached me, requesting for an interview saying:

"I expected you'd be seven feet tall and tough. You're not seven feet tall, and you don't seem tough to me either".

I spontaneously answered:

"Never measure a man's soul with tape or his toughness by hand".

The men from the Special Anti-Terrorist Unit laughed. The young reporter walked away blushing. It took me a while before I understood what had happened. What to me had been a momentary reflection, she had interpreted as a sexual innuendo! Talk about a breakdown in communication ...

The following day, a local newspaper featured a libel against me, written by a reporter who had attended the trial. From what had been said, he took it that I was showing off and giving lessons as an experienced gunman. I never expect objectivity from journalists, but to replace the contents of their inkpots with their own faeces, that's just utter decadence. Show some respect to the sacred quill.

Oh ... I forgot to mention the verdict: twenty-four years combined sentence. No kidding!

The Patra-Parga trial

In a while, in the mixed Ioannina court, the trial process would begin for the case concerning the car chase and exchange of fire at Parga junction. Although the Patra incident was more severe (given that we had escaped from a well-guarded place, taking a cop as a hostage and shooting at an unmarked police vehicle) the officers from Patra secretly reduced the case to a misdemeanour. They tried it in absentia, charging us with the aimless firing of weapons. In other words, they presented us as two gun-obsessed armed men who just walked into the port, took out their guns and began shooting aimlessly in the air. A director's cut of the events, serving the needs of the police force, which the prosecution accepted precisely as it was.

The two cases were linked by the Scorpion submachine gun, used in both incidents, so some police officers from Patra were summoned to attend the trial and testify as witnesses for the Parga case, since it was their testimony which identified Nikos and me as the perpetrators at the port of Patra. These testimonies proved enough for the authorities of Epirus to charge us with four attempted murders (one for each passenger of the Alfa Romeo).

In all the cases in which Nikos was my co-defendant, I found it hard to talk about the actual events and assume responsibility for them. The reason was that if I pleaded guilty, then Nikos would automatically be incriminated too as they saw us as an inseparable duo that did everything together. At the time Nikos remained free, we didn't have direct contact to discuss such things. I didn't know if he wanted us to take responsibility. So, I had decided to not plead guilty in the cases in which Nikos was also involved. In this particular case, however, there was an even bigger problem. The Scorpion used in both incidents hadn't been found and I had no control over where it was while in prison. The prospective sentence would allow the authorities to pin whatever crime the gun might be used for in the future on both Nikos and me.

The session began. The presiding judge did a roll-call of the jurors to make sure everyone was present. Everyone was there. Then he did something unheard of — he announced that the court would adjourn for one-and-a-half hours so that the jurors could go to their homes and return adequately dressed for the occasion. When the now decent-looking jurors returned, the presiding judge called the names of four jurors to take their positions. I rejected two men, so in the end, three women and a young man remained. I asked the presiding judge to remove the cameras from the courtroom.

"Why don't you want the trial to be recorded, Mr Palaiokostas?"

"The trial can be documented without the cameras, your honour! I find it impossible to concentrate, having cameras over my head. And, in any case, as a defendant, I have this right".

"The court will adjourn for ten minutes to deliberate on your request", he said, then stood up and headed to the deliberation room. I started to think that he was going to give me a hard time. After fifteen minutes, the courtroom's back door opened and his glowering face appeared, followed by the rest of the court by way of hierarchical order. They took their positions, and justice's rat spoke:

"The defendant's request for the trial to not be televised is made for some fraudulent purpose the court is unable to determine at present. Lack of sufficient explanation of the real motives behind this request, in conjunction with the severity of the trial and its social interest, force the court to reject his request".

From what I had learned during my legal saga, I knew that the request I had made for my trial to not be televised wasn't supposed to be deliberated by the court but was every defendant's inalienable right. But this presiding judge had everything arranged.

In this trial, he'd be the protagonist. He'd give a once in a lifetime performance. He was determined to succeed, using all means available, legal or not. Emptying a bucket of water into the ocean so the unremorseful castaway who refused to make landfall for years would drown was a heroic act, and had to be televised. His life vision was taking shape right before his eyes. He needed a way his children could witness this moment and feel proud of their father. When human beings manage to distinguish between what is right and their own malice, then the world will have taken a step towards collective self-knowledge.

I tried to remain calm upon hearing this decision. I didn't want to get into an argument with the presiding judge. I had to stay focused on my goal, which was nothing more than being acquitted. The presiding judge was digging a pit for me, but in the end, he'd fall into it himself. I could already sense him negatively influencing the jurors, and I was counting on them. The court assigned a lawyer for me. The trial began.

The four cops who took part in the car chase in Parga testified first. To their credit, they said nothing more and nothing less than the actual events. To the judges' persistent inquiries they replied that they never saw the perpetrators' faces, that they didn't take down the Lada's license plate number and that their service didn't manage to find any evidence other than the Scorpion shells. As far as the officers from Patra are concerned, only one of them gave a somewhat interesting testimony. The narration of the events, as he lived them, was quite vivid. Reaching the point when he found himself with a machine gun pressed against his neck, he said:

"Allow me, your honour, to publicly thank him for not killing me although he could have!"

"He threatened you, and now you're thanking him, officer?" the embittered presiding judge protested.

"I'm not doing it as an officer, but as a man towards a man, your honour. That's how I feel".

"From what you're saying, we ought to conclude that you're one hundred percent certain that the defendant is the man who held you at gunpoint?"

"Beyond all doubt, yes, it was him, your honour".

"If the defence counsel or the defendant himself don't have anything to ask, you may take your seat. The court needs nothing more".

The appointed lawyer, their own guy, wanted to put on a show. I stopped him with a single nod. I stood up, having some questions of my own.

"What was the type of the gun the man who threatened you held, officer?"

"An Uzi submachine gun".

"Are you certain?"

"Absolutely. I'm a policeman, I know all kinds of guns. After all, it was right in front of me. Its barrel was pressed against my chest for quite some time".

"How do you explain the fact that all the shells found were 7.65 mm?"

A deafening silence. The presiding judge took the floor, convinced that my question had no merit.

"Explain to us, Mr Palaiokostas, where are you going with this?"

"The officer told us that because of his profession, he can tell the type of every gun and that the gun used to threaten him was an Uzi. It's just that the officer is clearly unaware that no Uzi using 7.65 mm bullets has ever been manufactured".

"And how do you know this, Mr Palaiokostas?" the presiding judge asked, fishing in troubled waters.

"Oh, come on … I'm not just a pretty face! Ask the guys from the Special Anti-Terrorist Unit, they know their stuff" (these guys were my allies in cases like this one).

The smart presiding judge didn't dare ask them, knowing what they'd tell him. My following question was also on point:

"Officer, would you like to tell me when exactly you realised it was me? Because I haven't quite understood. Did you recognise Palaiokostas the moment he pressed the Uzi against your chest? Or are you identifying me just now as that man?"

"No, no! The rest of my colleagues who came face to face with the perpetrators and I identified your faces from the pictures they showed us when we returned to the station to give a statement".

"Did they show you other photos as well, or just ours?"

"They didn't have to show us any others. Yours were the first. We identified you at once".

"You see, officer, I have a terrible habit of reading the newspaper every day and watching the news on television. So the day after the incident, every newspaper and every news program featured the sketches of two dark-skinned men. The reports said that it was two unidentified men who entered the port to either commit a robbery or a terrorist attack. Do you have something to say about that?

This question of mine seemed to cheer him up. He turned to face the presiding judge and began boasting that the two sketches were his idea and that he had made them himself! He also said that sketching was his favourite hobby and that if he had to place it at the service of the police force, he'd gladly do it even if he got nothing in return.

"Your hobbies are of no interest to this court, witness", said the presiding judge, looking bitter. "This isn't what the defendant is asking. Could you make your question more concise, Mr Palaiokostas? Because the witness clearly didn't understand it".

"What I'm asking is this: since the perpetrators were identified the day of the incident, why did the Hellenic Police release, the following day, the officer's hand-drawn sketches searching for some unidentified men and not our photos and our names? By the way, the sketches looked nothing like us!"

"That's a good question", said the presiding judge, oddly enough, asking the officer to answer.

He said that it was not his call to make, that these matters are handled by the head of the police. I had no further questions for the witness. It was now my turn to speak. Aiming directly at the hearts of the jurors, I said pretty much the following:

"I will narrate a quite real incident that took place in a meeting room of Israel's notorious Mossad. Two hundred of the best-trained agents of the world were attending a special seminar. Suddenly, five men barged in the illuminated chamber holding Uzi submachine guns and began emptying their magazines into the bodies of the 'innocent' agents. They fled at once. A massacre. Men dead, others injured, ambulances, paramedics. Five men were arrested in the surrounding area as suspects. The agents, one by one, were called to identify the perpetrators. Not one identified any of them. And we're talking about the world's best agents. Needless to say that this incident was a test, an experiment to determine whether a human being, when their life is threatened, can focus and memorise the features of a perpetrator. The police officer told us that he himself remembered the features not only of the man who pressed an (according to him) Uzi against his chest, but also of his accomplice. Right afterwards, he identified the perpetrators as the Palaiokostas brothers out of the only two pictures they showed him at the police department of Patra. What can I say? Perhaps the officer possesses some special skills, superior to those of Mossad's agents, and he's wasting them making sketches.

"I don't know what my conviction or my acquittal would mean to this court. To me, sentences are now nothing more than years added to a tally. To be honest, it's been a while since I last counted to see what they add up to. A conviction or an acquittal will make me neither a better nor a worse human being; it also won't make society better or worse. What to me is essential in this trial and what the court has to take perfect note of before reaching any decision, is that there's a gun out there that has been used twice against police officers. Someone has taken hold of this gun. We don't know when and where they are going to use it. A conviction would set the ground for other cases to be built against us in the future. Because of my experiences, I have no trust in the methods of the police force, and I'm very sceptical about the judiciary. In no trial have I asked for leniency or presented any mitigating factors, because I've always been conscious about my actions. This isn't going to change now; so I urge you, in case I'm found guilty, to give me the maximum prescribed sentence".

The prosecutor talked big as usual, the lawyer followed suit, and then they were off to reach a verdict. It was taking them too long. Judges are stiff. After two hours, the lawyer came down to the holding cells to tell me that during this time the presiding judge and the prosecutor were trying to change the jurors' minds, because they stood for my acquittal. After a while, entering the courtroom, I saw the jurors' smiles, which came in stark contrast with the judges' glum faces. I didn't have to wait for the announcement of the verdict. It would be the first time I would hear the word "innocent" coming from a judge's mouth, despite being guilty. To me, my acquittal was just a formality; it didn't actually mean anything since it wouldn't change anything for me. In legal terms, I was guilty, and I was found innocent. And yet, the Greek judiciary already owed me and had (ten? I don't even remember) long sentences in store for me, for which stood the exact opposite, to even up.

Scheming "colleagues"

I couldn't believe that a lousy bank robber schemed against us (Nikos and I). The shitty bank robber had some "inside" info that there was plenty of money in the safe of a well-guarded agency. He armed his team, grabbed some guns himself, threw some hats belonging to the agency in the back of a Mercedes and brazenly drove past the agency's guarded gate. He committed the robbery, and when he was leaving, panic-stricken as he was, he broke the gate's boom barrier.

The Mercedes was found hours later in an alley in Peristeri and with it, the solution to the mystery of the robbery and, in addition, the scheme of its perpetrators.

An above-suspicion, upright family guy and concerned citizen, who owned a workshop in that very alley, twenty yards from the spot where the car was abandoned, happened to be having a smoke outside his workshop just as the robbers were dropping the Mercedes there. Two of the four robbers crossed the alley and walked right past him. They were each holding a large sack, wearing sunglasses, jockeys, and looking quite upset. Naturally, they seemed dodgy to him. And to whom wouldn't they? The always clued-up citizen wasted no time. He turned on the TV he had in his workshop and saw the flash of a news bulletin about the robbery, which, coincidentally once again, had taken place in the agency where he had been working until recently.

The mere thought of such an insult infuriated him. He decided to take matters into his own hands. He called for a taxi, went straight to the robbery unit of the Hellenic Police's headquarters, and told them everything. The whole story. The brains and the chiefs of the agency that secures the safety of the public sent a dispatch to verify whether the Mercedes was the one used in the robbery. When they got an affirmative answer, they offered the godsend do-gooder some coffee, advised him to calm down, and asked him if he was ready to identify the men he saw by looking at suspects' photos. He was ready and waiting. After all, this was the main reason he had paid them a visit. Dear reader, I don't imagine you're still wondering whose photos they showed him first and whom he recognised ... don't wait for me to tell you everything!

We had committed no crimes in the Attica region, let alone an armed robbery. Yet I faced charges for five or six of them, and I was convicted for at least three. Some were tried the same day; including the above mentioned, which wasn't exactly a bank robbery. I was hearing all this for the first time. The judges called the concerned citizen to testify as their main witness and the only one putting the finger on me. The presiding judge asked him if he identified me as one of the two suspects who walked by his workshop that day. Afraid to repeat his lie in front of me, he awkwardly replied that now that he was seeing me from up close, I didn't look like either of those two men. The presiding judge took out my photo from the holy case file and addressed the witness:

"This is the photo shown to you by the police and by which you identified the defendant as one of the two suspects. Can you confirm that now?"

"Yes, your honour, it was him in the photo!"

The court needed no more proof. That day my throat had closed shut; I couldn't even speak. All the better for "blind" lady justice — the mutes are her favourites. With a sentence of about eighteen years in prison, this robbery was pinned on the Palaiokostas brothers. Case closed.

I had already begun suspecting the witness from the moment he took the stand to testify. There were too many coincidences in his story for it to be plausible. He seemed, in a way, guilty — I suspected he deliberately acted this way to muddy the waters. A man previously fired from the same agency where the robbery occurred happened to be having a smoke outside his workshop, and right at that moment a Mercedes stopped only twenty yards away, and the robbers walked in front of him, upset and in a hurry, wearing backpacks. Then, without being asked to, he ran to the robbery unit and identified the two most-wanted bank robbers in the photos shown to him. What could be more suspicious? However, the officers at the robbery unit didn't notice anything out of the ordinary. They only cared about closing the case.

Two years later, I found out the truth by accident, from a roommate, himself a bank robber. When I told him the story he was surprised, because he knew who had committed that robbery, having been asked to participate (he declined for his own reasons). He also told me that this robber had gotten the information about the money from one of his uncles, who had been recently fired from the robbed agency, and who had a workshop in some alley in Peristeri!

If it walks like a duck ...

Total degeneracy. Among bank robbers as well. If "colleagues", even shitty ones, scheme this way to pin their crimes on others, how can we expect the police and the judiciary not to do the same? That's why I'm not holding the latter two responsible in this case.

You'll be wondering what happened to the scheming robber. A while after the robbery, he died of a drug overdose.

"When God's angry, it rains dicks," as a friend of mine used to say.

RETURN TO KORYDALLOS AND THE FIRST ESCAPE BY HELICOPTER

Blueprints, solitary confinement, and the sketch artist's nephew

Night fell, and all doors in Corfu's medieval hellhole were locked. I laid a blanket on the cell's concrete floor and was ready to do some sit-ups when, suddenly, I heard the key re-entering the lock and turning twice with its distinct metallic noise. At once, the door opened to reveal a deputy warden followed by four prison officers.

"Palaiokostas, let's go to the guardhouse. The warden wants to see you".

"What the hell does he want at this hour?"

"He didn't say. He must have something to tell you".

I put on my shoes and my coat, and followed them. The warden maintained a neutral position; he neither caused nor created tension. I'd say he was bearable. He was sitting at his desk when I entered. In front of him was a blank piece of paper.

"Sit, Vassilis".

I sat in a chair opposite him.

"What did you want me for, warden?"

"Nothing much. I just wanted you to tell me if you know anything about this ..."

He grabbed the blank piece of paper and turned it, pushing it towards me. It was the detailed prison blueprints that I had drawn a few weeks before and which I had given, along with a somewhat encrypted letter, to a Romanian cellmate of mine to mail, not disclosing to him its contents but underlining how dangerous they were. They were to be received by a friend in southern Greece. I didn't panic.

"What is this, warden? Why should I know anything about this?"

"It's the prison's blueprints. Whoever drew it did a hell of a job. Do you, by any chance, know to whom this handwriting belongs?" he asked me, opening his drawer.

He got out and handed me my letter.

"Many misspellings ..." I observed. "Yet it doesn't ring any bells".

"Look, Vassilis, in case you really don't know, this letter was mailed by Danny from your wing. The recipient wasn't found, so it was returned. Thinking it may be a trap, Danny refused to receive it. He denied it was his. I was obligated to open it, and so I did, and I found what's now in front of you. Then I called Danny here, while the prison was still open. He confessed to me that you asked him to mail the envelope without him knowing its contents or its recipient".

"Do me a favour, warden. Send someone to fetch him, so that he can say here, in front of both of us, what he told you".

"Prison regulations forbid me from doing that, but even if I went ahead and called him, we both know he wouldn't repeat what he said in front of you".

"And what are you willing to do?"

"You understand this is a severe matter for the administration and that's exactly how it will be handled. We're talking about planning a breakout. The prosecutor has been notified, he'll be here shortly. He has ordered that your cell remains locked to be searched by a special police unit and that we sweep the whole wing. You'll wait in the guardroom until he comes to see you".

"On what grounds will I stay in the guardroom?"

"It's the prosecutor's order. You can ask him when he comes to see you. I hope it's temporary until the wing and your cell are searched, and the necessary statements are taken".

Corfu Prison's guardrooms were, in essence, six or seven small stone tunnels, about five feet long and thirteen wide, with a small skylight high above their heavy, iron-coated ancient doors. Right outside the window there was a low-wattage light bulb, which barely lit the inside of each cell. On the dirty floor was an even dirtier mattress, on top of which were two equally dirty blankets. In front of the cells a longer tunnel served as a hallway, with a door at one end similar to those of the cells, which led to the main part of the prison, while on the other end there was a communal squat toilet without a door. I'd spend the next ten days inside one of these tunnels, without any formal charges and without the disciplinary board having reached a decision. Just because.

The prosecutor arrived a day late. He came to see me along with the warden two days later, following my loud protests. The moment I saw him I gave him an earful.

"Tell me, sir. Are you aware that I'm in the guardroom? Who gave such an order?"

"Yes, of course. I gave the order for security reasons".

"Whose security, sir?"

"Your own".

"Are you saying there is no other place inside this prison that an inmate can be safe in, except for these guardrooms?"

It took him a while to reply.

"We're taking measures to secure the prison, Mr Palaiokostas. You won't re-enter the prison. The ministry has been notified. In the following days, the Supreme Council will meet to decide in which prison you will be transferred".

"Can you tell me how long this will take?"

"I don't know, they don't tell us. Your case is rather unique, there's secrecy. Be patient. We want you to leave as soon as possible too".

He turned around, ready to leave, but then he stopped. He turned again to face me and asked me:

"It doesn't really matter since you're going to be leaving, but if you want, you can answer me to satisfy my curiosity. Did you make the prison blueprints?"

"I won't answer that".

"Do you know why I am asking? I'm KYR's* nephew, and so I have an interest in anything that has to do with sketches. I also found this in your cell".

---

*   KYR (Yannis Kyriakopoulos) is a famous Greek political cartoonist.

He opened his leather briefcase and handed me my own sketchpad, on the first page of which the prison blueprints had been engraved from the original drawing. I wanted to slap myself for my blunder. The intelligent prosecutor had caught me red-handed.

"You already know enough. I don't think you need anything more to satisfy your curiosity", I said to him.

With the air of a victor, before he left, he shook my hand for farewell and wished me good luck. I can't deny it, he knew what he was doing. He knew how to not complicate already complicated situations. He could have demanded a disciplinary hearing, or he could even have filed charges against me. He didn't. Palaiokostas was planning an escape. Nothing new there!

The warden remained in the tunnel. He agreed to bring my stuff over from my cell and, since I wasn't punished but only waiting to be transferred, he also decided to leave the door of my cell open during the day so that I could walk in the small hallway. Yet the warden proved even more generous: he gave me access to a phone booth, as long as I phoned my friends who were searching for me and told them to stop threatening him. Everyone has their buttons.

Descent into Korydallos

On the eleventh day, at six in the morning, the usual transfer convoy boarded the ship to Igoumenitsa. Nosy passengers were gathering around us, trying to sneak a peek inside the prison bus through the steel barricaded windows and discover the reason behind all this commotion. The fact that the police officers discreetly held them back only aroused their curiosity even more. Reaching the port of Igoumenitsa, the convoy disembarked first and turned right on the beach road towards Arta. At once, I ruled out the possibility that we were heading to some of the prisons in central or northern Greece. Ruling out Korydallos too, only three possible destinations remained: St. Stephan Prison in Patra, Chalcis Prison, and Nea Alikarnassos Prison.

When we reached Missolonghi, the officer in charge of the transfer was notified that there would be no ferries from Rio to Antirrio due to bad weather. The convoy changed course. We headed to Nafpaktos. As they neared Itea the four armed officers, sitting with me in the back of the truck, protested to their superiors that they wanted to use the bathroom. It was made clear to them they could use the bathroom when we reached Korydallos. Through the superiors' answer to the Hellenic Police's pariahs, the final destination of this secret transfer was revealed. It was the last thing I expected to hear. Me? In Korydallos Prison? How? Why? Why were they putting a convicted man in a prison for inmates awaiting trial? The convicts who remained in Korydallos or returned there after being tried and prosecuted were thought to have pulled some strings to achieve it. How those in charge of the mixed council of the Hellenic Police and the Ministry of Justice had decided to transfer me to Korydallos, only they knew. Time would prove if their decision was right or wrong. For the time being, I didn't feel good about this at all, and as far as the States' intention to oppose one of its citizens was concerned, it seemed my enemies had done well.

Late that afternoon, I found myself outside 'A' wing, being welcomed by the all too familiar sense and smell of the sick atmosphere of mass confinement. In the one hundred and fifty cells that the dictator Papadopoulos had constructed, each designed to house one inmate, the founding fathers professing democratic ideals after the regime change had squeezed five hundred souls. How come a free democracy has more than double the inmates than a cruel dictatorial regime? At some point, the bright, open minds that are nourished in this hyper-free democracy have to offer a scientific explanation to this question.

The only thing I can testify to is my personal experience, being artfully and greedily carved for years on my destiny by life — and that would answer "because it needs enemies to sustain itself". So it invents them by inventing crime and even more so petty crime, trapping a big part of society in artificial guilt claiming that "these are your children, you are responsible for them, and you're going to forever be paying for their actions by remaining outcasts". The construction of a social-class enemy, who will be fiercely fought to ensure the citizenry's peaceful coexistence, working as a smokescreen, bringing people together around those in power, who in turn sponge off them worse than any humble thief ever does. Spreading fear is the favourite tactic of those inadequate for the tasks that the people have entrusted them with. Maximising the severity of the pariahs' crimes, they underplay their own sins and responsibilities to society. They are like a drunkard who, late at midnight, outside a public house in a dark alley, is beating his shoes because he stepped in poop, but his damaged liver won't allow him to get back home. When society's liver is underperforming, society lumbers; it won't go far, it can't set goals. It is doomed to live in darkness, beating its children for its own predicament.

The more harsh the laws the legislative body votes in, the more corrupt and further from democratic practices its legislators are. The more zealously a judge exercises these laws, the deeper he is plunged in the cesspool of corruption, with his career depending on how harshly he enforces them. And the more kick-ass cops are, abusing power given to them by the constitution, assaulting people, and fixing indictments, the more certain their financial (and other) transactions with the underworld are. An ideal regime and an elaborate scam are mere inches away ...

The warden, the cellmate, and the dream

When I entered my new cell on the second floor, I saw two bunk beds and three unknown inmates. I asked to see the warden, who accepted me at once. It was Thomopoulos, Aravantinos' right-hand man, who during the latter's reign had earned a reputation for beating inmates. He welcomed me warmly and then humorously complained:

"Why, dear Vassilis, did they pawn you off on me?"

"You must have a strong back, Thomopoulos" I answered, cryptically.

"Tell me what you want".

"I only want to share my cell with one inmate".

"What do you mean?"

"You know what I mean".

"Vassilis, the prison is full, I can't make allowances".

"Since, as you saw, they pawned me off on you, you should make sure that I'm as little a burden as possible".

"You'll have to manage for tonight, and we'll see what we can do tomorrow", he replied.

"I'll take that as a yes. I just don't want the two inmates to be kicked out before they can find a cell where they'll be welcome".

We coexisted with Thomopoulos for about a year and a half, and it was a peaceful time, with no conflicts. Thomopoulos, absolute and straightforward, and I, frank and confident, found a balance. I don't know if this had to do with our Thessalian origin or him knowing about Aravantinos' blunder, but the very few times we did have to talk, we understood each other perfectly. In this initial case, the warden didn't have to do anything. The very next day, the leader of the Pontic Greeks* came to my cell, and the matter was settled. Two of my three cellmates were Pontics, and they found a solution on their own. I was left with a poor, half-sized Greek man who had been set up by some crooks who wrote bad checks in his name, made big money out of it, and left the unfortunate fellow to pay the price. And a high price it was; a sentence equal to mine. "You should have known better", was the response of both the crooks and the judiciary.

This little man was left to the mercy of the prison officers. They had warned him that a troublemaker had arrived in his cell from some wild, remote prison, whose only goal was to cause turmoil and threaten the inmates' peaceful lives in Korydallos Prison. And when turmoil comes to prison, transfers usually follow. He'd have to find a way to remain here and in his position (he had some duties during visitation hours). Unable to bear the correctional officers' pressure, he decided to become a double agent (wherever the ball lands) and began telling me everything. The most notable tidbit was that every day before finishing his shift, they'd remind him, "Be careful! He doesn't walk, he flies!" Such was the pressure they were putting on him that one night he suddenly woke up, sweaty and wide-eyed, and shared with me the happy news.

"Vassilis! I saw your escape in a dream!"

"Come on, speak ..."

"Well, there was wind, strong wind, blowing. And all the prisons' doors broke. The inmates and the staff ran inside to save themselves. But you walked against the wind, you got out, and you vanished!"

"Wait for it, man ... now go back to sleep, I'm still here".

---

*　　　Pontic Greeks are ethnically Greek, but they originate from colonies which were established on the southern shores of the Black Sea around 800 BC and came to speak a distinct version of the language over time. They were gradually pushed out under Ottoman and Turkish rule, and the largest remaining population can now be found in Macedonia.

The young lad

One evening, someone began persistently knocking on the door of my cell.
"Yes ... come in".
More knocking.
"Come in!"
It continued ... what the hell? Was it someone deaf knocking?
I got up and opened the door. A young lad with short blondish hair, spiky on top and shaved on the sides, was standing outside my cell. He was holding a huge lunch box.
He spoke to me quietly, in an almost conspiratorial manner:
"Mr Vassilis, uncle Giannos sends this for you", he said, giving me the lunch box.
Stunned, I took the lunch box and instinctively opened it. Inside was half a roasted lamb.
"Who are you, kid, and who's your uncle Giannos?"
"My name is Spyros. My uncle is So and So (he mentioned his surname), and he wants you to come and meet him. We live on the ground floor, in cell twenty eight".
"Let me put this somewhere, and we can go together". I closed the door and followed him downstairs. "What are you doing here, kid? Shouldn't you be in the minors' wing?" I asked him.
"No. I just look younger than I am. I'm twenty four years old".
"What are you in for?"
"Drugs".
"Doing them or selling them?"
"Both".
"I hope you do neither while in here".
"No, no ... nothing, absolutely nothing".
"You better not, poor kid".
I'd heard of Giannos, but I didn't know what he looked like. As we entered cell twenty eight, a seven-foot hulk with red cheeks got off his chair, extended his colossal arm and warmly greeted me. His countenance and speech called to mind border villagers. I was surprised to learn he was from the suburbs of Athens, an area about three miles away from the prison. Giannos was a well-meaning, unaffected, happy-go-lucky man, always distancing himself from the intrigues of the overcast inmates' world. He was fresh, he hadn't yet been contaminated by the sneaky venom resulting from the mandatory coexistence of different people in the asphyxiating prison environment. To me, relaxed people were always welcome. It was a way for me to rid my soul of the constant tension of repressive daily life.
Giannos didn't have a long sentence; he was released after a few months, leaving me to look after young Spyros. They were related, and he asked me to keep an eye on him because the lad was prone to using drugs. Yet the kid wasn't just

prone to drugs; he was also obsessed by what was being passed off, under a veil of mystery, as organised crime, to sustain a whole system of cruel anthropophagy.

When the cat's away, the mice will play. As soon as his uncle was gone, the young lad went wild. Dropping my name, he walked up and down the wing all day long. Up and down, back and forth, even getting inside cells — it was his thing. Some progressive ignoramus would say he was full of life (which he was) and there was no reason to worry. But in a world of twisted illegality, which the young lad admired and craved to be part of, life isn't taken for granted. In an arena where the fittest and possibly most devious man survives, life is in imminent danger.

Young Spyros was unable to distinguish (after all the system deliberately doesn't) between a criminal and an outlaw, between a lawless man and an autonomous man, between someone anti-authoritarian and someone authoritarian, etc. To him, all these were games in a vast, dangerous amusement park for adults, where everyone was free to try their luck, being responsible for any possible injuries they might suffer or even their death. He had a good, big soul which was in stark contrast to his lack of composure. He often lost control of the wheel, the brakes weren't working. He seemed like a Volkswagen Beetle with a Lamborghini engine on an incredibly tough track. It was clear he needed guidance before he went astray and down some dark path, as so many budding outlaws do, being swallowed and digested by the insatiable system. I have an innate inclination to protect younger men and keep them away from such places. So I decided to have a chat with him. I held him hostage several evenings in my cell for instruction, telling him pretty much the following (I'm providing a brief summary): "Kid, it seems you've got a lot of guts, and you like boasting about it. Good for you. You must know, however, that prisons are filled with people who came in front-loaded and exited through the back door. Having guts in illegality is a great virtue, yet when the monstrous civic hypocrisy comes in the shape of organised, suppressive mechanisms seeking to crush you, they don't prove enough. Then you're going to need morals, and brains. They are powerful assets that keep you strong and will never fail you. The way and the strength of a human being's thought is either their advantage or their disadvantage. The way we think defines our decisions, and the force with which this thought is expressed will determine the results of our choices. The power of thinking is what proves how much we want to achieve a goal.

"When your thought is expressed with a pencil, it is bound to be erased in the first storm that breaks. When your thought is expressed with permanent marker, nothing will erase it; it will become a little belief inside you, a faith. Small beliefs build consciousnesses and morals, which are nothing more than the boundaries we set to our actions. They define how we position ourselves, our attitude towards the things and events that unravel around us. In essence, they are our individual laws, our personal constitution, and our autonomy. And we say, I do this because my consciousness and my morals allow it, while they forbid me from doing that. Mine prohibit me from selling guns, protection to small businesses, drugs, my freedom, my friends, my mother, my soul. They also forbid me from entering a house to steal, to kill an old lady, to become a snitch, to cooperate with a cop, a politician, and many other things. What do they allow me? Only bank robberies, abducting rich people and being part of a revolution towards a more just world.

"So you see how my individual constitution forbids me far more things than it allows me. You also understand how all of them are considered permissible in the minds of thoughtless illegality. The people around you are willing to sell and be sold, to buy and be bought. If anything from this careless list attracts you then feel free to join them. But if you're interested in a selective, targeted, and conscious armed struggle with a vision, then I'm your man. Never forget that an armed man without morals is just a criminal, prey to the eminently criminal State mechanisms, cut off from the peoples' sense of justice. What I propose is to avoid a futile frontal confrontation with the guard dogs. A predator must not waste its sharp teeth devouring the plump flock; instead, it should sink them directly into the shepherd's neck. That's the goal. And remember that the sort of illegality I'm suggesting isn't thuggery or merely a pose; it isn't easy money and living big. Instead, it is a constant struggle that tests human resilience—an endless battle against your own self and your beliefs.

"Our desires and their actualisation are two completely different things. And yet we ought to fight for them if we want to be worthy of them. Your decision will be the foundation upon which you'll build what you truly desire. I advise you not to make such an important decision which concerns your whole life hastily. If you take a step down this road, there's no going back. When you build your own scales and sword of justice, you'll be forced to weigh and cut only with these, and by these it will be judged whether you'll be convicted or acquitted. So make sure that they're made out of the best material you have as a human being. You are called to become a raider of your own mind and soul, and bring to the surface the most precious materials for their construction. This road is very lonely, but having your own sword and scales, you'll never feel alone. The human herds who knowingly lost the individual tools most essential for building a fair society in which they'd wished to live happily feel lonely. A scale and a sword. Never give them over to anyone, because it is them that can set you free as easily as they can make you a servant".

I'm in no position to tell if he understood all of this, but he always had a big smile on his face. He was into it; he was a kid who lived life to the fullest, and he showed it. And he was right to do so. One day, he was eager to get out of the cell, happy as he was, but I stopped him.

"I forgot to tell you something equally important: our body is our only ally in this lonely road of ours. We live inside it, we move along with it, so we have to take extra care of it. We don't poison it with substances".

"No, no, I'm not doing drugs. I'm clean ..."

"Fine. Tomorrow morning I'll meet you outside, and we'll get some exercise".

In three months, the kid was ripped.

Becoming chief cleaner, Tarzan, and the dove

Thomopoulos honoured me with a position as chief cleaner in 'A' wing. I went by his office and demanded an explanation.

"Do you want to humiliate me, Thomopoulos? Why did you give me an officer's position?"

"Clothes don't make the man, Vassilis. The people are officers, not the position itself. Jobs don't rat out anyone; the people who have them do".

"Well said. Yet if a position is dirty, whoever gets it gets dirty too".

"Nobody will dare say anything about you. You're restricted, everyone can see that. Where should I have placed you? I have been given explicit instructions not to let you past the barred gate without supervision. You'll be formally the chief cleaner since you can't move outside the wing. I thought it best for you to take this position because you won't have to work and the inmates will listen to you because they respect you.

He had a point but ...

The same night, after lights out, I gathered the cleaners on the ground floor and, as the deputy warden watched, I made it clear to them that I didn't ever want to see a cleaner go past the barred gate without reason. "For as long as I'm in charge of cleaning, no more ratting out and sucking up. If I suspect anyone doing either, I'll cut your balls off", I said.

It was the first time, in more than four years, that I was making use of the law concerning in-prison work for the reduction of one's sentence, and I didn't feel very good about it. What truly interested me was for my cell to remain unlocked in the afternoon and until late in the night so that I could escape its stale air for as long as possible. I couldn't take advantage of this benefit to plan an escape, because I was restricted inside the wing. And even if I could, I don't know whether I would have at the time, because of my fixation on my word of honour.

I would spend two pointless years in Korydallos, making escape plans that went nowhere, having officers constantly search my cell, and exercising vigorously. My only companion was Tarzan, my pampered ginger cat that enjoyed my food and protection inside the wing. Every night, I'd throw him a kombolói bead through the door's peephole, and he'd play with it all night long, making creepy noises on the yard's terrazzo and getting on the inmates' nerves. Yet none of them ever came to me to complain. In the morning he'd follow the officer who unlocked the cells, and as soon as he reached cell number thirty-two he'd sneak in and jump on my warm blanket, rubbing himself on me, meowing, and purring. He was my alarm clock. He'd take his breakfast, and we'd go out to the yard together, I to exercise and he possibly in search of a female cat. He was the only one I'd really miss if I happened to clear off.

At one stage Tarzan had to coexist with a little dove. He didn't like that at all. It first arrived through my cell window and sat on the top bed; it had probably been electrocuted or hurt by some hawk. We built a little house for it using a carton, and adopted it until it got well enough to decide its own fate.

One day, after it had begun to heal, it started flying inside the cell. It was then that I noticed a tiny little ring on one of its feet, with a phone number on it. I called, and some guy picked up.

"I have a dove here that has your number on its foot. Do you breed doves?"

"Yes, where did you find it?"

"It found me, actually. In Korydallos".

"How did it get down there? I live in this area (I don't remember where), can I come and pick it up?"

"Of course, that's why I called you".

"Where do you live in Korydallos, so that I can come?"

"Do you know where the prison is?"

"So you live near the prison! But where? On which street?"

"Inside the prison. I'm an inmate".

He was shocked.

"And how will I get it from there?"

"You'll come to the front gate, and you'll say that Palaiokostas has one of your doves and that you want it back! I'll give it to an employee to bring down to you".

He never came. Perhaps he didn't believe me, or maybe he came, and they kicked him out because I forgot to notify the gate about the potential visitor, taking for granted that they'd take his unreasonable demand seriously. So the dove would have to make 'A' wing its new home. When it got better, it flew to the upper floor of the wing to escape from a jealous Tarzan, who was feasting his eyes on it. There it enjoyed the inmates' hospitality, although it soiled their hanging laundry. It, too, had an in with someone!

What happened to Tarzan? Yes, good question, reader. Shame! But I will tell you, making an introduction first, hoping you won't feel that bad, even if nobody knows. For better or for worse, those who sow the earth have to first confront one another. It doesn't matter if you eat canned tuna or smoked turkey, if you don't have a spine someone else will take advantage — that's the rule of life. Late one night a war broke out. A great, loud battle; the whole wing was awakened. Tarzan was defending his land from some uninvited intruder. He had a lot of supporters, but it was no use ... what a waste of a name. He left, ashamed, and I never saw him again.

Indeed, animals lead the way. How nice would it be if irresponsible people in responsible positions showed the same touchiness. I'd abandon illegality at once (so to speak). But they don't.

The hyper ...

My luck began to turn by the winter of 2005-2006, when the Ministry of Justice decided to appoint a warden for each wing, with one being in charge of the rest. Something like a hyper-warden the rest answered to. The day before he took over as leader, this top boss summoned the chief cleaners from each of the five wings to "E" wing's guardhouse to have a chat.

We sat on two wooden sofas facing each other, and after a while, the 'hyper" walked in. His expression and his movement foreshadowed nothing better than the formal announcement of an upcoming nuclear disaster. At one point, he opened his mouth, allowing his confined, suppressed thoughts to escape from the depths of his existence. "I've received reliable information that due to the expected change in administration there's going to be an upheaval inside the prison. It seems there will be an uprising, so I want each of you to report if anything of this sort is going to happen in yourwing".

There, right in front of me, completely unashamed, the chief cleaners from 'B', 'C' and 'D' wings tried to make a deal with the "hyper". This practice was a remnant of Aravantinos' progressive correctional policy: give us what we need, and you shall get what you want. They made it clear to him that they were going to be in charge of assigning cleaning duties among inmates and in return they assured him they'd control and suppress any uprising that may occur. The worst kind of backroom deals between aspiring people willing to make use of foul means to climb the ladder of illegality and a man in power wanting to establish himself as the ultimate lord of terror in this hellhole, always at the expense of the unsuspecting inmates' rights and wellbeing.

He skipped his own chief cleaner, since they coexisted in "E" wing, and he turned to me.

"What's up with 'A' wing, Palaiokostas? Could there be an uprising?"

"Luckily for you, warden, they don't have what it takes to ignite an uprising. But if it happens at some point, I'll be on the inmates' side".

"I appreciate your honesty, but I never doubted that".

The very next day, he relieved me from my duties. I'd relieve him of his, in turn, a few months later. You know what they say ... don't count your chickens before they hatch.

Unfinished Plans

It was around the end of January, or the beginning of February, in 2006, that I began working on one of the many versions of an escape plan, thoroughly thought out, which required external assistance. Shortly before, an inmate with whom I used to hang out had been released. He was a serious guy. Before he left, I went by his cell and spoke to him honestly.

"Renato, you know, just as most other inmates do, that my only goal is to get out of here. I want you to tell me whether you can help me with something when you get released".

"Of course, Vassilis! If I don't help you, then who? Tell me what you want, and if I can I'll gladly do it".

"I need you to search your country and find me some rocket launchers, some rockets, and explosives and bring them to me".

"I'm not familiar with this stuff at all. If you write down what you need, I'll find it, and bring it to you".

I wrote down what I needed in great detail and gave the paper to him, saying: "Just don't ask me for too much money, because after six years in prison I'm in deep shit financially".

"I'd never take money from you. You'll just pay the purchase cost and the labour of the guys that'll bring it over. I'm doing this for you, not to make a profit".

Indeed, after a month, one of my partners received a package full of weapons: rocket launchers, rockets, Kalashnikovs, magazines, bullets, TNT, grenades etc. and paid a nominal sum. Renato proved to be an honest man. He honoured his word. I didn't manage to repay him since we didn't keep in touch after my escape, yet I hope life repaid him in another way or it still remembers the debt. Still, Renato didn't do this to get something in return but because he wanted to. What a rare kind of man.

In the upcoming escape attempt, the two frontline guys who were going to assist me from the outside would be armed with Kalashnikovs and grenades. Why? Because one out of the four of them had vetoed the use of explosives and rockets, even though he would only act as our coordinator, being several miles away from the prison at the time of the attack. That struck me as odd. I couldn't comprehend this demand of his. My escape plans were designed in a way that minimised the possibility of human loss on either side. Never had I asked any of my partners to shoot a rocket directly into a guard post to eliminate a guard. Not even a Kalashnikov. When you attack a highly secured prison, you have to show your strengths at the outset. Show your strength and your determination so that your opponents know what they're dealing with. If you send the wrong signal in the first place, then things might take a wrong turn for both sides (most deaths are caused by a knife exactly because both victims and perpetrators underestimate it). This particular demand, aside from everything else, would compromise the safety of the two guys holding the line outside the prison wall, while we had the means to guarantee their safety and deter any interference from the guards.

The same guy would also veto my decision to take the kid with me. His justification was that he was too young. Obviously kids don't deserve freedom! These, along with some more vetoes, and my questioning his exact motives for participating in the breakout, made planning the inside part of the job even more difficult.

Spyros and I lived together in the cell where my night-time attempt would begin, and the plan called for two people to do it. Aside from having to tell Spyros that his dream would remain a dream, I would need to replace him with someone else who'd want to leave in this way, something that wouldn't go unnoticed by the administration. Spyros, although extremely sad, understood the position I was in. He knew this decision wasn't mine.

"Old one (that's how he called me), make sure you get out of here. After all, it's you who has the real problem. I have already applied for a furlough,* I don't have any disciplinary hearings, I'll get it, and I'll see you on the outside", he said to me to make it easier.

---

* The Greek prison system includes both short-term release (known as furlough or leave of absence) over a matter of days, usually requiring a regular sign-in with authorities, and the longer-term conditional release, which is notoriously difficult to get.

The problem of replacing him was settled the very next day, without even having to try, due to events unravelling inside the prison.

Self-confinement and a third cellmate

The next morning, inmates whose cells had been left with only three beds were carrying a fourth one from the forge to their cell, to place it over the third. It was a horrible image of the living dead carrying on their backs, without protest, their own coffins inside the group crematorium the non-vengeful State had given them to cremate their last remaining ounce of dignity. For as long as I had been chief cleaner, I'd had the sad privilege of watching those who returned from their short furloughs every night, their faces glowing as they walked through the wing's barred gate. Big smiles on their faces. They looked like men returning from the battlefield and seeing their own people after a long time. The very same inmates, now carrying their iron beds to their cells would, after some time, wait impatiently, a bright smile on their faces and a backpack in their hands, for the officer on duty to allow them inside the wing, because the ashes of their dignity were there, waiting for them.

You'll worship the rules of the world we handed to you, that you had scorned. You'll happily lay your pride before our feet. Such is the high price of a furlough and all other benefits that the correctional sewer provides. The suppression and the commodification of all human emotions place freedom and life itself under attack. The kind of society which Western subhumans espouse must be rid of all sorts of human wants. Dignity, honesty, morality, and all other virtues that constitute a rounded personality are only welcome when they're commodifiable and produce a profit.

A man who obediently returns to the worst place in the world, smiling instead of mourning, is the accepted member who will be returned to that ant-like society as a formerly-astray-but-now-reformed little worker, ready to be used. It won't be too long before offenders arrest themselves by their own volition, summarily convict themselves, and serve their own sentences unsupervised. The reason this hasn't already happened is that it would mean the collapse of a whole system that owes its existence to the maintenance of shameless society's institutional structures. Which lunatic's sick imagination, some centuries ago, envisioned automated, self-controlled communities of people living in concrete monstrosities and guarding them with the same zeal that a logical person would show in their attempt to burn them to the ground?

Just before afternoon rest time, while I was finishing a last game of chess with another inmate on the plastic table outside my cell, a prison officer, holding a notepad, walked to my cell and opened its door.

"Hey! Where are you heading? Who are you looking for?"

"I'm not looking for anyone. I'm a manager at the forge. I have an order to place four beds in each cell" he said with the air of certainty belonging to a man convinced that he's in charge and his word is the law.

"Does your task and the order you've been given give you the right to open whichever cell you want without so much as knocking?"

Silence. It was apparent he didn't know who he was talking to since I had never seen him before either.

"Whose decision is this?"

"The prison board's. The warden gave me a list of the cells".

"And is cell thirty-two on this list?"

"Yes. Look, it's right here ..." he showed me his notepad.

"And did the warden tell you who stays in this cell?"

"No. Why, should he have?" he said sarcastically.

"I guess so. Tell him to come with you when you come to place beds in my cell because you're in danger".

He unwittingly raised his voice.

"I don't understand. I'll come by myself, and we'll see what happens!"

"I don't think you'll have the time to see anything".

Some inmates laughed, overhearing our conversation, so the officer began to suspect something was off. He shot a look at me, looked around one last time, and left the wing. After they counted us and locked our cells, Spyros and I didn't take off our shoes. We were on the alert, ready to put on a fight if they attempted to put more beds in our cell by force. Throughout the afternoon, we could hear the blacksmith crews soldering beds. When they unlocked the cells, the crews had left the wing. At night, sometime after lock-up, the door to my cell opened. Two officers told me the warden wished to see me in his office. I had forgotten all about the afternoon incident, and I wasn't at all prepared. In the guardhouse, the warden and the wing's deputy warden waited for me. They were friends and had a good relationship with several bouncers from 'A' wing. Both from Piraeus, they knew most of those guys from the outside, moving in the same circles. Nothing reproachable about that. They'd never provoked me, aside from the frequent searches in my cell. After my escape, I accidentally bumped into them having drinks at some bar (probably on their pals inside). How could they have known Palaiokostas was sitting right next to them?

"How are you, Vassilis?"

"Fine guys, you?"

"What's got into you? Threatening officers now?"

"I did what? When?"

"This afternoon. About the beds".

"Oh ... I forgot. Well, I didn't threaten him, he threatened me".

"What do you mean? How did he threaten you?"

"He said he'd place two more beds in my cell. That, to me, is a serious threat".

"It is the prison board's decision to place four beds in each cell. Your cell is the only one that only has two beds".

"And I'm the only inmate with a life sentence, and yet I remain here in Korydallos. Get me on a prison bus tomorrow, ship me to whichever prison you like and it's problem solved!"

"Do you know how many times we've applied to the ministry to send you away? But all our applications were declined. Do you think we want you here getting in our way?"

"That's exactly my point, warden. When the ministry declines applications, it also has to make some concessions".

"Look, Vassilis. Everyone in your wing has come here to complain because there's only two in your cell".

"Since when did the wing's management pass into the hands of snitches, warden? You're free to send any inmate who comes to complain to you again to stay in my cell".

"Find a friend of yours and take him in for two weeks. I swear I'll switch his cell! Do it for me, I'm asking you as a favour", he insisted.

Then it dawned on me that this was an excellent opportunity for me to get Spyros' replacement for the planned escape into the cell.

"If someone is to stay in my cell, it must be a friend of mine, and I couldn't possibly kick him out after two weeks. He'd have to stay there. Since you're asking it as a personal favour, I'll accept it, but I don't want you to ever bother me again. Ever".

The escape that never happened

Yorgos, a guy I knew from another prison, arrived at my cell the following day. He had just been sent down for some robberies and really wanted to leave. I gave him one of the fretsaws which I always had hidden in several cells, and in the following days, he finished cutting a bar on one of the windows. He put some plaster over the cuts and painted it the same colour as the rest of the bars, so they became invisible. We contacted our allies on the outside, and set a Sunday night in February 2006 as the date for our attack.

My previous experience from the escape in Chalcis proved quite useful. I knew what we had to pay extra attention to while crossing the two iron net and barbed wire interior walls of the prison until we reached the exterior wall, which our allies had been tasked to demolish. We had prepared for the worst-case scenario in which the outer wall didn't fall. If our partners could hold the outer guards with their guns for one or two minutes, we'd climb that as well.

With Spyros keeping watch through the door's peephole until midnight, we made some hooks and wrapped bandages around ourselves on spots where it was likely we'd get injured.

By midnight we were ready, and waiting for the signal to finally set our plan in motion.

The signal never arrived. A bit after six in the morning, our allies informed us that when they went to pick up the vehicle with which they'd approach the prison's outer wall, they realised it wouldn't start, although it had worked fine when they'd left it the previous day. The next day, after a thorough search, they discovered dirt in the fuel filter.

The same man who vetoed two of my decisions told me on the phone that he had reason to suspect that the dirt in the fuel filter was put there by someone. Implying sabotage from within, he suggested we cancel the escape. As if this weren't enough, the same day, a trusted friend called me from Malandrino Prison to alert me, saying he had information that some of my partners were targeting my brother, Nikos. At the time, a large-scale police operation was ongoing for his location. Packs of rabid cops had delved into a merciless hunt throughout the country to arrest him. They'd do anything to get hold of him.

I was shocked. I didn't have a clear enough picture to be able to tell between what was deliberate and what was a coincidence, what was deceit and what was noble intention. Under these circumstances, aborting the plan was the best thing I could do. This way I could protect both my partners from a possibly unfair climate of distrust on my part, and myself from stepping over the line, accusing people who were willing to stick their neck out to get me out of prison. I never managed to discover the truth about all of this. What to do ... trust is an endless challenge in this world; it's fragile, it gets shaken too easily. A wrong turn of phrase, a different belief, a different way of handling things or even a random event can easily be understood as suspicious and leave you in a state of endless distrust.

The anti-terrorist

Just when I thought I'd seen everything.

One day they summoned me through the loudspeakers and, heading to the guardhouse, I came across the warden standing outside his office.

"Did you call for me, warden?"

"Yes. But it's someone else that wants to see you".

"Who?"

"Get in the office, and you'll see".

The office door was open. I entered and saw Syros, chief of the Anti-Terrorist Unit* sitting on the warden's armchair behind his desk. As soon as he saw me, he got up and walked over to me. He extended his arm, saying playfully, "Your reputation precedes you".

"It happens, sir. When it's this big, it precedes you. It's a matter of anatomy", I humorously replied.

"How are you, Vassilis? How have you been?"

"Aside from being in prison, everything's fine".

"Why did you want to see me?" he asked me.

"Me? I wanted to see you?"

"Yes. So and so told me", he mentioned the name of a lawyer and I immediately remembered.

---

* Syros gained national fame for playing a key role in dismantling the militant revolutionary organisation 17 November. The organisation's members accused him of using unorthodox methods during their interrogations to extract information.

For a while now, the same guy vetoing my decisions concerning the escape (he was an inmate back then), who also had inside information on the police, had been keeping me updated on the investigations concerning Nikos. As I came to realise, this information was intended to cause him confusion, panic, and suspicion, and destroy his defences.

The set-up was pretty much this: we know approximately where he's staying (he was bound to be somewhere). We have trusted information that on Easter Day he was roasting lambs with some friends in a secure location (one usually spends Easter Day with friends). A man very close to him decided to cooperate to cash in the bounty on his head; it is a matter of time before he is arrested etc. They'd also drop in the name of one of his former partners, and that was it. Of course, the inmate wasn't part of all this; he had good intentions communicating this information without knowing their goal. In one of our conversations, I had mentioned to him the constant harassment of my family by the chiefs of the Hellenic Police, aiming at Nikos' surrender in exchange for a minimum sentence. I had told him I was naturally surprised that, since their intentions were noble, they hadn't come to me in the first place. Unlike my parents, I could handle a supposed negotiation. Instead, they were giving empty promises to people that had no legal experience with such cases.

"My lawyer has a good relationship with the leadership of the police. If you want, he can arrange for someone to come and meet you," he had said to me.

"Yes, I'd like that, just out of curiosity, to hear what exactly they're offering. But that doesn't mean I will negotiate Nikos' freedom. After all, I have no such permission," I had answered him, and that's where the conversation had ended.

And so a month later Syros was sitting across me, asking me what I wanted him for. In such cases, my survival autopilot was turned on, in search of a way to directly tackle the problem.

"Look, sir, I didn't specifically ask for you. I was just wondering ... you're putting my family in a difficult position concerning Nikos' case. If your intentions were indeed honest, you'd do the obvious. You'd reach out to me to see whether there's any chance of negotiating Nikos' surrender. You never came to me because I know you better than anyone; I've experienced your retaliatory tendencies first hand, being now six whole years on the hot seat. If you want to show Nikos' your noble intentions, you can simply grant me the furlough I deserve, so that I can meet with him and tell him what exactly you're offering. This would demonstrate that your intentions are indeed noble". He nearly jumped out of his seat.

"What? No, no, no, no! No, that can't happen. I don't participate in, and I know nothing about, such negotiations. What I care about is protecting Nikos from the worst, given his frequent confrontations with the police".

"There's no problem if he is killed during an exchange of fire. It's something he himself accepts as possible. There'll only be a problem if you kill him in a dirty, cowardly way. Like that night ambush you set up two months ago in that byway, riddling his car with bullets aiming to kill him. He was lucky to walk out of there alive. And you didn't even hush up the incident".

"I'm not familiar with the incident you're referring to, but if it indeed happened let me say that I oppose such methods. I'm on the opposite side, but I want him captured alive".

At some point, while he was insisting that if Nikos ever decided to surrender, he'd be in charge of the procedure to make sure it all ended well, I questioned his trustworthiness.

"Sir, I never said anything about surrendering, and even if I had, you're here today and gone tomorrow. Your politician superiors use you as pawns. Whatever you say is just empty words, you don't have any official orders".

He was insulted.

"Just empty words, huh? Do you think the minister doesn't know I'm here talking to you? And do you think I'm just some random policeman to be used by politicians? I arrested the Revolutionary Organisation 17 November, everyone respects me!"

In his attempt to convince me of his unimpeachable character, he said something unheard-of:

"Just like you, I have my own principles. I'd never sleep with a woman younger than eighteen!"

I couldn't believe this. If a State's imposed laws are understood as individual morality, then career becomes an invincible ideology. This "fruitful" dialogue would go on for a while, before ending traditionally. He had placed his mobile phone on the table in front of him (perhaps he was cunning enough to be recording our conversation) and it suddenly started ringing, its loud ring tone playing a traditional folk song. What I gained from all this was a feeling of nausea until the following day. What business did I have getting involved in such complicated affairs? They had never been compatible with my character.

Dead on demand

It must have been less than a month later when the kid Spyros was granted his first furlough and, of course, he never came back. One night, two days after the prison officially declared him a fugitive, someone called my name through the door of my cell.

"Vassilis, come! I have something to tell you".

I walked to the door and saw Yorgos through the peephole. He was the leader of the henchmen* and newly assigned as chief cleaner. At the time, the wing was being cleaned by his crew.

"Hi, Yorgos. What is it?"

"Have you heard anything about Spyros?"

"I know what you know. He didn't keep in touch" (I lied).

---

*   Yorgos too became a victim of the bloody war raging these last few years between gangs, resulting in the deaths of dozens of people. He was assassinated in 2018, having been ambushed by armed men outside his house. According to the police, he had been the leader of a large group of blackmailers.

"Don't you know he's dead?"

"What the fuck are you saying, Yorgos?"

"Sorry, friend. But it's true!"

"How do you know this?"

"I've come straight from the guardhouse. The police sent a fax that he overdosed. I saw it with my own eyes!"

"Did you see the date of death?"

"No".

"Please, do me a favour and go back to find out. And also check when they received the fax".

As soon as he left, I tried to piece everything together. What he had just told me didn't make any sense! No more than two hours had gone by since I'd last spoken to the kid and he'd seemed fine to me. He couldn't possibly have done drugs, been found dead, identified, and a fax sent to notify the prison in under two hours. Something else was going on. However, until Yorgos returned, I couldn't even attempt to hide my agony. Yorgos said that the fax had been received that morning. The prison, as it ought, had requested verification and they had gotten a positive response. As required, they had erased Spyros from their list of inmates. After all, according to the police he had been found dead of a drug overdose just two days earlier in the centre of Athens. The police, in turn, had stopped looking for the kid. Everything was fine.

My suspicion that the kid had orchestrated this whole scheme through his family business would be disproved the following day when I contacted him. He knew absolutely nothing about all this! It was safe to assume that the kid's family had filed a missing person's report and that the police had picked up the first dead man with a syringe in his hand they could find in the trash-town's centre and had identified him as the formerly missing person. After all, they're all trash. For them, it was nothing more than another boring shift of listing trash, and look what happened!

An almost attempt

The kid was always in on every plan I had in mind. So I got him in touch with a friend of mine to proceed with a plan of escape similar to the previous one, only this time using explosives and rocket-propelled grenades. I'd assist them over the phone with practicing using the rocket launcher on a mountain near Athens, and they'd make a thick metal box, filled with explosives to be used on Korydallos' pyramidal outer wall. We, on the inside, were entirely readied from the last aborted attempt. The window's bar was cut, we had all other necessary equipment as well as an untamable desire to be free. There's no time like the present. So we arranged it for a spring night that year.

The human factor, however, once again had other plans, forcing us to call off this promising attempt. And when I say human factor, this time I mean my own inexplicable mental collapse in a matter of hours. Something like this had never happened to me before, and it never would in the future. Whoever was lucky enough to be by my side in a dangerous situation often accused me of being callous. That night, however, my callousness crashed into the sharp rocks of sensibility. By noon I had begun feeling anxious, something which to an extent was expected, seeing as I was going to be the protagonist in an "explosive" night after all this time. This concern gradually turned into an awful feeling, accompanied by unbearable anxiety and an undefined fear that brought me to my knees.

Whom could I tell? So much work had been done, we were so close to starting, everything seemed to be going fine, and because of this bad feeling of mine, everything would go up in smoke. But it would have been a mistake to hide my bad mood from my partners; Yorgos had already sensed it. The plan couldn't be set in action with me in this state, whatever might have been causing it. All the guys agreed not to risk it, so we postponed our attempt for a different night. That night would never come.

The following days, I tried hard to figure out what it had been that had caused me such discomfort, making us postpone a well-planned, promising attempt. I got my answer when I sent the guys to test the circuit without the explosives, and the detonator exploded at once. This meant that whoever would have gone to place the explosives would have been killed on the spot. This would have been the kid, and I'd have been the one responsible for his death. It was an excellent lesson for me, that we should never give instructions for building an explosive mechanism over the phone to unpractised people, no matter how simple the circuit appears to be. We never play with explosives. And we never question our bad moods ...

The firestorm, the strike and a word of honour

After a few weeks, a tragic incident would change things dramatically, bringing me one step closer to my first escape by helicopter. One night, a fire broke out in a cell in 'D' wing and three inmates were burned alive. The officers on duty, afraid to unlock the cell to save them without having orders to do so, waited for instructions from their superiors, who at this late hour were sitting on their arses in the guardhouse. Fire, in such a small space with so many flammable materials, doesn't wait for slow-witted correctional officers to make a decision. The inmates were dead within minutes. Some inmates from my wing, awake at the time, told me that the burning men's screams echoed throughout the prison as fire painfully consumed their bodies. No one was held responsible for these three horrible deaths; no one was ever punished. "What value do the lives of three foreign criminals have?" wonders selective justice.

The inmates from 'D' wing went on strike, demanding an explanation for the prison officers' decision not to open the burning cell, while the other wings went on hunger strike as their first reaction. Since morning, an inmate of questionable morality had begun trying to fire up the people around me, without me knowing. Some of them were anti-authoritarians who had been advised to approach me some time before. They were pure guys, their blood was boiling, they didn't know how prisons worked. They couldn't imagine that an inmate could gain from such tragic events. This, however, was the case …

They came to my cell and told me: "Vassilis, we spoke with Haris, and he told us we shouldn't take this lying down. We must react to what happened in 'D' wing".

"Did he suggest any ways of reacting?"

"No, but we must discuss and decide what we should do".

"Why didn't he come to me directly?"

"Probably because he doesn't know you. He might be afraid".

"I don't know him either, and I haven't heard nice things about him. So keep a distance from him. We don't need him to tell us whether we should do something. If you want us to react, we will. Every reaction is dictated by the incident causing it. In this case, it dictates that we go to the rooftop; every other reaction besides an uprising would be an insult to the memory of the three dead men. And I ask you this: who in this wing is willing and able to climb onto the roof?"

"But we have to do something. We can't let this slide!" they insisted.

I didn't want them to think I was indifferent, so I took action. I went to see Sasha, a Caucasian giant who was the leader of the Pontic Greeks in 'A' wing, and asked him whether they were willing to react and support 'D' wing.

"They'll do whatever I say, Vassilis. I'll go to gather them now. Feel free to tell me if you need anything else from me!"

He returned, smiling, after twenty minutes and reported that all his men were ready and awaiting orders. It was the Albanian leader's turn, who also told me they were all ready. Coincidentally, at the time, many of the best bouncers of Athens happened to be in our wing, all of whom were quite big I would say (none are alive now, because of score settling among them). I approached Yorgos, whom I had a higher regard for, and his response was that they weren't willing to lead any uprising, but that they wouldn't go against what the rest of the wing decided to do. In other words, they'd remain neutral. It was the bouncers' long-established practice not to pick sides in inmates' collective struggles.

Those closest to me visited all the cells one by one, notifying inmates that we wouldn't be returning to our cells, in protest against the deaths of our fellow inmates and to show our support for 'D' wing. We jammed the wing's door so that they wouldn't be able to open it from outside and made our intentions known to the administration. After a couple of hours they summoned about ten people from our wing to the guardhouse, among which were many bouncers, and Haris. I was asked last. I went and, before I had even managed to enter the guardhouse's door, I saw Haris exiting the public prosecutor's office. I wondered what he was doing there yet, deep down, I already knew. The public prosecutor would confirm my suspicion the following day. Nothing remains hidden under the sun.

Just as I entered the guardhouse, the bouncers left. I was determined not to get into a conversation. After an intense argument with the director and some wardens, I returned to the wing. Everyone was there waiting for me, except for the bouncers and Haris, who had vanished inside his cell. He'd never come out. And why would he? His job was done. I always said: whoever wants to meet the worst and the best man inside a prison can search for them, but it will be hard to find them. They're both hidden behind masks in this theatre of the absurd in which they're required to participate daily. The worst ones turn this game of masks into a science. Such is their mastery that it's almost impossible to distinguish between the masks and the person wearing them. They've got a natural flair for changing masks and roles fast. We're talking about real showmen; they can go from being Jesus to being Judas from one moment to the next.

The situation remained as it was until midnight when the warden arrived at the wing's barred gate to announce that the inmates from 'D' wing had returned peacefully back to their cells, after explanations were provided by the administration for the tragic incident. So, all of us supporting them had no reason to keep the strike going. I believed him. It would be unforgivable on a warden's part to trick a whole wing. He'd lose the inmates' respect. And yet the leader of the Albanians, who was in direct contact with 'D' wing (eighty percent of its inmates were Albanians), was vehemently protesting that the warden was lying.

I had a meeting with the people keeping the wing on its toes, and we decided that I should go and check whether the warden was telling the truth. If he was, we'd return to our cells. The warden was happy to accept my proposal. I took with me an Albanian, a Pontic Greek, and an anti-authoritarian, Yorgos.* We followed the warden and his henchmen until we reached 'D' wing's barred gate. The wing's interior was filled with papers and mattresses, yet its inmates were nowhere to be seen. They had all returned to their cells, and there was no indication that they had been forced to do so. Perhaps, the administration had used drugs. It was common practice to use drugs to repress a collective uprising of inmates. What an inglorious outcome.

The very next day, the public prosecutor and the prison board in charge of granting me the five-day furlough for which I had applied months before requested to see me. Every inmate was eligible for a furlough after their first five years in prison, and I was already in my sixth. The applicants' dependence on a sadist authoritarian who could grant them their chance in life or not, and whom the State supplies with sadomasochist tools that are supposed to set lost souls straight, is another step towards absolute correction.

"Palaiokostas, if you keep behaving like this you'll never get out of prison", the impudent prosecutor told me as soon as I took a seat at the meeting table.

He'd wanted to upset me, and he'd managed it quite well. It didn't take much.

I raised my voice, and I said to him, looking him straight in the eye: "Are you threatening me, sir? Do you have a problem with me? You're too small to decide whether I'll ever get out of prison".

The public prosecutor and the board were shocked. He tried to change his tune, so things didn't get out of hand.

"No, I never expressed any threat against you. I just meant to say that your behaviour during recent events doesn't help us to make a decision that satisfies both you and us!"

---

* He has since been released and continues his work.

"And how should I have behaved, sir? Tell me, I'm eager to learn!"

"Ask so and so (he told me Haris' surname, the guy who had fired up the guys and I had just seen walking out of his office). His trial is next week. Wait, and you'll see how well he'll do ..."

"I'm nothing like that son of a bitch, who makes deals with you while three inmates are dead because of your administration. And I'd never sell out the inmates' attempt to protest just so that you'd grant me a furlough".

"Wait outside for a moment so that the board can deliberate and we'll talk again", he said.

Outside were two girls. One of them was a social worker. When she saw me, she whispered to me, smiling, "You should know, I recommended that you be granted your furlough".

"Thank you, dear! You did what those cowards inside don't have the balls to".

The girl couldn't have been more than twenty-five years old, and I'd seen her for the first time when I had gone (according to protocol) to talk to her so that she could establish whether I was ready to behave properly if I was granted a furlough. It seemed quite funny to me that a young girl, who'd just finished her studies, could be in a position to judge a man who's gone through hell and back. I had gotten mad at her for asking me if I had regretted my crimes. I'd given her a crash course on crime and punishment, justice and injustice, truth and hypocrisy etc., making it clear to her that I felt proud of the way I was leading my life on this earth. The shock-seminar had paid off. She was a quick learner, good for her.

They summoned me back in the chamber and the prosecutor, with a conciliatory attitude this time, said to me: "Your honesty and frankness, Palaiokostas, don't go unnoticed. But they're kind of a double-edged sword. I can't prejudice the board's decision, but I want you to know one thing: if their response is negative this time, I'll take on your next application personally to make sure you'll get your furlough. Under one condition, though. You'll give me your word of honour that you'll return".

"As tempting as your offer might be, prosecutor, it conceals deceit. I'm honoured that you trust my word, but I don't know if I can use it as collateral for a furlough which I'm already entitled to. But if I do, be sure I'll honour it".

"I wouldn't have suggested it if I weren't sure that you honour your word, Palaiokostas".

I kept thinking about this whole incident all afternoon. We discussed it at length with Yorgos, walking up and down the wing's yard. Yorgos was an active anti-authoritarian who had found himself in prison for several offences. He believed that when dealing with people who have no honour and operate in deceitful ways to achieve their goal, entrapping a man by using his own moral code, one shouldn't feel guilty for tricking them.

"Vassilis, they're nothing but cruel authoritarians. Don't ever have reservations about what you're going to do. They're asking for your word for something they owe you and they have to justify their attitude towards you. You should have been getting furloughs for one-and-a-half years now. If you'd asked them for a furlough five years ago, then they'd have a reason to ask for your word as collateral, because they'd be breaking the rules. They're the ones who owe you something, not you them … If you return from your furlough it'll be a triumph to them; they'll take advantage of it to show everyone that even Palaiokostas follows the rules. Let's face it, you're a role-model of insubordination for many people; you have more responsibility to them than to those State bastards. Don't give them the satisfaction".

He was absolutely right, but he didn't know that, to me, keeping my word wasn't a simple ideology but part of my character. I felt that if I gave someone my word of honour and didn't keep it, a part of my character would collapse; that I'd never be the same again. It was a matter of soul and not logic. I thought that a human's word has value only when it is kept. History is full of examples of whole armies opening lines for the defeated to pass through, with the word of those in charge that they wouldn't be harmed being the only treaty signed. Fortunately, I proved lucky enough not to have to go through all this, because soon things took an interesting turn.

First escape by helicopter

As the yard was locked up, Yorgos and I entered the wing last, having discussed the subject in depth. The prison officer on duty was waiting for us by the wing's barred gate.

"Vassilis, the warden wants to see you", he said, opening the door for me.

I entered the gatehouse and, to my great surprise, saw the tremendous hyper-warden waiting for me.

"Sit, Vassilis", he said to me, pointing towards a chair at the opposite side of the desk.

After I took a seat, he adopted a pompous look and said, "Vassilis, I'm a leader just like you! So I understand you very well, but …"

I stopped myself from laughing. The "hyper" was comparing being a chief to being a leader, confusing apples with oranges.

"Leadership is the natural result of an influential figure being freely elected by the collective instinct to guide them. A leader has no choice. He is forced to lead the way, to guide, to envision … he isn't an elected official, a plain manager. Forgive me, warden, but I've never seen an appointed leader," I said.

"The fact that I've been appointed doesn't mean I've lost my ability as a leader. But let's forget that. That's not why I came to see you. I want to acknowledge that I made a mistake taking your position off you. It was a bad move on my part, and I'm willing to make it up to you. This week, the prison board is meeting to discuss job positions. File an application to be formally made a paramedic so that you can have a salary position and you'll come to my wing, 'E'".

"I'm not saying that I'm not interested in your offer, but I will have to think it over. I've been in 'A' wing for such a long time. I have gotten used to living there, I have my friends etc. If I apply, then it means I accept, and you should move forward. I just want to take with me someone from 'A' wing".

He agreed, as long as that someone was also a worker because 'E' wing was only for workers. In fact, I wanted some time to figure out where the trap was. Because I was sure that before coming to me bearing gifts, he had gotten the green light from both the director and the prosecutor. When they offer something, they have something in mind. I weighed up the situation; I decided to take the risk and went along with it. After all, 'E' wing was more comfortable in all respects. With me came Kostas, a boxer from the Mani Peninsula (from a well-known boxers' family) whom I had been exercising with. A nice fellow. When I made myself comfortable in my new cell, Alket came to see me.

We didn't know each other, just to say hello when we happened to meet in the prisons' common areas. He was officially a prisoner of Nafplio Prison, but he was staying in Korydallos, in 'E' wing, because of his ongoing trials. It hadn't been long since he'd received a life sentence for committing a murder, although no body was ever found. Only the Greek judiciary can pull off such magic tricks. Better to have a hundred innocent men in prison than leave a guilty one free in society. I assumed Alket would be looking for a way to escape. So, after visiting him in his cell a couple of times, I asked him whether he was willing to serve his time.

"Are you insane? Of course I'm not serving a life sentence! I'm searching for a hole or something to escape ..."

"Gone are the times when there were holes in prisons. Now we have to make them on our own, Alket".

"Why? Do you want to go?" he asked me, surprised.

"What do you think?"

"I'm just asking because you've already applied for a furlough and sooner or later you'll get it".

"There's a big difference between sooner and later. After all, I wouldn't be very proud to be escorted out. I prefer opening the door myself!"

"Do you have anything in mind? A plan?"

"Oh, I've got many plans. But plans need people who have the balls to see them through".

"I've got as many people as you want on the outside! Good ones, ready for action, willing to shoot to kill".

"We just need one, even if they're not shooting to kill. They just need to care for you personally, in a selfless way".

"I've got someone. A very close friend. He'd die for me".

"Are you sure?"

"Yes. One hundred percent sure".

"If you've got someone like that, Alket, trust me. We'll get out of this prison".

We agreed that Alket would get his hands on a new mobile phone which he'd use to communicate only with that friend of his and always in code. He'd come by my cell once every two days to talk, we'd never be seen walking together in the yard and most importantly, I made it clear to him that there shouldn't be any leaks. I considered the latter to be bad luck. Only those involved in the escape needed to know.

It would happen by helicopter. Alket and I would participate from the inside, and his friend and Spyros from the outside. From that day forward, everything went according to plan. Exactly three weeks later we'd go. After six-and-a-half years of incessant struggle to acquire her, here at the end she'd truly begun smiling at me, so full of promise. Freedom is female; she comes to you whenever she wants to.

Escaping by helicopter wasn't something that had just dawned on me there and then. It was the most well thought through escape scenario I had come up with. I'd been working on it since I was first imprisoned and I'd never come this close to putting it into practice. I'd discussed such a prospect with one or two fellow inmates in the past, but they hadn't been ready to get involved in so grand an undertaking. They thought you needed a pilot who was in on the whole thing or even your own helicopter for the escape to be crowned by success. On the contrary, I was more than confident that with one or even better, two, brave people who are willing to board a helicopter armed and take its pilot hostage, you're bound to succeed. You have an even stronger reason to believe your plan will succeed when nothing similar has ever been attempted before.

I had also convinced Spyros of this when we had shared a cell. I'd gotten him in an imaginary flight simulator for many hours until he understood that up in the air it's all psychology. That no rational human being would put their lives in danger, knowing that if something goes wrong, they're dead. We'd also discussed in depth where and how he'd rent the helicopter, that he'd need to have a test flight to get a sense of the altitude, the cabin, and everything else. So Spyros was perfectly ready, and we didn't have to talk about all this again. I had already given him plenty of firepower for the last aborted attempt, and I had hooked him up with a fake ID. After he met Panagiotis, Alket's friend, they ran the test flight two weeks later, and everything went as expected. At about six that evening, we went to the yard separately, and watched the helicopter flying about one-and-a-half mile away from the prison. We got back to my cell on the second floor to discuss. Alket was excited.

"My friend, we're leaving! Next Sunday we'll be out! We'll be free! I can feel it, I know we will!"

Alket's optimism had positive effects on me as well, helping me as I remained cautious so that I could deal with the whole situation without losing control. Another equally important positive thing about Alket, something which proved crucial to the success of our escape, was his complete lack of rivalry with me.

"Friend, I trust you completely. Whatever you say, you know what you're doing, so go ahead", he'd always say.

I raised an issue that had been bothering me. If we could, I wanted to take someone with us, an anti-authoritarian named Yannis who had recently been shot by the cops during a car chase after a bank robbery in the centre of Athens. He'd be sentenced to many years.

"Yes, my friend, the more of us on the outside, the better for us! And since he's an anti-authoritarian he must be a good guy". he answered me plainly.

He's anti-authoritarian, he must be good ... that simple! However, Yannis proved unlucky. The "hyper" was on holiday the whole week, and no one but him could transfer Yannis from 'A' wing to my cell. The train doesn't wait.

In that first test flight, Alket's friend and compatriot, Panagiotis, didn't participate. The kid went on his own. He booked the trip in the company's offices in Kifissia, which belong — as does the helicopter — to the Vardinoyannis' dynasty (this family unknowingly did something good in their dirty life), and he flew with two friends of his as a cover. When they disembarked on a rooftop in Glyfada (it was used as a take-off and landing spot) Spyros arranged with the pilot to fly again at the same time the following Sunday. He said he wanted to surprise a close friend of his on his birthday! And the deal was closed.

At six on Sunday, on the very same rooftop, the two lads, each carrying a small backpack full of guns, grenades, and a gas can, were ecstatically bombarding the pilot with questions about the helicopter. Looking down on them, he proudly and eagerly answered the foolish fellows' questions. He started the engine, and the helicopter took off. Panagiotis, as an excited guest star, sat in the co-pilot's seat while the kid sat in the back. This joyride included a wonderful tour of the southern suburbs, where refined primitive TV celebrities and businessmen lived, following the coastline until Faliro and then turning right, reaching the foot of deforested and burned Mount Parnitha before turning back. The pilot also acted as a tour guide, raving about the basin's concrete hellhole and the surrounding area.

"To our left, we see the Saronic Gulf and way ahead we can see Aegina and Salamis. To our right is Mount Hymettus and straight ahead is Piraeus, the port and the bay of Zea ..."

Reaching Rentis, the tour became a lot more interesting. The pilot, after proudly showing them how the Acropolis and all other similar carcasses of past glories look from that high in the air, went on to show them some more recent, inglorious ones.

"There, to our left, is Schisto and a bit further down is Korydallos Prison!"

He shouldn't have uttered these last two words! It was the pre-arranged signal for the two hijackers to act in unison.

Spyros, being in the back seat, swiftly removed the pilot's intercom from the pilot's head and placed his left hand around the man's neck, holding a grenade right in front of his face. At the same time, Panagiotis pressed a Tokarev against his head.

"We're going to Korydallos Prison, fucker. Now, if you do anything stupid, you're dead".

He turned white as a sheet. He turned towards the prison at once and in a while they were over 'E' wing's yard.

"Where do I land?"

"There!"

"Where? Where? Where?"

"There, by the red flag ..."

We, on the inside, were perfectly ready. We didn't need many things. Ten minutes before, I had talked with Spyros who'd said to me: "Everything's fine, mum. We're now boarding the helicopter. I'll see you soon".

We estimated how much time it would take them to get there and exited my cell together. Alket had a chain and a lock under his shirt. I was holding a plastic bag in which there was a big red flag. We also each had a makeshift knife on us, just in case anyone tried to be heroic. We stopped and pretended to be talking by the wing's barred gate. Less than two minutes had gone by when we saw the helicopter flying over Kifissos, heading north. For a moment we couldn't see it. I went to the bathroom, which was right across from us, and tried to call the kid. He didn't answer. As I exited, a deep rumbling sound reached my ears.

"Let's go, my friend. They're coming", said Alket.

We went through the door, and Alket closed it behind him. He removed the chain from his waist, put it around the bars and locked it. We headed to the yard's centre. We laid the flag with Che Guevara's face on it on the ground as a sign. Three inmates had frozen in the middle of the yard, staring at the helicopter. I approached them, and slapped the neck of the tallest one. They all turned to look at me, dazed, and when they saw it was me they ran away. The yard officer was a wrestling type of guy, yet he decided to stay put on the other side of the yard, next to the small fountain that was there. He didn't move a muscle; he just sat there, like the rest of the inmates, enjoying the unexpected spectacle.

The helicopter had arrived; it was but a hundred yards away from the prison's outer wall and within seconds, it was hovering over the yard. The pilot brought it into position for landing, and it began to descend. Dust and sand from the gravel flew in the air, creating a suffocating atmosphere. The yard appeared as though it had been struck by a raging sandstorm. The deafening, crisp sound of the helicopter's rotor blades, reverberating from the concrete wing building to the outer wall, was shaking the whole prison as though poised to destroy it. All our senses were alert. Adrenaline had kicked in. Everything seemed as though it was happening in slow motion, inside a virtual reality version of the world. I felt I could see every spin the rotor blades made, every grain of sand that flew in the air; I felt every soundwave hitting my eardrums. For a few seconds the helicopter hovered two feet above the ground until we got in and then it began to rise, making even more noise. In moments we'd left Korydallos Prison behind us, flying towards sweet freedom. The kids didn't relax, not even for a second. They were still threatening the pilot with the grenade and the gun.

"It's ok guys. Give us the guns. We'll take it from here".

Spyros took a Skorpion out of his backpack for Alket and a short-barrel Kalashnikov for me. I armed it and addressed the pilot.

"Relax. Don't screw it now that we're almost done. You'll drop us off in Schisto, at the cemetery, and then you can go home and we to work".

At once, the tension lifted, and the hijackers smiled proudly. They were brave lads. They'd proven the soul can fly without any aircraft, yet when one is found, it can lead to quite a spectacular aerial escape.

After a while, the helicopter landed at a parking lot outside the cemetery. The kid had gone there that same afternoon and left two stolen Enduro motorcycles, which we'd use to flee (he knew that place very well since it was related to his family's business). My three partners got on the motorcycles while I stayed back with the pilot until he switched off the helicopter's engine. I had with me a kombolói* that Yorgos had made for me. It was one of a kind. I had instructed him not to make another like it. Several deputy wardens had asked him to make one for them too, but he'd always refer them to me to ask my permission. None of them did, because they already knew the answer.

"You did great. Come, have this kombolói from Palaiokostas. It's collectable, and I don't need it any more. Oh, and don't you dare start that engine again, because no matter where you hide I'll find you and I'll tear you apart!"

I got off the helicopter and onto the kid's motorcycle. Alket and Panagiotis had already left. We raced behind them, and soon overtook them. Spyros was a master when it came to bikes. Somewhere in Haidari, a white Mercedes was waiting for us, stolen by one of Alket's friends and left there by Spyros. We got there almost at the same time. We abandoned the motorcycles a block away, and the three of us got in the car, while Panagiotis put on Alket's hat and walked away. Spyros, under my guidance, had done a professional job. We were surprised by how simply and carefully he had put our plan in action. This escape required madness and succinct professionalism to succeed, and the kid possessed both of those things. Of course, we thanked him and congratulated him on his accomplishment.

Twenty minutes later, we were driving uphill towards Mount Fyli, on the western part of Mount Parnytha. After such a long time in prison, the distances and the colours of nature didn't seem the same to me, and that wasn't even the worst part of my imprisonment. As we reached the valley of Thebes, the Second Programme on the car's radio interrupted its regular schedule to deliver a piece of breaking news. After sharing some initial information on the "unprecedented escape", the two radio presenters provocatively dedicated the next song to all fugitives.

Papazoglou's voice made us smile. We cheered up!

... and the fugitives of time,
are on to something,
they said it's not wrong to live life with passion
and that's why they saved themselves ...
... throw us a hook
give us advantage ...

Come on, fellas ...

---

*   Worry beads.

AFTER THE FLIGHT

Serpico, the bomber, obscure laws,
and political hypocrisy

Put in charge of guarding an entrance, a Greek man will install a toll booth and make a profit. And if you give him the power to enforce the law, he'll first adapt it to his finances and then enforce it mercilessly on everyone else. Given this reality, which the political system, as a collective consciousness, cultivated for many decades, a single bill voted through Parliament was enough to hand the reins of local crime over to the police. Not just to combat it but also to commit it, as long as its chiefs grew rich from it.*

An article of this law, given the chauvinistic title "undercover penetration", allowed the police to cover up the crimes committed by its officers and cooperating outlaws who were running undercover operations to dismantle all kinds of criminal networks. In other words, someone who has to penetrate the world of drugs is allowed to sell all sorts of narcotics to succeed, having immunity from prosecution. Someone who wants to penetrate a revolutionary organisation can plant bombs without facing any consequences. Someone undercover among bank robbers can participate in armed bank robberies. Someone undercover among blackmailing groups can become a protection racketeer etc. The law covers all kinds of crimes to produce the desired results. These unconventional practices aren't new, they were frequently used by law enforcement officials in the past as well, but they hadn't been covered by legislation. They were, however, accepted because of the nature of their profession.

Drugs are the best example of how prosecuting authorities understand and put "penetration" into practice. Senior officers (in cooperation with some lower-ranking initiates) from the drug enforcement administration give the green light to experienced and cooperative drug dealers of their liking (usually foreigners) to supply their pushers with drugs, under the condition that they'll rat out other dealers, who the police will bust, beat up, and arrest on all kinds of drug charges.

This simple method leaves everyone satisfied. The dealers, as lawful partners of the police, take out the competition, ratting out their unprotected rival dealers to the officers protecting them. The officers use their effortless, served-on-a-silver-platter arrests to present significant amounts of work in the fight against drugs and a large proportion of the profits end up in their pockets. Drug addicts keep multiplying, flooding the city, since they can find whichever drug they desire

---

* Author's note: corruption is the norm within the Hellenic Police and the political world rewards it, facilitating it by passing relevant laws. It is impressive how the justice system treats the cases of corrupt officers that happen to be brought before the court. Almost 90% of those accused are cleared of all charges and the rest get off with just a slap on the wrist ... For appearance's sake.

despite the constant dismantling of drug trafficking networks. Prisons, operating as pools from which the insatiable judiciary monster sups, are flooded with drug dealers, pushers, addicts, and all sorts of runners with life sentences, who were captured by the Hellenic Police's "beam trawls". And the corrupt legislative body of a country that has the sad privilege of having infinitely more drug dealers than addicts operates hypocritically to solve such a significant issue for society while shirking its responsibility, since it is on their command that the prosecuting authorities continue the relentless war against drugs.

It is quite common for inter-group wars to break out when conflicts of interest arise between the various cop gangs who enforce this particular law for their own personal benefit. Quite often someone cooperating with one cop gang is captured during a different cop gang's undercover operation with the same interest, finding themselves accused. So, protectors are forced to call or present themselves before the district attorneys in charge of the case to testify that the accused is no criminal, but their own tool of penetration.

So the undercover penetration article is one of the Greek Parliament's many gifts to police officers for their services towards the concealment of the widespread corruption that plagues all Greece; a country that itself gives birth to criminality. It is similar to the law concerning ministerial responsibility, guaranteeing that officers don't face any charges for their methods and, at the same time, making them complicit with crimes committed against the people. It's not a coincidence that the Hellenic Police's senior officers and the police trade union members have political agendas. Having the hot-button issue of criminality as a spearhead, they serve specific interests and, most commonly, right-wing political parties that always have open spots in the electoral register for when they're no longer active. Of course, the expenses of their costly electoral campaigns are covered by them, from their own savings from their meagre salaries. So crime constitutes a decisive factor in party conflicts and political developments. Something that can prove extremely useful; something to be exploited.

The corrupted group that infests the State reacts vehemently against the prospect of decriminalising the using and dealing of soft drugs, as well as the State-run specialist organisations which, under the supervision of medical staff, offer hard drugs to addicts in an attempt to get them clean. Because this way, the well-thought and highly profitable scheme of the contrived and incessant fight against crime that serves their whole dirty system will go up in smoke. Instead, they vigorously (as the naïve see it) and treacherously (as the clued-up see it) pass and enforce harsh laws against those trying to spoil their private party. Because they disrupt the order of things, which is nothing more than their sacred interests. They declare them terrorists, but they're social activists; and people with revolutionary ideas. The reason the anti-terrorist law was implemented was that some of them, without any personal benefit (nothing must be free in the capitalist world or it will be ruined) and having no other weapon, used some harmless bombs to awaken the people, those who live a life full of compromises, resigned because that's the way things are.

Things are the way they are because you are the way you are, little man. If you were different, things would be different too.*

A typical side effect of similar legislation can be found in the instance of the contemptible 'Law 13' (I don't know if it is still in effect), which provided preferential legal treatment, or even the dismissal of all charges, for someone involved in drug cases (among others) who had helped prosecuting authorities to solve the case in which they themselves were involved, as well as other cases of all kinds. Inmates who believed that ratting out their partners and cooperating with the police was a revolutionary act, along with their senior-cop patrons, had set up a side-business in and out of prisons, selling 'Law 13' services for as much as fifty thousand euros a head!

One of the many tricks they used was this: those inmates who wanted to make some money out of 'Law 13', with the help of their like-minded partners who had been acquitted by the same law, got themselves down to work. Tricking inexperienced outlaws and naïve Albanians, they planned drug trafficking from Albania to Greece. As soon as the unsuspecting traffickers crossed the borders carrying the drugs, ready to hand them to the rebels in a predetermined spot, they were welcomed by their pals, the cops. Aside from being rightfully decorated, the plotting cops stood in to profit from each 'Law 13' service they'd later offer. Meaning that they had another 'Law 13' instance in their hands, which they could use to "help" an inmate awaiting some important trial, who would benefit from a cop testifying that they had aided the bust and cooperated in the fight against crime. All this, of course, if said inmate had fifty grand and no shame. This fifty grand would be split among the snitching 'Law 13er' inmates who had arranged the whole thing and those tireless protectors of society, the senior cops. Of course, the unsuspecting young Albanians might still be in prison, since the judiciary vibrates with pleasure every time it utters the maximum penalty. Oh, fellow man! You're such a scab deep down, and that's the only thing that scares me in this life ...

Another example of law enforcement's corruption is the following series of events that clearly highlight my point.

After violating his furlough and to make ends meet, Spyros joined a group of three men, stealing bags and briefcases from moving luxury vehicles around the northern suburbs of Athens, while at the same time participating in several other kinds of robberies, including banks. While working with them, he discovered that the members of that team were being guided and protected by one of the many Hellenic Police's rogue cops, who at the time was chief of the Nikaia, Athens police department. For his valuable services, this ridiculous Serpico wannabe would demand — and receive — three grand per month from each of those he protected.

---

*   Vassilis may be referring to 17 November here, but his sentiment is likely more general, as unlike in Britain, bombings and arson attacks against buildings by revolutionary groups (as well as criminal and far-right gangs) are not uncommon, such as the 2018 bombing of Skai TV, or the bombing of an MP's house and arson attacks against a business owned by the wife of civil protection chief Nikos Hardalias in 2021 etc.

If any of his "lads" was arrested in action by a different police department he'd pay them a visit while still in custody, and request about thirty to fifty grand to make it disappear. He "honoured" his word. He'd take his precious "lads" by the hand and walk away with them from the district attorney's office. Note that they weren't the only ones who paid for his protection. At the same time, to show some work was being done, he'd arrest all outlaws that his roaming snitches told him to.

The following incident is indicative of the whole situation. During one of his informants' daily excursions, by total coincidence, they broke the window of the National Intelligence Service chief's car (he had stopped at a red light), and took a briefcase with classified State documents. Seeing the briefcase's contents, they contacted their mentor to guide them as to what they should do. He advised them to bring him the documents. Then, presenting himself as a Deus ex machina, he handed them to the chief of the National Intelligence Service. Since he wasn't obligated to reveal how he had come by the briefcase (informants' identities are confidential), he justified himself by claiming he maintained an excellent relationship with the underworld, from which he obtained useful information that helped him in the fight against organised crime. So he became highly respected within the police force, teaching his colleagues that no one goes far by playing nice ...

Spyros, still remembering my advice that he shouldn't trust any outlaw who did business with cops, didn't tell them anything about my impending escape (fortunately). In the final stage of the plan, he emptied and cleaned the house where he'd lived until then and followed my instructions to the letter. Some days after the escape, we parted ways with Alket, while Spyros headed back to Athens to meet his girlfriend. From her, he'd learn many details about what took place after the escape, which we had until then ignored. Disturbed by how much publicity the escape had received, two of the informants threatened Spyros' girlfriend. They had gotten her to the Nikaia police department, to their protector's office, to confess that she was one of the girls who had participated in the test flight. Of course, they'd also informed him of the house where Spyros had been living, in case we had hidden there after the escape.

The rogue cop had lost it.

"Why didn't you tell me sooner? I'd have gone myself to the cemetery at Schisto with my men, and I would have killed them the moment they got off the helicopter!"

Hold your horses, you cheap Serpico knockoff ...

This isn't a big revelation or anything. Everyone who cares to learn about such things knows about similar achievements. Everyone knows which politician ordered those bouncers to plant a bomb targeting Vassilis Michaloliakos,* and yet the police — after an in-depth investigation — accused the Revolutionary

---

*   Mayor of Piraeus. The New Democracy politician was injured in the 2001 blast, which he blamed on a political rival.

Organisation 17 November. The whole political world knows, as do all New Democracy party's officials, one of whom is this particular "bomber" who otherwise has a zero-tolerance policy.* Michaloliakos himself knows it even better, yet he doesn't talk. And what could he say, when he'd have to explain the motives behind this settling of political scores. So he chose silence, bound by the same omertà code imposed by the corrupted political reality he serves. A political reality in which political parties have the structures of criminal organisations, employ gangster methods and make sure people can't find a single one of them to demand explanations from. In which the police take on the role of a private army tasked to protect specific interests, and in which the majority of journalists become the bitches of TV station owners and get rich by selling themselves to whoever is in power, bound to keep their life and times a secret, lest the stench reaches people's noses causing undesired side effects.

It is common knowledge which politicians and members of the parliament are being bribed by drug-trafficking networks in exchange for immunity. It is also well known which esteemed prosecutor got four people out of prison, only a month after their detention, awaiting trial for five grand armed bank robberies because one of them happened to be his child, while during the hearing he made sure his son wasn't sentenced to prison at all. Despite all this, he continues to offer his valuable services, safeguarding the rule of law! In my cases, and I assume in many others too, his sleazy kind would summarily impose the maximum prescribed penalty for all offences. When, however, it comes to the criminals in power, it takes a couple of centuries of incessant sessions for the special parliamentary committees and the special courts to reach a final judgment. Which will be a judgment of acquittal, as usual. Talk about equality before the law! Those who commit an offence out of necessity are crucified, while the real criminals apply the punishments.

It is natural to question whether someone who has rejected the law wholesale cares if they are being followed by those who apply them. Let me be clear about this: I don't care about laws and their implementation in a State in which I don't want to actively participate, since they are built on the utmost amount of injustice and abuse. And still, these laws directly affect me. What I fail to comprehend is how these primates in power, obviously behaving like hungry apes in an open market within State institutions, are accepted by intelligent citizens as humans and even more so as being useful to their society.

Unfortunately, reality is cruel. It reflects desperate dwarves, their tiny hands erecting Cyclopean walls of laws around them, in an attempt to protect their lazy, helpless souls. They build a contagious and dangerous civilisation which is governed by greedy humanoids, who don't hesitate to steal their own children's future to satisfy their insatiable consumerism frenzy. If we imagine this civilisation as a multi-story building, and if I possessed such magical powers to

---

*   It is an open secret in Greece that politicians maintain open channels of communication with organised crime and use its power for their own purposes, which range from acquiring more votes to getting someone out of the way.

be able to decide its fate, I'd thoroughly renovate it. Most tenants perhaps would agree with me that it needs to be demolished, few, however, would accept the loss of their apartment.

Since I'll never accept that I'm being hunted down by sleazy bipeds, I'll uncover their corruption by posing a provocative question. How would they react in a hypothetical scenario where I participate in the next elections with a newly founded party consisting of various scumbags, where the electorate honours me with 80% of its votes (let's leave the remaining 20% for the scenario to make sense), and, as required by the constitution, I form a democratic government? Would a single one of them quit their prominent positions in protest? It doesn't take much thought or imagination to answer this hypothetical question. Absolutely no one! Forgetting my criminal background, professional politicians would graciously accept whichever ministerial position I offered them in my new government. Policemen would fight over a spot in my personal guard (as well as in those of my scumbags), holding their guns, ready to protect us from new imaginary bad guys; judges would keep on being fair, judging poor citizens based on my new laws. The system's concubines would fight over an exclusive interview where they'd refer to me as minister rather than "known criminal" while bankers, whose banks up until recently I would have been robbing, and businessmen, who would have feared that I'd abduct them, would beg me to accept briefcases containing their humble gifts, as democracy would steer its own course because it has no dead ends.

I don't know if the Greek constitution grants me the right to become a politician. Let them not worry — if I suddenly decide to turn myself into a joke I'll think of a more creative way to do so. Anyway, if I ever lose my mind (we're only human after all) and do become a politician, all Greeks had better vote for me. So many four-year periods of seriousness, industriousness, and responsibility have gone to waste thus far, let them give a chance to humour, carelessness, and irresponsibility.

Who knows ... we might all escape our collective depression!

The kid

In the summer of 2006, I came to Athens for a few months. It was a tough decision for me, I couldn't stand the place. Aside from not knowing it at all, it seemed to me — and it felt — like a concrete extension of Korydallos; its vast back yard, where people live in a semi-free state. This feeling only became stronger as I came to know some inmates who had lived in the city before being incarcerated. Their adaptability to this new reality was astonishing, as though they had already been ready for it. They gave the impression of tenants of an apartment building, who had been violently evicted from their luxurious and spacious 2,000 square feet penthouse, then moved to a humble, cramped, 300 square feet ground-floor apartment. Their struggle for freedom was directly linked to cemented square feet and everyday conveniences.

Escaping would never even cross their minds. Either way, an escape from a small prison into a bigger one isn't an escape at all, since it isn't worth the risk and it doesn't really change anything.

The reason I went to Athens was to locate, observe, and, finally, abduct Panagopoulos, a ship-owner who lived in a luxurious villa by the sea in Kavouri. Having been informed by the press about his illness however I crossed him off my list, and we set his son, who was around my age, as our new target. Every day he would arrive an hour after his father at the company's offices in Voula, in a brown Audi A8 (chauffeur-driven of course), using the exact same route as he too lived in his father's enormous villa. He was a relatively easy target, but it took us a few months of intensive surveillance to be sure about the route, because he went away (travelling obviously) from time to time. It was mid-autumn when we finished our surveillance, and we decided to have a break before moving on with the abduction in early December. We almost went through with it, but we were already too late. Such a waste of time. Perhaps, without me knowing, others had got to him first.*

I made it clear to Spyros that if the abduction ended well, I'd leave Greece. He was welcome to come with me if he wanted to but if not, he'd have to be his own man and make sure he remained out of prison for as long as he could. It is a hard fact that if we stayed in the country, there would always be a cell with our names written on it (as there eventually was). Spyros didn't last long under the pressure of being on the run. He revolted behind my back, ignoring safety rules which he was obligated to keep. I was surprised to find out that he was sneaking out to get drugs and meet his girlfriend, who had gone with him on that test-flight and who, when interrogated, had confessed that she and the kid were a couple. Right after the escape, knowing that this had taken a toll on him, I advised him to suggest to his girlfriend that she come with him, if she wanted to of course. Otherwise, he'd have to cut her off completely. The girl refused.

Understanding (or so I thought) the danger we were in, he promised me he'd never see her again.

Suddenly realising my closest partner was doing things behind my back, going down dark roads forbidden to fugitives, and not knowing how long this had been going on for, I was enraged. I was once again confronted with that invincible beast: the unpredictable human factor. Love is sacred, passions are understandable, but we had the entire police force on our tails, waiting for us to make a mistake. Wanting to somehow justify his unacceptable behaviour, I'll say this: youth's liveliness, the sudden change in his life, the age difference (he saw me as a father figure), his lack of fun, and his eagerness to take advantage of the cred his participation in the escape had given him, probably led to this dangerously careless behaviour. He thought the escape was the stepping stone

---

*   Ship-owner Pericles Panagopoulos was kidnapped by armed men in early 2009. He was released a week later, after his kidnappers received €30 million in ransom money. The police accused and eventually put on trial some inmates from Korydallos prison for orchestrating it.

towards a carefree life without rules and not the beginning of hardships which we had to overcome. He obviously couldn't handle all this wisely, and while he used to look up to me, now he saw me as a mere dictator. He thought I was responsible for the hardships of our situation and for being so focused on our common goal.

I am indeed coarse by nature. There's a sharpness to my speech which comes naturally, often without me realising it. It's who I am. I often spoke to him that way under the pressure of work, whenever he took serious matters lightly. Of course, the kid knew this aspect of my character well enough from having lived with me in prison for two years. Coming to get me with the helicopter, he knew I wouldn't leave this part of me behind. I was in a really tough spot. All this was too sudden, I didn't know how to handle it and I didn't have a solution. Who could, when we're talking about a rare soul, whose feet are deep in garbage and whose hands are reaching for the stars, a soul who crosses swollen rivers running. When he himself, who happened to have such a soul, couldn't handle it, how could I? Whatever rules I would have enforced on him, it would only cause more trouble.

And yet, after some four-letter words, I spoke to him earnestly, trying to fix things between us. We reconciled (or so I thought, once again) after he admitted that he was wrong. He promised me that it wouldn't happen again. His promise lasted only for twenty days. I realised (a little too late) that he had taken drugs before a bank robbery in which people almost got killed.

This was the straw that broke the camel's back for me. Now I could feel the devil growing near. It was evident that Spyros had no intention of defeating his demons. He decided to part ways, thinking he had already learnt from me what he could. He felt his wings were strong enough. He wanted to try them, free in the open air, away from my oppressive prohibitions. It was his right, after all.

Such a sad development. I felt responsible for him because he had put himself in danger for me, and I wouldn't have the opportunity to repay him. At the same time, however, I didn't wish to become hostage to a past heroic act while his present behaviour was becoming a problem. His behaviour created an adverse climate of suspicion which was alarming. I found no point in insisting; as I saw it, this was an impossible situation. How could I begin, focus, and carry out so demanding a job as abduction, given the circumstances? I was willing to repay him by getting him to the top, but not by allowing him to make me hit rock bottom, abandoning reliable safety rules which I had tested and put to practice living as a fugitive for many years, and which afterwards would be adopted by anyone who worked with me.

Another sad future development was that Spyros' case gave some poisonous toads, who had been standing by waiting for a long time, an opportunity to spew their venom, spitting against the wind, without really knowing the facts. This is one of the reasons I'm referring to this convoluted subject so extensively. Another reason is to tell my own truth as a tribute to a giving kid with a proud, pure soul; a truth that in no case reduces his worth, which was and remains one of a kind.

I'll bid him farewell, picturing him as I first saw him, outside the door of my cell, a huge lunch box in hand.*

Oh, kid. You went a bit overboard with the balance and the sword. You took my words at face value. I didn't mean it like that. How great you stood before life and death! You didn't give Charon a second chance, as you hadn't given me. You managed to scare him too. You ridiculed him. You exposed his worthlessness. You grabbed his scythe and showed him how brave lads should be claimed. At once, suddenly. Without mercy, in one stroke, standing tall, weapons in hand! This life was too small for you; they made it so, feeble and sick. A consumptive monster, whose mouth reeks of cheap, regurgitated lies. Greatly ornamented yet predictable to the end. You weren't meant for this toothless wretched life's mouth; a life which misses its virginity yet which has ripped its soul and body apart whoring them again and again.

Responsibilities, self-sacrifice, betrayal, mistakes, passions, lies and truth; fleeting life has it all. It was all too much for you, yet you tasted it all. I never dared unleash the chained beast inside me, forgive me for that, but I'm scared of wild human instincts. They're bloodthirsty; we must hold their reigns firmly. I had told you so: they kill people and in the end, they might kill us too. Don't bother with it though. What if our path is filled with fog, mist, storms; what if we are judged by the Law of Moses; what if we are up against the terror of the Plagues of Egypt? In the end, we'll beat our enemy. He's already knocked out on the canvas, but he refuses to admit it. He tries to stop the world from knowing we have descended to this earth. A battle of thousands against a single man is an outright victory for that man, irrespective of the outcome. That's just how history works. Nobody remembers, supports, and identifies with the fateful thousands but with the single individual who, sharp as a diamond, carves ways of thought and forms consciences, throwing in the blink of an eye his immortal seed in the river of human evolution. A seed which rulers detest. They furiously crush it in history's mortar, grinding it into powder and, not knowing how to get rid of it (even though they themselves feed on it in secret), add misleading flavours and make it palatable enough to be served to their hungry and controlled flock as their own invention and offer! We don't want our victories to gain a spot in the cesspool but to enjoy the heavenly dance floors where only large souls know how to dance. And your soul didn't only dance; it outdanced them all. Your short life is a shining star; you deserve a dominant position in the vastness of the starry sky. I'm sure it placed you high, as you deserve and from there you'll have a better viewpoint from which to judge things. But I think I can already see you smiling down at me.

Oh, my friend ...

---

*   Spyros was sentenced to seventeen years in prison for hijacking and served a large portion of his sentence until he was granted his first furlough, from which he didn't return. After months of being hunted down by the police over a series of armed bank robberies, and as the cottage he had been staying with his two (also wanted) partners was surrounded by men from the Special Anti-Terrorist Unit, he took his own life. Switching his Kalashnikov to rapid fire mode, he pressed its barrel against his jaw and pulled the trigger.

OUTRUNNING COPS
WITH RAMMSTEIN ON PLAY

Something would always happen to me at this time of year. It's inexplicable. It was a Sunday morning in spring, sometime before Easter. I was driving an X5 with tinted windows and at my side, in the passenger seat, was Lefteris. We were on the Farsala-Larissa road, headed in the direction of Larissa. It can't have been past ten o'clock when we came across a roadblock set up by officers from the Crime Prevention and Suppression Unit and the traffic police. We were about twenty yards away from making a right turn when, through a thicket and down the road, I saw police SUVs and black-clothed cops holding MP5s. There wasn't any other vehicle in front of us. I was sure they were going to pull us over. To the left of the road, I could see the first houses of the village, which spread over the whole barren hill. Right at the turn in front of us (which was now only ten yards away), there was a left exit towards the village square. I stepped on the brakes, and the heavy vehicle came to a standstill. I drove it off the main road a bit clumsily, following the road leading to the village. The cops could see the road's turn and got wind of my sudden movement, which hit them as suspicious. It was.

From what I could remember, there was no other road we could use to escape to a nearby village, and even if there had been a dirt road somewhere nearby, it would have been hard to locate it if you didn't already know where it was. For the time being, we had no other solution than to try, in case we got lucky. Sure that the cops wouldn't just stand there and watch, I kept on driving down the narrow village alleys until I reached its northern side.

"Lefteris, we're in trouble. Prepare the 'kala' and be ready for a confrontation".

"I'm ready, pal ... I've released the safety already, don't worry".

Indeed, he was holding the AK-S in his hands. The first police vehicle appeared in the X5's mirrors. As soon as they saw us, they turned on their emergency lights and their siren. The situation called for us to make our intentions clear before the SUVs could arrive and trap us inside the village.

"Fire a round over their car to make them stop".

Lefteris leaned out of the open window and shot five or six bullets. They were scared shitless — they stopped there.

This didn't solve any problems. We reached the edge of the village, but we didn't find any dirt roads we could drive on that would lead towards the village's exit. Having no other choice, we turned left and followed a paved path which seemed to be used as the village's back road and which led us round to the road from which we had first entered the village. To our great surprise, the roadblock wasn't there. There was not a single police vehicle to be seen, and the one we had just shot at was only now entering the main road towards Larissa. We followed close behind it, then turned in the opposite direction, heading towards Farsala. They didn't seem to be in the mood for a car chase, unless they'd panicked so much that they didn't realise we had entered the main road right behind them.

After a few miles I turned right on a paved road going through several other small villages in the plain of Larissa, which led to the Karditsa-Larissa road, and from there to the main Larissa-Trikala highway. Despite its horsepower and its pickup, the X5 wasn't very manoeuvrable along the narrow, winding local roads. Aside from everything else, it was so big that it could be easily spotted. A huge black SUV with tinted windows moving at high speed along the barren plain's roads in broad daylight was like an elephant in the city centre. Yet I didn't intend to get rid of it, because it wasn't stolen. One of Lefteris' relatives had given it to us so that we could travel. We had just switched its license plates with those of another similar X5. If we abandoned it, the man would get in trouble, so I was willing to do anything in my power to stop it falling into their hands.

We drove fast for a few more miles and, having left several villages behind us, on a stretch of the road, we saw an oncoming police vehicle with two cops inside, its emergency lights turned on and its siren screaming.

"Don't let them get near us. Climb out that window and shoot".

Lefteris did just that. He didn't need to fire many shots, because they pulled over at the side of the road, crouched in their seats, and never got back up.

"We won't get away easily from this cursed place. The whole police force is after us. Be ready for many confrontations!" I advised Lefteris.

Instead of answering me, he put a Rammstein CD in the stereo and turned it on full volume.

"They got sirens, we got Rammstein!" he said, smiling.

Although this was his first car chase with gunfire, he was doing fine. After a while, as we were driving down one of the many barren hills of the plain, we saw a Vitara police car on the opposite end of the winding road coming towards us at full speed. They noticed us right on time. They stopped on the road, without blocking the way, got out of the car holding their machine guns, and hunkered down behind it. At my signal Lefteris began firing from a distance, one shot at a time, so that they couldn't stand up. As we got near them, he suddenly stopped shooting. He bent over, trying to do something.

As we drove past the stopped Vitara, the officers suddenly got brave. They eagerly opened fire on us. I thought the X5 had been hit several times because, after about a hundred yards, it stopped in the middle of the road. The engine was running, but the car wouldn't move. I looked at the gearbox and realised the stick was in neutral. This is what had happened: while Lefteris had been shooting against the cops a bullet had misfired. Lefteris, not knowing much about guns, had thought the magazine was empty. Trying to change it, he must have accidentally knocked the gear stick, putting it in neutral.

Because of this brief stop, the cops thought they had injured me and kept track of all the people being admitted to the area's hospitals, in case I sought treatment. That's what they announced on the news, overjoyed at their exploit. They would be mortified to know that not only was I uninjured, but the X5 hadn't taken a single bullet. It was truly unbelievable. We had either been extremely lucky, or the cops we had met were moral and didn't want to shoot two fugitives in the back, deciding instead to fire into the air for the sake of firing. How else can I explain the fact that they missed an X5 driving so close by? If neither of the two is true, then we're talking about a unique exploit that calls for an award.

I shifted the car into drive, and we drove away without them following us. They were convinced that soon I'd bleed out behind the wheel, having been mortally wounded. I, Palaiokostas, not some random guy. They mentioned my name later that very same day. An outlaw like me justified any careless risk. An almost here, an approximately there and everything is explained. Who else could it have been after all? And let's say for a moment they did shoot me. How did they come up with the story that the passenger who shot at them was Spyros, making serious accusations against him? When the police are at liberty to justify their extra-institutional methods and their arbitrary courses of action, and this is accepted by the citizens as one of the difficulties of the profession, let them not wonder why they are being deprived of their constitutional rights. Let's not forget, I'm the outlaw, not the Hellenic Police! God forbid they take our crown! Unless I'm terribly wrong here …

After ten minutes or so we found ourselves driving along the main Larissa-Trikala road, in the direction of Trikala. Ahead of us was the bridge going over Pineios River and after about two hundred or three hundred yards there was the junction leading to Elassona. The truth is car chases don't usually involve police vehicles with their emergency lights and sirens turned on, pursuing a car in a sensationalist way, with everything coming down to the driving skills of those involved, when firearms are used by those being pursued. Nobody goes against a Kalashnikov's bullets, because nobody is that mad. Fortunately. From the start, it takes a turn towards a dangerous game of chess for sharp, all-or-nothing kind of players. On the police's part, all police departments and stations in the surrounding area are notified so roadblocks can be set at main junctions. At the same time, police vehicles are dispatched to the area to locate the pursued vehicle.

Knowing from experience that the junction ahead of us was very likely to be swarming with cops from the surrounding police departments, I warned Lefteris to be ready for a fight, taking out my own Kalashnikov and placing it on my lap, ready to use it. We needed to pass through, even if that meant having to put up a fight. Otherwise, we were at risk of being trapped in the eastern villages of rural Larissa in broad daylight, and then we'd be playing a losing game. Crossing the bridge, I remembered about a dirt road of sorts, after about a hundred yards, which led to the Elassona ring road. I drove the SUV onto it. It got us there.

After about half a mile I realised we had a flat tire.

"Fuck! Why now?"

"There's a pickup truck coming, pal. Block the road, we'll take it and leave", said Lefteris.

Indeed, a 4x4 pickup truck was coming our way, but I had a different plan.

"Forget it … Let's not draw attention to us now that we managed to escape. We'll change the tire and keep on driving!"

It was a great risk, but a necessary one to save the vehicle. I drove the X5 into a path-road covered by thick bushes, and we changed the flat tire to the sound of Rammstein. Perhaps we were the first people to ever do such a thing while a hot pursuit was underway nearby. Despite all this, we won the match. We escaped, and the X5 didn't fall into their hands.

Checkmate.

KIDNAPPING MYLONAS

Thessaloniki. I knew the city well; at least as far as picking a target was concerned. Ten years ago, before kidnapping Haitoglou, I had considered targeting several other businessmen from the area. With some of them I had reached the final stage of surveillance, knowing their cars, routes, houses etc. In this decade, no other company had grown as much as Yorgos Mylonas' Alumil.* According to its published balance sheets, the company turned over vast amounts of money each year with a steady increase. The prior year the company had turned over nearly ten million euros. Following an aggressive policy, the company would acquire big aluminium companies in northern Greece, eliminating competition in the domestic market, while at the same time undertaking big projects abroad, like for example in the Arab countries. So Mylonas was deservedly called the king of aluminium by the financial press.

But Mylonas had another dominant position too. A position that allowed him to control the distribution of community resources, State budget funds, and money in the form of bank loans for the development of the local industry in its entirety. He was the president of the Association of Industries in northern Greece, and this automatically ensured a position on the general counsel of the Bank of Greece. Kidnapping a president of industrialists, aside from the apparent economic interest, would also have a symbolic value. Such a prospect really interested me. I preferred it, to be honest, and so I set it as a priority.

When I got to Thessaloniki, I found two great guys waiting for me. Two of the most remarkable people I have ever associated and worked with, real gems. Pavlos and Panos. They had never been caught, and so the police didn't keep track of them. I discussed my target with them, asking directly if they were willing to participate in any way they could. The guys decided to actively participate in the kidnapping, first to help me and secondly to gain some experience. Money was the last thing they cared about. That was a good sign. On the contrary, our fourth partner, Simos, was in it just for the money. A bad sign.

I'd met Simos through a remarkable family in Germany around 1991-1992. Since then, throughout my imprisonment and after my escape, we'd kept in touch. Every time we spoke on the phone he'd complain about his and his children's financial problems, never failing to remind me how willing he was to participate in any profitable illegal job that would get him out of this economic quagmire. In a bad moment, when a partner quit the team, I took the risk of summoning him to Thessaloniki with the prospect of making him the lessee of the house we'd hold the kidnapped businessman in. When he came, he was determined to participate in all levels and stages of the job. I went along with it.

---

* Alumil is the largest privately-owned aluminium extrusion group in South-East Europe, producing door and window frames, architectural products etc.

We found a house quite easily. A two-story detached building in a one-acre fenced block underneath the Souroti monastery, away from any other homes. It was an ideal hideout both to keep the abducted businessman and to act as our headquarters until we were through with planning.

The guys had no experience in such large-scale operations. Nobody is born as an experienced person. For starters, it was enough that they were zealous and that they trusted me — my experience was sufficient for all of them. The kidnapping plan was imprinted on my mind down to the last detail. It was my responsibility to communicate it in a way that would make them understand that our success depended on how seriously we were going to treat it and how dedicated we would be, from beginning to end, to achieving our goal. To help them get in the mood, we all agreed that they should have a say in what happened. They would speak their minds, disagree, and ask for clarifications whenever they weren't sure about the plan.

Moreover, coordinating the team would be my responsibility and my opinion, because of my experience, would play an essential role in any kind of decision. After all, the guys were also of the opinion that too many cooks spoil the broth. This helped them to get in the right mood faster, both psychologically and practically, getting down to work with more confidence. They came up with ideas, which they discussed with one another and took the initiative to make some preparations on their own etc.

Another part was their weapons training. Given that this was an armed men's operation, they had to learn some things about handling and using firearms. After several nightly excursions to the surrounding mountains and wasting a lot of ammunition, we reached a point where they could sufficiently handle and use Kalashnikovs, MP5s, Scorpions, pistols, as well as defensive grenades. Now gunpowder-blackened, the lads were ready for the main course!

Locating Mylonas' residence proved to be a difficult task since he had just moved into his new, luxurious house over the Panorama-Thermi road, and it had been listed as one of the aluminium company's warehouses. We fell flat on our faces against Greek business acumen!

After more than a month of constant surveillance at his old residence, the company's offices, and the factory at the Kilkis Industrial Area, we had no new information. It was as though he had vanished off the face of the earth. Then, just as we were beginning to lose hope, ready to postpone the operation for the fall, we found him!

It was night-time. Hunched, holding a leather bag, he was walking along an illuminated sidewalk in Panorama. I was driving a black Audi. I turned on the car's hazard lights and pulled over to see where he was heading. He turned left and took an uphill road, getting into a Mercedes 500. Here we go. I had to follow him. Taking the village's sideways, constantly tailing him, we were soon taking the road towards Thermi. After a while he signalled left and entered the yard of a detached house where some exterior reconstruction work appeared to be underway. Perfect!

The house's entrance didn't lend itself to physical surveillance. The very next day we installed several cameras, which we changed often. This continued for about a week with few results. Mylonas would always come and go at irregular hours, and so it would be impossible to plan an ambush and take him. But where there's a will ...

We finally focused on finding a safe place near his house that would provide us with cover to wait for him every night until we could catch him. Driving down the Panorama-Thermi road, and before Mylonas house's entrance, I noticed a small turn heading left. This cut through the hill, but there was no way we could see where it led. So, one night, the guys dropped me a few yards away and I snuck inside. It was paved, and it looked like a tunnel without a top. After about ten yards I came across a locked double gate, which appeared unused because the lock was rusty. This suggested that the road led to an abandoned house.

There was wire netting around each side of the cut hill. I climbed the right hillside and, reaching the netting, I used a wire cutter to get through it at a spot which wasn't visible from the road. Up from there, the reforested hill only had low vegetation, bushes, and some pine trees. Using a hand pruner, I cleared a path to the top of the hill, which wasn't more than sixteen yards away. The hilltop proved to be a strategic point, granting us cover as well as a clear view of our target. The northern side of the concrete wall surrounding the vast, luxurious "warehouse," which was fortified top to bottom with expensive red marble, was only five yards away. I could see the whole yard as well as the covered parking for the family's cars which was under construction to the left of the second entrance. This hilltop, above Mylonas' house, would become our lookout for many hours over the following nights, without much result. The only one who was always punctual was a fluffy, plump, greyish-black tomcat. As soon as we reached the hilltop every night, as though waiting for us, he'd climb up the concrete wall, curl up and refuse to take his eyes off of us. Perhaps when he was little, he had dreamt of becoming a robbery-gang member. He certainly wasn't a snitch.

As the days came and went we learnt that Alumil was due to host an event. It would take place at night, just outside Thessaloniki, and Mylonas would be the main speaker. We couldn't let this opportunity go to waste.

***

It was the night of the event, the sun had just set. Holding Kalashnikovs and wearing camouflage clothes, masks, and gloves, we found ourselves waiting for the elusive Mr Mylonas under cover of darkness in the forest. Simos was waiting at a village across the hill for a command to get to the point we had arranged for switching cars. After about an hour, I heard some girls talking in the distance. I stood up and, taking a few steps through the pine trees, saw two ten-year-olds heading down the well lit-road, coming from Panorama. At that moment, Mylonas' Mercedes appeared from the same direction. He slowed down and stopped near the pair. I heard one, among other things, call the car's passengers mum and dad. Realising it was their daughter and she might witness her father's abduction, I froze.

The Mercedes moved along, turned left, entered the house's yard and stopped at the covered parking. The guys were waiting for my signal to begin. They had sensed my indecisiveness, but they didn't know the reason behind it. Calculating, I made the signal they had been waiting for. We exited the dark forest and jumped over the wall. Mylonas was only then exiting the car while his wife, Nellie, was already standing behind the vehicle. I strode near him. I grabbed his arm, shoved him in the back seat of the car and said to him in a tone that didn't leave room for misinterpretations:

"Come on, Mylonas, let's go for a ride ..."

Both he and his wife, shocked, began pleading:

"Why? What's going on, guys? Who are you? What do you want?" etc.

"We'll have time to talk on the way", I said to him and, grabbing the car keys out of his hand, I got in the driver seat.

I turned the key, but the Mercedes wouldn't start. I hadn't driven such a car before and Mylonas, either because he was scared or because he was trying to buy himself some time, was mumbling without telling me the German's whims. Having the two girls in the back of my mind, I got out, upset. I opened the rear door and ordered him:

"Take the wheel and if you so much as think of trying something funny I'll empty the whole magazine on you".

He realised I wasn't fooling around. He sat in the driver seat, started the engine and turned the car to face the exit. I saw two heads appearing from the curved downhill road towards the iron gate. What I wished wouldn't happen had probably happened. To what extent? I couldn't possibly know.

Following my commands, we took the road towards Thermi. After about a quarter of a mile, we turned right into a deserted road. After a while, I ordered him to drive the car onto a dead-end dirt road. There, we covered his eyes, and moved him onto the back seat of the Land Cruiser which in the meantime had arrived, driven by Simos. I left an envelope next to the Mercedes' gear stick, in which we listed all our demands. I got in the Land Cruiser, sat in the passenger seat, and off we went. In Thermi, Panos got out of the car, because he had a mission. Our plan called for someone to reach the outskirts of Katerini and from there to inform Mylonas' wife where the vehicle had been abandoned. We had two reasons for doing so. The first was so that the car and our demands would be discovered quickly enough before any thieves managed to skim it, and the second was so that we could use the call to trick them as to our destination.

Next, the plan called for us to drive around the edges of the regional unit for about an hour, before heading to our hideout. And that's what we'd do. As soon as Panos was off, I tuned my wireless radio to the police frequency. You wouldn't believe what we heard that night. The most absurd thing was that a group from the Crime Prevention and Suppression Unit had located the Mercedes in motion on some road near Panorama. Police Headquarters ordered all the units that had swarmed the area to approach the target. They cornered "Mylonas' Mercedes", but they had gotten some of the license plate's numbers wrong.

Thankfully, it wasn't us, or there'd have been a massacre. When I mentioned this to some officers after my arrest, they explained themselves saying that at the time they didn't even know who Mylonas was. Ignorance can be quite dangerous.

The further we got away from Thessaloniki, the more confident Mylonas grew. He shyly began asking questions.

"Why me, guys? Why not somebody else?"

"We saw you covered in flour and we took you for a miller"* I joked.

"No, I really want to know your motives, in case I can help," he insisted.

"Don't worry. You'll help with your money, Yorgos. What did you think this was all about?"

"Politics, perhaps ..."

"Politics? Are there politics in Greece? Parapolitics and common illegality run everything. And don't tell me you, such a prominent businessman, don't know it".

This is how more than one hour of intentional wandering went by. At a predetermined time, we ended up reaching our hideout at Souroti. We led Mylonas inside a warehouse, the interior of which we had covered with a tarp, turning it into a room with a bed, a small table, a chair, a portable toilet with a folding screen and a radio permanently tuned in the First Programme.

I put on a hood and took his off. I gave him new clothes to wear, a pair of slippers, and I said to him: "Yorgos, here's how things are for you right now. If you cooperate, your stay here will be easy. We'll do what we must so that you return alive to your family. Don't force us to take a hardline approach which doesn't really suit us. There'll always be an armed guard outside. Whatever you need, just call him and ask for it. Try to relax, because this might take a while".

He assured me that he was willing to cooperate and that he too only cared about returning to his family.

The following days passed quietly enough as far as our cohabitation with Mylonas was concerned. We brought him food and newspapers so that he could keep up to date, yet the journalist dogs indulged in an unprecedented crescendo of misinformation. Each morning, hanging at newsstands, they'd preach their own personal fantasy as the only source of truth concerning the kidnapping. And each night, TV channels would stretch the subject even more, shamelessly, toying with the kidnapped man's life. An irresponsible police force and unaccountable news network of misinformation were mixing into a potentially deadly cocktail. We sent a recorded message from Mylonas to his wife, in which he said he was all right and I took the chance to send a message of mine addressing the people who had his life in their hands. Among other things, I threatened that the hostage would be killed if the prosecuting authorities didn't stop the media from referencing the kidnapping. The media bosses put an immediate stop to the "independent", "objective" loquacious mercenary journalists, lest the moral blame for the death of the president of the Association of Industries in northern Greece was put on them. So, the next few days would pass quietly in all respects until the night before the scheduled ransom pickup.

---

* Mylonas, in Greek, means Miller.

Along with Panos, we drove to a sideway near Mylonas' house. Inside a fire extinguisher box, which we had located the previous day, we left a bag, in which was a disassembled mobile phone, a turned-off wireless radio locked to a specific frequency, a big red portable emergency light for a car, and detailed instructions to be followed during the ransom drop-off. Our reasons for leaving these things so close to Mylonas' house were purely psychological. This way, we were saying: "Fairytales are good, but a dragon is lurking outside, watching you".

Afterwards, Panos left for the centre of Thessaloniki to contact Nellie and tell her to pick the things we'd left for her inside the fire extinguisher box. At ten the following night, we arrived at a feeder road of the freeway near Makrygialos, Pieria, to pick up the ransom money. The instructions were clear. The Mercedes SUV, with the emergency light on its top, driven by Nellie and one of Yorgos' friends as its passenger, the mobile phone and the wireless radio turned on, and the money in six military bags (that was the bulk of the thirty million we had requested), would begin at eight sharp from the Megara toll station, in the direction of Athens. They'd keep on the right lane at a maximum speed of 75 miles per hour. Based on these facts, the SUV would arrive in about twenty minutes.

Our ambush site had been strategically chosen. We could see at least a mile down the freeway in the direction the SUV would come from; a good spot if there needed to be a confrontation (we all had Kalashnikovs, grenades etc.) which also offered a quick and easy escape route. As it proved, all these weren't enough; we needed a bit more luck, and we didn't have it that night. About five hundred yards after the SUV started moving — it remains unclear how — the emergency light dropped from the top of the car and broke. If that wasn't enough, the SUV was stuck behind two trucks that were moving at a slower speed and so had to overtake them. They used the indicator, and as a result, the hazard lights turned off automatically. So the SUV came by without us realising it.

We didn't know all this at the time. Returning to our hideout, we discussed what our next step ought to be. Whether it was safe to continue or if we should terminate the operation. The guys thought that it would be foolish not to make another try after we first heard from the other side what had happened that night. I, on the contrary, having more experience and thus being more suspicious, feared the worst. I had no trust in a police force that ambushed "Mylonas' Mercedes" a few minutes after his kidnapping by three men, armed with Kalashnikovs, as though it was just routine. I wasn't at all sure whether they were treating this as a serious situation where a man's life was at stake or as a mere game between them and the devious kidnappers — where the only thing at stake for them was their personal aspirations. The mental state of a woman whose husband was taken right before her eyes is fragile and therefore easily manipulated by the officers that had set up camp in her house (we could see their cars parked in line outside Mylonas' home around the clock), making hypothetical plans at her expense and inside her palace. Of course, I had no trust whatsoever in their corrupted political leadership.

In the end, we decided Panos should travel to a nearby town the following day, contact Nellie, and ask her to explain why she hadn't followed our orders. I'd speak to Mylonas, in case I learnt something that could prove useful concerning our final decision. In the morning, Panos left to contact Nellie, and I visited Mylonas. Yorgos was having a hard time in the warehouse amid an ongoing heatwave. I was saddened by this, but there wasn't any solution. To treat someone you kidnapped as a human isn't a sign of civilisation, its civilisation, period. But they're also tattletales! As soon as you let them go they get loquacious, they spit it all out. I got him a fan to cool the room a bit, and I went on with the necessary interrogation. I explained to him that this was happening because I had some suspicions and that he ought to be honest with me since his life was at stake.

In essence, my question was one, divided into smaller questions: if there was someone who didn't want him to return alive and had the means to achieve it. He was perfectly sure about his wife and his friend, who had been in the SUV with her. As politics were concerned, he had sold his soul to the New Democracy party. He'd often eagerly stuffed money in its large collection box. He knew many of its government officials personally. One or two from northern Greece in key positions were good friends of his, so they had no reason to harm him. My question of whether there was a competitor of his who was in with the police force's leadership or the officers who were handling the kidnapping case and could sabotage its successful conclusion seemed to trouble him. Yet, he didn't manage to give me a definitive answer.

Panos' news was sort of reassuring. Nellie claimed that she had followed our instructions to the letter. Mentioning the emergency-light accident, she told him she had kept driving the whole night to the Afidnes toll station and back. No accidents are allowed in kidnappings. Kidnappers know this better than anyone else. The officers camping in the houses of kidnapped people and the masked political personnel acting as traffic controllers, regulating the route and the flow of money, should also know it. For a price, of course. Thirty million euros are a holy grail when in Mylonas' hands, yet they automatically become Satan's trident when Palaiokostas gets hold of them! It's only natural. Palaiokostas only fills the bowls of strays and nobody else's. That's why they were upset.

In light of this new information, things would follow their natural course. After two days we'd make another attempt to get the ransom money, which this time would be successful.

A notable incident that took place during the ransom pick-up, which I would later learn from police officers and study in length in my case file, is the following: Pavlos and Panos, dressed and armed like cops, had parked their car in a feeder road of the freeway until I contacted them to announce that the SUV was coming, so that they could get to the freeway and pick up the ransom money. At that moment, by total coincidence, a real cop happened to be driving his car down that feeder road, having just finished his shift at the Katerini police department. Driving back to his house, in one of the villages nearby, he saw his "colleagues" and slowed down to talk to them. They gestured for him to get out of there. When he arrived home, he phoned his department to ask if there was an ongoing operation in the area that he didn't know about. They assured him that there wasn't, since they hadn't been notified by the Thessaloniki police department which was in charge of the case. Anything goes! The cop took it to heart that two random guys were wearing the police force's sacred vestments and came back angry, ready to arrest these two blasphemous men for police impersonation. Fortunately for both him and Mylonas, they had already left. As for those responsible, or at least those who had presented themselves as responsible to Mylonas' wife, they'd come up with an excuse. This comes naturally to responsible Greek men, they don't even have to try.

At about half-past eleven, we parked the two cars on a mountain in Thessaloniki to check the sacks with the money, lest they contain any strange objects. When I opened the trunk, I realised the money was much less than what we'd demanded. Opening one of the six military bags, the first thing I saw was a large yellow envelope. I opened it, and inside I found a handwritten letter by Nellie, addressed to the kidnappers' leader. She mentioned her inability to collect the sum we had requested. Then she begged the man who was holding her husband to let him free etc. I opened the rest of the bags, and they all had similar envelopes in them, containing handwritten letters.

After we'd thoroughly searched the bundles of banknotes and the bags, we returned home. Until the morning, the counterfeit bill detector was working non-stop counting the money, while we were drinking beer to stay awake. By the time we'd finished, there was a whole wall of money bricks in one of the corners of the house. Until recently, these bricks had been adorning the vault of some bank branch, while their sum had been written on Mylonas' bank passbook. And now they were determining his life.

The fact that money is controlled by the few is the accepted brutality of trade and an essential component of business around the world. Not allowing people who have an immediate need for it to have access to it is not allowing them a decent life and a chance to survive. It shows the repulsive face of economic violence. There's no place for emotion in the capitalist Junta's absolutism; the money has more value than the real, daily needs of a plain human's life. Those dedicated to the doctrine of economic fascism are willing to become martyrs in the hands of a kidnapper as long as their bank account's contents remain intact. I was wondering what is more moral and, to an extent, more logical: for someone to die for something they don't need and they won't miss, or for someone to kill for something they immediately need and they're being deprived of? For the time being, Nellie's prudence partially freed me from having to answer this easy-to answer dilemma.

Ten million eight hundred thousand euros had been in the bags. It was less than we had demanded and needed. Throughout the operation, we had never negotiated about the money. In the letter we had left inside Mylonas' car the night of the kidnapping, we had made it clear that the amount to be paid was thirty million euros and that it was non-negotiable. So now, given the circumstances, we had to make a decision about what we'd do next. Based on my experience, I knew she wasn't trying to deceive us; she simply didn't have that kind of money. Mylonas himself led me to this conclusion when during his "interrogation" the subject came up. He told me not to expect more than ten million because all the company's profits were immediately re-invested in its development.

We held a meeting, and we collectively decided to set him free.

The following night, I went to see Mylonas, holding his washed clothes behind me. Quite solemnly, and with a morbid sense of humour, I said to him:

"Mylonas. I'm going to ask you a question and your life will depend on the answer you give me. Do you want to die or go home?"

His face suddenly lit up. He knew ...

"To go home, guys", he said, smiling.

"Then get dressed. We'll be off in an hour", I said to him, throwing his clothes and his shoes on the bed.

Then I said to him, just about, the following:

"Mylonas, money in society works like blood in a human body. When the heart retains blood, it becomes hypertrophic while the limbs atrophy, and as a result, they freeze. For a society to be healthy, blood must reach all its members so that they don't atrophy. Otherwise, the cardiovascular system fails. I'm happy that we temporarily fixed a blood clot affecting its circulatory system. At the same time, I'm sorry that you had to be humiliated for us to succeed. Believe me, there wasn't any other way.

"You must know, however, that thousands of your fellow people have lived for many many years in conditions much worse than those you had to endure these past twelve days, being much more humiliated by the system you serve, and yet not for a moment did you care about them. Given you'll be free in a few hours, you may once again feel invincible and decide to take revenge. You must know that whether we're free or inside a prison, we never lose our strength because we're not some random people who just happened to do this. In business terms, which you understand better, we're the Vardinoginnis family in our field".*

Kiss a donkey's arse to make him blush, a friend of mine used to say in situations like this one, and it fits perfectly here. My speech had been for nothing. The following day, the loquacious Mr Mylonas was deifying the police on camera, praising their perfect handling of his case. He had no idea.

As soon as night fell, with Pavlos in the passenger seat, Mylonas lying in the back seat and Panos following close behind in a BMW, we headed to Giannitsa. There, we drove the BMW inside a dead-end dirt road; we got Mylonas out and took him about fifty yards away from the car. I took his blindfold off, gave him the car keys, and said to him:

"Follow the dirt road without looking back. At the end of it, you'll find a car to drive home".

That's where we parted ways. And so the operational part of the kidnapping came to an end.**

---

* The Vardinoginnis' business empire is based primarily in its shipping and refinery businesses but also incorporates shipping, banking, media, real estate, hotels and publishing. Family patriarch Vardis is a billionaire with worldwide trading links and the family is perhaps the most powerful in Greece today.
** After being held hostage for two weeks and after his kidnappers received ten million eight hundred euros in ransom money, Mylonas was released. At court, he maintained a prudent attitude towards the defendants. He is still active president of his company, Alumil.

SAFEHOUSE SURPRISE AND ARREST

We split the ten million euros from the kidnapping in four, and each of us took his share. The remaining eight hundred thousand euros was saved in order to finance a similar operation in the future (since our mission was not accomplished from an economic perspective) and part of it would be given to friends and partners who had helped one way or another and would keep helping us in future plans. But when you make new plans after such a kidnapping God laughs devilishly.

Pavlos and Panos, a few days after the kidnapping, went on summer vacation. Simos, on the other hand, put his share inside a big suitcase and travelled to his birthplace, Crete. After Dormition Day,* the two guys bringing me supplies visited the house at Souroti. One was Poly, who identified himself as an anarchist-communist and whom I had met during my second stay in Korydallos, the other was his friend, Vangelis, a rebellious and capable lad with a punk background. For safety reasons we made a decision. Poly would stay with me until all the weapons, and the rest of money (that I had yet to bury) had been taken care of, with the prospect of cleaning the house and eventually breaking the lease. During this period, we wouldn't have any contact with Vangelis. So, that very same evening, Poly arrived with a bottle of Tsipouro and several carefully-selected films. He had gone by a video club in Peraia and registered there using his fake ID, which he had used long ago to rent a small apartment in the same area, and the mobile phone number that was always turned on inside the apartment in case his landlord called.

When he entered the house, he left the video club's registration card on the table, where it would remain along with the keys of the apartment. At nightfall, we sat in the ground floor's eastern veranda. We philosophised about the rights and wrongs of life, and drank tsipouro along with some suitable delicacies I had prepared. It must have been about ten when Poly went to the living room to put on a movie. I stayed outside, waiting for him to call me. That was when I heard what sounded like an agricultural vehicle rumbling near the entrance to the detached house. The entrance was down a concrete path, about a hundred yards long, which ended up in the house's yard. That stretch was a blind spot when looking out from the house, due to several almond trees that formed a natural wall, their branches intertwining, blocking the road from the property. I was naïve enough to believe that indeed some farming vehicle had stopped or was moving slowly along the main public road of Souroti, near the house's entrance. That happened quite often since the house was located in a rural area. In reality, the noise I was hearing was the Special Anti–Terrorist Unit's diesel Cherokees, driving down the concrete road with their headlights turned off, after they had cut the padlock on the entrance's iron double gate.

---

* A major day in Greek orthodox culture marking the death of the Virgin Mary. It takes place on August 15th.

Poly called for me to go watch the movie, so I got up and walked to the living room, but as I walked in, the noise grew louder, so I went back outside to see what the hell it was. The scene outside the house had drastically changed. About thirteen Special Anti–Terrorist Unit SUVs had encircled the house. Heavily armed hooded officers dressed in black were getting out of them, ready for battle. Behind them appeared police vehicles, their emergency lights and headlights now turned on. It was summer, and it was hot. I was wearing slippers and Bermuda shorts.

All my weapons were on the second floor. An attempt to react in any way would be a lost cause under these circumstances. I couldn't even hope to win an armed confrontation with them. It was time for me to notify Poly about the sudden change in weather.

"Poly. The police are here ... what do we do?"

"We surrender. What else?" he said and went out to see for himself what was going on.

When he saw the blackened scenery of the now illuminated yard of the house, he raised his arms and walked down the steps saying:

"All right, relax, we surrender".

Such words, in such moments, are like a dagger to the heart. To me, it wasn't surrender but a momentary capitulation, taking into account the odds, which at the time were strongly in our opponents' favour. Poly was a brave soul. He never lost his courage. He just now acted as reason commanded. He approached them, and they began yelling:

"Get down, get down!"

He fell flat on the lawn. Two or three of them jumped on him and handcuffed him. I went down and stood on the landing. All their weapons were turned on me. I looked like an alien with all these red spots on my body. Whether it was my refusal to accept the new circumstances or Mr Anestis' influence, I felt an urge to react.

"Who's in charge?" I yelled loud and clear, as though I was controlling the situation.

Silence ... I tried again.

"Who's in charge? I want him to come and handcuff me".

"Who are you?" I heard a voice coming behind the cordon formed by the Special Anti-Terrorist officers and all other sorts of armed cops.

"The one you want ... Vassilis! Are you in charge? Why are you hiding? Are you shy?"

"Get down, or we'll open fire".

"If you're men enough, aim right for the head!"

Absolute silence ... for a few seconds, the only sounds came from the special taskforce's metallic gear. Suddenly, the black human wall moved towards me, compact and structured. Knees bent, small, fast steps, and their guns aiming right at me, they soon reached my position. Someone pushed me, another tripped me, and I found myself handcuffed on the lawn. Not a minute had gone by when a sharp sound came from inside the house. They had thrown a stun grenade inside before getting in to make sure there was no one else there.

"Hey ... what the hell are you doing? I've got explosives inside the house. You'll get killed, and I'll get the blame!"

There was some panic.

"Where? Where? Where? Where are the explosives?"

"Inside the house. Stop the operation until the bomb squad gets here".

They froze. Then they shoved us in different SUVs. From there, they dropped us off in different holding cells — nothing new for me. Handcuffed throughout my detention, two officers from the Special Anti-Terrorist Unit always with me inside the holding cell, some visits by higher-ranking officers that wanted to see me from up-close and have a quick word with me, consolidating their authority in the eyes of their inferiors; that's how I spent the night.

***

On the afternoon of the following day, Mylonas entered the holding room accompanied by the Thessaloniki police chief and deputy police chief. He had supposedly come to identify me, but his ultimate goal was to beg me to return the money, or part of it, because the company had expenses, it employed so many people etc.

"Forget it, Mylonas. There is no money. There's a long sentence waiting for me".

He didn't insist. Instead, he stood for a while to discuss the days of his captivity. The officers would intervene from time to time, since they had participated in a way in the developments, admitting many mistakes on their part. There, in front of me, he had the nerve to ask the officers how he could contribute financially to the purchase of equipment, helping the police's work as a sign of gratitude for them having done such a great job with his case. Oh, for fuck's sake! The deputy officer's attitude was a pleasant surprise.

"How many employees do you have in all your companies, Mr Mylonas?" he asked.

He proudly mentioned a large number, which I can't quite remember now. More than a thousand though.

"How many of them are former prisoners?"

" I ... I don't have ... I don't know ... I don't ..."

"Hire some, and you'd have done your share. You have a duty to society as a whole, not just the police".

Mylonas didn't say a word. After he left, a motor officer against whom I had once opened fire (and then him against me), came to identify me through the small window on the door.

Here's how that incident had unravelled: one evening, sometime before Easter that same year, I was driving a newly-acquired white Audi, heading towards the house in Peraia. When I left Souroti and joined the main road to Peraia I stepped on it a few times to test the new car. As I've said before, the Hellenic Police is omnipresent, and a mile before I reached the first houses of the town, on the right-hand side of the road, an unmarked police vehicle was parked, with two plainclothes inside, holding a radar speed gun. Whenever they noticed a violation, they reported the type and the license plate number of the vehicle, so that it would be pulled over at the roadblock they had set up a mile down the road, which wasn't visible from that spot.

I didn't see them in time, I didn't slow down, and it was now too late to change direction. There was no exit until the roadblock, so I ran straight into them. It had been set up by two traffic police vehicles, a police vehicle, and a police motorcycle. From afar, the traffic policemen signalled for me and the driver of a BMW in front of me to pull over for inspection. The BMW's driver slowed down and complied as he ought with the police's orders, pulling over. I, on the other hand, turned on the hazard lights, slowed down and, pretending it wasn't convenient for me to stop there, drove past them with the intention of parking a bit further down where there was more space. Instead, I stepped on it. Through the mirrors, I saw the motor officer jumping on his bike and coming after me.

The Audi had a powerful engine. It was a fast car. If I was lucky, I had a good chance of escaping without a confrontation. A gunfight with the police in that area, with a kidnapping on the cards, was the last thing I wanted. I drove the car onto one of the first roads I came across to my right and, trying not to stay too long on a single path, I headed towards the sea. Some vehicles ahead delayed me quite a lot, and so when I reached the road that I knew led back to the freeway, the motor officer was still right behind me. I had no other choice but to use a gun. I slowed down, got my right hand out of the window and, using a Browning, I fired three warning shots without aiming. He must have thought this was a weakness because he kept following as if nothing had happened. I stopped the car, crawled half outside the window and, holding the handgun with both hands, fired another four shots aiming for his tires. I began driving once again. He didn't let it slide. He drew his gun, placed his hands on the immobilised bike's wheel and, aiming for the now moving Audi, fired six consecutive shots, a single bullet grazing the fuel tank's cover. But he stopped pursuing me. He was a motor officer, he wasn't stupid! On full throttle, lest they managed to corner me, I reached my hideout in Souroti. Until midnight, I listened on the wireless radio the humourous incidents during their extensive searches throughout Thessaloniki. It was that motor officer, with whom I had exchanged fire, who was looking at me now through the door's window.

"Yes, it's him", I heard him assure the officer accompanying him.

Until that moment, I had no idea what this was all about, and so I asked the officer.

"He's the motor officer you shot in Peraia", he answered me.

"Let the man in. I don't bite!"

"Do you want to go in?" his superior asked him.

He hesitated, but then he agreed to enter. He seemed taken aback by my invitation. He stood near the door, and he looked at me without speaking.

"Tell me. Are you holding it against me?" I asked him.

"No ... but you almost killed me".

"Ok. These things happen between different armed worlds. I had no intention of killing you. I just wanted to escape, and you wouldn't let me. I only fired some warning shots".

He got a photo out of his pocket, in which three bullet holes were clearly visible on the lower parts of the motorcycle he had been driving. One on the headlights, one on one of the sirens and, if I remember correctly, one low on the fork.

"Do you call these warning shots?" he asked me.

"Nooo. These are deterring shots! The first ones had been warning shots, but you ignored them".

"And how could I have known it was you in the car?" he answered quite disarmingly.

"Well ... you have to be careful. Once in a while, Palaiokostas goes for a ride!" I joked.

"If I had some colleagues for backup, you wouldn't have gotten away ..."

"So it's good that you didn't, because we may not be having this conversation right now. I had some backup of my own, you see, but I didn't use it. A loaded Kalashnikov in the passenger seat".

He seemed to understand. Either way, he left satisfied that I had given him the chance to talk face to face. The officers from the Special Anti-Terrorist Unit relaxed. They now entered the holding cell without their hoods on. We'd talk until their two-hour shift was over and I learnt the first bad news when one of them said to me:

"This Cretan is a real piece of work! Where did you find that piece of shit?"

"Why are you calling him that?"

"Don't you know anything? He's such a prattler. He just won't stop talking. Not even the officers can make him stop!"

Until that moment, I was in the dark about what had followed our arrest. I had no contact with the outside world. I didn't even know whether the other guys had been arrested too. To learn from the special officers that one of my partners had made a deal with the police and the prosecuting authorities to save his arse hurt me even more than the fact I had been arrested. By night, I'd have learnt enough details about what led to our arrest to be able to piece together the puzzle of the events which preceded that fateful night.

After the kidnapping, and before we parted ways, we had all agreed that none of us would use the ransom money before we met again to make a collective decision concerning its laundering. When Simos arrived in Crete however, the first thing he did was to visit a Mercedes car dealership. He bought himself a luxury SUV, paying in cash. Then, he began thoughtlessly spending the rest of his share for coke and comforts, opening a door for the cops to arrest us.

Aside from Simos' uncontrollable spending spree, there had been (already from the beginning of the operation) another backdoor leading directly to us. The police had discovered it by accident and had silently followed the thread along this underground route. A few days before Mylonas' kidnapping, the four of us had been in the SUV, driving up the Thermi-Panorama road.

I had asked Pavlos to turn on the phone, which Panos would use to phone Nellie the first time. Pavlos saw a pizza restaurant advertisement by the side of the road, turned on the phone, and called the restaurant's landline. Without waiting for someone to pick up, he hung up — everything was fine until then. Yet the devil is in the detail.

Four months prior, one of the guys (I don't know who) had in the same way turned on a phone which I was using every fifteen days to contact a friend in prison, and called the same pizza restaurant, having seen a similar advertisement in a different suburb of Thessaloniki. A month before kidnapping Mylonas, throughout his captivity, and for a month after he was released, that mobile phone remained turned off. I used many mobile phones and replaced them from time to time for security reasons. Pavlos and Panos had been tasked with turning them on. Always away from my hideout. Obviously, at the time, the one who had turned on that mobile phone didn't remember that he had, or perhaps he thought it was an advertisement for a different restaurant. A severe shortcoming, when I had become annoying, always telling them to be careful with mobile phones. It was a mistake, yet an understandable one; they couldn't have predicted it. After that first phone call to Mylonas' wife, the police subpoenaed the pizza restaurant's phone records. They discovered that, a few months earlier, a suspicious phone number which was used once in a while to contact a specific prison had been turned on the same way.

Having no knowledge about that fateful coincidence, I thought it was safer to use that particular phone instead of turning on a new one. Being sure they would be all over those phones, and knowing my voice, I decided not to use a mobile phone again, unless there was some emergency. Afterwards, I gave the mobile phone to Vangelis, so that he could talk to my friend, under the condition that he' wouldn't turn it on very often and that he'd always speak in code. If you don't know you have something and what that something is, you don't take the appropriate measures to protect yourself. It was a matter of time before the damage was done.

For a long time, Pavlos and Panos had been complaining about Simos — his repeated blunt lying, his erratic behaviour, his mental instability etc. I, on the other hand, was so focused on the kidnapping's details, that these complaints (which after all would prove well-founded) seemed to me childish, and so I didn't pay them enough attention. Simos' moral compass and ideology didn't differ much from that of the average corrupted man of our time; he was a man without ideals who, trapped within the dominant consumerist ideology, tried to get rich any way he could and as easily as he could. That made him a weak link in a possible arrest. For that reason, I had given him many lessons about how he should behave in such a scenario. I had hoped the fact that we'd known each other for so long and that we had some mutual friends would stop him from crossing the line. When a man loses his shame, everything is easy for him. He who betrays himself will betray everyone around him with a clear conscience. Responsibility and dignity are too much of a burden for little decadent human beings, and they get rid of it at the first sign of trouble.

The Cretan police force would be the first to get to the bottom of this, arresting him on the morning of the day of our arrest. They got him in a C130 and rushed him to Thessaloniki. His defensive system wasn't working. It collapsed during his interrogation and, as usual, he turned in his friends and partners. He named Poly and Vangelis as the main orchestrators of the kidnapping, and he led the cops to a vault at the edge of the property, where I had temporarily hidden about one million euros from my share. Because of this incident, a war would break out between the police departments of Thessaloniki and Crete. The Cretans wanted some more credit, while the ones from Thessaloniki weren't willing to share anything.

"Big deal! You did nothing! You only got a snitch!" they'd say.

This war of stars was also raging inside police headquarters. The burning question was who would reap the benefits of this great success. The stardust even reached my holding cell, in the form of complaints and innuendos. Feuds and intrigues between senior officers about who would get the lion's share were still going strong.

The following day, they transferred us to the district attorney and then to the examining magistrate. It was the first time I was going through this with my co-defendants. I cared for them more than I did about myself. It was the first time they were up against the thick-skinned, stone-hearted monster called State, facing such serious charges. We got ready to be transferred to court at eight in the evening when our trial would be broadcasted live on the evening news.

Along with us they were pillorying a family, keeping all of them handcuffed, because a small part of the ransom money had been found buried in their yard; a gift from us to their son who was a prisoner. They themselves knew nothing about where that money had come from or who had gifted it to them — the State's shamelessness in its most disgraceful form.

This celebration of authority enraged me, and I took it out on the group's demure maid, the cunning examining magistrate. Entering his office, I jumped on him, blaming him for the media's rigged games and the pillorying of innocent citizens. He was disturbed, and he promised me that next time he'd transfer them separately from us so that they wouldn't be exposed to TV cameras. The guys requested additional time to prepare, and so the hearing was rescheduled for two days later. Returning to the holding cell, one thing was stuck in my head. What had happened to the apartment in Peraia? I had no convincing answer to the questions swirling in my mind. Why hadn't they already located it, since its keys had been on the kitchen table in the house in Souroti, along with the video club registration card? Those could have led them directly to it. And why hadn't Simos told them about it? Had he forgotten? Experienced snitches don't forget such things! Three million euros from my share of the ransom money was in that apartment as well as a large number of guns, some of which had been used in an attempted robbery of a G4 cash transport, outside a supermarket to the east of the regional unit.

Perhaps this was the reason behind Simos' selective memory. If he told them about the apartment, his made up story that he'd participated in the kidnapping only in order to repay some money he owed me would go up in smoke.

Inside the apartment, the police would find his fingerprints too; possibly on the guns as well. One thing was for sure. Sooner or later, they were going to find it. What was troubling me was when and how. So, I put into action a very ambitious plan to trick the officers into allowing me a meeting with Poly and Vangelis in my holding cell, without supervision. I asked to speak to the deputy chief since we understood each other better. He came at once. I cut to the chase and told him I was strongly considering returning some money to Mylonas.

"How come? Why now?" he asked, surprised. He didn't expect such a move from me.

"The guys are young, and I'm partly responsible for the situation they're in right now. If I can help them, I'll be glad to do it. But first I have to inform them about my intention and ask for their approval".

"So you won't return the money if they don't agree?" he asked.

"Of course not. I have no other reason to do it".

"I can't give you an answer right now. Tomorrow, when the whole administration is here, we'll have a meeting to make a decision", he said to me and left.

I knew the inducement I was offering them was such that they couldn't say no. The following morning, they brought Poly and Vangelis* to my holding cell. During our court transfer we hadn't gotten the chance to talk to each other, so the first thing I asked them was whether the police had used violence. They assured me that they had treated them and were still treating them nicely. They seemed to be okay. The guys were just as surprised as I was that the apartment had yet to be discovered. I asked them if any of them had kept a spare key so that I could send someone to get the money and the guns. Their answer was no, so the apartment was a lost cause, we couldn't save it. If we didn't do something about it, it could prove dangerous for many reasons. Simos could at one point decide to tell the cops about it, cementing his credibility in front of the court even more, at the expense of the guys. On the other hand, if it was discovered at some point, the police could appoint officers to guard it, resulting in the arrest of any people I would have sent to break in. Additionally, a potential break-in by common burglars was equally probable and unwelcome because of the previously used guns.

The most important reason, however, was the possibility of the apartment being located by the police after the kidnapping case was closed, leading to a new case being built against us. That would result in two separate trials. Based on the legal system, that would automatically mean a longer cumulative sentence for the guys. If, however, it was located now, then there would only be one trial resulting in a shorter sentence. Let alone all the fuss of being dragged to testify again etc. None of us wanted to leave the apartment to chance with all this in mind. We had two options: either for someone from the outside to place a call to the police and anonymously tip them off about the apartment or for us to do it, under the pretence of returning money to the victim. We decided on the latter.

---

* Poly and Vangelis were sentenced to prison for their participation in the kidnapping of Mylonas. They served their sentences and were subsequently granted parole under restrictions.

But there was a serious problem. I had nothing to gain out of it, all this was happening for the guys, but it could actually do them more harm than good since they weren't accepting the kidnapping charges. How could they explain returning the money? It would be like pleading guilty. Also, in a fast-moving ideological world, this gesture could be misinterpreted without accurate reporting.

Some (thankfully very few) sclerotic, constipated minds, entrenched behind their paper castles of anti-authoritarian and rebellious literature, lurked, to shoot poisonous arrows against those with faster feet at their first misstep, even if this was just a diversion created by the enemy. Those of struggle must be light, they must fight light, and they must be allowed to be versatile, not fearing they'll be castigated for making a transaction with authority, when in fact they're extracting a gun from its belt to turn against it. That's precisely what this was. A weapon we had the chance to turn against authority. This was clearly our call. This move wouldn't have an effect on anyone but us ... and only a positive one. We'd take some years of the guys' lives out of the authorities' hands. After all, we weren't in a state of total war to be indifferent about life. Those who understand ideological conflict and unarmed shadow-boxing against the State as war don't know and can't even fathom what real war is. In a real war, heavy ideological armour is totally useless; they'd be forced to get rid of it, revealing that inside lay nothing but a naked, skeletal human. I've got nothing against human nudity, only against those who cover it with a veil of theoretical revolution because they're ashamed of it.

After this dead-end, I took things upon myself.

"Forget it, guys. I'll take it from here. I don't owe explanations to any couch rebel ..."

The guys left, and in a few minutes, the chief and the deputy chief arrived.

"What have you decided, Vassilis?"

"We'll return three million euros to him".

"Where will we find it?"

"Get Mylonas on the phone so that I can talk to him and I'll tell you".

"We can't do that".

"Of course you can! Call him now, or I'll give him nothing!"

I knew I had them right where I wanted them because right now, they were the ones committing an offence. They had to summon the district attorney to be present for this. And yet they wanted all the credit for themselves. That suited me well.

Not long after ...

"Yes, it's me, the chief, Mr Mylonas. Vassilis wants to talk to you".

I took the chief's mobile phone.

"Hey, Yorgos ..."

"Hi, Vassilis. How are you?"

"Let me cut to the chase, Yorgos, You came and asked me to return some money. I've reconsidered! I'm willing to give you back three million euros if you promise to help the guys in court. They had no involvement in your kidnapping".

"Yes, Vassilis. I'll do everything in my power, I'll do what you say, thank you very much (etc)".

"Just make sure you don't try to trick me, you poor man, or you'll find yourself back on my target list!"

We laughed ...

"No, of course not. What are you talking about? Consider it done. I now know who I'm talking to!"

In the background, I could hear his wife's voice, shooting wishes fast as a machine gun:

"God bless you, Vassilis, God bless you! I hope you get out of prison soon!"

That last one must have been heard.

Giving the chief back his phone, I said to them:

"You lucky, lads! There are many guns where I'm sending you!"

They were rubbing their buttocks in glee. So that was done.

The following day we were transferred to the district attorney and the examining magistrate once again, now with the two cases consolidated. Returning in the evening, when everything was over, they threw a celebration at headquarters in my honour. Some of them were even kind enough to offer me a few glasses of wine (I would have also treated them to some tsipouro if they hadn't been so many and so anxious the night of my arrest). I drank to my freedom! The deputy chief arrived to ask me if there was anyone I wished to leave all the furniture and the appliances in the house to (which were many). It would have been more interesting if he were to ask me to whom I wanted to leave the Kalashnikovs and the RPG, yet the Hellenic Police officers lack in humour and imagination.

"I really don't care. Give it time, and you'll ask for my will", I said to him.

"Do you want to give the furniture to a children's home? And the rest to the so-and-so monastery?"

"I always give what I can to children. But to a monastery?"

"Yes, they're doing some charitable work" (I don't remember what exactly). The unbeatable predator of thought and grand magician of the slippery tongue came to my mind. "I carry a heavy load on my back, so what if some bugs climb on it too," wondered this German masquerader.

The following morning, just before I was transferred, the monastery's and God's representative came by headquarters to pick up my written permission and, by the way, came to thank me.

"May God protect you from the devil, Vassilis" he wished me, gentle and a bit lost".

"Those two don't bother with me, old man. They've got more interesting things to do. One of them rips your robe, and the other sows it".

After this, I needed some Corfu. United authorities can never be defeated! Devils and gods, all on the same side, fight so that man can never stand up because then they'll all be left unemployed.

SECOND ESCAPE BY HELICOPTER

Prison guards and paedophiles,
one and the same

It was the end of June 2008. After my arrest in Souroti I was transferred to Corfu Prison. It was night. We crossed the hallway on the wing's second floor and stood outside the door of the last cell in line. The deputy warden unlocked it, and we were met by a humid, warm distillery smell. At the back of the cell, a forgotten lifer was boiling some must in a plastic bucket. Standing half-naked, and dripping in sweat, he was tasting the quality of his yield in a plastic coffee cup. A one-and-a-half litre water bottle filled with a hot, transparent liquid testified that the distillation process was at an advanced stage. I entered the cell and he, surprised, kicked the bucket and the "thief's" wire out of the way to make it easier for me. My chaperones left, locking the door as though they had seen nothing. It couldn't be more obvious that I had entered a monitored cell. I hadn't been expecting a better welcome.

"I apologise for the mess, Vassilis, but they didn't tell me they were bringing you in here".

"Don't worry. I'm not a rookie".

"Just have a little patience until this bucket's done too and I'll put everything away. It'd be a shame to throw them, I'll get some phone-cards out of this".

"Throw it in the toilet. I'll give you as many phone-cards as you wish!"

"It's been pre-ordered. What will I tell the guys?"

"That I bought it. And that they should come to me if they have a problem".

"I also have this", he said, uncovering a big plastic washtub, half-filled with foaming must from various fruit, juices and sugar.

"Put that on my bill too".

He emptied its contents in the toilet, put away his distilling equipment, wiped his sweaty body with a dirty towel and sat on his bed. He pointed at the tsipouro-filled plastic bottle.

"Should I put that on the bill as well and drink it together?"

"You can drink it if you want, it's on me! I only wonder how you can drink warm tsipouro in this heat!"

"It's my only solace. I've nothing else left in this world. I've been in here for seventeen years already, and I owe them many more. It's been tough …"

He was drinking shots one after the other, listing his pain and his suffering. I was so tired from the days I had spent in the holding cell and the lengthy transfer I fell asleep at once. I was awoken by the morning metallic sound of keys and the unlocking of the cell's door. I sat up and saw the most characteristic sight of the results of the Greek correctional system. Lying face-up, still holding the empty plastic bottle in his arms, half up and half hanging down from the bed, my cellmate was snoring, sound asleep.

That old dog! He had taken a handful of psychotropic drugs (they are generously handed to inmates), he'd drunk one and a half litres of tsipouro, but he was still alive just to spite Death and the disgusting State!

I really had to switch cells, so I got down to the yard to meet the rest of the wing's inmates. Some of them and I went way back. They told me that the prison's administration was utterly impersonal and couldn't care less about their daily problems, but switching cells was relatively easy, as long as you told the warden which cell and which cellmate. With their help, both were found. Now I only had to go tell the warden. I went to meet him and mentioned it.

"Palaiokostas, what you're asking is quite simple. Because of your situation, however, I can't make that decision on my own. I'll discuss it with the director and the prosecutor. I don't think they'll refuse. You'll have an answer within the next few days".

The only thing I asked was for them not to put out my new cellmate, because he had been in his cell for more than two years already and he had gotten comfortable there. That's precisely what they did. Instead of giving me an answer, they ordered an inmates' switch. They transferred my current cellmate to a different wing and brought the new one in his place. I believed these were the administrations' antics so as not to show they gave in to me that easily, so I let it slide. After all, my new cellmate was easy-going; the perfect kind of man to live in a cell with. clean, studious man of a few words, a man above suspicion as the average citizen would say. Having tact enough, I didn't immediately ask him why he was in prison. That would happen a few days later, when he grew more comfortable around me and suggested I should write a book about my life with the prospect of him posting it online, as he was web-literate and all.

That suggestion struck me as suspicious. Only a few days had passed since, using one of the prison's payphones, I had contacted a friend, asking for his help to edit a future book of mine. Also, his mention of web literacy brought back to my mind an incident that had taken place in Korydallos, the last prison I had been in. Then, a noble, educated old man with white hair and beard, about sixty years old, had come to stay as the fourth inmate in the cell next to mine, where some of my guys lived. So far, so good, yes? Until, one day, I was sitting outside my cell, reading a newspaper at the table which both cells mutually used. He came and sat next to me to read his book. Eventually he was summoned for an appointment with his lawyer, leaving the book he was reading open on the table in his hurry. I read a few lines out of mere curiosity, and was appalled. The author was describing the thoughts and emotions of an old man, who had an eight-year-old boy on his lap, caressing the tender white skin of his legs etc. I grabbed the book and skimmed through it, lest this had been just a random page. The whole book was child pornography.

I tried my best to relax so that I wouldn't hurt him when he got back. He was a man of a certain age, and for that reason, my hands were tied. Returning, he saw me from afar holding the book in my hands. He approached me, smiling awkwardly.

I grabbed his neck, shoved him inside the cell and rubbed the book on his face. "What is this fucking thing you're reading, you creepy old pervert? For fuck's sake! Where did you find this?"

"From the prison library", he moaned.

"Pack your things and ask to switch wings right now or I promise I'll gut you!"

I released him, and he ran to the wing's barred gate without his stuff. Only a few minutes had passed when they called me from the loudspeakers. The old pervert and the deputy warden waited for me inside the wing's gatehouse, sitting across from each other at a table.

"Why are you terrorizing other inmates, Vassilis?" the deputy warden asked me (as he ought).

I placed the book on the table in front of him.

"Read!" I said to him.

He opened it on a random page and began reading. He turned to look at me.

"What is this?" he asked me.

"Don't ask me. Ask this nice old man you're protecting. He took it from the prison's sex shop! It's not enough you bring them in my yard, you make sure they're well entertained too!"

The nice old man, naïve enough to now feel safe, stood up to me.

"You don't know anything. You don't know who the globally acclaimed author of this book is," etc.

"I don't give a damn about this author. I just want to know who you are, you old fuck. Sitting at my table, reading child pornography".

The deputy warden, realising things could get out of hand, sent him to pack his things. As soon as he left, he tried to justify the unjustifiable.

"Please, don't make an issue out of this book. We get donations of whole boxes full of books; we can't possibly check them all. I promise that I will order the whole library to be inspected".

And he concluded:

"What can we do? They're everywhere, and we are forced to protect them!"

This incident had been swirling in my mind when I asked my cellmate why he was in prison.

"For financial stuff, but I don't like to talk about my cases".

His diplomatic answer made me even more suspicious.

"Understandable. I respect that. I just want you to know that I have a big problem with snitches and people who have committed sexual crimes that involve children. Or, to put it better … they're the ones with the problem".

He didn't respond.

I enlisted the wing's inmates to shed some light into this case. Having spent more time in this prison, they had some connections. They sent someone to the wing where he had been living before he came to my cell. It wouldn't be long before I heard back, and the news he brought me was the worst possible. The guy had been convicted for circulating child pornography on the internet. From that moment, I had no doubt about the administration's true intentions for me.

They had put a dirty plan into action, attempting to provoke my violent reaction so that they'd have a reason to remove me from their prison. They couldn't bear my weight, and they were plotting to get an excuse to ask the ministry to transfer me.

The Corfu police force's administration was probably in on it too. The fact that the chief of the island's police had visited me not once but three times, with no apparent reason, only strengthened my belief. He told me that he had been visiting me because he liked me, being from the same area and all (he was from a village in Trikala). And to make his professed likeness more believable, every time he came to visit me he'd bring me a book as a gift, which I always threw in the first bin I came across on my way back to the wing. One time, the "politically oppositional" deputy warden escorting me back noticed me doing this.

"Did you read it already?" he asked tongue in cheek.

"I'm used to reading between the lines", I replied.

"Beware of Greeks bearing gifts, Vassilis!"

"I'm afraid neither of Greeks nor of their presents. I'm just not the type to insult my fellow men".

"They fear you'll escape again", he said to me in secret.

As things were turning out, I needed to be extremely careful. I had to deal with a scared, hostile administration that hadn't hesitated transferring a child molester in my wing, in my own cell, just to achieve their goals. He, obviously blinded by everything he had been promised in return and unaware of the danger since nobody had informed him about it, had agreed to play their disgusting game. They had literally thrown a lamb inside a pit full of hungry wolves. The "good" news quickly spread, and all the inmates were waiting for my signal to attack.

"I have reason to believe this is a trap the administration has set for me and me alone. To avoid walking right into it, I think I have to deal with it personally", I said to them to calm them down.

I got the man of the hour inside the cell to interrogate him.

"Tell me, you motherfucker, why are you inside?"

"For child pornography".

"And why did you agree to come to my cell with such a conviction, you stupid fuck?"

"They forced me to come".

"You came by force, but you'll leave willingly. Go now to the warden and ask him to switch wings. If he refuses, ask for his protection because here you're in imminent danger. I'm barely keeping the others from ripping you to pieces".

He left, never to return. In about an hour, they summoned me to the guardhouse. It was a spacious chamber which housed not only the warden but all other administrative offices as well. Walking in, I felt the inquisitors' searing eyes burning through my skin. Directly ahead of where I stood, the prosecutor was sitting behind her desk. I was seeing her for the first time. To her right, at his own desk, was sitting the dirty, old buffoon, the director. Chronic malice, suspiciousness, and cunning had soaked his existence to the bone and were oozing out of every pore on his skin. A living fossil of different times and practices, he seemed as though he had just emerged victorious through the screams of the tortured souls who had passed through this hellhole he'd been governing. To his left, at her own desk, sat an elderly social worker who was the spitting image of him. The warden, as though he wanted to distance himself, was sitting in a chair far from all of them. At the chamber's corners stood several huge morons, legs apart and arms folded, with their mentor the warden (also a huge dickhead) at the centre. They were creating a forced air of tension inside the chamber, for which only one title was suitable: "Libation to blissful stupidity".

I stepped inside the chamber, stood close to the director's desk and the argument ignited.

"Why did you summon me here?"

"Palaiokostas, what will we do with you? Why are you kicking out all your cellmates?" the director began first.

"Because you're playing treacherous games at my expense and I won't let you have your way".

"Nobody's playing games at anyone's expense. It's just that this prison doesn't grant any inmates privileges!" the prosecutor intervened.

"Since when is the peaceful cohabitation of inmates considered a privilege? What business did the child molester have in my cell?"

It was the social worker's turn to take the floor and deal me a low blow.

"You call yourself a broad-minded man, and yet you judge people by their offences!"

"You obviously don't get it, lady, although you're a social worker. I'm more broad-minded than you think. Since you have your society worked out this way, so that I'm your mortal enemy while he who fucks your children is your once friend and your once valuable partner, I suggest you take this guy into your homes, to watch over your children and your grandchildren while you're away".

She began squawking like a trapped crone.

"Look, Palaiokostas", jumped in the director. "There's no way you're getting whoever you want in your cell. If you escape, it's me who'll get in trouble!"

"No matter which snitch you put in my cell, you'll be the last to hear about my escape! You're going to lose your position no matter what excuses you come up with. All you're doing is prejudging and bringing forward what you don't wish to happen", I said to him.

This tense argument would continue in the same vein for ten more minutes, without any chance of reaching a common ground. Returning to my cell, I found a new cellmate waiting for me there. They had sent him from a different wing once again. Thankfully, he was an old-timer and a nice guy, so I didn't address the issue again. Yet when you toy with confined nature, you ought to expect adverse reactions.

Premature awakening

This argument with prison management awoke the beast inside me prematurely. Thinking it was still too early for any "sneaky" plans, I tried my best to keep it under control, and it appeared to be understanding. And yet, the moment it woke, it wreaked havoc on everyone. Its howls were its excruciating speech saying what a thousand wise men couldn't. It would pierce through my ears, taking me over. I couldn't hide it. It was visible in my every move. In my step, my gaze, my speech. It demanded its right to freedom, right there and then. How could I silence it? How can you restrain such a will to live? This wild beast plainly refused to kneel before its chains. It forbade me to live as a captive man, let alone accept my captivity as a normal condition. It kept me alert, constantly searching for a way out. Willing to dig, to saw bars, to set the walls ablaze, to build a ladder and climb to the stars, until it discovered an exit.

It wanted to get rid of this circle dance those human vampires were circumscribing around me. Until it got out, far away. Until it could stand in the forest and breath the fresh mountain air; until it could hear its voice echoing under the starlight.

Confinement doesn't have the same consequences for all living beings. People with more powerful instincts, broadened emotional worlds, restless minds, and a strong sense of freedom, experience a much worse captivity. Western legal "culture" never cares about this. Categorisation takes place only as far as offences are concerned and the answer is always more prolonged confinement. There's no benchmark more infallible than that of nature. It teaches life and death, even cannibalism, but never captivity by one's own species.

Captivity is a construct of "civilised men"; it isn't accepted by the creator. Whoever commits it is a criminal. We're talking about a continuous collective crime. The hefty price modern men burden themselves with to maintain the privilege of cohabitation in organised societies has many names. The rule of law, jurisprudence, justice, correctional policy. These are the first velvet layers of sugar-coated barbarism, which people never managed to shake off. But when you can't get rid of your shit, you had better turn it into a creative necessity and, finally, a useful science! Over the next few weeks, I tried to sound out those inmates I considered friendly about the idea of planning and putting into action an escape plan. I had one in mind that required the participation of some more inmates.

The wing housed several lifers and long-term convicts. All those I spoke to were willing to take the risk and before I knew it, winter had arrived. November, in all prisons, is a month of action and upheaval, in which we too participated. December coincided with the murder of Alexandros Grigoropoulos,* resulting in increased supervision measures both inside and outside the prison. So our plans were put on hold. In early January the trial for my first escape by helicopter was to begin in Athens, so I knew they would transfer me to Korydallos Prison. We thought that, while I was gone, things would be much more relaxed and they'd be able to work on the plan better, so that when I returned we'd be ready to put it into action.

---

*   Grigoropoulos was a 15-year-old student shot dead by police in the anarchist district of Athens, Exarchia. It's hard to overstate the impact the killing had on Greece, sparking riots in the capital and several other cities which lasted for most of a month. The revolt electrified the country's anarchist movement, as Greece's youth participated in and were radicalised by unrest which expressed a generational rage against not just police brutality and corruption, but the broader economic malaise which underpinned high unemployment and a sense of hopelessness. The boy's death is commemorated annually on December 6th.

It was mid-December when an inmate arrived in the wing from Korydallos. Big deal. But this inmate, although it was his first time coming to a prison where security on entering was very tight and inspections quite thorough, managed to sneak in a mobile phone, a charger, and enough drugs to treat the whole wing for a week. His behaviour showed that this bush was dreaming of becoming a plane tree. He'd give his mobile phone to anyone who wanted it, to talk for as long as they wanted without asking for anything in exchange. He'd get into arguments with prison officers with no apparent reason, acting tough etc. And yet, when it came to me, he'd bow his head, he didn't even dare greet me. I was more than certain that he had been sent here by the police, with the consent and the help of the prison's administration. Prisons are filled with willing, guided suppositories, waiting in line to take on a mission among inmates to reduce or eliminate their own sentences, revealing and reinforcing the decline of the human soul. Such little people's worth isn't justified by the quality of their struggle and their position towards life in general. It is granted to them by prison administrations in the form of privileges. And this little man was trying to become someone on their dime.

I was right. One afternoon, there was a knock on the door of my cell, and he appeared holding his mobile phone.

"Vassilis, it's Alket ... he wants to talk to you!"

I signalled him to hang up. After he did:

"Don't ever do that again. How dare you come into my cell and ask me to talk on the phone to someone without having asked me first?"

"But I thought ..."

"Don't think anything. Do you know what my relationship with Alket is?"

"I just wanted to do you a service".

"Who do you serve exactly? Would you like to tell me?"

The following day he got beaten up by some other inmates. The employees came and took him, putting an inglorious end to his ambitious mission. The only thing he'd be able to tell his principals was that I wasn't getting along with Alket, which was true. I was angry at him because of a particular incident.

The first days after our escape, as a precautionary measure, I requested that for as long as we stayed together we wouldn't keep in touch with people we didn't trust completely. Alket and the kid agreed with me, they were of the exact same opinion. Later, when we parted ways, Alket sought shelter — until he was arrested — with some of the people we had previously rejected. Now one of those men, Vassilis,* had appeared in our case file as having arranged the escape! This arranger, and now co-defendant, learnt from someone that I had badmouthed him, and was angry at me — with good reason. Such misunderstandings are

---

*   Vassilis Stefanakos, nicknamed "King of the Night," was said to have been involved in smuggling and racketeering. The author notes: the police granted him the title of boss of the country's organised crime. After his release in 2016 [as part of a prison overcrowding relief scheme] he was murdered outside his office [in 2018], when two armed men riding a high-powered motorcycle opened fire against his armoured BMW, right after he had gotten in it.

common in the world of outlaws, but for me it was the first time, and until that moment I couldn't put my finger on the exact reason.

Being a wanted man, I had a sacred duty to secure my freedom. Among the many other things I had to deal with, I had to sort out the people with whom I would keep in touch. When I didn't trust someone (because they were careless, chatterers etc.) I avoided them as I ought to. However, there's a huge difference between "I don't trust someone" and "They're working with the police". Snitches are clearly enemies. They require different treatment. Even if I had well-founded suspicions, without substantial evidence I would never badmouth someone, though it could come to bite me in the arse later. That's what my sense of justice dictated. If I had to accuse someone of something, I'd say it right to their face, directly, so that they wouldn't have to find out from somebody else who might twist my words. I was resolutely opposed and abstained from any practices that caused friction and animosity. My path was set out for me, with its own cunning enemies. I certainly didn't need any more.

The man who had communicated this malicious gossip did so deliberately. He had this exact result in mind. Until that moment, everything suggested that this man was Alket.

Returning to Korydallos and the first false step

The suppository inmate's bosses, learning I had issues with Alket, made their first and decisive false step, in the process falling in the pit they were trying to dig for me. When I got to Korydallos, in early January, they transferred me to the guardroom in 'C' wing, to place me in his cell. Let them have a go at each other, they thought. This was also part of their correctional process. It was noon, a bit before we were allowed to exit to the yard when the deputy warden escorting me opened a cell in 'C' wing's guardroom. Inside was Alket, with another inmate. I hadn't seen him for two-and-a-half years since our escape in 2006. He stood up and came to hug me. I stopped him.

"First we need to talk", I said to him.

He was puzzled. I saw it in his eyes. When my escort left, I signalled for his cellmate to get out.

"What is it, friend? Why are you like this?" he said to me as soon as we were alone. I told him.

"What do you have to say?"

"My friend ... how could you possibly think I'd ever do such a thing?"

"When we discussed this, it was just me, you, and the kid. It must have been one of you two, adding their own stuff".

"What reason would I have to say these things? Whatever men discuss stays between them. Spyros, for his own reasons, is trying to pit us against each other. Remember he's in their cell, they talk to each other. What don't you understand?"

What he was saying made sense, but I didn't know whether I should believe him. I didn't want to be biased, so I decided to talk with Spyros who was indeed staying in the same cell with our two co-defendants in 'A' wing.

Our trial would begin in a week. The fact that Alket had been offered shelter by people the police knew justified their wild fantasy that some other people must have planned the escape. And they found these other people, preparing a real monstrosity of a file. The monstrosity, resulting from the Greek prosecuting authorities' imaginative jiggery-pokery, said that the escape was orchestrated by the same man (Vassilis) who had been hiding Alket all this time, with the sole purpose of getting him out of prison so that he could have him kill his opponents! Only the Hellenic Police are capable of such monolithic thinking. As if there weren't any people left out there willing to kill for peanuts, that his only option was to organise such a risky operation. Even the most unversed person can understand that when two armed men have the will and the ability to rent a helicopter and use their guns to force its pilot to land it in the yard of a prison, a fixer is only useful for waving them off!

Despite my experience in the way case files are prepared, based on a muddle of targeted rumours and whispers from the underworld, I was often surprised by the prosecuting authorities' boundless inspiration in their attempts to expand on this imaginative talent of theirs. In this case, their targeted conspiracy suited and served, in the best possible way, a brand-new piece of legislation aimed at criminal organisations, which they had ordered and been handed by the always-willing-to-fight-crime Greek parliament. So they decided to adapt its implementation in the lives of both fair and unfair men.

And here is the case file: to make sure the recipe succeeded, and to make the charges more palatable, they took me out of the picture as an orchestrator. I was being presented as a lucky man just passing by. A guest star of sorts. They were saying I didn't know anything about the escape, that I noticed the helicopter at the last possible moment and just barely managed to get on it! For that reason, they were simply accusing me of the minor offence of escaping, with a maximum prescribed sentence of about eight months. Instead, Vassilis, having offered Alket shelter, was being accused of having planned the escape, with the two hijackers, Spyros and Panagiotis (the latter hadn't been arrested yet), under his command. He was also facing charges for being the moral instigator of one or two murders committed by Alket, as well as other criminal charges that had to do with the criminal underworld.

Waiting for the trial, I decided to pursue a meeting with my co-defendants to discuss and coordinate, if possible, our defence. After consulting with the prison's director, our meeting was set for nighttime, two days before the beginning of our trial.

Rumors, misunderstandings, and tension

As we entered the chamber next to the guardhouse our three co-defendants were waiting for us, sitting behind a large table. I hadn't seen Spyros in about two years and the others since the summer of 2005, when we coexisted for a while in 'A' wing. There was tension in the air. To avoid making things worse, I left the subject of the malicious gossip until the end and focused on the upcoming trial. The first surprise came when Spyros told me he was going to deny all charges, although there was substantial evidence against him. The second was when he demanded that I take responsibility for orchestrating the escape!

"Since you're planning on pleading not guilty, why do you care who takes responsibility for the orchestration of the escape? And why should I be the one to do it? Alket can take responsibility for it". I said to him, quite curious.

His response wasn't convincing. On the contrary, it was rather suspicious. Although I was facing only misdemeanour charges, I had no problem with taking responsibility for organising the escape. I owed it to him, as long as this was in his own interest and his decision, unaffected by others. That didn't seem to be the case.

In our time together outside the prison we had worked out a basic defensive plan in case of arrest, based on our own dignity, and he was now moving in a completely different direction without any reason. It was apparent he had crossed to a different side, taking on the role of the intermediary so that the charges against Vassilis were dropped. That pissed me off. I thought it dishonest of them to be plotting their defensive plans without me, taking advantage of the moral obligation I had to Spyros.

I overreacted, and Vassilis stood up, ready to leave, saying:

"Let everyone say whatever they want and be done with it".

"Of course everyone will say whatever they want and they'll be judged based on it. I never forced anyone to plead something they didn't want", I responded.

He opened the door and left the chamber quite upset.

I had actually already met Vassilis the last time I was in prison, when he'd stayed in 'A' wing for a few months. It had been his first time in prison, and Giannos had suggested he come to find me. I had never heard of him before. He was a lively, happy-go-lucky sort of man. And intelligent too. In the little time we spent together, we grew to respect one another, and that's why when he got released I asked him whether he'd want to help in any way and however much he wanted in a possible plan for my escape. He was honest with me. He told me not to expect his active, let alone physical, participation in something like this. But if I found some willing people, he could help materially, by finding us a car etc. To his credit, when the time came for him to help in a planned escape (that never came to happen), he did. Always with respect to the needed materials and to the extent possible.

Associating with him — even from a distance — I realised we were quite different when it came to the moral and practical treatment of active armed struggle. This difference had to do with our backgrounds and our goals. We came from very different places, and were heading in different directions. Our motives were different. He, a supporter of office strategy, had come to know and commit crime through the night clubs he owned. While I, my feet scarred from the sharp stones of Pindos, was walking down a tough and quite different path, with a Kalashnikov in my hands, always out front.

As an answer to my natural questions about the way he handled these situations I'll use the words of a friend and partner as he told them to me: "Don't be surprised. Vassilis isn't an outlaw. He's a businessman, with illegality as his hobby!"

The planned escape that brought our irreconcilable differences to the surface made me realise that any such plan involving Vassilis, even at a remove, would be doomed from the start because despite his total lack of previous experience, he wanted his requests to be heard and always vetoed my decisions without reason. Not wanting to jeopardise our acquaintance, I separated it from my actions, deciding not to include him in any future escape plans. So, when after a few months my first escape by helicopter took place, Vassilis knew absolutely nothing about it. He heard about it, like all Greek people, through the media — but nevertheless appeared in the case file as its orchestrator.

And yet, he wasn't totally innocent. For personal reasons having to do with his prestige in the world of illegality, he had been boasting that my escape was his doing. He didn't think that, since we live in Greece, he'd have to refute these rumours as being valid in a trial, facing several criminal charges. Because rumours are a lot like balloons. The more you blow them up, the bigger they'll become and the higher they will go when you release them. The higher they get, the more people see them and talk about them. Vassilis proved to be a hobbyist balloon-blower too.

But he'd gone too far here. He blew up this balloon too much and the trained eye of the police force had noticed it. An eye that, unfortunately, fails to tell the difference between a real helicopter and a plain balloon. A balloon that still floats over the prison, carrying a load of rumours.

Aside from trying to take credit for our success, that had been the result of a lot of effort — something which revealed a lack of respect for the necessary personal experiences related to the struggle for one's own freedom — these otherwise "innocent" rumours had other, darker aspects. One of them was that I appeared to be in his debt, within the world of illegality and out of it too, since these rumours had turned into substantiated charges, and therefore into an undeniable truth. They trapped me in a debt which in reality I didn't have, while to him they worked as credentials, opening closely guarded doors. His participation in the liberation of an inmate was an act of high moral worth and symbolism. This reputation of having co-ordinated such a difficult escape to liberate a prisoner with a specific history of struggle and life stance, could on its own work as a pool of Siloam, washing away any sins of the past, and also as a future passport to avoid any control towards the top.

The sad thing was that Spyros, now attached to him, wasn't refuting these rumours. On the contrary, his stance strengthened them, not doing justice first and foremost to himself, since this golden badge of honour was all his. He'd won it fair and square, and he should have never taken it off his chest, never given it to someone else. Alket, on the other hand, feeling that he owed them for offering him shelter after the escape, avoided the subject. After all, he didn't find it that important.

On the contrary, I wasn't willing to appear so ungrateful as to badmouth those who'd helped him escape and avoid responsibility towards Spyros, because of these rumours. What was even more tragic was that since they had become a case file, nothing could be changed. Even if I refuted them, it would appear as a mere line of defence of those involved to avoid their criminal liability, and nothing more.

I said all this to Giannos* who stayed behind, asking him to explain how I had appeared in their case file which included murders, blackmails, score-settling etc. I, who was entirely opposed to such practices. Giannos was convinced that it wasn't them spreading these rumours and it was all a plot conceived by the prosecution to tie the indictment, charging them with as many crimes as possible.

I had a different view of how things had really gone down. Already from the first days after the escape, I had been informed that Vassilis was spreading these tales. I hadn't paid much attention then, thinking they were innocent rumours in an attempt to increase his shares in the illegality stock market. I had gone through similar situations in the past, like after I escaped from Chalkis when some robbers spread around rumours that they picked me up with a Porsche as soon as I jumped from the prison wall, while in reality, I had walked for two whole days. Thankfully, then, such rumours didn't become a case file. Now, however, one of the two cops presented in the case file as Vassilis' partners had testified that Vassilis himself had confided in him that it was he who orchestrated the escape. When I mentioned this to Giannos as proof, he said to me:

"And you believe what a cop says? He's trying to save his sorry ass, and he's saying bullshit. Even if it's true, why do you care? Does it affect you?"

"Giannos, it's my honour that some people want to be included in the most important moments of my life, as long as it's true. After all, I want to know to whom I owe in this life even if I never manage to repay them. As far as I know, the only one to whom I owe for this escape is Spyros, and no one else".

"Did we tell you that you owe us something? We're just asking, if you can and want to, to take responsibility for the escape, first and foremost to help Spyros. What do you care if this also helps us to get cleared of the charges they pinned on us? It won't cost you anything. If I had your sentence and I could, I'd help the whole prison!"

"It bothers me that you came to talk, having already made a decision. Why didn't you just come and ask me?"

"Didn't I just do that?"

"I'll take responsibility for the kidnapping because the kid asked me. It's the least I can do for him. But to really help I have to make a plea, accepting and answering their questions by telling a bunch of lies. And that would be humiliating. My problem isn't assuming responsibility, but entering a plea!"

"Why don't you want to enter a plea and give answers? I don't understand", he insisted.

---

*   Giannos was accused by the police and subsequently convicted as one of the men behind the 2009 kidnap of shipping magnate Pericles Panagopoulos,, pulling the strings from inside the prison.

This argument with Giannos saddened me. He was an outspoken man, I liked him. I always had something nice to say about him. Since Vassilis hadn't stayed to talk, Giannos got hell instead. And yet he maintained his usual, plain way of thinking over such matters. They play their game, we play ours, no matter who wins. The end justifies the means. To me, however, things weren't that simple. I felt that an attempt to contradict the charges made by the same set of people who would summon me to enter a plea would mark the willing abandonment of my conscience at the sight of the firing squad's guns. It would be the same as putting it there for the systemic schemers to shoot it, legitimising their crime. Something like this would be humiliating for me. I'd feel the same way even if the charges weren't just the dishonourable construct of prosecuting authorities, but included actual details of the escape. I couldn't even fathom that I'd have to apologise to the State for taking back the life it had deprived me of. This unfeeling beast. The sole liable!

I've always been transparent. They all knew my beliefs, especially Spyros. He knew them even before he came to free me with the helicopter. I'd say they had been his key motive. Unfortunately, he disagreed when it came to putting them into action. During my previous incarceration, I'd never attended any trial that concerned a co-defendant. It was at my own discretion to decide how to handle entering a plea or not in every charge, in every trial. What I'd say, how, why, and if I'd say it was my own decision, nobody else's. It wasn't affected by and it didn't affect anyone but me. Now, however, the exact opposite was true. In this cesspool of a case file, I found myself lumped together with half the "underworld" of Attica.

In the end, although I was sure that, based on the charges and the evidence, this line of defence would harm Spyros more than help him, and since this is what he wanted, I agreed to take responsibility for orchestrating the escape, without responding to the courts' questions.

Before the meeting was over, I addressed how my words had been twisted, resulting in this attitude towards me. Giannos, understandably, didn't want — and it wouldn't have been right to — point at the one responsible since neither Spyros nor Alket owned up to it. I was now more than certain that it had been the former, and that all this time I had been unfair to Alket. It's impossible to guess what is happening within the soul and the mind of a person. Later, I'd make the safe and yet bold assumption that he had acted immaturely (turning our co-defendants against me) thinking and fearing I'd turn against him because of his life and actions on the outside. And because he thought I'd suspect it was him who handed these early birds the results of my three months of hard work surveilling ship owner Pericles Panagopoulos. At the time his kidnapping was ongoing, and the authorities' suspicions were falling on me since his name had been at the top of the list of acclaimed Greek businessmen they had found in my hideout in Souroti.

As soon as the meeting was over, I took the kid aside and asked him if he had given information on the ship owner to other people. He said he hadn't. I never managed to learn if he had told me the truth.

Lies and truths, a tangled mess

I didn't enjoy any of the events I just narrated, and the same stands for those that follow. I resented all these rumours, the lies, and the conspiracies, woven so masterfully that they appeared like the one and only truth, making it impossible to untangle and refute them. This absolute truth would prove to be but the beginning of a chain of events. Still, as they were unfolding, I couldn't have possibly guessed that they were mere scenes in a masterful script, written and directed by this always creative and unpredictable life. The shooting stage had already begun the moment I arrived at Corfu, without me knowing, and the end would be written on the 22nd of February, during my second spectacular escape from Korydallos by helicopter.

Life conjures its own scripts and takes the plot wherever it wants. Chooses the cast and crew, casting whomever it wants in whatever part it wants. All those of us involved were doing a pretty good job playing the parts it gave us a long time before. Without Vassilis' overblown rumour-balloon and the kid's erratic (in terms of their target) lies, the escape could never have happened. According to this line of thinking, they both helped in the escape. Vassilis always had wanted to be part of it, after all!

The chiefs of the Hellenic Police and the Ministry of Justice that had been tasked with supervising us didn't know what villainous life had in store. So they were making their own dirty plans, enjoying the role of shadow protagonist, pulling the strings with us as their puppets. Their rationalised scenario dragged the administrators of Korydallos prison into this tragicomic delusion. Now, they all believed that another escape by helicopter, by the same fugitives, was impossible because the orchestrator and one of the hijackers from the first escape were in a cell in 'A' wing, while the "guest star" along with the "hired gun" were locked in solitary, both completely harmless. A big mistake! Accumulated lies can become the drug that puts to sleep, first and foremost, those who produce it. It is also a fuel that can provide great impetus; it can momentarily cause lift-off — albeit perilously because it can easily explode, and those who have created it are usually the first to pay the price.

Their own little tale would put them nicely and soundly to sleep, only to be awoken in terror by the strong, continuous rattling of the rotor blades.

Great ceremony for this cesspool of a case file

The trial began with great ceremony, offering plenty of stimuli to cartoonists so as to guarantee them a brilliant career. Each morning ten defendants (most of us strangers to each other) would get on a bulletproof prison bus, and we would set out from Korydallos for the Piraeus Court of First Instance. Security measures were high. Heavily armed officers from the Special Anti-Terrorist Unit with Cherokee Jeeps, and numerous police vehicles filled with armed officers would accompany us from and to Korydallos.

Reaching the courtroom, we'd be meeting several other defendants. Because their charges against us wouldn't be complete if they weren't adorned with all the colourful ornaments temptress night had to offer.

Bouncers, crime bosses, goons, bullyboys, unaccountable cops who shamelessly identified as double agents, common informants of both sides, even likeable pushovers. Some had been arrested because they'd gotten tired and had sat on the stoop of some apartment building where a suspect under surveillance happened to be staying. However, the case file didn't specify their exact role in the so-called criminal organisation. So now the psychotic — and always willing to serve the blue uniform — justice system had to rule on the level of their involvement, while at the same time reaching a verdict for tired passers-by. Of course, their conscious perversion intended to use these poor guys. By acquitting them, the judges established their impartiality for convicting everyone else. It was apparent that the State was using the institution of justice, the key to guaranteeing its cohesion, to deceitfully harm the lives of citizens.

The trial commenced, and nothing would become something, and something would become life sentences. A flood of absurd lies would be transformed into an unshakable truth by those who had made them up in the first place. A truth that legitimised and necessitated these convictions. The judges who took on carrying through this crime were all pomp and circumstance and very happy to do it. Strict, serious, lenient, making jokes, compliments, whatever they saw fit to build their lie. The renowned lawyers of most defendants — instead of throwing these large case files in the faces of the judges, reporting them as an insulting, lousy legal construct, and walking away — were diligently fixing their silk ties to appear before the TV crews that were swarming the court, hoping to get a precious statement from them.

Crime reporters, gunpowder-blackened from combat reportage, fighting their own war fellating information from the Hellenic Police's higher-ranking officers and spitting the extracted contents, warm and fresh, on the faces of their viewers, blurring their window to the world, were walking up and down the courtroom and the hallways outside.

Following their superiors' orders, they were recording the faces of organised crime and presenting them to ordinary citizens, at the same time informing them what and whom they should be afraid of, and how much. One of the many renowned reporters present, in one of the many recesses, managed to approach the courthouse's holding cell with the help of a higher-ranking officer. Using vulgar language to fit in (or so he thought), he began summoning the defendants one by one to have a chat. Nobody said no. Alket was the last to go. Returning, he said to me:

"Go, he wants to talk to you!"

"Who says I want to? Screw him!"

The reporter, seeing I couldn't care less about him, yelled:

"Palaiokostas! Come on mate ... I want to tell you something!"

"Don't 'mate' me, you prick!"

Everyone laughed.

He took this public snub hard. He began accusing me of all the things he had written in his "quality" reportages and other ravings of this sort.

"Fine ... come by Korydallos whenever you want to get your prize!"

Since then he has been spewing hate on every 'impartial' and 'objective' article he writes that happens to mention my name in it.

Even the officer in charge of the holding cell's security congratulated me!

"Good job, Vassilis. You served that snitch right", he said.

A crazy proposal

In the meantime, Alket seemed to have been waiting for my arrival quite anxiously. He wasted no time; cutting to the chase at once. He began trying to convince me to orchestrate a new escape. Doubting his intentions at the time, and having left my cellmates in Corfu working on a similar plan, I avoided the subject.

"It's too soon for me to plan an escape. Not even six months have passed since they got me. They're keeping a close watch. They're trying to locate the rest of the money, the guns, and any other involved partners", I'd say to him.

And all this was partly true. Yet he wouldn't give up. Convinced that it wasn't a coincidence that we found ourselves together in solitary confinement, whenever we returned from the court he just wouldn't leave me alone. Despite his proneness to prison's "trivialities" there was still a spark burning in his wolf-like eyes. All it would take was a small blow, and they could set the world ablaze. After I stopped suspecting him, I decided to hear what he had to suggest. He proposed a second escape by helicopter! Alket was always this generous. Based on the facts, I thought such a plan would be unrealistic. Aside from being together in the same space, there was no other reason to justify being optimistic that such an attempt would be successful again.

We were in solitary confinement (meaning in a closely monitored space), inside a prison within a prison, with five or six highly suspicious inmates who were there for protection (perhaps some of them had paid to be there). There was no way we could trust them. There was only one payphone in solitary confinement, and every conversation was recorded. Nobody had ever managed to sneak a mobile phone into solitary. and even if we pulled it off, it would be extremely dangerous to use it. In such a small space, those put there by the administration would notice at once. Aside from weekends, all other days we were at court since the trial was ongoing. We'd return late in the evening, exhausted and having little time at our disposal.

Under these circumstances, it would be almost impossible to orchestrate a successful escape, even if everything else was already in place, which wasn't the case. We hadn't even found the people who would hijack the helicopter. We didn't have weapons, cars etc. We didn't have anything. Everything was up in the air, with no hope of success.

Alket mentioned that a brave woman was willing to take the lead, to be one of the hijackers. Nothing more. I didn't pay much attention. I wasn't optimistic at all, but I didn't want to hurt his feelings.

"For the time being, I can't orchestrate such an escape. The only things I can provide are money and my brain. If you think you can take care of all the rest, we move forward. When you're ready, tell me to take action", I said to him.

Oddly, he was excited. He promised he was going to take care of everything himself. I had come to know Alket's excitement from our first escape, and yet, in this case, I found it rather undue and unreasonable. One of the following days, he managed to slip a watch mobile phone onto his wrist, and with it, he began trying to get in contact with people. He'd been in prison for quite some time and having the connections he did with compatriot outlaws, it wouldn't be that hard for him to collect the arms and cars that we needed for the escape. He'd only need money, and we had plenty of that. Yet I was still very sceptical about his ability to find the proper people who would manage to pull off the hardest part of the escape — renting and hijacking the helicopter. Such a humble incentive as money wouldn't suffice for this. It needed something more. And miracles don't happen every day.

Love in the clouds

It was a weekend afternoon, we were both in the cell, and Alket was still communicating with the outside world using his watch phone. He was talking with a woman named Voula.* She was the one he had mentioned to me repeatedly as a willing, available hijacker, but their discussion was a bit tense. They seemed to be having an argument. After a little while of this, without warning, Alket gave me his handsfree saying:

"Talk to her, please, she doesn't understand!"

I grabbed the headphone and placed it in my ear, quite taken aback.

"Hi, Voula ... how are you?"

"I'm fine!"

"Do you know who I am?"

"Who doesn't?"

"Have you fully understood what you are about to do? The consequences it will have in your life?"

"Yes. I've thought about everything. I'm determined to do it. I want it more than Alket!"

Pure love, how can you not take a bow at that! Here's a reason why it should exist in our life. Because it flies!

---

*   Editors' note: not to be confused with Soula Mitropia. Mitropia was noted by court reporters as Alket's "glamourous girlfriend" (now wife) when she made a splash during his trial and has since become a source of some media fascination. After their escape she was later detained and accused of being involved in a bank robbery, as well as carrying out the helicopter hijack plan, being convicted for the latter. Both she and Alket have consistently denied her involvement.

But I was always strict:

"Voula, this isn't a game. Are you sure you can press a gun against the pilot's head and get him to Korydallos?" I asked her, testing her in cold blood.

"Yes! I'll get him good".

Her way, her attitude, her tone, the certainty of her response, made my stomach give a prolonged hard kick. It was that familiar joyful ringing that promised only good things ahead. Her spontaneous answer, the way she spoke, stressing every letter, every syllable, and every word, made me sure she meant it. I was now confident there was a woman out there, completely aware of what she was about to do and at the same time poised to succeed. She believed in herself but, first and foremost, she believed in us, and we had no right to let her down. I had nothing more to say with Voula. I bade her farewell, saying:

"Since you want this, we will do it. You'll receive instructions within the next few days".

Hanging up the phone, I saw Alket looking at me quite impatiently.

"So? What do you say, my friend?" he asked me.

"I think she can handle this. Where did you find her? I didn't know women like her existed".

"I told you, my friend, and you've given me such a hard time! Now come on. Do your magic and get us out of here!" he said.

"Leave it to me. I'll take care of it. You just find her a partner".

He trusted me, and he showed it. He never argued when it came to making decisions. He never questioned my planning skills. And I, in turn, trusted him completely when it came to his intentions. He wouldn't just wake up one morning to tell me he had changed his mind. He was standing by my side, my equal.

Voula's last words had turned the hourglass upside down, starting the countdown for the big exit. After a few days, she'd meet an acquaintance of mine to receive plenty of money to cover all the expenses of the operation, an aerial image of the prison with the spot where the helicopter should land marked on it, and a handwritten letter with the full and detailed escape plan. Alket provided her with a fake ID, and the first test-flight to Arachova went pretty well. She followed the plan to the letter except for one small deviation: that day there was a lot of snow in the region, so after they landed the pilot wouldn't let Voula get off until someone came to pick her up (that's what the flying protocol dictated). So Paris, who had been waiting for her a bit farther away, was forced to approach them and the pilot got a glimpse of him.

He had the hood of his windproof jacket on and was wearing a scarf that only left his eyes exposed, and yet we thought it wise to push the second flight a week backwards so that his face would be forgotten. Paris was a brave and rebellious young lad. After I spoke to him, he agreed to pick up the lady after the first flight to Arachova and be her armed companion for the second flight to Korydallos. A woman who desires to obtain something, if she remains focused on her goal, becomes very diligent. Aside from everything else, she also goes unnoticed. Voula would prove to be much more than a dedicated woman; she was multitalented, she had guts. She did all the preparations by herself without complaining even once. A great asset. Necessary for such operations to end well. Returning from the test-flight, she focused on collecting the cars and the weapons Alket told her to. She did great!

The snitch, the decoy attempt, and the construction site

In solitary, we had our own, pretty serious problems, which became larger by the day. A young fucker, who wanted to be transferred from solitary to 'A' wing, took advantage of the administration's fears to achieve his goal and lied that he heard Alket talking to someone on the payphone about an upcoming escape, though not how or when. Of course, the administration was alarmed. They couldn't just ignore a testimony that confirmed their fears. They transferred him to 'A' wing, as he desired, and they began thoroughly searching our cell daily.

If this wasn't enough, two inmates of similar quality, whether inspired by our exploits or instructed by the administration to justify their stricter surveillance measures, thought they'd take their chances and try to become the next most wanted men in the country. What do Palaiokostas and Rizai have that we haven't? We all got two hands and two feet!

The solitary confinement wing was an enclosed, open-plan space, about twenty-five yards long and eight to ten yards wide. There were about ten cells built one next to the other along the chamber and in its middle, leaving enough space for two corridors in both sides which were connected, forming, in essence, a Pi-letter shaped corridor around them. All the cells had two doors, each leading to one of the corridors. All the doors on the side that led to the yards were always locked. They never opened. So if I wanted to go to the yard, living in the last cell, I had to go around all the other cells to reach the end of the other corridor, where the door leading to the yard was located. Meaning that, if I somehow managed to open the always-locked door of my cell, I wouldn't have to walk all that way because I'd be right across from the door of the yard. Crossing the corridor that led to the yard — on my left — there were some other doors that led to other small yards, but they were always locked.

One night, after taking some of the psychiatric drugs freely handed by the prison, these two guys made a rope from sheets and a hook, managed to open the locked door of their cell and one of the doors leading to the small yards, and exited. When they were done looking at the winter stars in this state of "liberty", they thought things over. Not giving a damn about who would pay the price for their momentary rebellion, they got rid of their makeshift ropes and the hook in the yard, locked the doors again, and returned to the comfort of their cells to continue their peaceful sleep. A for effort, right?

Early the next morning, not knowing anything about the previous night's events, we left for court. On our return, we found the solitary swarming with blacksmith and electrician crews. Wires, buffs, welding machines, impact drills, screwdrivers, and other similar tools had turned the solitary confinement wing into a construction site. Until that moment, they had sealed up all the second doors of the cells and all those that led to the small yards. The only door that remained unsealed was the one that led to the yard we usually used. All along the corridors they had drilled holes to place new, additional railings which the administration could open electronically. They were also placing wires to install more audio-visual cameras in strategic spots inside the chamber. This commotion would continue until a few days before the escape. We, as was natural, asked what all this was about. We never got an answer, except for the usual: "Administration's orders!"

Knowing that Alket and I would be blamed for their exploits, the wannabe fugitives didn't even bother to inform us about their nightly venture that had threatened to spoil our plans. We'd only learn that some ropes and a hook were located in one of the yards the following day, inside the courtroom, from our 'A' wing co-defendants. Putting a plan of counter-attack into action, I requested to speak, and the presiding judge granted my request. I asked him whether he knew that Alket and I were in a state of solitary confinement because of the ongoing trial involving us etc.

"What you're asking me, Mr Palaiokostas, is not under the court's jurisdiction. It's the ministry's and the prison's decision. The court can't intervene". the presiding judge said.

"How defendants come to the court and whether they're in a position to participate in the process is under the court's jurisdiction, your honour. It is illegal for us to be kept there during our trial, and I want to believe you're against illegality. If tomorrow they brought us in with our hands cut off, would you continue the trial as though nothing has happened? So how can you say it's not the court's problem? It concerns the court too ..."

"Why? Is there a chance they'll bring you with your hands chopped off?" he asked with a naïve sense of humour.

"Who knows? They might decide to abolish handcuffs and for the time being, this is their only use! My question remains one of great importance. What I'm saying is that we can't fully participate in a trial that concerns us because of this particular state of detention we are illegally subjected to. I've grown tired; I'll not attend any more hearings. Until the time comes for me to make my plea, my lawyers will represent me".

"It is your inalienable right to do so, Mr Palaiokostas. If you can't, or don't want to, you don't have to attend the trial as long as your lawyers represent you".

I never stepped foot in there again. And I had my reasons for the decision. For one, I had realised that while we were away at court, prison employees would enter our cell and search it (something which is forbidden by the correctional code if the inmate isn't present). I also wanted to send them a message that not only weren't we planning an escape, but it was them illegally holding us in solitary confinement, while we were persistently asking to be transferred to a different wing. Rocking the cradle one last time, lest the baby wake now, so near the end. We didn't have any milk, and we couldn't stand listening to it!

In the following days I asked to see the wing's warden, and he accepted. We had an argument about the situation in the solitary confinement wing because of the crews. He insisted that the makeshift rope and the hook found in the locked yard were proof that we were trying to escape.

"Warden, do you think I'm stupid? It's not us you give the pills to! If you're so sure, why don't you accuse us of attempted escape? Are you trying to cover it up?" I needled him.

"I'm not covering up anything, I just can't prove it!" he said, looking guilty.

"Call for forensics. Only aspiring fugitives have reason to visit a locked yard. No fugitive wears gloves! That would be a first. What do you say?"

"Forget it. I don't want to take things further. The director and the warden from 'A' wing are against me. They burdened me with you two. On purpose".

"I don't want to get involved in your personal disputes. I'm just an inmate temporarily accommodated by your prison for my trial. We said that we'd let it slide, that we won't make an issue for being illegally held in solitary confinement. Yet there's a limit to everything. We just can't stand returning late in the evening after the tiring trial process and being welcomed by the creepy machines' sounds any longer. Not to mention the almost daily inspections! How far will this go? You have us in the most secure place in the whole prison. What more do you need to relax? This isn't plain anxiety, this is obsessional neurosis!"

"I'm not searching your cells for fun, Palaiokostas. I don't wake up wanting to search your cell. I'm doing it because I have some information!"

"You call the imaginary desires of those snitches you filled the solitary confinement wing with information? Do you think you'll discover anything in my cell? Even if I had something to hide you wouldn't find it in my cell! Check my folder; if you find that during my seven-and-a-half years in prison, a suspicious object was ever discovered in my cell, I'll allow you to search my cell every day. So you're searching in vain. If I decide to leave it won't simply be an attempt!"

"I have been informed that Alket took a mobile phone from 'C' wing and I can't find it in your cell. That troubles me a lot".

"It doesn't have to. Because we don't have a mobile phone. It's just your snitches toying with your fears. They feed them, to make themselves seem useful to you, to achieve their goals. Take them all away and then, whatever you find will be ours!"

The homestretch and the second escape by helicopter

I left his office feeling particularly concerned. It had only been a few days since we had procured a mobile phone from 'C' wing. During one of my visitations, I'd unexpectedly run across a lad who I knew from my last stay in 'A' wing. He had been released and then arrested and convicted again. He was one of the guys I felt bad for not remembering, and at the same time happy to realise that the only thing he wanted was to strengthen our acquaintance, whatever the cost on their part. The "insignificant" yet pure-hearted inmates were my incomparable advantage over the key holders and their sleazy partners.

He came right up to me.

"Vassilis ... don't you remember me? I'm Kostas. I used to hang out with Mitsos and Yorgos ..."

"How could I? There's so many of you, after all!"

"I'm in 'C' wing, and we're in charge. If you want a mobile phone ..."

"You'd be doing me a great favour if you could. I want it to be unused, both the device and the SIM card".

"It goes without saying. I'm expecting to receive some new ones soon. I'll keep one for you. I'll give it to Alket".

Indeed, after a few days we had a new mobile phone, and it arrived just in time. Voula got her hands on a new mobile too, which she'd use only for our communications, and everything finally began falling into place. The very same day I met the warden when Alket returned from court, he told me that some of his compatriot inmates in 'C' wing had complained to him about repeated inspections in their cells looking for mobile phones.

"Go now and give him the watch. Without the SIM card. And tell him to stop the inspections since he now has the mobile phone he's been searching for", I said to him.

"Are you mad? Do you want us to make fools of ourselves?" he reacted.

"Do it, mate. He's not going to give us a break otherwise. If he locates the phone, then we can forget about the escape. Things are getting tough. I'm afraid they're going to place wire netting over the yard. If we manage to leave, the joke will be on them".

He went and threw it on the warden's table, quite upset.

"Take the fucking phone and leave everyone alone!" he said to him and left.

The warden bought it. The following day, he gathered the wing's employees to inform them, showing them the watch phone so that they knew what sort of phones were being smuggled into prison now, and to be aware!

With all this happening, the middle of the week came, only a few days before our upcoming escape. Everything seemed balanced on a knife-edge. The solitary confinement wing had turned into a fortress. We were under unbearable pressure. They transferred Alket to a separate cell next to mine. One of the new gates they had installed along the corridor separated us. Throughout the night, every half an hour, an employee would come to inspect all locks (those of our cells too), waking up Alket in the process.

"Hey! This is becoming fucking annoying ... we have a trial tomorrow. Go back to your office and whack off, you arsehole!" he swore at the employee.

Although it seemed the odds were against us and our escape plan stood no chance, an unstoppable force was pushing me to go against the facts. It was an almost deadly force. Another thing that bothered me was the issue of Spyros. I didn't want him to think I hadn't helped him in court, so we arranged the escape for after I'd entered my plea. And yet things were getting out of hand, and we couldn't postpone the escape any longer. I discussed with Alket the possibility of informing Spyros a day before the escape, in case he managed to climb to the roof so we could take him with us. But our fear that our plan might leak was too high, so we didn't dare do it.

Alket, as usual, was unreasonably optimistic.

"Everything will be fine, friend! Come Sunday, we'll be out, you'll see," he'd say to me again and again, full of energy and passion. At the same time, to convince me, he presented various shaman tricks with numbers and symbols that backed up his optimism to me. I never really got any of them. Instead, I felt as though the whole world was against us.

Our cells were inspected for the last time two days before the escape. It was the first time that the warden was in charge of the search himself. Obviously, this time his information had been clear and specific, so he wanted to take credit for any findings that would prove we were indeed up to something. He arrived with about ten lock-lovers and turned the cells inside out. Throughout the search, I was arguing with him. In the end, I advised him that if he ever came back, he should be wearing boxing gloves because I'd beat his sorry arse.

Sunday came, and everything seemed to be going according to plan. Outside, everything was working fine. The only obstacle making things a bit harder was that it was still snowing non-stop in Parnassos and the helicopter couldn't land there. Luckily, I knew that area very well. Itea has a football pitch, and there was rarely snow at such a low altitude. I thought it — correctly — to be a perfect alternative.

Around three in the afternoon, after Voula and Paris were already on the helicopter, we received a text message that everything was going well. The countdown began, and the half-hour wait seemed to last a century. The feeling of suspense, knowing that a helicopter would soon arrive to free us from the living tomb they had forced us in, can't be described in words. Yearning and suspense had taken over our minds and hearts. We were wigwagging between "everything we'll be fine" and "if not, let us be the only ones to pay the price". Of course, we were more than ready to welcome it like a kiss of life!

The helicopter would have to land on the solitary confinement wing's rooftop because the yard was too small. To make sure it would land in the right spot, we had arranged to throw a blue bag with clothes there, so it would be visible from the air. That would be my job. Alket had taken on the task of sealing two of the three doors separating the yard from the solitary confinement wing. We had a small rebar for him to place inside the first door's lock, and he would tie the second one with a strap from a bag.

Our agony would come to an end about twenty minutes later when we received the final text message that they'd soon be here. I grabbed the prepared bag and exited to the yard. I could already hear a distant, hollow buzz and at once, I threw the bag onto the rooftop. In a few seconds, a loud wave of noise began to steadily spread around the prison complex. The culprit of this disturbance appeared and hovered near the rooftop's end. Its door opened, and I saw Voula holding a folded rope ladder. She tied one end around the helicopter's landing skids and, as though she was spreading out a blanket for a picnic, she let it unfold perpendicular to the isolation wing's wall.

In the meantime, Alket had arrived, but he wasn't alone. A few seconds after he got there, four or five prison guards appeared through the yard's door. He hadn't placed the rebar properly inside the first door's lock. A guard had cut the strap from around the second door, using a straight razor he had had on him, although this was forbidden inside the prison. When mistakes happen at such a critical moment, they can prove fatal, with one acting as a domino for the rest. Alket didn't even follow the plan (according to which I'd climb the ladder first, get my hands on a gun, and seize control of the situation). Returning after having chased the guards down the solitary confinement corridor, I saw he had already reached the roof. Priority wasn't necessarily a bad thing, but since he hadn't mentally prepared for that role he climbed into and sat inside the helicopter, losing visual contact with me. Besides that, he had a small makeshift knife on him. I didn't.

So I was left alone, unarmed, with the correctional officers getting cocky. I chased them down the corridor once more, but they ran right after me to stop me from climbing. Half the ladder was stuck inside the steel wire netting due to the extra weight of Alket's climb. I grabbed it and began climbing using only my hands. About half-way up, I felt a hand grabbing my ankle. One of Hades' guards was making a last attempt to trap me in his realm. I kicked him once and kept on climbing. He wasn't that determined.

Voula was holding strong. She was brave and instrumental in our attempt. She waited for me to get there, and only after I had untied the ladder and got in the helicopter did she get in herself. Taking her time, of course, as though we were sightseeing! Life requires a degree of madness. The aircraft took off from the roof. I don't know if it was just my imagination, but through its imposing sound, I heard and felt a long round of applause from more than a thousand inmates.* And then we were flying into the frozen grey horizon. An intense explosion of uncontrollable emotions illuminated our, until then, dark interior skies like colourful fireworks. As if it were the beginning of a grand celebration. This is how we said goodbye to that piece of concrete human shame.

The pilot was a real tough guy.

"You're the pilot now, I'm waiting for orders". he said to me as though he'd known me for a long time.

"Follow the freeway in the direction of Lamia, and I'll tell you".

"Don't you have a kombolói for me?" he asked me, tongue in cheek.

"Of course, I have — Palaiokostas has something for everyone!"

I got my white ivory kombolói out of my pocket and threw it to him.

"Here, catch my friend. But don't let the cops take it, it's collectable!"

"Do you take me for a fool?"

That's the kind of pilot that escapes need! Reaching the Afidnes' toll station, I ordered him to lose altitude. We landed in a sandlot, near one of the freeway's byways, where a friend of Alket's was waiting for us with two cars.

---

*   There was in fact prolonged applause and celebration as their helicopter took off, which was recorded by a nearby resident — footage of the escape is still available online.

Everyone got out and ran to the parked vehicles. Paris and Voula took the RAV and drove off at once. Alket entered the Golf and waited for me to finish with the pilot.

"Turn off the engine. I'm going to put a hood over your head. You can take it off in five minutes".

"Don't worry. I'm not going to cooperate with the cops!"

"Nice ..."

I jumped outside, holding the Scorpion. It was snowing pretty hard. I ran and sat in the back seat of the Golf.

"Off we go!"

Sitting inside a charcoal-grey Touareg filled with guns, wearing new clothes, and with the A/C turned on full blast (oh, how bad is technology), after half an hour, and while it was snowing hard, a young girl would wish us a nice trip at the Isthmus toll station. Tensions had now eased. We could hear all the world's fates laughing their arses off!

We instinctively looked at each other, and we kissed each others' cheeks. We couldn't believe it. What we had just accomplished was a real feat. We hadn't just left the prison, we'd escaped its solitary confinement wing and under very adverse conditions. Nothing united Alket and me more than our inextinguishable passion for freedom. And this shared passion of ours, when we joined forces in these two short encounters of ours, was transformed into two decisive moments for both our lives. Two spectacular aerial escapes. Karma ... *

Freedom is a precious, everlasting struggle for any decent human. There's nothing more beautiful and real than the attempt to achieve the impossible. And when the impossible becomes possible, it's just magic. The few who have lived, even only once, something as intense, know precisely what I tried to describe. The indescribable ...

---

* A few months after the escape, Alket was located at a country house on the outskirts of Attica and re-was arrested by the special task forces. Although he was heavily armed he didn't resist his arrest because his lover and another couple were in the house. About two years later, he attempted to escape once again from high-security Malandrino Prison. His attempt was unsuccessful and he is still in prison at time of writing, serving two consecutive life sentences.

MY ATTEMPTED MURDER IN ALEPOCHORI

I had just finished making some necessary phone calls in Loutraki, and was on my way back to our temporary hideout, where Alket was waiting.

I was leaving the outskirts of Shoenus when I came across an Attica taxi.* It was unusual for a cab from Attica to be moving around these areas on a weekday, though not so rare as to be automatically considered suspicious. Not a week had passed since, driving along one of the area's roads, I had come across a similar (perhaps the same) taxi, once again with two passengers, parked outside a small church. The driver had gotten out and was spray-painting the church's sidewalk.

"What an arsehole … of all the walls out there he had to pick this one, which the villagers whitewash and look after," I thought, but didn't pay any more attention, continuing on my way.

Returning later out of mere curiosity, I parked my car outside the church to find out what reason those men had to defile it.

"Those motherfuckers! That's how far they've come", I said to myself, seeing the white wall filled with swastikas and slogans of the Golden Dawn fascist party. Since then, I have observed many similar freshly-painted slogans on walls in the surrounding area.

I drove past the taxi to visually inspect its passengers. They were two men around forty years old. They weren't acting strange at all. I remained close by, just in case I noticed something that would link them to that incident. I couldn't recall the other taxi's license plate numbers or the faces of the guys who had been in it, so there was no point. I stepped on the gas. The taxi sped behind me, with no indication that they were specifically following me. I was driving a Tuareg with slightly tinted windows and a license plate number that corresponded to the same brand and model. Shoenus connects to Alepochori via a six-mile, narrow, ill-formed, unmaintained, serpentine road, which didn't afford the Tuareg an advantage over smaller cars with lower horsepower. In fact, I'd say that because of its size it was at a disadvantage because of the many twists and turns of the narrow road, which didn't provide sufficient visibility ahead.

During the ride we didn't come across any oncoming vehicles, and I didn't notice any others following behind. There was no apparent reason for me to risk driving fast to test the taxi. About one-and-a-half miles before we reached Alepochori, as a precaution, I turned the Tuareg down a small opening on the right side of the road to let the taxi drive off. One or two minutes had passed since it disappeared around the first curve of the road, when behind me appeared, in order: a black Audi, its front license plate hanging from only one screw, a white Peugeot, and a silver car, probably a Citroen. As they passed by me, I saw that in each were three people of a young age.

---

* Taxis from different areas of Greece have different colours. Taxis from Attica are yellow.

Following the same course as the taxi, they disappeared behind the curve of the road.

It was dusk. I stayed put for a few minutes, trying to process everything. There was only one question, yet a crucial one: were those guys cops? If they had located me, why hadn't they cornered me where I had stopped? It would have been the perfect trap. There was a big vertical rock (cliff) to my right, on the side of the mountain, the sea was ten yards to my left, and I was trapped inside the car by the side of the road. Had they located the house and were on their way there? They were outnumbered considering who they were going to try and arrest! Unless there were others in the area too, converging on their way to the detached house. It could also have been that they were small, versatile units in search of suspicious vehicles assigned to perform on the spot inspections to locate us. Perhaps they had already invaded the house. And all this was if I assumed they were cops!

When someone lives as a fugitive, such incidents (and even more suspicious ones) occur many times, raising a state of alarm. They have to reach conclusions using only the facts in hand and their experience. Usually, these incidents prove to be just coincidences, but frequent coincidences add up to form a huge trap, into which people fall that one time which is not a coincidence.

In that particular case, it would be reckless and unprofessional to take the identity of those on board the three cars and the taxi for granted. It wasn't easy abandoning our house and leaving the area just because of a suspicion. It could have been a group of kids going to some feast or returning from Loutraki. The Audi's license plate, hanging as it was from one screw, could be an indication that they were a group of thieves. After all, it would be nighttime soon. I really needed to find out what was really going on. I had to learn if Alket was in danger and if it was safe for me to return home. If I didn't follow them, I'd never learn. Inside my waist bag, I had a Glock 9 with spare magazines and two grenades. In the passenger seat, I had a small backpack with some necessary supplies in case of an emergency and a Scorpion. In the back seat, inside a travel bag, I had a Kalashnikov with several magazines.

I caught up with the three suspicious vehicles in the outskirts of a small, sparsely populated settlement before Alepochori. I was about thirty yards behind the last vehicle. We moved like this for about three-hundred or four-hundred yards when I saw a random (?) car parked by the other side of the road. A bit further down, I spotted the taxi, now parked too, its passenger peeing against a lamppost. Suspicious! Let's see ...

We travelled another four hundred yards. There, to our right, began the one-piece stone wall of some house, more than a hundred yards in length and more than seven feet tall. To its left and towards the sea, the road descended about four feet, surrounded by salt cedars. It was a natural trap in which to corner a car. They'd launch their attack there. As it turned out they had performed this trick successfully many times in the past. Without Palaiokostas!

Suddenly the road became impassable. The Audi drove to the far left of the road. The Peugeot drove on the dividing strip, stopping right behind the Audi, and the Citroen followed suit, stopping right behind the Peugeot. I didn't check the mirrors; I was sure the same thing was happening behind me.

The doors opened, and at once they all jumped out holding guns. The drivers were carrying MP5 machine guns. They stood outside their cars. All the rest quickly approached me and pressed their Glocks and USPs against the Tuareg's windows, swearing at me.

Even if I had had any doubts about how I should act in this tight spot I had found myself in, the swearing of those Hellenic Police arseholes banished them. As though my quick decision became a magic command, at that precise moment, like a mirage, the one-piece wall on my right split in two for a car to appear and stop behind the Citroen. I shifted the car into 'S', stepped on it, and the beast sprang forwards growling, amid a barrage of point-blank shots.

When life loves you, you shouldn't fear death! Hitting the "vehicle ex machina" broadside, I entered the narrow road. I could feel bullets flying around me. I drove for about a hundred and fifty yards until I reached the end of the narrow road, shots still hammering the Touareg ... and turned right straight into a dead end. It didn't matter; the car was already damaged, it couldn't have gone much further. I grabbed my backpack, got out of the car, and climbed a forested hill. Having escaped from the bounty hunters' ambush, I'd make sure they never saw me again. One of them would testify to it when I crossed to the opposite, bigger, and also forested hill.

Night had almost fallen. I sat under a pine tree to catch my breath. I could vaguely see the settlement from up there. It was about two hundred yards away. I stood there watching the miserable fascists for a while, holding their guns, running up and down the settlement's streets trying to find me. I regretted not having taken the Kalashnikov with me. I was in the perfect spot to make them fall into the sea dancing the Dance of Zalongo.* Through the commotion from dogs barking trying to defend their yards from these strange invaders, I heard someone yelling to the rest:

"Let's go. Nobody can catch him now".

He got that right!

I now had no doubt as to who the guys writing slogans on the church's wall had been. The Hellenic Police had equipped their fascist friends,** turning them loose to hunt people.*** I was more than confident that they didn't know who was inside my car. The Touareg's tinted windows and the falling darkness couldn't

---

*   During the Souliote War, on December 16th, 1830, about sixty women from Souli and their children committed mass suicide so as not to be captured by Turks. According to tradition they fell one after the other off a cliff, while dancing and singing.
**   This was not uncommon. In the late 2000s in the wake of the Grigoropoulos riots Athens Indymedia, an anarchist news outlet, published multiple photos documenting direct collusion between police and fascist groups in the repression and harassment of radical and migrant areas of the city.
***   Many uniformed men are favourably disposed towards far-right political parties and some of them are even directly involved. In the 2015 election, the neo-Nazi political party Golden Dawn received more than 60 percent of the votes from police stations' and police academies' ballot boxes.

have allowed anyone to make out the number of passengers, let alone their faces. However, I found the small backpack I had in the passenger seat and took it with me, riddled with bullets. If there had been a passenger with me, they'd be dead. Not for a moment had I threatened them to justify such an armed attack. Even their bullets had felt too ashamed to hit their target.

One of the fascists had actually appeared as a witness for the police in the trial we had left unfinished because of the escape. He had been the leader of a team looking to locate Alket, before his arrest in Aspra Spitia, Boeotia. I recognised him at once because of his unusual build. He was dragging a whole acre of arse behind him! I had wondered how such a back-loaded man had been hired by the police and whether his XL buttocks had played a crucial role in that decision. Now I understood … he knew how to swear ("get out, you arsehole!") and how to shoot people in the back. These two skills are an essential precondition for someone to be hired by the Hellenic Police. All other imperfections, if they can't be fixed, can be easily overlooked.

For those who don't know, for a specific kind of armed man of my temperament, swearing causes a reaction. All modern police forces know this, it is taught in police seminars worldwide. These scumbags knew it too. That's what they had been counting on. That I'd react (as it happened) so that they could seize the opportunity to finish their mission. This had been their premeditated attempt to murder me, since more than ten guns had been turned against me from that short distance. The barrels of most of them had been pressed against the Touareg's windows.

They'd justify my possible murder with the usual method: he opened fire against us first. Of course the media would cover everything up. The covering up of the real events of the attempted murder leaves no ground for misinterpretation for their actual role and their intentions.

I must remind you here that all this is written by the same man who, surrounded by officers from the Special Anti-Terrorist Unit, urged them to aim for the head. I want and must say that then I didn't hear a single swear word and there hadn't been a single act of violence on their part. Instead, they had shown some respect to the two people whose freedom they were about to rob.

I've never feared death. In fact, I'd say that although I've chased after it for years, it consciously and deviously avoids me. I'm not making such an extensive reference to that incident because the possibility of dying scared me, but because of these fascists' clear intentions. Their murderous intentions. They had been given the green light to kill me by their superiors, who, in turn, had received it from their political leaders. Markogiannakis,* the political shame of Crete, was still Minister of Public Order. So I'm focusing on the political responsibility for the decision to have me killed.

About a year later, I sent a letter to a newspaper on a completely different topic and, as a side note, took the chance to address this incident and how the media

---

*   Christos Markogiannakis is a disgraced former New Democracy MP.

cover up such events. The Hellenic Police's reaction came through one of its reps, who appeared on television to say that the police won't enter a conversation with Palaiokostas, adding: "What did Palaiokostas expect? That we'd tip him?" The Hellenic Police representative was clearly urging people to kill a fugitive. Although this statement was reproduced many times over the following days on television, not a single journalist commented on what he had said. After all, this kind of fascist speech is quite common, and it's overlooked with a slight smile as an on-point one-liner. One that kills.

Similarly, about a year later, another parapolice representative, taking advantage of his free screentime, announced that the Hellenic Police had declared war on Palaiokostas! It is perhaps a world first for the police force of an entire country to declare a one-sided war against a single citizen.

I'll answer to all fascist representatives of dark thoughts and intentions, who only know how to play their dirty games off-stage and are given the floor to speak as such. I've never asked cowards for anything, let alone their word. I just want to know who they represent and who is after me. In this one-sided and unethical war they have declared against me, I have never responded and I never will. They are thousands while I stand alone. Yet they disregard the basic principles of war. In this case, I'm the general determining developments and events. Until now, I haven't come across any warriors, only jams of mercenaries who collectively shoot for the back. In no case do I consider them my equals. War requires morals, and to be a warrior, you have to be brave. They don't possess either of these qualities. Their morality is limited to shooting men in the back, and their bravery is trapped inside the black spray which they shake vigorously before defiling the walls of churches.

And a strong suggestion to the chiefs of the Hellenic Police: if they want the cheerful dispatches of their various SUVs that travel Greece from time to time to be of some use, they should be accompanied by painter crews, to whitewash the walls their brave lads defile with Nazi symbols and Golden Dawn slogans.

To the civilian personnel elected by the people I'll say one thing: by providing nurture and shelter to these armed fascists because they do dirty work for them today, they are cultivating tomorrow's armed force of executioners and torturers of dissidents. By urging these dogs to bite their fellow people, they ensure a time will come when not only will the animals bite them too, they will rip them apart. In the times we're living in there's no reason for tanks to appear on roads to enforce a Junta. Their caterpillar tracks have been driving freely through the minds of television-bound people for a long time now, and they have become necessary to citizens' mental balance. It's easier and much more efficient for fascism to be gradually inserted through the wide-open backdoors of fake democracy and then slowly and steadily incorporated in its unsound ideals.

I want someone to tell me, for example, how the State, which managed to "tele-arrest" one of the many mountzas* I, as a true Greek man, addressed

---

*   Mountza or moutza, also called faskeloma, is an insulting gesture among Greeks, when an individual spreads their fingers and shows their open palm to the person they intend to insult.

towards the authorities, found a whole embossed palm-print of mine on an A4 piece of paper in the streets of Katechaki.* If the rumours and the articles are indeed true, then totalitarian regimes around the world have a lot to learn from the innovative, ground-breaking, methods used by Greece's modern European democracy to create false incriminating evidence . A mind-set of the type "this is what we suppose, this is what we understand, so this is the truth, and we have every right to use all sorts of unfair means to support it", is deeply rooted in the country's law enforcement and shared by every member of the Greek police force. Let's wrap him inside an A4 piece of paper and be over with it! He's a fugitive, he can't defend himself, and we'll never give him a chance. We put a bounty on his head, we unleashed our well-fed fascist dog with a black spray can in its mouth to do him over, so the case never reaches the court, our scheme is never revealed, and we continue our justice spree undisturbed, they thought. And they acted accordingly.

I want to let the cowards behind my incrimination know that my mountza is a bit bigger than an A4 piece of paper. They should remove it the same way they planted it there, or perhaps cut a finger out. Otherwise, this palm-print might blow into their deformed-from-lying faces like a loud slap. That whole affair might go down in history as the most severe and blatant construction of incriminating evidence, ordered from high within the System and then concocted and served by the dark mechanisms of the Ministry of Citizen Protection, since the regime change.

If by chance an honest judicial (or any other for that matter) authority still exists, steering clear of the unsolvable network of dealings and interdependence that drives the abusive force of the State's structures, and being more interested in whether State institutions are blatantly used by authority-addicted egomaniacs (to frame citizens among other things) than whether a fugitive is arrested or not, then this case has to be scrutinised. In great DEPTH and in great HEIGHT!

If, again, there are any honest, brave officers who know something and haven't lost their active citizen status, refusing to serve a force that employs non-transparent methods and has vague and dark motives, let them speak. If not for me, if not for the truth, if not for the conspiracy, at least for the sake of the relatives of their dead "colleague". So Greek citizens can learn who ordered such a conspiracy and why, how it was executed, ,and with what evidence.

We know at least one of its moral instigators and orchestrators. He is the great guardian of all democratic institutions and then minister of citizen protection, Michalis Chrisochoidis.

---

*   This is a reference to the 2010 Katechaki bombing case, which led to €1 million bounty being placed on Vassilis' head making him, at the time, the most wanted man in Europe. The letter bomb, seemingly intended for controversial politician Michalis Chrisochoidis (see overleaf), killed a postman when it went off prematurely and authorities claimed they had found Vassilis's fingerprint on a piece of the remains. Critics point out that generally bombs, by nature, don't leave that sort of evidence and he has no prior history of attempting political assassinations at all, let alone of doing so in such a clumsy manner with a high chance of hurting random civilians. The bounty remains in force as of the time of publication.

The man who built his political career on the ruins of the Revolutionary Organisation 17 November.*

In fake democracies, there is no way for someone to protect themselves from ruthless rulers, let alone when that someone is a fugitive. For those citizens who trust law enforcement and the judiciary, thinking that similar tactics belong in the past, the following chapter might change their mind. If not ... there's nothing more I can do!

---

*   Chrisochoidis was a controversial political figure. He served as the minister for citizen protection for many years and under various governments. His first term coincided with the dismantling of the 17 November organisation in 2002. To many Greek people his name is synonymous with extreme police repression. In 2010 a bomb exploded inside his office in the Ministry of Citizen Protection, killing his assisting officer. The Greek State offered him a legion of trained police officers for his protection. The war he declared against crime included raids inside cinemas in Athens to arrest and detain underage people that had committed the heinous sin of watching the new Joker film with their parents.

SOME FURTHER STORIES

Road trip, vignettes and final thoughts

ROAD TRIP ON TWO WHEELS

Hellenic Police: a charges industry

From December 1991 until April 1992, and from the autumn of 1992 until April 1995, Nikos and I were abroad. For the former period, I don't have proof, only testimonies. For the latter I have hard evidence. This evidence had been in the hands of the Hellenic Police since August 2008. During my arrest at the hideout in Souroti, among other genuine documents (as, for example, an ID), the police found and confiscated my Brazilian passport, stamped from entering and exiting more than twenty countries to which I travelled during that period.

Through my book, which is my only way of addressing the public while living as a fugitive, I dare the chiefs of the Hellenic Police to release this passport to the public (as it is, without any tampering). The passport that their predecessors have kept hidden for so many years so that the people don't know how easily they can forge charges against fugitives (among other people). Note that the Hellenic Police know absolutely nothing about these trips. The only thing the people in charge cared about was to hide the passport away, lest it became public, and several of their charges against me were revealed to be false. Aside from that, when talking about me, they refer to me as "the infamous criminal", although to them I'm a complete stranger.

I hope the prosecuting authorities find their lost dignity and do the obvious: investigate all aspects of this issue. Not for those responsible to be held accountable (it's the last thing I care about, and it doesn't really matter). But for citizens to learn what the hell happens behind this protective iron curtain, where prosecuting authorities act with impunity. To learn which para-institutional methods and unfair means are employed by those tasked with ensuring respect for the Constitution. It would be a sort of moral catharsis for the more than ten forged charges against me that they themselves adjudicated and the eight or ten convictions that pinned on my back a sentence of about a hundred or a hundred and fifty more years in prison. These numbers are approximate. Five more, five less ... who cares, really? These are but minutiae for the Greek justice system.

Because I always want to be perfectly clear: the period to which I am referring is from my escape on Dormition Day in 1991 until the 20th of December of 1999 when I was arrested in Livadeia. During that time, I was accused of three armed bank robberies, of which I was found guilty and convicted. Two of those were the one in Kalabaka and the one in Ioannina, which I have already mentioned. All the other armed robberies of which I was accused (banks, supermarkets, the Hellenic Telecommunications Organisation, the Hellenic Post service, and many others) were the products of the Hellenic Police's conspiracies. To this very day, I have never committed an armed robbery anywhere aside from banks. I haven't spent most of my life as a fugitive to tell lies. Unfortunately, in a society where lies rule, only fugitives can tell you the truth.

The reason I'm vague about the number of forged charges and the summary of the sentences resulting from these additional convictions has to do with my inability to access these case files. And honestly, there are so many that I can't recall the exact numbers. I don't want to mention specifics that aren't true. Neither do I find it necessary. From a simple search in my case files, based on the charges and the dates I was abroad (aside from all the others when I was in Greece, and they pinned them on me "because that's what they wanted"), one can draw some safe conclusions.

Forging an extra charge against me on the part of the prosecuting authorities could be partially justified. They're people too, they can make a mistake — even two.

Shall I spill the beans? Even three! Ten more forged charges make for an organised crime consciously, repeatedly, and deceitfully committed by the State at the expense of one of its citizens. It's a State crime that will forever remain unpunished. And it certainly doesn't have to do anything with democratic ideals but with dark methods and practices of corrupted prosecuting authorities that serve totalitarian regimes. After all, it's common knowledge that the serving of justice in a country defines the quality of its democracy and, in essence, the type of the regime. Of course, all this is but a wish and a hope of mine ... just in case some of them feel ashamed. In a place where shame is viewed as a defect of the weak.

The trip

After my last trip in northern Europe (England, Ireland, Scotland, and all the Nordic countries) the idea of a longer, more adventurous trip grew inside me. My travel record already included several tours of Europe, the Iberian Peninsula, and six countries in Latin America. On some of these trips, I was accompanied by Yannis. He loved travelling and had nothing to do with illegality.

"Your job is tough, whoever thinks that living as a fugitive equals an easy life and profit has no idea what outlawry actually means!" he'd always say to me.

He would have been my first choice for this adventure. Two years before, we had met again in a country in central Europe, planning a tour of Africa on a 4x4 trailer. We chose Africa because it fitted both our adventurous characters. We didn't make it, because of some issues that came up concerning the vehicle's license and most importantly, because of a different unexpected event. As we were working out the logistics and trying to overcome the problems that arose, among which was the fact that I was a fugitive still using a forged Greek passport and driver's license, Yannis, fed-up with everything, indirectly suggested a different way of travelling.

"All this is bullshit, the best way to travel is by bicycle! You can buy one whenever you want, without any papers. It doesn't need insurance, license, documents, license plates of any country, fuel, and all that ... if it breaks, you fix it on your own. If it can't be fixed, you simply buy a new one in the country you're in, and if you get bored of it, you throw it in the rubbish, and the trip goes on!"

"All this sounds fine, Yannis, but there's a disadvantage ... pedalling".

"Do you think sports are a disadvantage? Do you know how much your lungs train if you travel about a hundred miles each day? If you get tired, you can load everything onto a car, a bus, a train, a plane. You can even carry it if you have to! One can travel by motorcycle when you're sixty and by trailer when you're eighty, we wouldn't have any problems pedalling. We're both athletic, we're young, and we have plenty of time and money too. If we don't try this now, when will we ever be given a chance again? We only need to make a decision and get our hands on some passports".

Yannis' words stuck in my mind. Two years later, now with genuine travel documents as well as some experience in travelling, they had grown on me. So, feeling restless, I phoned him. I hadn't contacted him for a long time and he was really bored. When I announced my decision he took the first plane to join me as fast as he could so that we could plan and begin our trip. Yannis had no reservations concerning my initial thought, which was to start from Germany, travel across Poland, Ukraine, and all the south countries post-Soviet States, to end up in Mongolia. If everything went smoothly we'd then enter China, through Tibet, to finish our trip in south India. Too ambitious a plan to come true.

Crossing the Netherlands border to Germany, the first big city you come across is Cologne, where we'd buy everything we'd need for our trip. Mountain bikes that wouldn't limit us to tarmac roads and were durable enough for the challenging terrains we would be travelling on, a light rainproof tent, good sleeping bags, cycling clothes, thermals, raincoats etc. The employees of the huge cycling store helped us a lot, knowing everything about travelling by bicycle. The results were near perfect. The only things we didn't buy were helmets — you know us Greeks, we're always disobedient!

Our initial plan was to cycle out of Europe, starting from Berlin, where we hoped we could get visas for the countries we were about to cross. So, we got our bicycles on a train and reached Berlin, where we spent a weekend until the Russian embassy opened again on Monday. There we came across the Russian bear's stubbornness, and we had to change the direction of our trip (though not our destination).

The former Soviet Republics had just become emancipated from mother Russia and therefore didn't have their own embassies abroad yet. They were still served from the Russian one. For someone to travel in these new countries a Russian visa would do, which was valid for strictly two months. You also had to have booked a hotel and have proof that you had gotten a series of vaccines. A blond Russian was in the visa-issuing office and his grey-blue, glassy, husky-like eyes hinted at what we were getting ourselves into.

Yannis tried to reach an understanding with him.

"We have planned to travel to Mongolia by bicycle, and a two-month visa isn't enough. We don't need a hotel, we're road-trippers, and we'll sleep wherever night will catch us etc".

"NYET".

But this, but that …

"NYET".

It seemed that even if we booked a hotel and got all the vaccines required to get that precious visa, we'd still face trouble with these countries' authorities since there was no way we could make this trip in less than two months. And we didn't want to make it with our hearts in our mouths. We were sad to discover that we were still too early for this kind of trip in these new countries and I wasn't patient when it came to such things.

Thankfully, the planet is enormous. So we changed our plans — we'd reach India through the Arabic countries.

There's no time like the present, so we set off at once. Enjoying the beautiful springtime German countryside, we cycled south, heading to Bavaria. Yet where I went, trouble followed. It was fluttering day and night over my head like a winged demon. Ignoring Germany's laws against fishing, in one of the many lakes we came across, we bought a fishing kit from one of the stores nearby, went near some other fishermen, and began trying to catch some fish, which we did — two big ones! We didn't get to enjoy our admittedly incredible feat however because the "lake police" arrived in an SUV. As they pulled up, only Yannis was holding a fishing rod and they rightly arrested only him (Greek cops would have arrested everyone, even the fish). Of course, our protestations that we simply didn't know the country's laws, being tourists, didn't do us much good. They got him in the SUV and transferred him to the nearest ranger station. There they fined him four hundred Deutsche Marks, without giving him a payment receipt (I'm sure they pocketed the money for themselves) and let him walk a mile to get back. All pigs, no matter where they are, have the same face … only some of them keep up appearances.

A bit before we crossed Germany's borders and entered Austria, by mistake, we got onto the autobahn (a federal controlled-access highway). We hadn't travelled more than a mile searching for an exit when we heard a siren from behind us. It was a traffic police vehicle, with a single cop in it. He pulled us over and checked our passports. Mine was Brazilian. He was excited. He was a fan of Brazilian football, and so he didn't give us a ticket as he ought to. He escorted us for about three miles until we came across an exit and enthusiastically wished us a nice trip. Coins always have two sides. Not all cops are pigs…

The German people are great. Honest, incorruptible, direct. They have everything taken care of. Calculated, controlled. No skylight for dreams …

Over the following days we climbed the amazing German-Austrian Alps. I'll never forget the thick, medium-rare beefsteak and two big glasses of Weiss Beer we enjoyed sitting on the balcony of a tower, overlooking the clear, green Alps. It was my first reward after having cycled through Bavaria, and also my first affirmation that this adventure we had just begun would be an extraordinary one.

We had made a plan to spend the night a bit outside each town that interested us, to be able to get there early in the morning and have the whole day to explore. Bicycles are the best means of transport in residential areas, especially in flat towns where cycling doesn't require much effort. We spent a whole day in Vienna and another in Budapest. Beautiful cities, with great architecture, and lovely people. On our way out, we crossed the flat farmland of the Magyar — we soon got tired of eating schnitzel and potatoes …

Yannis' idea would gradually prove rewarding in all its aspects. Travelling by bicycle gives you the privilege of becoming an active part of nature, not just a passive observer locked up inside a cage with windows that just zooms from one place to the other making a racket. This slow way of travelling granted us a better perspective and allowed us to take everything in. We could feel the breeze, the sun, the scents, the sounds … and that had a positive impact on us. Truth is that neither Yannis nor I had ever been fond of cycling. I could barely remember how to balance on a bike from when I was little, so those first days were tough. We were both fit enough, but the long miles sapped at muscles we weren't used to using, a sudden change that shocked our bodies. We travelled about sixty to one hundred and twenty miles each day depending on the terrain, the stops we made, and the weather, which fortunately had rolled out the red carpet for us. It was the end of May, and we weren't facing any weather problems.

The first rains welcomed us when we left Timişoara and began climbing the Carpathian mountains of wild beauty, covered by virgin forests. Under a light rain, surrounded by the lush environment, and with a strong fire burning outside our tent, we'd rest for almost a whole day in a clearing on those heights, so near and yet so far from civilisation.

Rolling back down to the south, we stayed in Bucharest for a day. A beautiful, interesting city. There, we'd learn what organised begging really looked like. There was no way you could leave without giving something! Of course, a pickpocket stole a hundred Marks from us outside an exchange bureau, even though I did keep an eye out! But everyone has their job, I suppose.

It was afternoon when we set off for Constanţa.* Before leaving Bucharest, we sat in a coffee shop to have one last coffee for the day. It was then that a beautiful waitress gave me her phone number; the first of this trip. We had just paid, and were getting ready to leave when she wrote her name and her number on her pad and gave it to me saying:

"Call me anytime you want".

Yannis was a tease as usual.

"You're giving your number to him? I'm more handsome!"

"But I fancy him!" she shut him up …

It was too late for flings though, we had to pedal. Such are the drawbacks of cycling.

The frequent honks, cars' emergency lights, and bad roads reminded us that we were now very much in the Balkans. Something that amazed us in Hungary, and even more so in Romania, was how many horses they had and how neat and ornamented they all were.

---

*   Romania's largest coastal city on the shores of the Black Sea.

You could see them everywhere, even in the middle of the street. I hope someday people will use only horses and bicycles to travel. The world will undoubtedly become much more beautiful. Yet people are always in a hurry going nowhere.

By nightfall we reached the Danube. Just as we were about to cross the bridge, we saw some young lads by the side of the road selling the fish they'd just caught in the river. We bought the largest ones; got ourselves some cold beers and followed a dirt road along the river to camp in a quiet place near the banks of the Danube. Among gigantic willows, under the clear, spring, night sky, and with the vast river's murky waters silently flowing next to us, we spent a memorable night grilling fish, drinking beer, and babbling in Greek. Our minds were free from any cares, and so we didn't mind that we were tired. We felt that something undefined, something of greater importance, was charging our souls. It was so effortless, so natural, and yet so addictive that each day we searched for it harder.

Our decision not to take any travel guides for the countries we were going to travel through was proving to be a wise one. We didn't want to fall into the trap of having a prearranged travel program. We both had experience in travelling; we knew what interested us. We had good maps, based on which we decided our route. Leaving Constanţa, we enjoyed a seemingly endless road along the Black Sea until we came across an organised camping area with small wooden bungalows next to the water, several miles from Varna. We stayed there for two days to get some rest, and were taken aback when the owner spoke to us in fluent Greek! Thank goodness he did, because we sometimes loosened up thinking nobody was listening, and then some Greek word would slip out.

A young biking couple from Holland would also stay for two days in the same camping area, who happened to be heading to India too. They had done their homework on all the obstacles they were going to come across during their trip. We'd learn many useful things from them, for example that a female biker crossing theocratic countries was in danger of being sexually assaulted even accompanied. The girl had every reason to worry, a friend of hers had been sexually assaulted by some men from a village in Iran because she had been wearing biker tights, despite being accompanied by a male companion. For that reason, the couple had arranged to travel by train after leaving Turkey, until they reached India. They'd only stop in big cities and the capitals of these countries. What was of practical help to us was their knowledge of solutions concerning all sorts of problems that could arise with our bikes. They knew everything about them, from difficult-to-fix damage to easy ways of cleaning a bike chain.

These two days of rest by the frozen waters of the Black Sea were a breath of fresh air after about two weeks on the road. It was something we needed, and gave us the strength to continue with our trip. On the first hills of the mountains which mark a natural border between Bulgaria and East Thrace (European Turkey), we came across an odd traveller. He was a man, in his mid sixties, dragging a two-wheel cart behind him that looked a lot like a miniature racing chariot. He had its arms stabilised at the sides of his waist and was slowly but steadily climbing up the hill. Out of curiosity, we stopped and began chatting with him. He was French.

He had started his journey from Paris, two months before, and had walked all the way to the Black Sea. He was heading to the Holy Land and estimated he'd reach his destination in a month. He had vowed to himself to undertake this pilgrimage many years before, and had now been given a chance to do it. He said he had made the cart himself. It was really light, made entirely out of aluminium — a very bright idea, so that he wouldn't have to carry all his heavy belongings for such a long time given he was going so far. Realising there were even more extreme ways of travelling than riding a bicycle, we kept him company through all the uphill paths. In the end, after taking some pictures to remember him by, we wished each other a nice trip, and parted ways. Although I didn't agree with his motive and destination, I preferred him over the million other grey-haired old men who sit in coffee shops for hours lusting after youngsters. All of them longing for Death to come and release them of their rotten fate and their boring selves.

We stayed in cosmopolitan Istanbul for a couple of days. We visited what remains of the Hagia Sophia (a real mess),* the Grand Bazaar, and at night stood on the Bosphorus Bridge to see the city's illuminated streets reflected in the waters of the strait. We ate like horses every chance we got. The Greek and the Turkish cuisines are so similar, even the names of the dishes, and I had missed Greek food a lot, so I didn't even bother keeping up appearances. I got right into it. During the fifteen days we'd spend in Turkey we put all the weight we'd lost since we had started our trip back on.

We crossed the Bosphorus by boat. While we were on the dock, a lady of a certain age, who was about to board the same boat as us, heard us speaking Greek, and approached us.

"Are you from Greece, guys?" she asked us softly.

"Yes! You?"

"Greek, yes ... born and raised in Istanbul! But keep your voices down, these aren't nice people, they don't like hearing Greek". she whispered.

We were surprised. Over the few days we'd been in Turkey we hadn't noticed anything like that. But it's one thing travelling to a country and another living there daily as a minority.

Reaching Asian Turkey, we got on our bikes and headed to Ankara. We'd arranged to stay there for two days, but ended up staying three more because I got sunstroke. What saddened me wasn't the sunstroke or the additional days, but that I couldn't taste their foods, which were all delicious. In secular Ankara, we rarely saw women wearing hijabs. If one ignores the many military building complexes (even in the city centre) and the terrible gridlock, Ankara seemed a Western capital of an Asian State.

---

*   The Eighth Wonder of the World was in serious disrepair in the 1990s, and while a major series of restoration works were undertaken in the 2000s many areas remain poorly maintained. Originally built as the patriarchal cathedral of the Byzantine Empire before being turned into a mosque by the Ottomans, it became a museum from 1935 to 2018, when Turkish president Recep Erdogan designated it as a mosque again. It retains strong symbolism as an icon of Greek orthodox Christianity.

When I was feeling better we set off for the coast of Asia Minor. The heat now made it impossible for us to travel more than half a mile per day, and we didn't want to push ourselves. We'd stop at every beach we came across that we liked and have a swim. The same stood for every tavern we came across, which offered great views and good food. Trying to guess which Aegean Island we were looking at across the sea, we'd eat seafood and drink raki. How can you cycle after that?

Steadily heading south, we made several stops to visit archaeological sites, among them Ancient Troy, Ephesus, and Halicarnassus. At a small tavern by the sea, in some seaside resort near Marmara Island, we heard a male voice speaking to us in fluent Greek:

"Are you from Greece, guys?"

The voice was coming from the table next to our own, where a group of five people were sitting, all of them speaking Turkish up until that moment.

"We like to think so, yes". I said to him, tongue in cheek.

"And are you travelling by bicycle?" he asked, obviously surprised.

"Cursed Poverty!"

"Where are you heading?" he continued his absolutely-normal-for-the-occasion nosy questions.

"Wherever the road takes us ... we're thinking about reaching India".

"India? That far by bike?"

"Alexander the Great got there on his horse Bucephalus, and he became a hero".

"Fair enough ..."

We stopped talking for a while until suddenly, the guy and the girl sitting next to him got up, came to our table, placed their hands on our shoulders, posed, and directly asked us:

"You wouldn't mind taking a picture, guys, right?"

"Of course not!" I said, taken aback.

They must have thought I was a fugitive or something. The camera flashed again and again; they took many pictures. Only then did we ask them who they were. They told us they were high-ranking officials from the Greek embassy in Turkey, taking a vacation in the area — at least that's what they told us. In the end though they treated us to some raki. Great ... it's all on the Greeks then!

Throughout our journey along the coast of Asia Minor, we'd realise how much Greeks and Turks are alike, we only spoke a different language. It's impossible to understand how the stupidity of the two countries' rulers managed to plant hate in the hearts of these two peoples, entangling them in an endless defensive absurdity, subverting their peaceful cohabitation. As well as undermining their financial, cultural, political, and mental development ...

We spent half a day exploring Smyrna and then sat at a small restaurant in the port of the city. No matter how hard we tried to imagine the devastating war at the beginning of the century* and the pain of the people who'd tried to escape

---

* The Greco-Turkish war of 1919-22 saw Greek forces, backed by the British, land at Smyrna in an attempted invasion of Anatolia. Smyrna burned in September 1922 when a Turkish counterattack retook the city.

through that very same port, we failed. After all, these images are so grey and so distant … the modern world has permanently left them behind. We saw it a few years later in Iraq, we even see it today, a century after that massacre. Thousands of people killed, and millions of people turned to refugees because of the terrors of wars between the States of the Mediterranean.

Where is the dynamic mass peace movement in the Mediterranean, in Europe, in the whole world, driven by young people? Perhaps the disoriented generations of the internet, walking in a trance around a wired world seeking for fleeting happiness in fake consumerist paradises, will soon be awoken. And perhaps they'll realise that a giant guillotine is hovering above their heads, ready to behead them at any moment. Maybe they'll understand that all the political, religious, financial, and military vampires of this planet are feeding on their blood and will stop giving it that freely.

No blame rests on a generation slowly dying on websites, only on those who have the moral responsibility to awaken it. If there's one thing this global means of hypo-information could prove useful for, concerning humanity's future, it's the coordination of a global scale uprising and revolution that will thwart the plans of its blind and ruthless bellwethers. Surrounded by hordes of cymbalists, the planet's pitiful rulers don't feel comfortable with such a prospect. They know there are no proper tools, and they don't have the strength to fight youth's united wants. That's why they keep on rhythmically rocking the cradle.

We took our last breath of the Mediterranean just outside Attaleia, before we dived deeper in Easter Turkey. Knowing what was to follow, we made a two-day break to get some rest at a pine-clad organised camping area by the sea, which provided spacious military-style, fully equipped tents for rent. It was the end of July or the beginning of August, and the heat was unbearable.

The sun would rise hot about six in the morning and would set even hotter at about nine in the evening. We could only cycle for four hours early in the morning and three late in the evening. Between times we'd always find some beach or some small port on the coast of Turkey to rest at during the necessary hours of summer siestas.

We had to cycle for two-and-a-half more days through a landscape that seemed like a fiery furnace before we reached the Syrian borders. On the first night, we found ourselves travelling through a sandy heath. The wind was blowing hard, and it was impossible to set up our tent. We barely slept, because the wind would shoot sand and small, dead, thorny bushes at us. The closer we got to Syria's borders, the more the area became militarised. We came across many military bases and remote army outposts — small guardhouses made of sheet metal and painted camouflage, guarded by soldiers in full armour (combat boots, camo, bulletproof vests, cartridge pouches, helmets, rifles etc.). We felt sorry for them. It must have been torture standing there under the blazing sun, with temperatures well over forty degrees Celsius or even higher inside their tin coffins.

***

These images brought to my mind memories from my military conscription in the regional unit of Evros.* The armoured warfare camp's commander was a short, restless man. Although I was disobedient, I can say he liked me a bit. It must have been because I was quite good when it came to using and handling weapons during military exercises. More than once instructors let me train the "newbies". I'd show them how to use grenade launchers, rifle grenades, throwing training with hand grenades and using LOW anti-tank grenades. During assault rifle shooting exercises, to have some fun, I used a pretty simple trick. I placed the soldiers who were the worst at aiming to my right and to my left, and therefore my target sheet would end up with many more bullet holes than the bullets inside my gun's magazine. It was common, if a soldier's shots proved to be one hundred percent accurate, for honourable time-off to be awarded. Not to everyone, however.

During a large scale military exercise, a real battle simulation where armoured cars, artillery units, and engineering units participated, my SUV and my crew were entrusted with a hard and essential mission, which would decide the outcome of the battle. Our mission was to locate and reach a vantage point from where we could see all the troops involved. From there, we had to inform the command centre on the positions and the movements of both friendly and enemy forces. They didn't show us the spot, we had to locate it on our own, in an area we weren't at all familiar with. My crew, aside from me, comprised a sergeant and a corporal. They were well-educated city guys of a certain age (having deferred to finish their studies), who got anxious because of the importance of our mission. Being in my element during exercises, I tried to calm them down: "Don't worry, lads. We're going to see this mission through. Leave it to me!"

Looking around, on one of the many forested mountains surrounding us, the top of which would be the perfect spot for our mission, I spotted a barely visible line. This line began at the end of a path going up a barren side of the mountain, crossed the forest, and reached the summit. Driving the tough military SUV, despite my crew's protesting, we approached and began driving up the rough mountainside. Entering the forest, I realised I had guessed correctly. The line I had spotted was an old, hastily constructed road that crossed the forest, unused for years. Perhaps, at some point, it had been used by loggers. Among the abandoned road's scattering of pomegranates several oaks had sprung and grown, now being more than three feet tall. The surrounding trees' branches had interwoven above, turning it into a continuous natural tunnel, which was why it couldn't be spotted from afar.

The sergeant, who was the crew chief and, supposedly, in charge of our mission, got excited. He took a military axe out of the SUV's survival kit, got out and began chopping off any thick branch that blocked our way. The one who paid the price was the corporal, who was acting as deputy crew chief and gunner. He was in the back seat, holding both grips of the 30mm rotary machine

---

*   All male Greek citizens between 19 and 45 years old are required to do six months of military service.

gun that was placed on the SUV's raised platform. The tree branches often reached low enough to get tangled on the machine gun's barrel. As the SUV moved, they pulled him to the left or to the right. Twice he fell flat on his face trying to control the vast machine gun. Every time he complained, the sergeant would make fun of him: "You're not a bride on the way to her wedding, you're at war, my poor fellow", he'd say laughing.

In less than half an hour, we reached and seized the mountaintop, which was a natural lookout. It afforded us a panoramic view of the surrounding land, where the mother of all battles was about to take place. It began the moment the sergeant proudly reported through his wireless that a lookout had been found and that he was now ready to inform them on both friends and enemies, giving their coordinates at any time. I brought the binoculars up to my eyes and followed the movement of all the troops. At the same time, I communicated everything in great detail to the sergeant so that he could convey them to the command centre. I have to admit what I was seeing was really spectacular. But I didn't understand many things … I didn't know where it was heading.

Coming from different directions, their guns spitting fire and smoke from the blank ammunition, various types of armoured vehicles and machine gun-carrying SUVs headed towards a riverside where the engineers had set up makeshift bridges. Armoured personnel carriers followed close behind, while crowds of ground troops were running, lightweight rifles in hand … and the artillery's cannons were thundering from the surrounding hillsides. War!

I shouldn't babble any more about this lest I accidentally expose sensitive military information, so let me skip to the end. After several armoured vehicles were immobilised, damaged or because of some accident, we defeated them … we ate those Turks alive! Long live our army! Long live our nation! And even longer all naïve people! Our crew was nominated by those in charge of the successful military operation for a ten-day honourable leave, as a reward for our contribution to this great victory. I had been punished several times and according to military law, all soldiers having gotten detention in the past aren't entitled to any honours. And yet the honorary proposal was for the whole crew and for it to be awarded to the other two, I had to be exempted. The problem was solved by the camp's commander when he summoned me to his office.

"My child, it is a common secret among military officials, and also a historical fact, that disobedient soldiers are the best warriors in real battles. Your case is, I might say, quite paradoxical. You disobey your superiors' orders, and yet you're disciplined and practical when it comes to making your own decisions".

"Do you think this is a weakness, sir?"

"No, my child, not at all. But this is the army, and there are rules!"

"Rules and initiative are as contrasting as obedience and freedom, sir!"

"You're right, my child. It is wise that every man finds a middle ground in such difficult dilemmas. And yet, so that the rest of your crew isn't deprived of their leave of absence and since you're at odds with your captain, I'll send you to the outpost by the river, where things aren't as tense, to get some rest".

So he sent me to an outpost at the Evros River to get rid of me. The outpost was in charge of guarding a watchtower by the riverside and foot-patrolling along the river banks. Life at the outpost was relaxed, and it became even more so after my arrival.

Later that summer, while I was on guard duty along with a pot-loving soldier, we made a bet that I'd manage to convince the two Turkish soldiers patrolling the opposite riverside, to cross to our side. I partially won.

I used three pornographic magazines as bait (the poor guys didn't have any) and indeed, after hesitating a bit, one of them left his gun, took off his combat boots, folded the bottom of his military pants and stepped knee-deep in the river. I approached him and greeted him. He seemed calm and quite badass! Giving him the precious gifts, I asked in gestures whether he could bring us some weed the following day. He promised he would ... at least that's what I understood.

The following day, having our own reasons, we asked to be on guard duty in the morning. Of course, nobody denied us. We spent the whole day waiting, with our eyes locked on the opposite side of the river in case they came.

Nothing ...

"The fucking Turks sold us out! You should have arrested him! We'd have taken a twenty-day honorary leave of absence! And then I'd have brought you the best weed you'll ever have from my village!" my fellow pothead soldier raved angrily.

The sight of the Turkish soldier leaving his gun behind and crossing the river is representative of how much young people want to abolish artificial borders to communicate and co-exist. Still, the States' military and political interests don't allow it.

I'd experience the full extent of the relaxed security measures of the outpost, alongside the military camp's commander, when he decided to make a surprise inspection of the outpost and the patrol along the Evros River. That day, a corporal and I had been on duty on the watchtower. If I remember correctly, we had two-hour or four-hour shifts, but we never really followed them. The watchtower, at least fifty feet tall and eighteen by eighteen feet long, had a small house at its centre that looked a lot like a treehouse. Its floor was made entirely of wood, and it was surrounded by iron bars. On the side overlooking Turkey, small sacks filled with the river's sands were placed halfway up the bars to protect the guards from enemy fire.

Around noon, finishing his "shift", the corporal got down and approached the bank of the river, where some willows cast their shade, to take a nap. For the last while I meanwhile had been thinking about sunbathing. I got up on the watchtower, hung my G3 on a nail, took off my helmet, my cartridge pouch, my combat boots, and the top of my camouflage suit. I opened four sacks, pouring their sand on the iron floor to make a small beach, and lay down to enjoy myself. No more than fifteen minutes had passed, when I heard a diesel-powered car approaching on the dirt road. For a moment I didn't worry, thinking it must have been one of the area's beekeepers, who was coming to check through his powerful military monocular the state of the sunflower crops further inside Turkey, where their bees often roamed (bees don't respect borders). This was strictly forbidden by the military and often punished by incarceration, but when I was on duty they were free to do as they pleased. And they never came empty-handed; they'd always bring me plenty of honey.

Whoever it was though, I thought, shouldn't see me like this!

Lying as I was, I put on my combat boots, then I got up and turned to face the direction of the noise. At that moment, a well-polished military Mercedes SUV climbed the embankment and drove down the few remaining yards until it reached the watchtower. The first thing I did was throw my military flask, which was filled with water, at the thicket where the corporal was sleeping, in case he somehow managed to get away ... No use, he was out cold. I didn't really try to cover myself. The men in the SUV, now right underneath the watchtower, saw me half-naked, without my helmet, my gun, etc.

"Nothing I can do about it now", I thought.

I slowly began dressing up again; I put on my helmet, then my tunic (I didn't button it up), and finally I grabbed my rifle. The passenger door opened, and the military camp's commander got out. It was the worst thing that could have happened. For a few moments, we stared at each other, him on the ground and I high on the watchtower. He was waiting for me to tell him which soldier I was, the area's coordinates, and then to mention if there had been any incidents during the day, as dictated by military protocol.

Giving up, he asked me:

"Who are you, my child?"

"Palaiokostas!" I answered boldly.

"Is that you, Palaiokostas? What happened to you? Is this how soldiers are supposed to present themselves?"

"Why, sir? What's wrong with me? You're scaring me!"

"Your tunic is unbuttoned, you don't have your cartridge pouch, and your helmet isn't fastened. Do you know you're defending the country's borders here?"

"Totally, sir!"

"Where is the corporal?"

"He went to the bathroom, but it's taking him a while".

Certain I was lying to him, he began searching around to find any spots where the corporal could be sleeping. He soon found him. The corporal, despite all the shouting and the diesel-powered military SUVs noise, was still sleeping like a baby! I couldn't see his "bed", but I could hear the commander yelling at him as he woke him up. At least he was lucky enough not to have a heart attack, waking up to find the camp's commander raging over his head!

"You'll report to the camp first thing tomorrow! Both of you!" he barked at us before leaving in a huff.

The following day, at the break of dawn, they shipped the corporal back to the camp. News reached the outpost late in the evening, and they were in stitches. Aside from twenty days of detention for misconduct, the commander also said to him: "Corporal, you left Palaiokostas guarding the borders and went to sleep?"

***

That day I narrated many stories to Yannis from my time in the military, just so that we could forget about the heat as we cycled towards the south-eastern borders of Turkey.

The closer we got to Adana, the more the indigenous population's appearance changed. We came across many folk who looked like Mongols but also many Kurds living in purely Kurdish villages. The first time I got to meet some Kurds was in 1991, in Patra Prison. It was two of the four or five guys who had escaped from Ioannina Prison a few weeks prior. In their attempt to make it, they had injured a correctional officer with broken glass. After a week, they were discovered by Albanian soldiers across the border where they were arrested and handed to the Greek authorities at once. For a whole week then they had been left at the mercy of the correctional officers at Ioannina Prison, who tortured them daily to avenge their like-minded friend. When they came to my wing in Patra they could barely stand on their feet. Their bodies were covered in bruises, and their faces were deformed. They couldn't eat, and they peed blood. These people had travelled along the Greek-Albanian mountains for a week without food, hoping that the neighbouring Communist regime wouldn't hand them to the Greek authorities. Then, exhausted as they were, the sadistic face of the Greek correctional system took out all its rage on them for another week. And after that, because of their injuries, they couldn't eat for a week, until their wounds had healed. They were little guys, a hundred and twenty to a hundred and thirty pounds at most. Despite having suffered like Christ, the spark for life and freedom still burned in their eyes. When they got a bit better, they said to me:

"Vassilis, if you have an escape plan, count us in!"

Real warriors, that's what they were.

Several years later, while I was a fugitive, I heard on the news that a small group of inmates, most of them Kurds, had escaped during a transfer, opening a hole on the bottom of the prison bus. From the names released to the public, I was sure that among the escapees were those two guys. I was happy for them, they truly deserved freedom; they were real fighters. Their people also deserve freedom, fighting alone for centuries to secure the bare necessities, fighting against the Middle Eastern financial behemoths clashing over it. A Battle Royale of the planet's powerful States, all preaching freedom and self-determination of peoples, as long as it suits their geostrategic interests.

On the last night before reaching the border we camped in the middle of a valley that looked like a miniature of the Thessalian plain, between Adana and Syria. Surrounded by Kurdish villages and high mountain ranges, the valley was full of cotton and grain fields. We cycled away from the main road and set up our tent in a vast, recently harvested area. We brewed some coffee on the camping stove and sat outside to enjoy the quiet of the night. Darkness had already begun to fall, and the clear starry sky was seemingly held high by the surrounding mountaintops, stretching high as they could.

The small, dimly illuminated villages scattered on their hills and their slopes seemed like hanging fairy lights ... and far in the distance, from beyond the mountains, we could hear from time to time the sounds of flock bells, disrupting the silence, adding something unique to the calm nightly landscape's symphony.

We hadn't experienced such serenity since that night we'd spent at the banks of the Danube. No matter the comforts resorts offer, it's impossible to compare them with nightly landscapes like this one and the feeling they offer you. Where you feel your soul grow, reaching as far as the eye can see and even further ... becoming one with the landscape. At the same time, the mind empties; it is released from the weight of the waterlogging of our minds, to which modern people are daily and wilfully subjected.

We stayed there for hours, half lying on the ground, our minds wandering in the nightly eastern landscape. Until we noticed that the flocks we'd heard from far beyond the hills had intruded into the surrounding harvested fields. It seemed that the shepherds had found an opportunity to get their flocks down into the valley for some night-time grazing in the recently harvested fields, which were filled with crunchy, nutritious brushwood. The starlight was just enough to vaguely see about a hundred to two hundred yards away from our tent. A bit further away, we could make out a very long white wave approaching us. About ten proud, gigantic eastern sheep dogs arrived first. All their tails and ears were cut, and they all wore wolf collars.* They seemed very mistrustful and sure of themselves. Circling twenty yards away from our tent, walking slowly, they surrounded us and lay on the ground so that we didn't come into contact with the flocks which, in a few minutes, swarmed the whole area. They were flocks of sheep and they were so many, hundreds, thousands maybe ... they were everywhere. We didn't see the shepherds, definitely more than three, but we could hear them. We could hear them whistling, and we're not talking about plain shepherds' whistling. They were continuous, and they weaved a sweet nightly melody, as though written and orchestrated by a composer specifically for the flocks' peace of mind. I'd never heard anything like it. The East has a different, unique soul.

"We've got ourselves some good guards, we have some quality music too, let's get some sleep!" Yannis said to me.

We slept like babies, and at around ten the following morning, we reached the Syrian borders. There we were in for a big surprise. The Syrian border patrol agents refused to stamp our passports because, as they said, they had no such orders from their government. We ought to have gotten a visa from the Syrian consulate in Ankara.

"We're so and so, we travel this way and ..."

Nothing. They were adamant about it. The country's safety comes first! Which, in this case, was endangered by two bearded cyclists! Borders don't mark anything else than the boundaries of a State authority's influence. The most heinous mass crimes in human history have been committed because of borders.

---

*   Spiked around the outside to protect against attacks to the neck.

If glorious Greece's borders were ever to reach Northern Korea (I hope they never do), proud Greek soldiers would stand guard, heavily armed, looking over the Sea of Japan, sure they're protecting the land of their fathers ... oh, this is a mad world, indeed.

Just in time, four lads arrived (rich kids from England) in a Land Rover Defender, its roof pulled back, safari-style. With an air of superiority, they tried to get through passport control. Nothing. The customs officers told them to pull over and wait. They drove backwards and parked their car right next to us. Yannis began chatting with them.

"Hi!"

"Hello!"

"Where are you from?"

"We're British!"

"You don't have visas either, huh?"

"No, but we'll get them!"

"How can you be so sure?"

"This lad's dad is an ambassador (or consul, I don't remember) in the British embassy in Ankara and he's contacting him now to find us a solution".

"Oh! This changes things ..."

"Where are you heading?" they asked us.

"India".

"Oh! Perfect!"

"You?"

"Jordan".

"Anyplace in particular?"

"Yes. We're going to the place where that Indiana Jones movie was filmed!"

"Oh, I see!"

"Yes. It's a lifelong dream to see the place where this historical figure once lived from up close!"

Perhaps, fellow reader, I should put an end to my journey and a full stop to this book. There's no point ... yet, hope springs eternal.

"Try again, Yannis. Perhaps you got something wrong".

Yannis was very fluent in English, but for me, he tried once again. The results were the same ... Indiana Jones was a real person and a hero. Humour is the antidote to despair ... Speaking with a heavy accent, I said to Yannis:

"Tell these fucking blond kids that they have Palaiokostas right in front of them, and they're seeing him in the flesh! Let them not search in deserts for Hollywood ghosts, or else I might steal their SUV and get out of here!"

We couldn't control ourselves, we burst out laughing. We waited for another fifteen minutes in case they were allowed passage so that we could "attack" the customs officers for preferential treatment of tourists etc, on the off chance we could avoid a return to Ankara, but the Syrians gave no favours to anyone — not even the entitled kids of British ambassadors. They handed them back their passports and sent them back to Ankara to get visas.

We lost all hope that we'd cross the border, it was now clear that the customs officers had a jurisdiction to allow foreigners to enter their country without an official visa, issued by a competent authority.

Until then, throughout our trip, we had entered and exited eight countries facing no similar problems. To demand that cyclists return from the Syrian borders to Ankara and then come back with an official visa is twisted, to say the least. We were gradually realising, to our great disappointment, that the countries we were about to cross between Turkey and India had no interest in travellers. The Arab States, Syria being the first, received us quite indifferently and, to an extent, treated us like we were not welcome. Been there before ...

Of course, we weren't keen on returning to Ankara by bicycle. And the worst thing was that the nearest city connected by rail to the capital was Adana. Given the circumstances, we'd need a whole day to get there by bicycle. In the end, we left at once, and reached the city late in the afternoon. The next direct train to Ankara was scheduled to leave the following morning which wasn't necessarily a bad thing. We found a nice hotel in the city and had a great time there.

Early the following day we boarded the train to Ankara, which was another whole day's journey from the south-eastern border. The train moved slowly across the mainland, crossing breathtaking landscapes. Deep gorges and pine tree forests, desert landscapes, fertile plains, picturesque villages small and large where the train often stopped. It brought to my mind the time when I was young, when we'd travel across Greece by train. You needed two days just to get from Thessaloniki to Athens!

What bothered us was whether our decision to travel across the Middle East in the middle of summer, in countries where we were bound to face visa-related issues, was the wisest. Another incident that took place right in front of our eyes in the central railway station in Ankara troubled us further. When we got off the train we stayed on the main platform for a while, to pack up our things on the bicycles. While we were doing so we heard a commotion, and we saw some female tourists running away in panic. Looking around, we spotted the reason behind their fear. A Muslim Imam, holding a willow switch, was hunting any female tourists who had dared come to the land of Muhammad wearing shorts and vest tops, hitting them on their thighs and anywhere else he saw bare skin. Turkish hijab-wearing women, with the consent and help of several stupid Muslim men, were ecstatically applauding him, while all the male tourists accompanying the girls targeted by the rogue Khawaja did absolutely nothing.

"He's such a prick! I'm going to go and head-butt him twice, make him forget his name!"

"Are you insane? You escaped in Greece, and now you want to be arrested in Turkey for beating up an Imam?" Yannis reacted.

"What's gotten into him, beating girls?"

"He thinks they scandalise morals and his religion!"

There's nothing more shameful in this world than the establishment and operation of religions. They're the most scandalous thing human civilisation has to offer.

And because there are lots of other fish in the sea, we didn't visit the Syrian embassy, but the Chinese one instead Our new travel plan was to travel across mainland China, head up to Tibet and then down to the coast of south India.

China had just begun to slowly open up to the Western world at the time, so we were a bit worried it would be difficult for us to get visas, but in fact the exact opposite happened. We didn't have to wait more than five minutes in the air-conditioned visitors' hall in the embassy. A beautiful young Chinese woman welcomed us by asking us some questions for the sake of formality: what was the purpose of our visit, how long did we intend to stay, and how we would be travelling. We, in turn, asked for our visas to last long enough for us to be able to travel across such a large country. The Chinese woman, with our passports in her hands, climbed a flight of stairs and disappeared. After a while, she reappeared, smiling. Giving us our passports, she wished us a nice trip and a pleasant stay in her country. Great! The visas would last long enough for what we needed.

Since back then Turkey didn't have a direct link by air to China we'd have to stay in Ankara two more days before taking our flight to Beijing, making a stop in Paris where we changed aircraft. In this case, too, we'd come to realise how flexible travelling by bike can be. We simply took off their wheels, placed them in special sacks and checked them in before flying.

The early morning found us flying south-east of Ukraine and north of the Black Sea. This air travel worked as a small compensation for everything we'd been deprived of by the cancellation of our initial travel plan. The aeroplane followed the exact same course, only high in the air. From high up there and with an unobstructed panoramic view as our ally we couldn't get enough of watching an endless mosaic of continually changing colourful landscapes, slowly unravelling right before our eyes for hours. High, immense mountain ranges. Thick green forests. Calm, shiny lakes. Long, winding rivers. Vast steppes ... and the malignant human tumour was entirely out of sight. I had taken many transatlantic flights in the past, some of which passed over places such as the Amazon rainforest, but never before had I seen such widespread natural beauty on the surface of the Earth. The clean atmosphere (we didn't see a single cloud) contributed to our visual pleasure, allowing us to clearly observe landscapes and colours from our window seats.

After landing in Beijing we assembled our bikes and headed to the city. We had barely left the airport when a helmet-wearing, fully equipped cyclist made a loud appearance next to us. He began talking to us in English, pedalling by our side. He was from Luxembourg and had arrived on our flight. He wanted to chat, and we couldn't say no. We were all hungry, so we decided to make a stop and grab a bite at one of the first restaurants we came across on our way to central Beijing. There we'd learn that every year our unexpected "companion" would, during his one-month vacation, pick a country and travel across it by bike. This year it was China's turn. His plan was to visit the Great Wall of China and then Hong Kong — the classic tourist way.

"Where will you two go?" he asked us.

"We haven't made any specific plans. We'll head further in the mainland, and we'll see ... wherever the road takes us".

"Aren't you going to visit the Great Wall of China?" he asked, surprised.

"We're not architects, nor archaeologists, nor historians! And we're not in the mood of travelling that far just to get photos with the wall in the background!"

"And what will you do in the mainland?"

"We want to be near plain Chinese villagers, see what their lives are like, their habits, feel their aura, their land's aura".

"I'm sorry to say this, but there's a problem in the mainland, they have nothing to eat, there's real poverty in these villages".

"Where did you hear that? Who told you?"

"The travel guide says so". he said, getting out of his backpack a deluxe travel guide of China, written in English.

He opened it, skimmed through it, found the pages testifying to his comment and handed it to Yannis, saying:

"It's by the most reliable travel-guide publisher in the world".

Yannis read the pages in question, which offered the necessary advice-instructions and turned to face me, saying:

"It's true. It says that all hopeful travellers who dare reach the depths of the Chinese mainland should know that they'll face serious hardships concerning food! The rural population is on the verge of famine".

"Do you believe this?" I asked him.

"I don't know. We won't know until we get there. If you're asking for my opinion, a travel guide for the Chinese provinces is as useful as bike helmets for the Chinese!"

We laughed ... right on time, our order arrived. With the help of the English menu, the Luxembourger and I had ordered "legs of duck". What they brought us looked like a vegetable soup, in which several boiled, yellow flippers (duck legs) floated. Really gross! Yannis on the other hand, who had ordered from the Chinese menu at random, ate well. I guess we were at higher risk of starving by sticking to travel guides and English restaurant menus! We let the Luxembourger head to the Great Wall, and booked a room in a downtown hotel. Its luxury restaurant offered delicious, traditional Chinese cuisine and we didn't pass up the opportunity ... Thankfully, the waiters spoke English and we kept clear of the sweet and sour pig trotters.

The whole following day, with the help of local cyclists, we toured around the centre of Beijing. Among other things we took the necessary photos with the Great Hall of the People in the background, at historic Tiananmen Square, we visited some museums, we wandered in the Forbidden City and in a vast, impressive Chinese park full of ponds and everything. We went by the Silk Market, and enjoyed some outdoor-restaurant delicacies. What we ate ... now that's a whole other story.

Two days later, at noon, we set off from Beijing. We were planning on cycling south-west and then, at some point, begin heading east, ending up in the port city of Shanghai. In essence, we'd be making a great V in the Chinese mainland. The route we'd chosen, based on our calculations, was about one and a half to two thousand miles and it would take us about twenty to twenty-five days of relaxed cycling to get there.

Night had begun to fall however and we hadn't even exited the city's beltways. The expensive road map of China, which we'd bought at the Paris airport and had been by another "best in the world" publisher, didn't correspond at all to the reality of China's streets. In the end we made the bold decision to leave Beijing's beltways entirely, hoping that further away from the city we'd be able to read the map better. Crossing under a huge bridge, we followed a smaller and straight road to the city's exit, heading south-west.

We had travelled far from the outskirts of Beijing when, straight ahead, by the side of the road, we came across a small restaurant. We thought it wise to take one last proper meal before the great famine so we placed our bikes by the restaurant's wall and went in. At the back of the long illuminated chamber, and in front of the kitchen, stood two young Chinese girls dining with a middle-aged Chinese man. It seemed they were a father and his daughters, and they owned the restaurant. At different tables, two groups of three people were eating. When they realised someone had entered the restaurant they turned and stared at us like we were elves or something. And rightly so. Before them stood two bearded white guys with jockey caps and biker tights! At that time, twenty-five years ago, Chinese people weren't used to such sights outside big city centres.

The two Chinese girls came to welcome us shyly, showing us to a table. They didn't understand English, so we tried to make an order with gestures. Failing, Yannis went to the kitchen so that the girls' father could show him what he could prepare for us. When he returned, the two Chinese girls came back, each holding a small metal bowl filled with water as well as a folded towel. They stood there, in front of us, waiting. We'd never seen anything like this until then, but we understood we were meant to wash our hands. Like true Greeks, we dipped our hands in the bowls, got a handful of water and splashed it on our thick beards ...

... pfrou, oh, nice!

The two girls broke out in laughter. They showed us how we were meant to do it. You dip the towel in the water, you wring it out, and then you clean your hands and face. We began laughing at our blunder, making everyone else in the room laugh as well. This funny scene had broken the ice of communication. We got into a signing conversation with all the patrons, who I guess wanted to know "where we were from and where we were heading". We were called to answer in gestures and words unknown to them what no human has ever managed — and will never manage — to answer, no matter how many languages they speak. So we decided to do something simpler, to make them understand that somewhere on this round Earth is a small place called Greece, Grecia, Griechenland, Hellada, Hellas. Nothing! Yet we persisted. Acropolis, Socrates, Pericles, democracy, Mykonos ... no luck ...

When we'd finished our pork and vegetables that the cook had prepared for us, and drunk the two Chinese rice beers one of the groups had treated us to, we opened our map and asked the two girls to help with our trip. No matter how hard they tried, they couldn't figure out the roads depicted on the map. Finally a truck driver stood up from one of the groups and came to our table to help us, knowing the area's roads well. He too failed to read our map, the best map in the world! The driver left the restaurant for a moment, returning with a map of the whole country, which was big as a book. He showed us where we were, how to get where we wanted to go and, finally, the proper way of reading the map, since he was gifting it to us! The map was in Chinese but was clear enough, easy to read, and it would prove lifesaving during our trip. For the most part of our journey, we cycled along dirt roads, and we never lost our way. The best gift a Chinese person could have given us at the time. Without this map, we wouldn't have gone anywhere.

The following days, our suspicions concerning the part played by behemoth companies in directing global mass tourism and controlling travelling would be confirmed. In countries with different styles of life and development, like China, which the governments of powerful Western countries can't control, these companies, cooperating with their governments, operate like battering rams for the propaganda mechanisms of aggressive Western expansionism. China, a country up until then untouched by capitalist markets, which had to show modern and even more so ancient cultural wealth that could be heavily exploited by the tourist trade, as well as the active manpower of more than two billion people operating on solid social foundations and State structures, was very financially attractive to the organised piranhas of the West who are attracted to and follow the smell of fresh money.

The following days were days of reconnaissance and acclimatisation to the new environment of the Chinese countryside. It is true that upon our arrival in China, we'd had a hard time because of the heat, which became even more unbearable because of a complete lack of wind and high humidity. The deeper we got into the mainland however, the better the climate became. We didn't face any problems cycling, since throughout our trip we were on the flat ground of a country where bikes are the people's preferred means of transport!

Every few miles we'd come across a smaller or larger village, a small town or a city ... The Chinese countryside was inhabited. You understood what it really meant for the country to have a billion residents. Yet a paradox was visible. The villages and the small towns weren't groaning under the weight of high population density but the exact opposite, because the population was scattered. Travelling about one-and-a-half to two thousand miles across the Chinese mainland, we didn't see an inch of uncultivated land. Every small mountain, every hill, every valley was filled with thousands of sown fields. It was impressive. Even more impressive was the fact that there weren't many agricultural machines. Seldom did we see a tractor, it was as though the crops were planted and grew by themselves.

The only thing we saw poking through all kinds of plantations were countless straw hats ... it gave you the impression that the Chinese were communicating with their plants!

Lined up by the banks of a river, fishing equipment by their sides and each holding a fishing rod, calm fishermen waited patiently to catch some fish. Groups of elderly Chinese men with thin white beards were sitting on the ground, smoking their long pipes while nearby water buffalos grazed peacefully in paddy fields. Others, as though putting on a performance of unorthodox walking, were strolling around followed by flocks of ducks. Some would even call us from the roadside offering to treat us to some hot tea from a steaming kettle on some fire. Cyclists, lugging colourful vegetables on their bike' racks and with huge straw hats on their heads, appeared silently from the narrow dirt roads of the valley. We were treated daily to such unique sights in the Chinese countryside, which had its own slow pace.

One morning, waking up near the bank of a river where we had camped the previous night, we saw about eight or ten Chinese men practising martial arts on an arched stone bridge. Such a wonderful sight ... we had come across an outdoor karate school. We didn't manage to watch them for long because they got wind of us and the students stopped obeying their teacher — our presence there was far more interesting a lesson to them.

Nothing at all reminded us of Western civilisation. Their packaged food, their clothes, their bikes, their cars, their home appliances were all made in China. Not a single word was written in another language. When we were planning our initial voyage across the emancipated countries of the former Soviet Union, including China, this had been our goal. To get to know them before the Western lifestyle's husked cynicism managed to crush them. We were thrilled to have achieved that ... at least in China.

Cops? Not a single one! In Beijing, when we had seen some, we'd noticed that none of them was armed. It was a surprise ... youth, youth, youth ... so full of vigour. That's what we saw wherever we looked. Not a single overweight or disfigured human being. Two out of the many small examples are the following: at some point, cycling along a freshly paved road, we came across three hundred young villagers lined up by the roadside, paving the road using shovels. That's when we understood that the Western world was taking a considerable risk in its attempt to enforce, on its own terms, the Western way of life in such a populous society with great social cohesion and history, deeply rooted in their land. Hastily crossing the yellow river on an old bicycle, a young Chinese man approached us ...

"Hello!"

"Hello!"

"Where are you from?"

"Greece".

"Oh! Yeah ... Greece ... Greece! Pericles ... Socrates ..."

"Yes, yes ... you?"

"Chinese!"

We laughed. More than five minutes passed, and still, he refused to leave. I let Yannis deal with this, hoping that the man would at some point feel tired and abandon his friendly talk. His bike couldn't keep up with ours, so he was forced to constantly track stand. After about ten (perhaps even more) miles Yannis, now fed up, stopped his bike, opened his arms, looked at the sky and cried out in Greek:

"Oh for fuck's sake, what have I gotten myself into? Hasn't he got anything better to do?"

The likeable Chinese man realised Yannis was frustrated and apologised:

"Sorry guys. I didn't want to annoy you. I'm just studying English, and I thought it was a good chance to practice!"

"And did it have to be us, my friend? We're not a mobile workshop (in Greek)!"

We laughed … and in this case, the dynamics of this country's youth spoke for itself and said: "When in the depths of the East a young Chinese man is track standing for ten consecutive miles just to practice his English, the West shouldn't feel so secure".

The Chinese women were another revelation to us. Born and raised in the Western world, we only had a vague idea about them. We confused them with Japanese and Filipino women and anything else that had to do with women from these parts of the world. The Chinese villager women were a special category. It appeared that they were privileged in terms of social standing compared to men. We didn't know if this already existed in the traditional culture of Chinese agricultural societies or if it was a result of the Communist revolution or both. It was highly enjoyable. We forgot our fatigue whenever we got ourselves in the middle of a group of young female bikers. Their reaction was always the same since they'd never seen white people from up close. After the initial shock, they'd look at each other to make sure they were all seeing the same thing and then they'd break out in laughter. An attempt to communicate would follow, which resulted in more laughter. Whenever they made an appearance, they were always clean, ethereal, and glowing with pure beauty … whenever we'd stop somewhere to have lunch, they'd gather around us. They'd touch our hair, our beards, to feel what they were like. And without asking, they'd get on our bikes to cycle around their village. At least we didn't miss the positive female aura and pure smiles on this trip!

In every village we came through, loudspeakers would deafen us. A penetrative voice would always have something important to pompously announce. Afterwards, a Chinese song-march would always follow and so on and so forth. Communism, my friends! And yet they were imaginative and practical. They'd lay their rice and all their cereals on the main road of the village so that oncoming vehicles could do the threshing for them.

Until that point, the travel guide's propaganda scenarios about an upcoming famine in the Chinese countryside hadn't been verified, and they never would. The exact opposite was true. We'd always come across one or two small restaurants with plenty of food at the centre of each village. Summer fruit, like melons and watermelons, were being sold even on the streets outside settlements.

Yannis had taken on the difficult task of exploring the fridges of all the restaurants we chose to dine at. All of which were filled with food of all sorts. Each time he'd describe a new product to me that he had seen in the fridge. Sometimes it would be giant worms, other times snakes, or locusts, or ants, or even cockroaches.... I never felt the need to see them for myself. I was absolutely fine with sticking to the basics: duck, pork, vegetables and rice. There's nothing better for cycling. They were fresh, well-cooked, and really cheap. A glass filled with scalding water and a handful of longleaf tea floating in it was their usual treat. We couldn't get used to drinking hot beverages in the middle of summer though, so we settled for cold rice beer.

The preparation and cooking of food was clearly men's business. Not once did we see a woman cooking. On the spot, right in front of us, they'd light their charcoal stove and cook whatever we'd ordered inside a big wok within a few minutes. Most of them were young, and they really wanted us to leave their restaurant satisfied. They had a strong desire to communicate with us. All those lucky enough to have been gifted by nature with five or more hairs on their chins used them to break the ice between us. They'd stroke them, giving us a meaningful stare: "Hey, we're not that worthless, we've got some too!"

We gradually became quite skilled in communicating directly and wordlessly. Using only gestures and loads of humour, which is the key that unlocks each peoples' soul. And, here and there, some Greek words that only led to more laughter. Because laughter is the same in all languages around the world, as long as it is pure.

Older Chinese people would either show great interest in our presence there or no interest at all. One day, while we were in the middle of nowhere, the sky darkened, and a strong wind began to bow. Within minutes it stopped and then it started to rain. Yet those were not like the raindrops we were used to; each of them was the size of a ping-pong ball. They'd fall on the dry dirt of the road and splash two feet high in the air. We were terrified. For a moment we thought this had been a monsoon or something like that, as we vaguely remembered seeing on the TV. By the roadside, underneath a big gazebo, about ten men who had been working in the surrounding fields were gathered to protect themselves. We approached them and got under the cover with our bikes. They didn't pay us any attention, it was as though we didn't exist. They stared at the dark horizon, talking to each other with these short screams that make one think they're arguing. Their behaviour got us even more worried.

"Something must be terribly wrong with the weather, and that's why they're not bothering with us at all", we thought.

Ten minutes later, and while all this time we had been trying to understand from their stares and movements how bad things were, the sky cleared and the rain stopped, as suddenly as it had begun. The villagers all flounced away towards the fields without even looking at us, as though holding us in contempt or thinking us responsible for bringing this sudden rain over their land. We were wondering if all this really happened or if it had been a game of our imagination.

We'd experience some similar behaviour, which we never really understood, from other Chinese people of a certain age. Perhaps it had to do with their opposition to the opening to the Western world attempted at the time by the ruling party. Maybe the villagers were trying to make their feelings about this known by ignoring anything strange to them. A sort of silent protest.

In other cases though the exact opposite happened. A family with two kids invited us to their home. They made us tea, showed us around their house, gave us a tour of their warehouses where they had huge clay pots filled with rice and cereals and from the roofs of which hang corn, onions, garlic etc. They urged us to stay for dinner and sleep at their house for the night, but their very young kids couldn't get used to us. We seemed scary to them, with our beards and all. They ran to hide, crying, whenever they saw us. There appeared to be two contrasting worlds in the Chinese countryside: one that desired to be left at peace and another that yearned to communicate with the rest of the world.

One morning, in the yard of one of the first houses of a Chinese village, we saw Western civilisation's weak spot being brutally assaulted. Surrounded by five or six women and men, a skinner holding his curved knife was skinning a dog that was hanging upside down from the thick branch of a tall mulberry tree. We were horrified. There's a limit to everything, even to the cultures, habits and customs of people. They say that human meat is delicious, and yet we don't see people being skinned, hanging from mulberry trees (which we'd deserve). Each people must have moral boundaries, even when it comes to food. If our travel guide had proved to be right, only then perhaps such an atrocity could have been justified.

Full of countless experiences from the traditional and grassroots-level organised Communist Chinese countryside, we found ourselves cycling along the Yangtze River when we finally spotted Shanghai from afar. It looked like an endless worksite. The cranes outnumbered the multi-storeyed buildings. A real construction orgasm was underway in this city. Wearing a Communist cloak, China's metropolises were in a rush to enter the shiny, and yet so dark, world of capitalism. We'd stay in Shanghai for three days, enough for us to rest and get ready to continue. We had a great time.

The end of our trip was unexpected and a bit comical. Having had enough of the Chinese countryside, we thought we'd reach Tibet by train. We got our bikes up in a special wagon, and after a one-and-a-half day's journey (in the train's restaurant we accidentally ate snake, thinking it was eel) we reached our destination. But when we went to get our bicycles, we realised they were missing! Obviously, some employees must have liked them and had stolen them, forgetting about their Communist ideals! Ideologies and stealing are two different things. Communism means to eat, and capitalism means to steal! The Chinese were on the right track.

We couldn't communicate with the employees of the station or the train. None of them spoke English. They were playing dumb. So we had two options: either return to Shanghai and buy new ones or continue our way to Tibet by train and then make it up as we went.

An unexpected event would give the answer to our dilemma, completely changing our plans. A family matter forced Yannis to return to Greece. So we had to indefinitely postpone our trip to Tibet until we were given the chance again. After a few more days in Beijing, Yannis flew back to Greece, and I took a flight to Latin America. To fill some more travel pages in the book of my life.

Top: Repair works at the Hagia Sofia in 2001. Above, a typical entrance gate to the Siheyuan of Beijing. Pics: Tyler Bell and Snowy Owl

ROLLING FIREFIGHT IN KOZANI

It was nearly the fifteenth of August, and boiling hot. The trip was long, and I had miscalculated the time. I was about an hour late for my appointment. When I got to the parking lot of the supermarket in Kozani, Ivan was waiting patiently for me in the passenger seat of an old black Mazda. I grabbed my backpack, locked the Renault, opened the Mazda's door and sat in the driver seat. Since Nikos, I trusted no one else to drive in the countryside.

"Let's go, the guys are waiting for us, and they're loaded". Ivan said to me.

I started the old Mazda and realised the tank was running low. Whenever I was on a mission I wanted it full, so I filled it up at a central gas station and drove until we reached the northern side of the city. I didn't know the place well, so I drove around the streets to locate any ways out that would come in handy if things were to go awry.

Finally, we turned right into the road behind the Technical Education Institution of Kozani and, after less than a mile, left onto an uphill dirt road. Our appointment for collecting a batch of guns and ammunition was set for a small church on top of a hill at the end of this dirt road. Ivan's friends were supposed to be waiting for us there. Driving up the path, I saw a black Octavia heading to the Institution. I thought it wise to prepare Ivan for a possible confrontation.

"Ivan, there's an Octavia down on the road. Perhaps it's an unmarked police vehicle. Inside my backpack, I have a Kalashnikov. Get it out and be ready. Have you ever shot one of these before?"

"Against cops? Never!"

"I guess now is your chance. Have you got this?"

"Yes ... don't worry".

As I expected, the Octavia turned and entered the dirt road behind us. I could see it speeding up the road through my mirrors. When it was a few yards behind us, the occupants turned on a portable emergency light on its dashboard and: gang gang gang ... nee-naw ... nee-naw ...

"Take it easy, you'll give us a heart attack!"

They got next to us, repeatedly barking through their open windows:

"Police ... pull over for inspection!"

"Yeah, sure! Wait for it!

I stopped the car, turning to look at what was taking Ivan so long. He was still trying to get the Kalashnikov out of the backpack. He was moving at a snail's pace. There were two plainclothes in the other car, one quite young and the other a bit older, with a surprisingly large head. The young cop, full of confidence, got out holding an MP5, his finger on the trigger and the barrel facing the ground.

Under my right thigh, I had a Glock 17 loaded and ready. From such a short distance it would have been easy to execute him on the spot. Looking at him, without saying a word, I let the Mazda slide down the dirt road and turned it to face the paved one. He rushed back to the unmarked cop car and, doing exactly what I had just done, they began pursuing us. We were ahead of them, but I got delayed by traffic at a crossroad and they managed to see which way we had headed, towards the old Kozani-Ioannina freeway.

The Octavia was a much faster car. Since they knew where we were heading, it was only a matter of seconds before they got right behind us. Knowing that the man next to me was holding a machine gun in his hands, we had to clear things up. Ivan had yet to release the safety! It was one of those moments where you wish you were alone in the car. Such situations aren't for everyone, and he needed some help to get over the sudden turn of events. I reached out, released the gun's safety, made an abrupt U-turn to face them and ordered him to shoot the moment they appeared. When he saw the Octavia, instead of shooting from afar to make them stop, he asked me whether he should shoot through the windscreen! For fuck's sake ...

"No, Ivan. Lean out of the window and shoot".

He did it, although a bit late, when the front of their car had almost touched our own (thankfully we didn't crash). At the sight of the Kalashnikov the two plainclothes reacted as they should, ducking down to protect themselves. The Kalashnikov was short, and it misfired upwards. I saw many bullet holes beginning from the middle of the windscreen to the top. Barring any accidents, nobody had been hurt. Emptying the magazine, Ivan got back in his seat and didn't bother to do anything else, thinking it was over.

I backed up and turned again. Then the young plainclothes opened his door and opened fire at us (thankfully with his pistol). Although no bullet hit the Mazda, I was surprised by his immediate reaction. Stepping on it, within a few minutes we got to the Kozani-Ioannina freeway. At the end of the road a young man and woman from the Motorcycle Police waited for us. Taking advantage of the road opening on the left, I pulled onto the freeway in the direction of Kozani. They didn't move a muscle. That was the right thing to do. About a mile or two further down we saw two oncoming SUVs (a police vehicle and an unmarked one), their emergency lights and sirens turned on, full of cops. They drove past us and ... they didn't see us! I swear ...

When we had gotten far away from the Kozani regional unit, an incident that had taken place during one of my transfers from the Kozani police department to Diavata Prison came to mind. The officer in charge of the prison bus had refused to take off my handcuffs, as he ought and was obliged to by law. As a result I made a two-hour trip with my hands tied behind my back inside the prison bus which was speeding like crazy, making abrupt manoeuvres, hitting the brakes etc. This decision of his was utterly thoughtless. He had no reason whatsoever to act this way. The prison bus was surrounded by SUVs of the Special Anti-Terrorist Unit and the Crime Prevention and Suppression Unit, as well as several unmarked police vehicles. There was no shortage of security. He was obviously doing it from uncontrollable personal meanness.

At the time I had threatened to go public about his reckless abuse (and to myself: If I bump into you outside, you fucker, I'll kick your arse).

"I don't care. Do what you want", he had said to me with the nerve of a fucking cop who uses his authority any way he pleases.

If he had been in that police vehicle, I don't know if I would have managed to control myself or if I'd have planted a bullet in his fascist head. But he wasn't. Such cowards, making decisions and giving orders that affect the whole force, hide in the security of their dark offices. And always someone else pays the price.

.. AND AGAIN IN LIVADEIA

It was a morning in February. Sitting behind the wheel of an Audi, and with Fotis in the passenger seat, we were driving along the Livadeia ring road in the direction of Arachova when I got wind of a grey Fiat with two passengers acting strangely. They'd overtake us, and then fall behind, following us and looking at us offhandedly. Such modern tricks didn't work with an old dog like me.

With their constant manoeuvres we were almost out of the ring road. I didn't tell Fotis about the guys circling us. I didn't want him to get scared. I had just picked him up from the place of a good friend of mine outside Thebes to get him to a village in Phocis. I didn't know anything about him, and that included how he'd react in a confrontation with the police. After all, I thought I could take care of the two rough guys on my own. They had an ace up their sleeve, however. A big, hidden roadblock by the ringroad's exit, which was constantly being notified about any suspicious vehicles moving their way. Several black-clothed goons jumped in front of us about a hundred yards before the ring road's exit, holding submachine guns. We were in for a treat.

Unfortunately for them, a Mercedes SUV was driving ahead of us. Its driver panicked upon seeing this sudden gathering of armed, State, road pirates. He suddenly hit the brakes, thinking he was their target, which allowed me to manoeuvre, overtake him from the left and keep driving at full throttle. The Fiat was exposed. Without turning on their siren, they began silently chasing. Fotis got upset.

In front of his feet, in a travel bag, I had a loaded Kalashnikov. I rolled down the power windows and said to him: "Fotis ... grab the Kalashnikov, switch the selector to the middle position and get ready to shoot when I tell you!"

He did exactly what I told him, with a slight deviation: he opened the collapsible stock of the gun. As I understood it, and as he'd say to me later, he had never used a gun against policemen before, and he had been improvising.

The ambitious plainclothes took their roles too seriously and indulged in a wild pursuit. There weren't many exits on the road ahead. There was one on our right leading to Davleia and one on our left leading to Distomo, but both had police stations. After those, there weren't any other exits. We'd have to reach Arachova, and the police department there would surely have set up its own roadblock. Given that the officers from the roadblock we had just escaped were tailing us, we had to get rid of the Fiat. I had decided to turn right and drive onto a narrow country road after a few miles that would lead us to Chaeronea, and I didn't want them to know that.

Taking everything into account, I didn't think the two officers chasing us were a real threat, but the longer they remained on our tails the more dangerous they could become. And I had no intention of getting involved in a game of cops and robbers, putting ourselves in danger by driving recklessly. Thinking that a blast would be enough to send them a message and put an end to their attempt, after a few miles, on a downhill road, I hit the brakes, and the Audi stopped dead. At the same moment, I gave Fotis the order he had been waiting for.

"Get out now and shoot!"

I meant out of the window, but he took my words literally, and acted accordingly. So he opened the door, got out of the car, took a firing position and opened fire against them. Through the mirrors I came to a second horrible realisation. The two police officers too had made the same mistake. They had stopped the Fiat fifty yards away from the Audi and as soon as they saw Yannis firing against them, opened the doors and run away! Mayhem ... they lacked both basic training and common sense.

It was the first time in all the years of fighting my pursuers that I feared there might be casualties. My only hope was in Fotis' inexperience using such a military weapon. I wished all the bullets would miss them. As soon as the magazine emptied, Fotis did exactly as every newbie does in such situations. He got in the car and sat in the passenger seat, relieved.

"Get another magazine, arm it, and be alert", I continued with the necessary commands.

He did exactly as I told him. After a while, free from any pursuers, I drove the Audi into a byway that I knew led back towards Livadeia, right at the site of the roadblock. I was under the impression that the road I was looking for,leading to Chaeronea, began from that byway. I was wrong. Reaching the end of the road, I realised my mistake. I took the risk of exiting into the ring road, hoping the roadblock would have been dismantled following the car chase. Turning right to exit onto the ring road, I saw two police vehicles and an unmarked car. They saw us too. Perhaps they had been waiting for us.

I made a U-turn and began driving the opposite way. We were trapped, and there was no way to turn the tables now. I had no other options than to follow some random dirt road and see where it led us. So I turned into the first road I saw on our right and kept driving uphill towards Chaeronea for a while. The dirt track was winding, wet, and in a terrible state. The Audi had four-wheel drive, but it wasn't built for such roads. It was struggling on the uphill, muddy, twisting dirt road and I was stepping on it so as not to get stuck in the mud. At some point the road began descending and, lo and behold, behind the hills, down below us, I saw a monastery, by which I knew the road I was looking for ran. Indeed, in a while, we found ourselves driving along a paved road. But just as we were beginning to feel positive, the gear shift stuck. I had burnt the clutch disk driving so fast on that mud path!

The road was downhill from there until Chaeronea, so I let the Audi slide until we reached the first houses of the village, and there I parked it down the first road on our left. We grabbed two bags, with all the guns I had had in the trunk, and headed to the village centre to get a new vehicle. We didn't care what, we just had to get away from there at once. At all costs. As soon as we reached the village centre, as though it had been waiting for us, we saw a Fiat with its keys still in the ignition. As though it was ours, like nothing strange was going on, we dropped the bags in the back seat, got in the car and off we went.

Fotis begged me to pass by the Audi once more, in case he had forgotten something inside. I did as he asked and when he finished searching the abandoned car's interior we continued driving to the road's end, where we would have ended up if the Audi hadn't broken down. Parked a hundred yards in front of us, right at the exit and to the right of the road, was a police vehicle. Standing next to it was a cop, wearing a bulletproof vest and holding an MP5 machine gun, waiting with his finger on the trigger for the Audi to appear so that he could empty it on the bodies of its brazen passengers. Driving by him, we gave him a wave, and he waved back!

When we'd gotten far enough, and were no longer in any danger, Fotis, thinking we had escaped, turned and said to me: "I'd heard many things about you, but I didn't believe them. You truly are a ballsy, brave dude!" In this case, I'd say we were both lucky more than anything else.

Driven by this incident and the injuring (as it happened in the end) of one of the two policemen that took part in the car chase, the authorities tried to spread hate about me, first and foremost among the police. They also seized the opportunity to better serve up my planted "mountza" to public opinion, as incriminating evidence for the bomb that went off in their hands inside the Ministry of Citizen Protection. So the ministry's leadership found a way to place a bounty of half a million euros on my head, in the middle of the economic crisis! The leaders of this land are always so generous. It's not as though they're going to have to go without them. The people are doomed to pay for their dirty business forever.

Thankfully, most people aren't like them. They know precisely what unethical apes the authorities are. They have great pride and a unique primal root of justice that scorns their gifts. They'd drink a glass of wine with me ... they only mess things up when it comes to voting. Perhaps they understand their duty to vote as an unbearable authority that doesn't suit them and that they have to get rid of. A sort of moral cleansing, a more profound inward purging. That's why they hand this burden to the worst! To keep evil away. But evil, like a kallikantzaros, will always sneak down the chimney and mess them up ...

This incident exposed the police force's nakedness. How ridiculous its experts are, scheming and forging charges against all those they have no other means to touch.

Inside an A4-sized envelope, which I never saw, never touched, and never mailed, and which exploded destroying half a floor in the Ministry of Citizen Protection, the police managed to find a whole palm print of mine!

Inside a whole Audi (A4) which I had long used to get around and which I had touched multiple times with bare hands since I took no precautionary measures — as I usually do with the cars I use for my daily transportations, something the police know — and which was abandoned in a hurry during a car chase, they only found a single fingerprint somewhere in the trunk.

You're slipping up, gentlemen! Keep up appearances! Control your venom you little darkened-background, serpent-like men ... or you'll choke on it!

A RETROSPECTIVE AND SOME HUMOROUS INCIDENTS

The nails

It was night, just before eleven. We were driving down the western side of Veria. No sooner had we turned onto the old uphill road to Kozani than we saw emergency lights and heard the siren of a police vehicle. At the same time, they were turning their headlights on and off (a signal to pull over for an inspection). Kostas drove the van in the middle of the road so that they couldn't overtake us and kept on driving up the village's road. Holding a shotgun in my hands, I moved over to the van's back door, which we'd modified so it opened from the inside too, using a rope. I lay on the floor, face down, and pulled on the rope. The door opened outward and upward revealing the police vehicle only five yards behind us. Its headlights and emergency lights blinded me; its siren was at full car-chase volume, really deafening. Right next to me, for a situation like this one, we had a big box full of steel nails, specially made for slashing tires (Kostas' idea). As I lay there I grabbed it, and emptied it right at them. Because of the van's speed, the nails spread all over the road, forming a thorny carpet for those trouble-makers to step on ... and they did. They were utterly taken aback. Seeing the van's back door suddenly open and someone throwing the unknown contents of a lug right in front of them, they were confounded. After a few swerves and a final nee-naw which echoed as they turned off their siren, they stopped in the middle of the road.

That's what they get for wanting to perform inspections whenever they feel like it ... we nailed them!

Narration of a car chase

Once at a restaurant in Amfissa, I heard some policemen describe a lengthy car chase in the country roads of Phocis which ended similarly to the one narrated above, only with Nikos and Kostas as its protagonists.

It was noon on a Sunday when I reached Amfissa Prison, on my way to visit Nikos. At the entrance, holding pans and several lunch boxes of various sizes covered with colourful checkered towels, was a crowd of women of various ages. At first, I thought they were relatives of the inmates, waiting to enter for visitation. But at that moment the prison door opened and two employees appeared.

"Hello, girls! What goodies have you brought us today?" asked one of them.

"Don't lick your lips. They're not for you," a feisty one scolded him, in a thick accent.

"Why, Mrs Lena? We have souls too!"

"You also have homes and wives to cook for you. The prisoners don't!"

"I know, Mrs Lena. But no matter how much they eat, there'll be some leftovers for us too ..."

"Enough talking. The stuffed vegetables will get cold, and you'll have to eat them like that," she answered with her unique sense of humour, uncovering the tray she was holding and handing it to him.

Talking with the employees in a similarly witty way, one by one the women politely handed their home-cooked foods to them, always mentioning what each food was and what trouble they had taken to prepare it. In the end, they warned them:

"We want our pans back spick-and-span, huh!" Then they all walked away from the prison and scattered in the streets of the city.

What I understood at that moment (something which Nikos would verify a while later when I paid him a visit) was that the women from the neighbourhood would cook and bring home-made meals for the inmates each Sunday. And they wouldn't take no for an answer. From the way they were treating the employees and how comfortable they felt around them, it seemed they thought of this as an earned right of theirs. Why has this sort of humanity been lost? Where have these kind human beings gone? Why did they run out of emotion? That's what I wonder, three decades later ...

Every day that goes by, today's humans lose a small part of themselves. The arid lives they lead, as though sleepwalking, dehydrate their souls, emptying them of feeling, crippling their souls. Their lives are now pointless, a mere end. Because they didn't resist and they let themselves be carried away by the waves of the cunning modernising current. And now they find themselves sailing swampy tides.

Nikos would be tried the following Monday at the city court for his car chase, and I thought it would be a good chance for him to pick up some blades that I'd place in the courthouse. When, after the end of the trial, I saw him getting on the prison bus to be transferred back to the prison, I went back in to check if he'd gotten them. He hadn't managed to. I picked them up, and since it was way past three o'clock in the afternoon and I was starving, I went to a restaurant to grab a bite.

As soon as I ordered two men, around thirty years old, came and sat at the table next to mine. With them were two women, a bit younger than them. To my great surprise, the moment they started talking I realised that next to me were sitting the officers who had been in one of the two police vehicles involved in Nikos' car chase. They had been witnesses for the prosecution in the trial, and after it ended they did as I had done — come to the restaurant to eat. I almost choked three times that afternoon trying to stop myself from laughing at what I heard them saying. The two officers, seeing the young women were quite interested in the car chase, and trying to impress them, did their best to embellish the story, making themselves sound like heroes.

"We located them after receiving information from headquarters, we signalled them to stop for inspection, but they didn't comply. They tried to flee! At once, without hesitating, we began pursuing them, with our colleagues in the other crew following and ..."

The women would often interrupt them, quite anxious to learn the outcome of the car chase: "And? Did you catch them?"

They didn't answer them, because the essence was in the car chase itself. They kept on bombarding their companions with the accomplishments of men who are fit and able to only serve one force. And so they continued.

"We were pursuing them, but they were driving fast. So we wouldn't catch them. They turned left at a crossroad, and we pulled the handbrake, trying not to lose them ... we entered at full speed ... thank god we didn't die!"

Womankind, always impatient, was anxious for the finale, forcing the two heroes, after a final attempt to narrate in detail the car chase through dirt roads in Phocis, their fingers always on the trigger, to conclude their story.

"At a turn of the dirt road, they threw nails at us and slashed our tires!"

The young women broke out in laughter! Shit ... disaster! Yet the guys didn't give up. They wouldn't let criminals who take flight to avoid being inspected by officers of the law steal the girls' hearts!

"Arseholes, that's what they are ... they should have robbed a bank and then fled the country. Now they'll never get out of prison".

Greek policemen have an opinion about everything, solutions to any problem, and above all else know the course and the end of everyone's life.

Rita

It was just before midnight when I walked into a country dive bar near the centre of Alexandreia, Greece. The room had the shape of a crescent moon. Sofas with pillows and armchairs lay around the bar, which was in the middle of the dimly lit space. I went straight to it where two young women were preparing the orders of its few customers.

"What will you have?" one of them asked me, smiling.

"Nothing. I came to see Rita".

"Where is Rita?" she asked a different woman sitting on one of the stools nearby.

She silently looked around the bar and got down from the stool. She walked to the back where a group of youngsters were sitting on a sofa, drinking their cocktails. Among them were two young women. She wasn't alone when she came back.

"Hello!"

"Hi. Are you Rita?"

"Yes!"

"I'm Nikos' brother".

"Yes!"

"Do you know he's in prison?"

"Yes!"

"I came to grab his stuff".

"How do I know you're telling the truth?"

"That's easy".

I took my ID out of my wallet (yes, at some point, I abided by the law) and gave it to her.

"You can also ask me whatever else you want", I said to her.

She took the ID, looked at it for a second, and then handed it back to me saying: "What I do with Nikos is our business. When he gets out, I'll talk to him directly!"

"I think you don't understand. Nikos wants his stuff now, not when he gets released".

"I don't want to discuss this. Now go, or I'll call the police!" She turned her back and walked away to join her friends.

I saw red! She truly enraged me.

"Can you please tell me when the bar closes?" I asked one of the women at the bar.

"It depends on how many customers we have. I'd say about half-past three or four".

I got out and walked towards the end of the road, where Kostas was waiting for me in an Opel Ascona.

"What happened?" he asked me.

"She's a real bitch, that's what happened".

"Why?"

"She told me to leave or she'd call the police!"

"That fucking bitch! What are we going to do?"

"Let's drive somewhere outside of town to wait, and we can come back after three when she gets off. If we can, we'll grab her and get her in the car.

At three, we had parked the Opel at an ideal spot from where we could see the bar's entrance. Just after four, Rita exited along with two burly guys and they all got in a black BMW. The two barflies sat in the front seats, and Rita sat behind the driver. We followed them. They exited the city heading towards the freeway. They seemed to be heading to Thessaloniki.

"We have to overtake them before they enter the freeway".

"I know a spot a bit further down. I'll corner them there".

A mile later, Kostas attacked. It all began as a simple overtaking, escalated into a rough cornering at gunpoint and ended up with them abruptly pulling over. The bulky barflies were stupefied. As our attack was unravelling, I had the passenger window rolled down and was pointing at them with the sawed-off repeating shotgun. Rita, recognising me, calmed them down. I heard her reassuring them that she could take care of this without their help. She opened the BMW's rear door and got out alone. I got out too, opened the Opel's right rear door, she got in and sat in the back seat. Before I got back in, I threatened the two guys.

"Don't even think of calling the police, or this won't be the last you see of us!"

Rita was now all sweet and cooperative. We set an appointment for the very next day somewhere in Thessaloniki. We dropped her off near Alexandreia, saying to her:

"If your friends called the police and they interrogate you, you'll tell them it was some customers you had a misunderstanding with but who you'd never seen before".

We headed to Veria. We switched the car's license plates on the way, and by the tracks, we came across a deadly roadblock. Surprisingly, they didn't ask us to pull over, although we were the only vehicle on the road at that time.

The following day, taking all precautions, I met with Rita. She gave me a small bag; I took it and was ready to leave. Rita had other plans. She took my hand and began walking with me! After apologising for her behaviour, she told me she wanted to see me again, to get to know me better. She had already seen me at my best, there was only worse from there.

Arrest and escape

It was past midnight and we were driving along a small road, ready to enter a small town in West Macedonia. We parked across the street from the first construction site we came across and turned off our headlights. I got out, crossed the road, turned on my flashlight, and began searching the three floors of the unfinished building for any crowbars and, if I was lucky, some metal-cutting scissors. We needed them to break into a local gun shop, which we had located long before and for which we had travelled all this way. I didn't manage to find what I was looking for. I got back down, and was ready to cross the street when the headlights of a vehicle coming from the centre of the town, about twenty yards to my right, illuminated me. I stayed put, waiting for the car to leave so that I could do my job ... as if. The car was a police Land Rover. They turned on their emergency lights and stopped right in front of me. There were three policemen inside. The driver remained at his seat, while the officer sitting next to him and the one sitting in the back got out, the latter standing right in front of me.

"What are you doing here?" he asked me sternly and snobbishly, as the other officer walked around the SUV to assist him.

"I came to get some air ... is that so bad?"

"What's your name, and where do you live?"

"Will it do you any good to know?"

"Speak! Who are you? Do you have an ID?

I gave them a name and an address just to stall them and buy Kostas some time to come and blindside them, since none of them were keeping an eye out for such a possibility — they were all focused on me. I was a law-abiding citizen back then, I didn't carry a gun. Abiding by the law was not the reason I wasn't armed, admittedly; I just didn't have any easy-to-conceal firearms, and at the time I thought it would be a bit much to take a sawed-off shotgun with me just to find a crowbar at a construction site. Yet here we were, life already training me, testing my resilience. Already from back then, she'd given me a good-luck charm against its unexpected situations and its coincidences.

While they were still asking me questions and I was still answering them, I peeked across the street, at the parked Opel, to see Kostas. But I couldn't see anyone inside the car. The blokes, when I told them I didn't have ID with me, asked me to get into their Land Rover and go to the police station with them for identification. I overreacted and at once, they grabbed me by both hands to force me inside the car.

"Come on, you guys ... there's no reason to be violent! If you want us to go to the station, we'll go to the station", I said to them, trying to sound convincing, while I offered to get into the SUV by myself since its rear door was already open.

That's when they eased their grips, releasing my arms. I suddenly jumped between them and got away ... I kept on running for about ten or twenty yards along the road, in the direction of the town's exit, and jumped down the dark, downhill, left side of the road. Turning my flashlight on and off, I continued running along the road, until I put the town's last houses behind me. Nobody followed me. The police vehicle slowly drove towards the end of the town ... I could see the blue emergency lights on its top and the bright beams of the cops' flashlights sweeping both sides of the road, which from that point on were forested. They reached a spot and then turned back, doing the same over again, until they'd vanished towards the town. I was sure they wouldn't even report the incident to headquarters. I climbed the hill again and got back on the road just as Kostas was exiting the town with the Opel. I repeatedly signalled him with the flashlight.

At last, he saw me, and he stopped, seeming surprised. When I reached him and got in the car, he asked me obviously puzzled:

"Didn't they take you to the station?"

"Didn't you see what happened?" I asked him in return, even more puzzled.

"No. I ducked down so that they wouldn't see me!"

"I was waiting for you to come and sneak up behind them ..."

"I thought about that, but then I thought it would be better if they took you to the station for identification. You're law-abiding, they didn't have anything against you, they'd let you walk".

His response sounded logical and convincing, but I didn't like it at all. Sure, they'd have let me walk if they didn't have any unsolved cases in their town or the surrounding area in the last month to pin on me. With a brother in prison for burglaries and not having a convincing answer for being in their town though I was the perfect victim to pin anything they wanted, from petty crimes to who knows what else.

In the short time I had cooperated with Kostas at that point, I'd never thought of utilising my law-abiding status. Neither would I have done then, if I had been in his place and he in mine. I'd have grabbed the shotgun, I'd have gotten out of the car, and I'd have held them at gunpoint. It wasn't as though they were from the Special Anti-Terrorist Unit, they were just three little men pretending to be policemen. But back then, I was only at the start. Those were my very first steps in illegality.

I could sense the qualitative difference of our approach, but I couldn't possibly grasp its details. When you can't locate the roads that lead you to a result, you doubt the result itself. So, I too had my doubts about whether what I felt about my partner was right or not.

Laughing stock

We drove past the first houses of a village in Karditsa and parked the car about a hundred yards away from the one which Kostas would visit. We had only recently escaped, and we didn't have any guns. Kostas knew someone in that particular village who had held on to some Steyr Mannlicher-type submachine guns from the days of the Resistance. He kept them in perfect shape. From him, we'd gotten the one I'd used during the assault at Larissa Prison, and it had been as good as new.

It was early September, past midnight. Kostas was ready to get out of the car when we realised an SUV had parked right behind us, with its headlights turned on. It remained there behind us for more than a minute, without turning off its engine and headlights,nobody getting in or out. Just to be sure, we decided to go for a drive, checking whether this was something random or something more serious. We pulled out and drove straight ahead. The SUV began following us. About a hundred yards ahead, the road took a right where the residential area ended, giving over to the sown valley and its various dirt roads. One of these began right at the turn ahead of us and stretched into the verdant valley and, just to be sure, we drove onto this dirt path and trundled down it at a low speed. Once again the SUV drove onto the dirt road too, following fifty yards behind us.

For fuck's sake.

We now had no doubt that the SUV was an unmarked police vehicle. What we couldn't possibly know was how many cops were inside it, and whether they knew who they were dealing with or if they'd just found our behaviour suspicious. From the moment this realisation struck us, I found myself holding a seven-round pump shotgun filled with six-bullet cartridges, ready for a confrontation. For the time being, still not being one hundred percent certain about the identity of our "followers", I decided not to start a war, because on the dirt road we had just gained a useful advantage — the good earth itself! The road was in decent shape, allowing Kostas to speed up. The surface was comprised solely of red clay, ground like flour from the summer drought. The thick dust cloud we were leaving behind us soon swallowed the SUV. At night-time, with their headlights turned on and a wall of red dust in front of them, they couldn't possibly drive, let alone pursue us. They'd have to keep their distance.

We drove for a mile or so like this when we noticed the headlights of a vehicle, about two hundred yards to our right, moving in parallel with us. We thought they had called for backup and it had finally arrived. For a few minutes, we continued our parallel courses until we came across a crossroad and turned left. Soon we saw in the distance the headlights of an oncoming vehicle, approaching fast. We made a U-turn, stepped on it and after a while, turning off our headlights, snuck into the first narrow road we came across, which led to a cotton field. The vehicle drove past us without slowing down. Hah, we'd fooled them!

After a while, we bumped into another set of headlights. This time they weren't moving. Because this four-hour nightly car chase, with all its funny incidents (to write about all of them I'd need several pages) ended up being a real fiasco, I won't continue describing it, but I'll flash forward to its end, where the essence lies. Exhausted from the nightlong, real-life Pacman game in the maze-like dirt road system of the Thessalian Plain, and running short on fuel, we finally decided to risk exiting to a paved road. Despite our frequent changes in direction, in the darkness and in an unknown flat land, we hadn't lost our sense of direction. It was about half-past five to six in the morning as the day began to dawn. With our headlights turned off, we chose a bridge as an escape point, and drove towards it. It was well lit, so we could observe it from afar, and for ten whole minutes, any suspicious movement.

To our surprise, it proved to be a much quieter place than the fields. We didn't turn on the car's headlights until we were driving along the paved road, two hundred yards away from the bridge. We crossed it fast and on the alert, without any problems.

After a while, we came across a petrol station which had just opened, parked next to the pumps, and I got out to open the gas cap, lest the employee realise I didn't have the keys for it.

When I saw the car's exterior, I freaked out! Not only couldn't I see its colour; I couldn't see it, period. The whole car was buried under a thick coat of dirt; in fact, the only thing testifying that this was a car was its shape. It was then that I realised I was covered in the same dirt too, since we'd had the front windows open throughout the night. How would I explain myself to the slow-moving villager working at the petrol station, who was now coming my way to fill my tank? Well, I was always prepared. If he asked, I'd tell him we were participating in off-road racing and we'd just finished from a nightlong practice. The calm villager seemed cheerful; he didn't even comment on the pile of dirt that had arrived at his petrol station.

"Morning, guys! How did the watering go?" he asked.

"Good morning to you too ... fine, fine!" I answered him without having really understood what he'd asked me.

"It didn't rain at all this year ... hard times for raising cotton. Are you watering many acres?" he continued.

"About fifty!" I answered him, still not having completely understood what we were talking about ... but the direction our conversation was taking suited me well.

A four-wheeled farm-track arrived at the petrol station. It was too covered in dirt, and its gigantic owner even more so. The employee asked him the exact same question, the only difference being that he knew him.

"How did it go, Michael?

"Same as every day! I've been out since one in the morning. I've driven through the whole valley", the giant replied groggily.

The pure villagers' conversation awoke my memories. When I was younger I had worked many times in cotton harvesting, and I remembered that cotton, which is the most cultivated product in the area, is watered after midnight during the dry months of summer. And given that back then there were no automatic watering systems, people had to do it all themselves.

I really started to doubt whether there had ever been a real car chase, or if it all had been a trick of our imagination.

We drove away from the petrol station, discussing the previous night's events, which now began making more sense. After coming across a police vehicle that didn't pay us any attention whatsoever, and given that all roads were empty and quiet, we concluded the following.

The SUV that became the reason for this one-sided car chase must have belonged to some villager who was heading to his fields. For some reason, it had parked behind us, and coincidentally started moving again the same time we did, following us towards the fields for some night-time watering. We, being fugitives and having gotten to that village with the sole purpose of acquiring some guns from that neighbourhood, naturally thought the SUV was an unmarked police vehicle because of its strange behaviour. When it began following us in the middle of the night, this suspicion grew into a certainty. Being in the dark about the villagers' night work, we thought all the lights we saw in the valley belonged to police vehicles, and we acted accordingly. Although we knew we couldn't have reacted any other way in this one-of-a-kind car chase, and although it ended well, we couldn't believe how easily we'd fallen for that. We felt like the laughing stock of the entire cotton valley!

Throughout my active struggle, experiencing countless similar adventures, I thought and felt they were unnecessary and, to an extent, unwelcome. Now, being a detached observer and free from any emotions, I firmly believe they were the best obstacle courses life could have laid in our paths without notice, as a sort of sudden tough training. Each time, each course was different, but they all had the same goal: victory.

Many victories in life's unwelcome obstacle courses operated cumulatively throughout the years as a real education of experience and knowledge, which in hard times that call for something more than a man of struggle, proved quite precious. Going over this unique, four-hour, night-time car chase, without an enemy and an object, and trying to decipher what practical knowledge it has granted me and how I have benefited from it, I'll say this: the decision not to use a gun in such a critical moment, when our certainty of the SUV's passengers' identities would have allowed it, is a life lesson itself. Especially for a man who has chosen, because of circumstance, to live armed, but to not let guns guide him. Also: it is impossible to evaluate the benefits of another lengthy, extreme awakening of those senses which are tasked with securing human survival.

It is hard to assess their contribution to the enrichment and quality of emotions that, in the long run, might change them as human beings. The help and the boost they give them to perceive and feel freedom more deeply as an individual right, but most importantly as a precious duty, are priceless. Because in such cases, the value of a fugitive's freedom is confirmed by their pursuers. The pursuers who are willing to sacrifice and be sacrificed … it would be hubris for him not to do the same.

Stop … Go

It was the end of fall. At half-past four in the morning, we parked the vehicle at a semi-main road in Ioannina. Wearing full-face hoods and holding shotguns (I also had a big metal cutter, and Kostas a crowbar), we got out of the car and stood outside the gun shop we'd had our sights fixed on.

It was freezing. The straight wide road was completely empty. I began cutting the four padlocks that secured the rolling shutter. When I'd finished, Kostas and I pushed it all the way up and Kostas, using his crowbar, shattered the storefront. I walked inside and cut the padlock of the gun locker. I pulled the long rebar locking the guns, and at once we began grabbing shotguns and throwing them in the back of the car.

That's when a motorcycle with two passengers appeared at the end of the street. We were outside the gun shop, standing on its front steps. The motorcycle's pillion rider saw us as they passed. We heard him shouting at the driver three times: "Stop … stop … stop!"

The bike was driving at full speed, and its driver perhaps had more pleasant things on his mind at the time, so it took him a while to react. After about two hundred yards however they turned and now they were coming in a hurry to meet death.

"Leave it to me. You finish what we started", I said to Kostas, so he kept on working.

I was holding a black sawed-off shotgun in my right hand, pointing at the ground. The two rebel riders and aspiring heroes were coming from the left; they didn't see it from afar. The moment they got in front of me and were ready to get off the bike however, I brought it to the front … crack-crack … I pointed it at them, aiming at their heads.

"Are you looking for someone, lads?"

Instead of an answer, I heard the pillion rider scream in a panic:

"Go … go … goooo!"

They stepped on it, never to be seen again. We burst out laughing.

***

Meeting migrants

Every moment for a fugitive is a moment of action. Although the following short narrations aren't strictly action-themed, they enclose the slightest signs of humanity on behalf of fugitives towards their fellow people ... and they're not humorous at all. They're just some of the many short stories we picked up during the flow of immigrants from Albania that happened to coincide with our own struggle, which took place in the countryside.*

Travellers in the dark

It was nighttime, and Nikos and I were driving down the Grevena-Kalabaka freeway when we both felt the need to use the bathroom. It was our chance to stretch our legs for a while, so we turned the car left onto a small dead-end dirt road, at the end of which was a small clearing surrounded by young oak trees, growing back after being cut by loggers. We turned off our headlights and, each holding a Kalashnikov (we never parted with them, not even when taking a leak), we walked in different directions.

We were in the middle of relieving ourselves when from the side of the forest we heard the noises of twigs breaking. For someone who isn't familiar with the nightly sounds of the forest, a hedgehog walking on the foliage would seem like a bear attack, but what we heard didn't sound like a bear attack but an elephant stampede! We stopped our business and switched on our flashlights, turning them in the direction of the noises. We couldn't see anything. The noises suddenly stopped.

After a few seconds, we heard a voice.

"Hey! We're Albanians!"

"Hey! We're Greeks!"

After a few more broken twigs, a worn-out face appeared in front of us. Behind it, another appeared, and another, and then three more. They were all young men ranging from twenty to thirty years of age. They were wearing dirty, worn clothes and carrying makeshift sacks on their backs. They seemed like tortured elves. They hesitantly crossed the clearing, reached our car, and formed a line across us, quite uneasy. As long as we were pointing at them with the flashlights, they couldn't see we were also holding guns. Nikos, as always, took it upon himself to try and communicate with them, but to no end. They knew and understood only a few Greek words. Communication goes through the stomach, I thought, so I walked to the back of the car, opened the trunk and brought out a large crate full of food. I put it on the hood of the vehicle.

---

*   With the collapse of the Soviet Union Albania followed suit in rejecting the Communists in 1991. The election of a conservative Democratic Party and introduction of gangster capitalism caused economic chaos however, leading to the 1997 civil war. This in turn sent a sustained wave of migration into Greece — around 500,000 ethnic Albanians have permanent residency there as of 2021.

"Go for it, lads!"

"They did. And they didn't leave anything, except for the crate. I turned on the car's headlights so that they wouldn't feel uncomfortable with us pointing the flashlights at them and so that we could see them better.

Only then did one of them notice that their benefactors were armed. They began talking to each other, quietly and sharply. They were terrified. They couldn't understand who they were dealing with and what our intentions were, and we couldn't explain it to them. This incident took place before the Albanian Rebellion. Kalashnikovs were still hard to find in Greece, and the illegal night-travellers had every reason to worry. On our part, aside from providing them with food and water, we had no better way to ease their fear, since we couldn't verbally communicate. What could we tell them? That we were the Palaiokostas brothers? They wouldn't understand. As soon as there was no food left, they wanted to go.

"We go ... we go ..." they repeated many times, as though they couldn't even believe it themselves.

"Yes, ok. You go. You go ... everything's fine!"

They began falling back, without turning their backs on us, not for a second. When their backs touched the oak trees, they panicked. They suddenly ran into the forest, in different directions, making a lot of noise, sure we'd open fire against them. They did exactly what any rational being would have done, to protect themselves from an irrational human world that opens fire against any sort of unprotected life. We waited there, puzzled, for a few moments, listening to the noisy paths each of them had taken. After a while, there was complete silence. Afterwards, we heard some whistling and signal cries. The group was gathering its pieces that had scattered in the dark forest.

Shame is a sudden emotion that awakens the morality of a human who has unfortunately lost it. Because the times do not allow for morality and emotions. It's a waste of money and rudeness. Two of the most useful tools for the establishment of modern sub-humanity. I knew how these kids felt; I too had walked the path of fleeing, I'd gone down that road myself. Being a teenager, along with my pals, we'd followed the Sirens' songs, calling us to an endless feast of joy and plenty. We'd woken up with our hands on our hard dicks inside a cinema in the centre of Athens screening some pussy on repeat; a cinema we'd just been using as a cheap hotel, to trick our lethargy for another night.

Blizzard

We had been driving along the Ioannina-Trikala freeway when, high on Metsovo, it started snowing, and we saw a line of parked vehicles by the side of the road. Their owners were putting chains on their tires as instructed by some officers who, as a precaution, wouldn't allow anyone to drive past them without snow chains. We pulled over and installed chains on the SUV's back wheels to keep moving. After the Katara plateau, as we were driving down the road towards Kalabaka, we came across a blizzard accompanied by a strong chilly wind. The car's thermometer showed an outside temperature of minus five Celsius. It would be a miracle if we made it to Kalabaka.

At a wide left turn on the road, against the tail lights of the truck in front of us, we saw two people crossing, walking with great difficulty against the wind.

"Stop, Nikos. They'll die if we leave them. Nobody is going to pick them up".

Nikos, being even more sensitive than I was, turned on the hazard lights, and pulled over. We'd already driven past them. I got out of the car and signalled them to come close. They were looking at me suspiciously as the snow was pummelling them from every direction. I started to get angry.

"Stop staring and come inside!" I yelled at them.

They slowly approached and got in the back seats. They were eighteen to twenty years old, yet they looked like they were fifty. That's how exhausted they were. The shock of the transition from the minus five degrees outside, to the thirty degrees inside the car, made them fall asleep at once. They smelled of melted flesh. Thankfully for them the ride lasted for one-and-a-half hours because of the heavy snowfall. Reaching Kalabaka, we tried hard to wake them. When we finally succeeded, we got ourselves in real trouble! They wouldn't get out of the car. They tried to give us money, urging us to take them to Athens. They thought we were traffickers.

"Come on, come on, out!" I ordered them.

I had a backpack full of food, and I gave it to them. They took it, yet they still refused to move. Outside, the temperature was below zero ... I opened the trunk and gave them two special sleeping bags for alpinists (we'd later shed many tears for those). They stared at them, looking bereft ... in the end, they took them and got out.

German Gifts

It was the beginning of summer, early in the morning. We were outside the parking lot of a hotel in Kalabaka, and we were trying to steal a light blue Audi with German license plates. In the end, we did it. We ditched the old one just outside town and headed to Grevena. Partway there, we drove off the road to check out the interior of our new acquisition.

In a German-style organised trunk, aside from everything else, we located two cases with forty Swatch watches, a purse with seven hundred Deutsche Marks in small bills, and three large suitcases with men's clothes. What should we do with all this?

"Let's give them to a poor migrant", said Nikos. We were moving on byroads that ran through villages when we located a group, heading to Kalabaka. There were about fifteen of them, all male of various ages. We parked and offered them our "confiscated" merchandise, but they were suspicious of our motives, and ran downhill into a barley field. We got out of the car and called them to come over, but they all stood in the middle of the field, looking at us suspiciously, without talking.

To gain their trust, we took out the suitcases, the watches, the money and the food. We left everything by the side of the road, got back inside the car and drove about two hundred yards away, up the road. The most daring youngster among them approached the things we'd left, took the cases with the watches and the purse with the money, yelled something to the rest and went back into the barley. Yet he didn't go near them; instead walking in the opposite direction. As he was the one who had dared do it, he thought he deserved the lion's share. Half his companions began chasing after him, stepping on the four-foot-tall barley, while the rest ran towards the suitcases, just in case they too contained watches and money. It was a hilarious sight and at the same time tragic too ... I wouldn't blame the field's owner if he got a bit racist after this. They really destroyed his field, not a single cob remained standing! Yet it was us and our gifts that were truly responsible.

Reward

When law-abiding citizens (many times with support by the police) profited by ruthlessly taking advantage of the needs of migrants, we tried to help them any way we could, despite our situation, and they repaid us in a moment we really needed it.

One afternoon, we parked our car under a huge, old sycamore to get a nap. We pushed back our seats and woke after about an hour. Without getting out of the vehicle, we set off to finish our trip. After the first few yards, we heard a loud noise; we felt a sudden jerk, and the car stopped. We got out and saw that the two front wheels were aloft, inside a three-foot-tall and four-foot-wide ditch! We'd seen it before falling asleep, and we had taken for granted we'd remember it when we woke up, something that apparently hadn't happened.

The way the car had fallen, given it was front-wheel drive, we couldn't possibly get it out without help. And we were in the middle of nowhere.

Just as we were about to give up, ready to abandon the car, a group of Albanian immigrants appeared. There were about ten of them, all men, all over forty. After hesitating for a moment, they came near us. They spoke Greek.

"Could you lads help us get it out?" we asked them.

"We can! Why not?"

They spoke to one another in Albanian, they coordinated, grabbed the car, raised the whole thing in the air and moved it to the opposite side! Real hulks ... they accepted the food and the water we offered them, but they were insulted when we offered to give them money for their help.

Proud people.

***

Commandeering a car

It was early summer, half-past six in the morning, and we were driving along the Trikala-Larissa road in the direction of Larissa at ninety miles per hour when suddenly, our white Opel's electrical system failed. Impetus kept the car moving until we fetched up outside a carpentry shop, the owner of which had just parked his car and was ready to enter. We had some basic knowledge about cars' engines but nothing about their electrical systems. After a quick check of the battery, the wires, the fuses etc. we entered the carpentry shop. We had no other option. We had to commandeer the owner's car instead. When I walked into his office, I found him sitting in his rotating chair. I got my CZ out of my belt but didn't point it at him.

"We want your car", I said to him, grabbing the keys that were on the table.

He tried to tell me something, but seeing Nik behind me holding a .357 Magnum, he just stared at us. Being more social and humorous, and knowing that his Magnum was empty, Nikos stayed behind to keep the guy company as I went and started moving our things to our new commandeered vehicle. By coincidence, in the trunk, inside two sacks, we were transporting a large number of guns, aside from our own.

After five minutes, I re-entered the office to discover that the atmosphere had radically changed. Laughs ... jokes ... everything was fine! Nikos had taken control of the situation. He had even placed the empty 357 back on his belt. Leaving, we asked the carpenter to postpone the call to the police for as long as he could, because if we came across a roadblock, there would be a car chase and exchange of fire, and his car would be the first harmed.

"No, my friends, don't worry! How much time do you need to get where you want to go?"

"One ... two hours tops".

"Fine, fine... but like we said, you'll give it back to me tomorrow?"

"You have our word!"

He explained to us the car's basics, begged us to take care of it, wished us good luck, and off we went.

The following night, just as we had promised, Nikos called him so that we could return his car.

"Your car is in the parking lot of the medical centre at Sofades, and the key is in the exhaust pipe ... hurry, or someone might steal it!"

"Thank you, guys, thank you very much! The police had only nice things to say about you, they know you well. You should stop what you're doing, you're nice lads ..."

"Don't worry. This was our last wrongdoing. We'll join a monastery now!"

The barefoot fugitive

I don't remember exactly where the following short story took place (the area was unfamiliar to me at the time). Still, it was near the sea somewhere between Thessaloniki and Kavala.

We had approached a secluded beach we'd seen the previous night, to get some rest and have a swim. I remember we had a watermelon with us, so we made a makeshift port out of stones near the sea, to stop the current from drawing it in, and left it there the whole night so that the sea would cool it and we could eat it the following day.

When we woke up, we saw the watermelon had set sail, floating far away in the sea. Even though we weren't great swimmers, we managed to apprehend it and return it to its place — but it was a waste of time. The salt and the multiple swells of the sea had softened it like a sponge. If you're from a mountain ...

We didn't let that ruin our mood. We enjoyed ourselves swimming until late in the afternoon, took an afternoon nap in our dropped-back seats and, after we'd woken up, decided to leave. We didn't bother getting out of the car, we just closed the doors and set off. That's when I made a mistake, as I would realise after it was already too late ...

We chose to drive along a byway, heading to West Macedonia. It was scorching hot. Having all our windows open so that the summer breeze could sweep in, we were enjoying our trip when in the middle of a stretch of the road, in a secluded spot with no human in sight, we saw a police roadblock. I instinctively turned to grab my shotgun but bending over, I realised I was barefoot. That's when I remembered that, leaving the beach, my shoes were on the car's hood! Shit! For fuck's sake!

"Nikos ... I don't have shoes, so be careful. I'm counting on your driving skills, or I'll have to kill one of them to take theirs".

"Relax, they won't pull us over", he said to me, sure and calm as a Buddhist monk.

The road continued downhill for a quarter of a mile, and then it climbed up a hill to vanish behind them. There was no other vehicle on it at the time. The roadblock was right in the middle of the visible part of the road, next to a dilapidated lonely building.

It didn't seem that big of a deal ... an SUV with three policemen from some local police station.

As we got about a hundred and fifty yards away from them, one of them slowly walked to the rim of the road and lazily raised his hand, as though he was greeting us. Without slowing down, we drove past him, and reciprocated his gesture. He stayed there for a while, staring at the car driving away, and then walked over to the other two and held a short meeting to decide how they should react. We had reached the end of the stretch of the road when we saw them clambering into their SUV to chase us. They surely weren't in a hurry.

Driving down the hill, the road started to become winding, so we did what we do. We drove left, off our path. Then at the first small town we came across, Nikos entered the first shoe-shop on our way, and bought the first pair of sneakers he saw. And so I stopped being the first barefoot fugitive the Hellenic Police has ever pursued.

You can't even relax for a moment.

Mercedes 300

That night we were out in search of a car in the streets of Trikala. It was still quite early when we located a Mercedes 300 sports-coupe in a narrow road outside a hovel, with its headlights on and its engine running. It was a rare piece, too good to be true. I suggested that Stelios, who was driving, roll around the block and drop me off at the corner of the street, fifty yards away from where our potential victim was parked. He was to keep an eye on me at all times and if he saw me take it, follow behind me. If anything unexpected took place, he'd come by so that I could get back in the car.

I grabbed my backpack and strolled down the sidewalk until I reached the Mercedes. I looked around; there was complete silence. I opened the door, threw my backpack in the passenger seat and got in the driver seat. That was when the first surprise came up — the car had an automatic transmission; I'd never driven one before. I thought it would be too risky to try and learn then and there, so I didn't stay more than ten seconds in the car. I grabbed my backpack and opened the door to get out. At the same moment, the hovel's door opened, five yards away , and a man appeared holding the hand of a five-year-old girl.

He saw me getting out of his car. I grabbed my gun, making sure he saw it and kept walking back down the sidewalk to reach Stelios, who was still watching and waiting for me. I had gotten two yards away from the man when he left the girl and attacked me from behind. I caught wind of his movement in time and shot once onto the sidewalk to make him stop, but he was already too close and running too fast. He fell on me, and I found myself kneeling on the sidewalk with him on me.

I was enraged! I pressed the Glock against his stomach and pulled the trigger. It didn't fire, because I had pressed it so forcibly that it had accidentally locked. That moment, however, I thought it had merely misfired, and I couldn't possibly reload it during a fight. That, plus the fact that the little girl was screaming the whole time her hero father was fighting with me, enraged me even more. I grabbed him and turned him, pressing his back to the ground. He realised I was strong. He couldn't take me on.

He got up, but instead of going back to his child, the fucker ran and hid behind a car across the street. I reloaded my gun, walked to his hiding spot and pointed the gun at him. I wanted to shoot him right in the head really badly … but the abandoned girl's cries and Stelios, who arrived next to me, screaming for me to get in the car and go, saved him.

I experienced Greeks' deification of a piece of metal first hand when I was in Germany, a real obsession. They were working from morning till night so that they could drive to their villages in summer with a fancy car. And this guy had exposed his daughter and his sorry arse to danger just to protect his fancy piece of metal, which in reality wasn't at risk; he had clearly seen I had abandoned it.

Stupid people are unpredictable. If they took care of themselves as much as they take care of their cars, at least they'd be of the same value.

Accident

I was still for a while. Holding tight to the Renault's wheel, I was trying to figure out if I had been hurt. My legs and my hands were all right, but my shoulders and my back were aching. And my mother had warned me … always fasten your seatbelt. I searched my belt; the Glock wasn't in its place. I looked at the passenger seat, the Kalashnikov was missing too. I searched in the back seats, and the only thing I found was my small backpack. I grabbed it and tried to open the door. It was stuck.

"Are you all right?" I heard a voice from outside!

I turned my head a bit left and saw two men about thirty years old, looking at me.

"I think so … but I'm having trouble getting out. If you can …"

One of them was about two hundred and fifty pounds. He grabbed the door and opened it.

I got out, anxiously scanning the surrounding area for one of my guns.

"We were behind you … we saw the accident and stopped to help … we called the police, and they're on their way … do you need anything else?"

While they were talking, I had located the Kalashnikov on the sandy soil, and I was already holding it. I armed it to see if it was still working, and at once, I answered their questions.

"From you, no. You can wait for the police to tell them what you saw."

I walked towards the road, where they had left a BMW with its engine running. I threw the Kalashnikov and my backpack in the passenger seat, and I grabbed the wheel. My two surprised benefactors hesitantly approached the window and made an attempt to change my mind.

"Come on, pal. Are you taking our car? Why?"

"You shouldn't have called the police, guys … don't worry, you'll have it back by the end of the day".

First gear, second gear, and off I went. I hadn't driven but a few miles when my right hand became paralysed. I kept on driving using my left hand, from Chalcedon to Grevena.

At court, the two robbed men lied that they had had five million drachmas in the car and that I had fired several shots before taking it. The presiding judge understood they were lying and scolded them.

"Have you any idea what you're saying? With your testimony, the defendant might be convicted for attempted murders. The police didn't find any bullet casings at the scene. Mr Palaiokostas, did you fire any shots during the incident?"

"The only thing I did, your honour, was test the bolt to see if the gun was still working. Nothing else".

"Here, dear witnesses, you're saying that you had five million drachmas inside the car. Where exactly was the money?"

"In a purse, under the driver seat!"

"Did you find that money, Mr Palaiokostas?"

"I took their car with the sole purpose of escaping. I had no other option, they had called the police. When I abandoned it, I had no reason to search under the seats".

"And where did that money go?"

"If it ever existed, perhaps someone stole it after I abandoned the car!"

Shooting range

It was an afternoon in the middle of summer, forty degrees Celsius. It was a scorching hot day and there I was, driving through the Thessalian Plain. It couldn't get any worse! I had been driving for three hours now, and it'd take me another three to reach my destination. I decided to make a stop so that both the car and I could get some rest, so I bought a cup of instant coffee and a bottle of cold water from a kiosk in Palamas, and after driving two or three more miles in the direction of Farkadona, I stopped off at a dead-end clearing, where some acacias cast their shade.

Turning off the car's engine, I began preparing my coffee. In the meantime, I saw that a bit further away, at an old, small quarry, at the base of a stony hill, there were some targets. But they didn't seem to be used. After all, who would be crazy enough to come out at this hour for shooting practice? And yet, you shouldn't take logic for granted, especially when it comes to Greek police officers. I've said it before, nothing stops them! They're all-weather, and they'd prove it right then and there. A brand new, well-polished Primera police vehicle appeared on the paved road. It slowed down, and slowly entered the gravel road. At the clearing, the gravel road split into a circle and then continued; the ring was covered with tall, dry grass. I was at the end of the circle.

Seeing the police vehicle driving down the gravel road, I grabbed my coffee (not having managed to take a single sip) and sat in the driver seat. At once, I started the engine and armed my Kalashnikov. Reaching the beginning of the circle, the police vehicle stopped for a moment, as I had parked my car in such a way that, no matter which way they entered the clearing, I could leave the other way. After hesitating for a moment, they decided to come in from my left. I began driving on the right side of the circle. They backed up and hurried to welcome me. I turned and drove the other way. Here we went again. They backed up and tried to come the other way ...

Fine. I wasn't in the mood for playing games in this heat. I drove right up to them. I drove half the car on the grass, and we found ourselves side by side, looking at each other through our open windows, three feet away from one another. There were four of them. The three passengers were older and highly decorated while the driver was younger and less so.

"What are you looking at, you dumb fucks? Fuck you!" I said to them, angrily. At once, I stepped on it, leaving them behind, staring at me. I got to the paved road and only then did they turn on their emergency lights and their siren. But they hadn't even turned yet.

They were taking their time. They didn't want to come face to face with a sun-cracked guy again. They had come there for some shooting, not for war.

I headed to Palamas and parked the car in one of the first streets I came across, trying to listen for the siren. As soon as they drove past me, I turned and continued driving towards my destination. I drank my coffee on the way.

Summit

It was a Sunday morning. Enjoying my fresh cup of coffee, I was driving a leisurely route along the Aridea-Edessa country road in a four-wheeled Nissan. How original, you'll say! Be patient ... surprises always lie ahead.

The winding road ran along the sides of a densely forested mountain, cutting into the forest every once in a while. I was already near Edessa and in front of me, there was another car moving slowly, which one moment I saw and the next I didn't. Less than a mile before I reached the first houses, the road followed the mountain's last curve before vanishing behind the opposite hill, hidden by the vegetation. The other car was fifty yards ahead of me. I saw it turning left at the brook. Then it vanished. As I got closer to the curve I could see, through the thick leafage, some movement on the opposite side of the road — and the moment I reached the end of the curve, everything turned blue and white!

Fifteen yards away, the road was filled with policemen. Police vehicles of various types were parked everywhere. To the right, I saw dozens of unmarked police vehicles driving down a narrow road, followed by countless police vehicles. The first unmarked vehicle was just then entering the road I was on. After they allowed the car in front of me to continue on its way, several cops walked in the middle of the road to stop me from passing. They were crazy! I slowed down and then stepped on it. They jumped to the sides. The unmarked police vehicle suddenly hit the brakes, forcing all the others behind it to do the same. I swerved to the left and managed not to crash into it, then kept on driving at full throttle, hearing all the cops yelling, raising their hands in the air:

"Hey!"

"Hey, my ass!"

I didn't hear any shots, but I expected there'd be a car chase. For more than a hundred yards, I could see policemen on both sides of the road. At the time, my eyes were just taking pictures without my mind processing them, because it was too busy getting ready for the upcoming pursuit which I considered more than certain.

Driving as though they were already chasing me, I entered the north-east side of the city and cut straight through, exiting its north-west, heading to Kozani. Surprisingly I neither heard nor saw any police vehicles coming after me. I drove until I was a safe distance away and started to play back the whole incident in my mind. I concluded that I had accidentally stumbled across some very important person, who was right at that moment being transported, and I had just happened to be the one they had stopped for him to pass. As was natural and expected, seeing all these cops suddenly blocking my way, I had thought it was some kind of roadblock, and reacted the way I did. This version of events was supported by the snapshots I'd observed and memorised. Shots that depicted police officers lined on both sides of the road, wearing white gloves. I turned on the radio and tuned in to the local station to listen, hearing that at that very moment the President of the Hellenic Republic, Kostis Stedanopoulos, was touring the city of Edessa and he had just left that particular spot, which was something like an archaeological site.

So that explained why there wasn't a car chase. And why they all were just as surprised as I was. They didn't make a decision fast enough, tasked as they were with the orderly tour of the president. That president had had the bad habit of not announcing his visits, otherwise, I would have known because even when I was on the move, I kept up to date through the State radio. If I had been a few seconds late, there's a big chance that there would have been a heated incident. And then I'd have to convince the impartial judges that this was a simple coincidence and not an attempted murder against the President of the Hellenic Republic. Talk about (bad) luck.

When I went to prison, by coincidence once again, a cellmate of mine had as his advocate Stefanopoulos' son, Ilias, who was a lawyer in Patra. I had many hearings in Patra back then, and my cellmate suggested that Ilias should work on my defence too, as a friend, without pay. I accepted and got to know him. Despite being the son of the President of the Hellenic Republic, he was the coolest and most calm lawyer I'd met until then, so I told him about the incident, to see how he'd react.

"You're insane! You'd have killed my father!" he said tongue in cheek.

"Since he's still alive and still the President of the Hellenic Republic and you're his son, tell him to do something about this disgrace of democracy", I said to him (meaning the detention and the justice serving systems).

"Do you think my father can do anything about this? The world of politics is like a drunken scrum aboard a ship in rough waters trying to find their balance and my father just presides over them". Ilias said to me.

Bottoms up then.

The Rambos

It was Holy Week, just before Easter. I parked my brand new two-litre Grand Vitara in the parking lot of a supermarket, outside a city in central Macedonia, and went to do some Easter shopping.

Not but a few days had passed since I and a guy from Romania, a good thief and safe-cracker, had stolen the car, along with its key, from a motor show. From the first moment I had realised this Vitara was jinxed. In motor shows, all new cars have as much gas as there is in their reserve. Fifty miles from the show, we broke into a secluded petrol station and filled it up, but when we tried to start the car it just wouldn't. Instead of diesel, we'd filled the tank with petrol! For reasons known only to the owner of the station, the pump that was supposed to have diesel had petrol instead. We realised it when it was already too late, yet we didn't give up. We pushed the car to a dark uphill ramp that led to the basement's door, and we parked it. There, in the darkness, we repeatedly stepped on the gas, flipping the switch until all the petrol ran out through the supply rubber hose which we had unfixed. Then we filled it up with diesel. This time using the petrol pump!

The Vitara was a four-wheeled SUV with a two-litre engine, something that suited my travelling style. Plus, it didn't have an owner searching for it or crying over it, so I thought about keeping it for my personal transportation. I asked some friends of mine from Athens to locate an identical SUV and take its license plate numbers so that I could forge some of my own. It was taking them a long time as this particular model had only just hit the market, it was hard to find. For the time being, until I found the number I was after, I put some stolen German license plates with an expiration date on it. Given that it was the Holy Week, I thought nobody was going to bother with the details.

I'd reckoned without my host.

When I finished shopping, I exited the supermarket holding a bag of groceries. I'd parked the car to my right, its front facing the parking lot's wall. Behind it I could see a black BMW, its doors open, slightly blocking the Vitara's way. A well-dressed woman around forty, holding a binder, was examining the license plates and two big guys with gun holster belts were circling. I paused to assess the situation. The black BMW, their appearance, and especially their behaviour suggested they weren't police officers but something close to that. I assumed they were from the Financial Crime Unit. They'd obviously spotted the expired license plate and thought this marked the end of Greece's economic problems. I didn't know if they'd given the plate number to the police already and were simply waiting for backup to arrive.

The armed Financial Crime Unit had at that time just been formed by the then Ministry of Finance. They'd dubbed their armed men "Rambos" and had unleashed them in the streets to combat financial crime. According to the people in charge of the ministry, each driver moving on the country's road system had suitcases full of cash in their trunks. Such is the audacity of bureaucrats, in their attempt to mislead people about where the money is really hidden and secure more votes by hiring Rambos. The Greek peoples' endurance for deceit is admirable.

The Rambos had taken their role too seriously. Many times I came across them setting up roadblocks on country roads. They were thoroughly searching all oncoming vehicles' trunks, in case they discovered some off-shore with millions in stolen money. Thankfully for them, they never stopped me, or I'd have sent them to the Acheron to look for it! All this, as well as many other things, crossed my mind like wildfire and I got really pissed. I got the key out of my pocket, pressed the unlock button and walked straight up to them. Hearing the sound of the locks popping and seeing the Vitara's hazard lights flashing, they turned to look at me. The woman with the binder was standing right in front of the rear door, and the two big guys were at the back corners of the SUV. When I got near them, seeing that the woman had no intention of moving, I spoke to her in a manner that left little room for arguing:

"Please step aside so that I can open the door".

"Is this your car?" she asked, taking a step left.

"Would it do you any good to know?" I asked her in the same manner, as I opened the rear door, threw the grocery bag inside, and closed it again.

"We're with the Financial Crime Unit", she said to me, confident that the mere mention of the Unit she was serving would make me shit myself.

"I neither asked you nor do I care about your profession, ma'am", I said to her and at once I walked past her and one of the big guys.

I reached the driver's door and opened it. The Rambos didn't move; they didn't even speak. I was ready and determined to react at the first sign of aggression on their part ... deep inside, I wished they would react so that I could test their "Rambo-ness" in action!

The woman with the binder followed me, asking:

"Where are you from? Where do you live?"

"From Moschofito and I don't have an address". I answered her, continuing what I was doing as though they weren't there. I sat in the driver seat, I put the key in the ignition, and I turned it.

She stood by the open door and said to me:

"Are you leaving? You can't leave!"

"Why? Who's stopping me?"

"Your car has expired plates! This is illegal!"

"If the only illegal thing you see in front of you are the license plates then you're not cut out for this job", I said to her.

I closed the door, turned left, backed up, and swerved to avoid their BMW. The Rambos jumped to the side. I didn't see any enthusiasm for showing initiative there. I turned the SUV around, stepped on the gas, and headed to the parking lot exit. I looked in the mirrors and saw them getting in the BMW to follow me, but I never saw them again. They were neither in the mood, nor were they equipped for a car chase. They certainly notified the police to try and locate me, and that in itself is an ongoing car chase, where one has to act accordingly and get away from the area.

The perfect citizen

In front of me, riding on an Enduro motorcycle, two helmet-wearing, heavily armed lads were leading the way. That morning we'd set off for a quick job , and I'd experience the most visually enjoyable thing I've ever experienced during a bank robbery. All because of a fantastic guy.

Thirty yards away from the bank, I drove my X3 to a preselected small opening by the right side of the road which afforded a panoramic view of the target, and opened the left window. I was to act as a guardian angel for these two experienced lads (one of whom was Spyros), who had attacked many banks. Calm, as though nothing out of the ordinary was going on, they crossed the road, drove their motorcycles onto the pavement, parked right in front of the bank's entrance, got off, pulled out their guns, and disappeared inside.

Inspecting the area, which had been my task all along, a guy around thirty years old caught my eye. He was standing to the left of the bank's entrance, wearing a short-sleeved shirt and jeans, holding a folded newspaper. He looked as though he was waiting for someone. When he saw the bike with the two helmet-wearing guys parked near the bank entrance he got upset. His eyes locked on them and followed them almost instinctively. Mine, in turn, locked on him and observed his every move. The guy, seeing the lads pulling their guns before entering, and giving him a meaningful glance, put on an unbelievable eye-witness theatrical act, which every screenwriter would wish to have conceived and written, every director to have directed and every cameraman to have recorded.

For a few seconds, his gaze and head followed the two robbers' movement. Right afterwards, being now sure of what was to follow, he leaned on the metal doorframe, crossed his legs, unfolded the newspaper he was holding, and began reading it, whistling casually (literally)! Every so often, his curiosity drove him to unfold his legs, take a step, and turn to look through the glass façade and the transparent curtains inside the bank. Then, just like a naughty kid, he'd abruptly and guiltily return to his act. Open newspaper, cross legs, casual whistling. The same scene was repeated more than four times until the lads got out of the bank, got on their bike, and vanished at the end of the road, where I followed them to pick them up. And the guy was still whistling; one eye on the newspaper and the other following the motorcycle.

What a guy! What consciousness! Never before had I met such a "concerned" citizen, and neither did I believe someone like this existed. I always saw them running away in panic, calling the police. I'm not in a position to guess his thoughts, but I'm sure about the purpose of his whistling.

"They robbed the bank; what is it to me? Good luck lads ..."

I'd like to get to know this guy, Even if they pinned the robbery on me. If, of course, they haven't already pinned it on others who suffered in prison.

Useful security guys

One afternoon, my travels found me outside a new department store in Larissa. Just out of curiosity for this new human creation, I decided to make a stop and have a cup of coffee. I drove my Fiat Punto into the store's parking lot, locked it, and entered a vast, air-conditioned hall. Aah, capitalism and deception are such a good match! Brilliant! Astonishing! I grabbed a coffee to go and began exploring the store from end to end. It was eight in the evening, and the department store closed at nine. I got anxious whether I'd get to see everything.

Just before nine, I got back to my Punto holding a suitcase filled with all kinds of useless, shiny shopping. The only thing I actually needed was the suitcase. All the rest had been to satisfy my visual appetite. I left the suitcase on the floor and fumbled in my pockets for the Punto's keys. I couldn't find them. I searched in the purse where I'd hidden my gun; nothing. I searched inside the suitcase; nothing. For fuck's sake ... just what I needed.

I walked back inside the fancy brothel and walked by all the stores I had visited before, lest I'd dropped them somewhere and somebody had found them—waste of time. I asked for help from the guys at the information booth. They called through the loudspeakers for anyone that had found a set of car keys to deliver them at their booth. Then, they used their wireless to call the department store's security manager. Before long, a guy around fifty arrived, wearing a well-known security company's uniform. I told him what my problem was and I asked him if I could and whether it was safe for me to leave the car in the store's parking lot through the night and for as long as I'd have to.

"Of course you can. The parking lot has a closed-circuit camera network and is being watched around the clock by men of our company. You have nothing to worry about. Your car will remain perfectly safe!" he said to me, a tad offended, as though I had questioned the honour of his family.

"Could you please also keep this suitcase in a safe place until I figure out what to do with the car?"

"Of course, security is our expertise!"

He took it and left without saying another word. I left too. Once outside the department store, I got in a taxi and reached the city centre. I tried to call some people that could help with my unexpected problem, but none of them answered. The car had both an alarm and an immobiliser installed. Inside it, apart from my personal armament, I also had many other things that ought not to be lost. I couldn't break into the car to take them without an escape vehicle. That was why I had the security officer watch it over for me. But it was too great a risk for it to remain in the department store's parking lot for a long time: its license plates were stolen. If by chance someone figured it out, I'd have an even bigger problem to deal with.

Having all this in mind, I had to act on my own. I grabbed a taxi to Trikala, and at the first kiosk I came across I got lucky. Some guy had left his Golf with its engine running and had gone to buy cigarettes. I took it and left. Yet, as I soon realised, I wasn't as lucky as I had initially thought ... I hadn't gone but a few miles when I realised the Golf's electrical system was problematic. In the end, I managed to reach the department store by morning.

For some reason, which I can't really remember, I had to get the suitcase I had given to the security officer the previous night. So I got in the department store and asked the first security guy I ran into to call the security manager, so that I could get it back. The manager hadn't arrived yet, so a woman brought it to me. On the suitcase's handle was a piece of paper saying: "This suitcase belongs to a man with thinning hair at the temples, about thirty-five years old from Thessaloniki, who lost his car keys and will stay at some hotel in the city. In his frustration, he forgot to leave his mobile phone number!"

Now, that's what I call punctuality and service! I took it, put it in the Golf and, holding a screwdriver, headed to the parked Punto. With some effort, I opened the passenger door and, as the alarm penetrated my ears, grabbed anything of value that had to be salvaged. Outside Elassona, the Golf died. Thankfully, Stelios finally answered the phone. Half an hour later, he came and picked me up.

In the following days I'd think about the security manager, about what would happen when the police realised to whom the car he was watching over that night belonged. I certainly wouldn't want to be in his position.

The author

It was a rainy winter afternoon and I was parked facing the exit of a dirt track, on a small raised headland. I had just buried a batch of guns, and was sitting behind the wheel, enjoying the misty, green fir-forest landscape. After a while, through the thick fog, the headlights of a car appeared, revealed to be a Land Rover with a bump on its roof, driving up the muddy dirt road. I grabbed my Kalashnikov, which had been resting in the passenger seat, and released its safety.

The Land Rover's driver got wind of my car in time and stopped about twenty to thirty yards away; its fog lights turned right on me. The passenger door opened and I could see the Ranger Service logo on it. Obviously, the ranger station's employees had located my car's fresh track marks on the wet dirt road, starting from the paved road about four hundred yards away, and had decided to investigate in case the vehicle belonged to illegal loggers or poachers.

A seven-foot oaf got out, put up his camouflage coat's hood to protect himself from the rain, and began striding up the road to reach me. I covered the Kalashnikov with a towel, and opened the car's glove box. I got out a leather binder, placed it on the car's wheel, opened it and began writing with devotion on the pad of paper inside the binder.

The lanky guy reached the car, pressed his face against the wet passenger window and began repeatedly knocking on the glass with his index finger. Pretending to be surprised, I turned to look at him. He looked like a figure straight out of shadow theatre, crouching outside the foggy car window. I pressed the button, and the window opened. Pressing his palms on the base of the window, he half-crawled inside the car and screamed at me, as though I was standing half a mile away from him:

"Whatcha doin' 'ere?" he asked in a thick country accent.

"Excuse me?" I screamed back, as loud as I could.

"Whatcha doin' 'ere, am sayin'!" he repeated, even louder this time.

"I'm an author, sir! Who are you? Is there a reason you're interrupting me?"

He stood still for a while, not saying a word, just looking at me, while his waterproof jacket's hood dripped all over the towel covering the Kalashnikov.

"We're from the Ranger station", he said after a while and continued: "And watcha writin'?"

"If you leave me alone I might write something ..."

"Fine, fine ... write, write!" he said to me, pulling his long body out of the car.

He began climbing back up the uphill road rather awkwardly, like a rickety crane. When he got half-way up, the Land Rover's driver stuck his head and his one hand out of the window and asked him in gestures:

"Who is he?"

"An author!"

"What?"

"He's an author!"

"And what's he writin'?"

"Go an' ask him yourself!"

He got in the car, and they backed down the hill until their lights vanished in the fog. So I finally got a profession. I was an author!

Fake interview

Around 1993-1994, Nikos and I were abroad. I was in central Europe and my brother was even further away but every once in a while, I'd phone Petros in Athens to see how he was and hear news from home. One day I called him and learnt that later that week, a recorded interview of Nikos would be broadcast on a show that had, as its sole purpose, the location and arrest of fugitives, and if I'm not mistaken was called "Wanted". How much cynicism and vulgarity have Greek people suffered.

Petros didn't know Nikos, so he had taken for granted that it was his voice on the advertising audio clips which the citizenry had been bombarded with all week. The two crime reporters who were about to broadcast this interview were doing everything in their power to secure as many viewers as possible for their upcoming show. And there, they'd certainly try to sell out at the best possible price the product that had unexpectedly fallen in their hands, firmly believing it was genuine.

I was dumbstruck by this piece of news. I couldn't understand how all this had come to be. I was confident about one thing: Nikos would have never done anything like this. He was just as allergic to mass media as I was. We detested stardom, let alone through shows as obscene as this one. Even if I assumed the worst, it still didn't make any sense.

Petros explained to me that the advertising spots said the following: "The notorious fugitive and wanted man, Nikos Palaiokostas, offers an exclusive interview from his hideout and talks about everyone and everything! He reveals the truth about life in correctional institutions and the ways drugs are smuggled inside ..." and other similar vulgarities. Right afterwards, a guy pretending to be Nikos, through a recorded phone conversation, talked shit, giving a strong sense of snitching.

I didn't talk to Nikos on the phone often; neither could I inform him directly so that he could deal with the matter, given it concerned him directly. So I had to carry the can myself. In no case could I leave so severe an issue unattended, hanging over us. Many questions arose. First and foremost, who was behind this phone conversation and what was his reason for using Nikos' name?

Were the police doing this in an attempt to force and assess a reaction? Were the cops working with the show's reporters to the same end? Were the two crime reporters acting on their own, aiming to increase their show's ratings, ignoring or taking the risk of such a ploy? Was it some inmate or ex-inmate, who thought that for his snitching to be heard and have a weight he could use Nikos' name? Many were the questions, with the latter being the less likely. No matter how naïve, an outlaw always knows that at some point he'll be exposed and he'll have to face the consequences of his actions. Either way, I had to act right away; I couldn't let this play out until the broadcast. When certainly — and even if I didn't interfere — the scheme would be exposed during the show. Outlaws and other friends who knew us were ready to call in live and reveal the truth.

Petros gave me the TV station's phone numbers, and I called its call centre.

"Such and such TV station here!" I heard a female voice on the other end of the call.

"I'd like for you to give me a number so that I can contact the show 'Wanted'".

"Can you give me your full name and a landline number?"

"No, I can't! I'm calling about something very important. It has to do with the Palaiokostas case. I intend to give valuable information concerning the subject to the show's producers. You understand my position".

Without any other questions or wasting any more time, she gave me two phone numbers for the show. Not even the Attica General Police Directorate would have been that willing to assist me! Only snitching throws doors and windows wide open in this fucking country. I called one of the numbers, and a girl picked it up.

"I want to talk to one of the journalists of the show concerning Palaiokostas".

"They're out at the moment. Let me put you through to their assistant partner".

"Hello".

"I'm calling you concerning your upcoming show focusing on Nikos Palaiokostas' interview".

"Yes. I'm listening".

"I'm about to reveal something very important. I need to know who I am talking to".

"I'm Vaios so and so".

"Can I speak directly to the producers of the show?"

"For the time being, it's impossible. They're out for a story. You're free to talk to me, I'm their assistant and their partner".

"You are planning on broadcasting an interview with Palaiokostas".

"Yes".

"How certain are you that you actually interviewed Palaiokostas? Nikos, I mean?"

After a pause …

"Why? Is there any chance that it isn't him? Who are you?"

"I'm Nikos' brother, Vassilis".

"And you're saying it's not him we interviewed?"

"That's exactly what I'm saying. And let me say one more thing: if the show is broadcast, all those of you who participate in this travesty will live to regret it!"

"Look, Vassilis … you have every right to be talking this way if things are as you say they are. I thought they had cross-checked it, I know nothing more than you do. I just want to say were compatriots … I'm from Trikala too!"

"Stop sucking up to me. Now you're from Trikala, huh? Where do you live in Trikala?"

"Next to the cemetery".

"Oh! You're going the right way then! Now give me the cell phone numbers of your superiors, and I'll talk to them directly".

"I'll give them to you. Just don't tell them you got them from me".

"Now you're insulting me. You're talking to Palaiokostas, remember?"

He gave me their cell phone numbers, and I immediately called one of them.

"Hello".

"Are you so and so?"

"Yes. Who is this?"

"This is Palaiokostas speaking!"

A moment of silence.

"Yes, what do you want?"

His tone upset me.

"What do I want, you arsehole? Who is giving interviews through your show using Nikos' name? How can you broadcast a show without checking who's talking to you? Listen, you poor fellows; the little games you're playing with the police will blow up in your face. If you don't stop the show's broadcast, I'll hunt you down and aim right for the head when I find you! Simple as that".

"Who is this? Who am I talking to?"

"This is Vassilis speaking!"

"No, Vassilis. I'm not playing any games with the police. I'm not a snitch".

"You're something even worse. You're a filthy crime reporter who hunts fugitives!"

"If the man speaking on that interview isn't Nikos, you have every right to be angry. I wonder who it may be ..."

"That's your own problem to solve if you want to sleep easy at night!"

"It sounds like you're calling me from abroad".

"That doesn't make you any safer!"

"No, of course not. That's not why I'm saying this. We won't go on with the show. We're ourselves the victims of fraud too".

"Fine, fine". I hung up.

Of course, the advertising spots for the show stopped at once, and the show itself was never broadcast.

During that time, all TV stations that wanted to be taken seriously had incorporated similar shows on their programs. They had created a climate of terror for any citizen who dared or thought about vanishing without permission. Investigations were led by known and successfully shameless journalists. Without hesitation, they'd set off on a merciless pursuit which reeked of cannibalism. Their participation in the psychopathic manhunt on TV required that viewers be in a state of constant vigilance and alertness. A few weeks after Haitoglou's kidnapping, after that bounty had been placed on our heads by the generous State, a known numpty with a similar show was tasked by the cops with an ambitious plan to trap and arrest us, with the help of all the venal snitches out there. In the studio, with two high-ranking cops by her side and brandishing her thirty pieces of silver, she conducted the law-abiding, venal citizens' unquenchable passion for snitching. At the same time, all police personnel were on standby throughout the country, waiting for that blessed tip to spring into action.

That very same afternoon, and while we were on our way to the Peloponnese, we learned about the calamity that would befall us, so to protect ourselves from television's fury, we acted against our own better judgment. We acquired a portable TV and got to a mountain in Attica to have a good laugh until midnight.

That night everybody saw us, everywhere, and at the same time! In Lagadas on an Enduro motorcycle. In Grevena in a 4x4 pickup truck. In Ioannina in a Cherokee Jeep. In Patra in a black BMW. In the centre of Athens in an armoured Mercedes. Outside Mouzaki, horse-riding on our way to Agrafa! And the cops ran hither and thither.

Throughout the show, the numpty claimed she knew where I was, but when I accidentally bumped into her, face to face, she didn't have a clue. The same thing stood for a morning-show presenter, who one morning informed his viewers that the noose was tightening around Palaiokostas but the same night, sitting next to each other at a coffee shop, we started talking about random things. What goes around comes around …

I ran across one of these many aspiring "Palaiokostologists", an acclaimed crime reporter, at a grocery store and I grabbed a ripe, red tomato out of his hand.

"I saw it first", I said to him, smiling.

I have many other similar stories and just as many unexpected encounters with such vile people who serve or suck up to the authorities. Little people, praying day and night to see me behind bars or dead. Because it is there, behind bars and in cemeteries, where their own disgusting abscess lurks: their soul.

I have many stories about my usual pursuers too, but I can't narrate them in detail either, even though enough time has passed for me to be able to talk about at least some of them. Like when someone broke into the house next to my own and the police arrived by accident at mine.

"Headquarters sent us for the burglary in your house!"

"When did that happen? Because I didn't see anything!"

A different time, right outside my house's gate, a stolen car was abandoned, and a group of eight double-riding motorcycle policemen arrived. After asking me whether I had seen who'd left the car, we began chatting about car thieves — it was very instructional. All my questions were answered!

In an apartment building this time, they broke into some apartment (what a pain these burglars are). Police officers were ringing the bells, lest the thieves were still inside one of the apartments. Thankfully I'm not a thief, and I don't look like one either.

MY PLEA

It's only you who I want to apologise to, fellow reader. To tell you the truth,: I'm guilty! And I'm guilty because:

I never formed nor served any political sects!
That's why I found myself charged, wanted, and pursued by them. With my every step, I could hear their exclamations about the beauty of democracy. But the only thing I could see was a dressed-up whore, in the living room of whom flocked together all the wealth and power addicted men, holding their offspring by the hand.

I never sold out, nor did I buy off anybody's conscience, including my own,even when they have turned selling it and buying it into a high science ...

I never started a war with anybody!
But they fought me like few others: with all sorts of weapons, all kinds of bullets. And, strangely, I'm still alive ... and free.

I never legislated., I never enforced, and I never obeyed any laws!
Laws dictated by the interests of a handful of rulers. I came across their rules everywhere, but I never found justice.

I faced hordes of agitated pursuers and as many avenging judges with hatred-filled eyes. Among them, I never saw a human or a sign of humanity — only ridiculous megalomaniacs dragging the pettiness of their laws on their turned-off souls.

I'm not holding a gospel but a rifle!
I've walked with it, and I still do, always showing respect to life, human or otherwise.

When they use the same gospel by which they swear my guilt, to crush lives without mercy. My rifle has never caused any pain; their gospel has caused immeasurable suffering. I've seen this suffering, I've heard it, I've felt it first-hand.

I'm guilty because: I used to rob banks!
But I never bankrupted a man, a household, a country! I always found empty safes, because those tasked with guarding their contents had made sure to empty them from the inside.

I kidnapped rich men!
Who still lead their lives lavishly while I still live as a fugitive. They say I'm a bad person ... so much that I corrupt the goodness of their work that wipes out entire generations.

I've injured policemen!
My human nature doesn't allow me to be controlled by others. I have self-control because I'm the master of myself. My disavowal was and still remains suspicious to them ... and a confrontation is inevitable. I was defending humans' paramount right to freedom while they were defending their salary and their deeply rooted lies. They were always on the offence, always shooting in the back. I was always on the defence, always shooting in their faces.

I escaped from prison!
All humans who are deprived of their freedom, irrespective of the reason, have this self-evident duty. They were embarrassed by my escapes. I never saw any of them be embarrassed for their one-size-fits-all, bloodthirsty justice or their correctional monstrosities. They consider a free human being to be the greatest embarrassment because humans' freedom is their constant prey, which they hunt incessantly and fiercely.

I never desecrated this earth by restricting horizons!
I consciously refused to be recruited as another unimportant worker in the construction of the global empire of money. I never laid a single brick; I never bought or used not a single square foot from their colossal yet flimsy monstrosity. They threaten people with the collapse of this very same edifice if they ever stop serving it Because they're the only ones who know how to maintain it, given they are its creators. They are the ones in possession of its complex blueprints, and therefore they control the future of the societies they have trapped in it.

I defend my truth!
They defend their lie. The lie that arms every hand. Their barefaced lie armed the hand that writes and narrates. It reared me; it is that which I'm fighting, that sustains me. They named me guilty from the moment I consciously chose not to serve it.

Innocence is the ultimate embarrassment at such times. A bullet in the heart of truth. Every innocent man, another slimy servant of their lie. Yet another person who identifies innocence with compensation for work, which is their paid guilt. It's self-deceit. A bribe to appease their conscience. A life hired for the completion of a horrible human work. Those eternally irresponsible prostitute their ideals, giving absolute power to the charlatans who present themselves as responsible, just, and well-intentioned protectors. And while the former, hunched and carefree, go to the jobs their protectors dictate, the latter join forces to come after the dreams of their children. Artfully guaranteeing their proper future use, they come up with new plans to quietly gain absolute control over them. They take their dreams as self-evident collateral against the perpetuation of this transaction.

So, the very existence of humans is trivialised, reduced to an everyday commercial transaction, the supreme duty and goal of which is to incorporate it as the smallest part of a gigantic voracious fungus that greedily devours the planet's skin. Because they haven't learnt how to take a chance, how to say no! Or to not be afraid and live on their own. But when the hour of judgment comes, they beg to be treated as whole beings and not like a worthless, small piece of it. But by then it's already too late. The monster nurtured by their paid work means business. It takes its role seriously, and that's why it doesn't deal with small things. Its self-preservation always comes first.

The mass paranoia of humankind which today, united and enslaved, serves the cruel dictatorship of markets, naming them the miracle of human civilisation, will have a heavy price to pay. Recent human history allows no optimism. Humanity's chosen leaders have always led it into the deepest darkness. And will continue to do so for as long as it needs them. Again and again. They know no other path. They have a single motto, a single cry: authority or death! It's us or a forest of huge mushroom clouds!

That's the extortive dilemma the peoples' oppressors pose as their suggestion for the planet's future. For that future's sake, they commit all their crimes.

EPILOGUE

I told him, don't go to the city. He didn't listen to me. Foolish, young, lone wolf; he followed a secret path in the middle of the night, got there and defiled the housekeepers' yards. I can still hear the enraged yells and the howls of the fattened animals. I can hear breathless, malnourished strays defending the pavements and the trash cans. The city is our concern! We don't need uncouth wildlings! They all scream at the top of their lungs!

Shut the hell up, you dogs! My speech doesn't serve ideas and doctrines. It doesn't care about the domination and the control of any system. My speech praises life and humans' substantial freedom. My speech dreams of pristine mountaintops that touch clear skies and gaze at bright horizons. Endless virgin forests, to the heartbeat of which dances the very joy of existence. Fast-flowing rivers, swelling with life, redeemed in crystal lakes and foaming oceans. Golden coasts, where pine trees' fair tears, precious wet amber, drip prodigally to the depths of a light blue sea. Silver full moons, urging lovers to feel the truth of life in an orgasm's unbridled force. It dreams of children's joyous voices, chasing their hopes in the fluttering of colourful butterflies and painting with their laughter their own treaty for maintaining life — a life free of prisons of rules, orders, coercion, self-restrictions ...

A life truly free.

***

And now, fellow reader, it's just the two of us.

If you felt me, we share one heartbeat; our heart's duty is as one. If you understood me, light might be the shared cells in our bodies ...

If you tried, never lose courage; my footprints will always accompany you.

If you're just another eternally happy and carefree human: I'll respect your sleep, but I can't stand your loud snoring. I hope and wish you to be one of the guests in Earth's great feast when at last it will be freed from the noise once and for all.

Until then, I'll remain with the unique ones; the uncatchables. Those that consciously chose to lead their lives normally, reacting to an abnormal world.

End.

ABOUT FREEDOM PRESS

The oldest anarchist publishing house in the English speaking world, Freedom Press was founded in London by Charlotte Wilson and Peter Kropotkin in 1886. A major player in British anarchist politics at the turn of the 20th century, publishing writers including Italian firebrand Errico Malatesta and historian Max Nettlau, it fell into decline in the 1920s before being revived by a group of anti-war activists in the 1930s.

The Press briefly became famous in a 1945 free speech case when the editors of its journal *War Commentary* were arrested and tried for writing anti-State and anti-war essays causing "disaffection in the armed forces". Although an all-star cast of advocates rallied to defend them, including Herbert Read, George Orwell, Benjamin Britten and E M Forster, all but one were jailed.

Post-war, Freedom was revived by a group formed around Vernon Richards. While Richards was sometimes a controversial figure the Press brought a number of successful writers and artists into its circles during his nearly 60 years as a publisher, including works by Marie-Louise Berneri, Clifford Harper, Donald Rooum and Colin Ward among many others.

Based in the heart of London, Freedom is often on the front line of major events and has been firebombed twice by fascists, in 1993 and 2013. On both occasions the press was saved by immense solidarity from the global anarchist movement.

Today Freedom Press runs Britain's largest anarchist bookshop at its home of more than 50 years in Whitechapel, and continues to regularly publish works on the philosophy and activities of anarchists. We run a daily anarchist news site at freedomnews.org.uk and continue to publish a free bi-annual printed journal, *Freedom*.

The full fascinating story of its 134-year history is told in *A Beautiful Idea* by Rob Ray (ISBN 978-1904491309), available from the Freedom Bookshop, 84b Whitechapel high Street, London E1 7QX and online.

freedompress.org.uk

and

freedomnews.org.uk

ALSO FROM FREEDOM PRESS

Why Work?
A provocative collection of essays by writers from the 19th century through to today dissecting work, its forms under capitalism and the possibilities for an alternative society producing for our needs, rather than mere avarice. Now in its third edition, with a new foreword from union and co-op activist Shiri Shalmy and three additional essays.
£9 | 184pp | ISBN: 978-1-904491-38-5

Fighting Women
by Isabella Lorusso
This series of interviews with Spanish Civil War veterans offers a unique insight into the two-front revolution that women were trying to achieve in the 1930s, putting their lives on the line to fight fascism (and Stalinism) while confronting men whose commitment to liberation too often stopped at their own front door.
£10 | 188pp | ISBN: 978-1-904491-35-4

History of the Makhnovist Movement
by Peter Arshinov
The Russian Revolution was a time when the old order was swept away. Everything was changing and in Ukraine Nestor Makhno's anarchist army was able to break the Whites. But nearby the Bolsheviks were moving, setting the stage for a gruesome confrontation. Peter Arshinov was there.
£9.90 | 275pp | ISBN: 978-0-900384-40-9

Invisible
by Andrew Fraser
Many writers and books talk about the homeless. Andrew has direct experience. His writing on life as a rough sleeper, interwoven through this scorching diary piece, offers a clear-eyed truth from the gutters of a year surviving Britain's housing crisis.
£10 | 208pp | ISBN: 978-1-904491-31-6

ACKNOWLEDGEMENTS

The following people backed our crowdfunder for this book at the highest tier, many thanks to you and everyone who helped make this project possible!

Sylvia Gran
Dimitrios Vouris
Joshua Rivera
Ishmael and Aurély
Iain Salmons

ETC Dee
Jakub Czarski
Stelios Amore
Mo Moseley
Aylon Cohen

Nigel Atkinson
Mike Melero
Light Record Media
Rosa Magalios
Rekky

Peter Gallagher
Mike Finn
Theoryfighter
Yanis Yanoulopoulos
Nikolas Alexis Yanoulopoulos

Trade orders may be sent to publishing@freedompress.org.uk or to our distributors:

Central Books	centralbooks.com	(020) 8525 8800	(UK)
AK Press	akpress.org	(510) 208-1700	(US)

A Normal Life was printed by Aldgate Press, a worker co-operative. Tel (020) 7247 3015 or email print@aldgatepress.co.uk

Typography: Big John, TheSans Typewriter, Caladea, Verdana